Infertility
Inferschmility

Aprill Fasino Lane

Published by Fountain Blue Publishing of California.
www.fountainbluepublishing.com

First Printing: December 2013

Cover design by Kim Barton
www.tymecaptured.com

10 9 8 7 6 5 4 3 2 1

AGC Scholarship Foundation:

For couples dealing with infertility, the staggering price of diagnoses and fertility treatments may make the dream of parenthood seem out of reach. The AGC Hope Scholarship, established in 2010, will make it possible for couples who do not have the financial resources the opportunity to fulfill their dream of becoming parents.

Please check us out at: www.agcscholarships.org

Facebook: www.facebook.com/Agcscholarships

THIS BOOK...

Sometime ago, I sent my blog to a few publishers. I'm not a writer. I didn't go to school for writing. I know nothing about the publishing world. I just found a few publishers (via Google) that I felt my blog content would suit their interest. I heard back from them all. One offered to publish it as an eBook. One said that they are only working with novelists. The other said they would like to publish my blog as a book. The third one didn't go into detail about eBook vs. printed book. So really I had two to decide between. There was something about the third one that I really liked. They just felt right. I felt like they would get it. Not many people can get it. Infertility is a hard thing to understand if you have never been through it. As hard as it is to understand, there are some fertile people out there that just "get it." I felt like M (right, another M?!?!) gets it. She gets the importance of this story. She gets the importance of making a difference. Who knows, maybe she has dealt with some infertility or maybe someone close to her has dealt with it... Or maybe she just gets it. Either way, I felt that from her right away... So, I signed the contract with the Publisher, Fountain Blue Publishing. The editor has been working editing all my posts into book format. At some point, they will start pulling the posts off the blog.

Aprill Fasino Lane

A NOTE FROM 'M', THE PUBLISHER:

I not only 'get it', I feel it. A friend of mine went through infertility. I remember her tears, her fears, and her feelings of worthlessness, failure, hopelessness. I listened to her cry. I watched her rock gently in her chair as she talked (cried) about the unfairness. She and I have been friends for, wow, 15 or more years now. At the time, I felt privileged that she trusted me with her emotions and at the same time I wondered, why me? Why would she want to talk to me? I am the mother of four and a grandmother. I am the 'picture' of what, at that time, she thought she would never get to be.

My wonderful friend has since had two beautiful babies and although the experience was hard for her (harder than I can ever imagine), I was enlightened. I came to understand how truly lucky I am to have been able to conceive my children without medical intervention. It is most women's deepest desire to have a baby. I don't know that I could ever have been as strong as my friend or Aprill if I had been told I had to deal with infertility. I am pretty sure I would have caved and bought another fur baby.

My heart goes out to all who want to achieve their hearts desire, but their bodies will not allow without a struggle. My hope is that this book brings hope and answers to at least one woman dealing with infertility.

HUGS!

Melanie Fountain

DEDICATION

This book is dedicated to my husband Brian, whom I love to pieces. Without your unwavering support, our family wouldn't exist as it is. LY-17.

And to my amazing little boys, Miles and Mark. One day you will understand the capacity in which you changed lives. Never has anyone been so loved before they existed. Never has anyone been so wanted before they were given. You brought us out of our lowest low. You proved that miracles do happen. You showed us that with determination, will, and perseverance, hope can become a reality. Now, you are the faces of hope. You are living proof that some things are totally worth the wait. I love you so much.

ACKNOWLEDGMENTS

Without the vision of Kim Barton and Melanie Fountain of Fountain Blue Publishing, my blog would never have become the book that it is. They have provided direction and encouragement - all while reminding me that this "is my story to tell." I am forever grateful for the faith that they have in me and the faith that they have in our story.

I never would have been able to handle the endless emotional stresses involved with our battle with infertility without Brian. At our wedding, there was one line that all of our guests remember us repeating. The line is often quoted at family functions. "To be the father of our children." When the pastor had me repeat that line, I ad-libbed my own version - "To be the father of ALL FOUR of our children." At the time, it was funny. We always said that, "Aprill wants four children and Brian wants two. So we will compromise with four." We had no idea that the line in our vows and the compromise we would joke about, would end up representing one of the most devastating struggles in our lives. Throughout every cycle, every negative Beta, every loss, Brian reminded me of why we were fighting. We were fighting to be parents. Being parents is in our blood. We never thought for one second that we wouldn't be parents; we just didn't know how we were going to get there. If it weren't for his constant reminders of why we were fighting and why it was worth fighting for, I'm not sure we would be in the place we are now. I am amazed at his ability to remind me of how beautiful I was - even though we all knew I was 20lbs heavier than my pre - IVF weight, I had acne, night sweats, bags under my eyes, bruises all over my body. Those things never changed his vision of me. It's one thing to feel like a failure as a female; it's another thing to feel like a failure of a wife. If I ever felt like I was failing him, he reminded me that we are in this together. Although everyone remembers that one line from our wedding vows, what everyone should remember is how we have proven our honor. "Through sickness and health..." Not everyone gets to experience a love like ours, a marriage like ours and survival like ours. Two P's.

Dr. Beth Plante - How does one convey appreciation in a few short lines for the person who holds responsibility of building your family? I don't know. When I would send Dr. Plante crazy articles about tests done in countries thousands and thousands of miles away, she researched it. When I found tests that were available in other states, she found a way to provide us with the capabilities to partake in those tests. She fought for us - she constantly fought for us. She was fighting as hard as we were. Although we were her patients, we felt like she saw us as something else... Parents. We never felt like a number. We never felt rushed. We never felt unsupported. She presented us at rounds to get advice from colleagues. She would stay up at night thinking about our next steps. Good doctors are not rare. Good doctors exist all over the country. What you don't see often, are good doctors that are patient centric - that go above and beyond to make sure you are okay. It's not often that you find doctors as personable, understanding and compassionate as Dr. Plante. We love her like a sister. Thank you, thank you, thank you... for all of it.

I'd be remiss not to thank the staff at the clinic. Dr. Plante may have been the front woman in our care; however, she was not the only player. Dr. Hottie, Dr. PGD, Dr. Jerkface (who I grew to like a lot and actually wasn't mean), were all instrumental to our care. We are forever indebted to that clinic. All the amazing nurses, receptionists, coordinators, financial department - they're all part of the team that makes the clinic so amazing. We love you all.

Endless love and support came from our family and friends. It's not easy to support someone when you don't know how to relate to them. We appreciate all the people who followed my blog in attempts to understand us a little better. We are so honored that time was taken out of your day to research what we were going through. We were given space when needed and smothering when required. You may not have seen our appreciation when we were hiding in our misery but it was there. Much love.

AGC Girls... I get choked up just typing our name. Our friendships are bound by loss and failures but built on a foundation of love and hope. Some of us have never met yet we the best of best of friends. You represent strength, will, and determination. You are what every person should strive to be, regardless of their disease. Seriously, my heart is melting just trying to write this. Celebrate Hope my friends. Some things are totally worth the wait (although, there is nothing wrong with mentally punching people in the face while you are waiting).

Faith. Hope. Love.

Shine. Grace. Peace.

Dear Aprill,

The path to parenthood has been anything but easy for you and Brian. The highs and lows are excruciating at times. The process feels like a marathon. The marathon is long, the marathon is raw, and the marathon is physically and emotionally exhausting. Nevertheless, Miles and Mark are now a source of unimaginable love and joy, and I know you would say that the marathon is absolutely worth running.

Any person who has ever stepped foot in a fertility clinic will be able to identify with some aspect of your story. This honest, uncensored account will bring laughter and tears to your readers. It will remind those who are struggling to become parents that they are NOT alone. Perhaps most importantly, your unselfish willingness to share your story will bring hope and optimism to countless individuals, couples, and families.

Aprill, Brian, Miles, and Mark, I cannot thank you enough for the opportunity to participate in your care. It has truly been a pleasure and an honor to be part of your journey.

Dr. P

Better late than never...

This blog is long overdue (2.5 years overdue). I'm not sure what I have been waiting for. I follow other bloggers, I participate in fertility forums... why not have my own blog?

I'm not diseased, therefore I'm not contagious. I'm not a mother, but that doesn't mean I don't know how to mother. I'm not jealous, so don't act like you have something worth being jealous over. I'm not broken, so please don't try to fix me. I'm just a girl who loves a boy. I'm just a girl who is excited to start a family. I'm just a girl who has a few things to say. I'm just a girl...

I'll update our history another time... here's where we stand: We're on our 3rd round of IVF. We have been waiting since our miscarriage in February to get started. Currently, I am on birth control to get my body ready to produce lots and lots of eggs. I have no problems producing eggs. As my AMAZING Doctor once said "She puts my other patients to shame." Maybe when people make condescending comments I should fire back "Please, you can only produce one egg a month. I can produce 20. Top that." On June 9th, I will start Lupron injections. Lupron basically induces menopause. The goal is to stimulate my ovaries to produce a lot of eggs. What we don't want is for my body to naturally ovulate and release the eggs on its own. That's where Lupron comes in. It prevents my body from releasing the eggs. On June 25th (yes, my birthday and the one year anniversary of Michael Jackson's death) I will start Gonal-f injections. Gonal-f will be my friend for about 12 days. After that, it's egg retrieval and embryo transfer time. I'll explain all of this in detail as time goes on.

Misconception #1:
Infertile means Sterile.

Our History

It's a long one...
It all started on our honeymoon. We were so excited to throw all birth control out the window. We were all grown up,

married, and ready to have children. The first couple of months we didn't "try" but we weren't being safe. After a few months of that, we then started trying. How hard can getting pregnant be as a newlywed? After months of ovulation kits and periods, I decided to talk to my OBGYN. My OBGYN didn't seem too worried, but since it had been a year of trying, she wanted me to see a RE (Reproductive Endocrinologist). She also handed me a script of Clomid and told me to take it while I waited for an appointment with the RE.

Seventeen months after getting married, we met with the RE. My first thought was, "Damn, he's old." Our heads were spinning with all the terminology that he was throwing at us. He gave us options; drugs and timed intercourse, pill form of drugs and IUI, injection form of drugs and IUI, injections and IVF. We opted for the pills and IUI (If I knew then what I know now, I would have gone right to IVF). My husband, B, needed a semen analysis and I needed a Hysterosalpingogram...a WHAT!?!? We left the appointment feeling overwhelmed, yet hopeful. Both our tests came back perfect...beyond perfect. Following the results of the initial tests came three IUIs (intra-uterine insemination).

IUI #1: Cancelled

I over stimulated from the Clomid. My cycle was cancelled. At the time I was crushed. I didn't know anything about fertility treatments. When Dr. Old-Face called me he said, "I'm sorry, you can no longer continue treatment." I thought he meant forever. I spent the night crying my eyes out (we also watched Marley & Me... not smart). We had a meeting with Dr. Old-Face about a week later. That's when he clarified that I couldn't continue with Clomid, but could continue with other methods of treatment.

IUI #2: BFN (Big Fat Negative)

I was and still am terrified of the needles. TERRIFIED. I have a HUGE fear of needles...even after sticking myself with hundreds of them. The first night of needle injections involved zero fun and lots of screaming. Anytime B came near me, I would shove him away. I sooo did not want to stick a needle in my stomach. Finally, he pinned me down and just stabbed me. The needle going in was scary and the needle coming out was painful. I Love my husband to death, but that was the last time I was going to allow him to do it. When he withdrew the needle, he took my skin with him. I ended up texting a few firefighter friends (we used to live across from the station) and asked if they could give me the shots. From then on, at 8:00 pm, I went to the fire station for my shots. The first time I went, they gave me a Teddy Bear.

IUI #3: BFN

On to IVF...

IVF #1: BFN

We were just a month away from our 2 year anniversary. In my mind, IVF was the answer to our struggle. In Vitro is the end all and be all of fertility. How can it possibly not work? For Insurance purposes, I had to undergo a sonohystogram (saline in the uterus to see if it fills normally). That's where I met Dr. P...You'll hear a lot about her in future posts...

I was so excited for my ER (egg retrieval). I wanted a good dozen eggs. When I woke up from surgery and they told me that they retrieved 15 eggs. I was ecstatic. 15!! We are SO getting pregnant! My excitement only lasted a couple of minutes. I heard a nurse telling the girl in the curtain next to me that they only got two eggs. TWO! Hearing her sobs just broke my heart. After the ER, we came home and did nothing. I basically slept all day. I called the embryologist the next day to get our fertilization report. Of the 15 eggs, 13 were mature and 11 fertilized. They were all 2-4 cells (which is perfect for the 24 hour mark). I went in for the ET (embryo transfer) the next day. We were giddy and excited....making jokes about how we were about to conceive in front of doctors, fellows, nurses, and embryologists. As I'm lying on the bed, legs in stirrups, they tell us that we only had two embryos of decent quality to transfer, one 4-cell and one 5-cell (not good). The cells should double every 24 hours. By the time you get to your transfer they should be between 6-10 cells. The doctor working that day had ZERO bedside manner. He was telling his Fellow a story about how he transferred terrible looking embryos like ours into a colleague...blah, blah, blah. I was fighting back tears the entire time. While I was in recovery, he came in and gave us advice on "what we should think about doing the next time around." I was a mess. I should have been excited and hopeful. Instead, I was disappointed and crying.

IVF #2: BFP (Big Fat POSITIVE)

Dr. Old-Face went on Sabbatical. He told me he would assign me to another doctor. I asked him if it would be okay if I could get the nice Doctor that did my sonohystogram...he agreed and that's how I ended up with Dr. P. She has been a GODSEND. We just LOVE her.

Shortened version of cycle: 18 eggs retrieved, 15 mature, and 14 fertilized. They transferred an 8-cell, 7-cell, and 6-cell all under 10% fragmentation. In other words, they were ideal for a successful outcome. This time around, I felt different. I was doing acupuncture, I was positive, we had a near perfect fertilization rate, I felt great. We had a ski trip planned with some friends. Every day while they were skiing, I was secretly testing with

POAS (Pee on a Stick). I had one POAS left. It was four days before my Beta was scheduled. I woke up at 5:00 in the morning, took the test, waited about 30 seconds before throwing it away. I woke B up crying to tell him it was negative. A couple hours later, we got out of bed. Everyone was up making breakfast. I, all of a sudden got nervous that they would see the test in the trash. We were sharing a bathroom with my best friend and her husband...I have no idea why I was worried about the darn test. Anyway, I went to the bathroom to get it out of the trash and I saw a faint pink line. My heart started pounding. OMG, it's positive!! I couldn't believe it. I had acupuncture that night. My acupuncturist called me to tell me she was running late. "No problem," I said, "I can run errands." The only errand I had was to drive to the pharmacy and buy another test. I bought a few line ones and a digital one. I told myself I would wait until the morning to test again. Yeah right. I ended up testing in the bathroom at acupuncture. The digital said "PREGNANT." We were psyched...beyond psyched. The next day, I could hardly stand it. I called the nurses line at the office and told them I had a work meeting on Monday (total lie) and was wondering if I could do my Beta early. They weren't happy about it, but they agreed. I went in on Sunday for my blood test. I knew it was good news when they called. Every result call I had before this one started with "Is this a good time to talk." This time, the nurse started the conversation with "How's your day going?" My beta was 83. They like them to be between 50-100. 83 is wonderful, especially when you're testing early. They don't congratulate you until you have a second Beta done 48 hours later. They want to see doubling numbers. My beta came back at 243. Thank GOD! I could go into the emotional rollercoaster of the miscarriage and the days leading up to it. It's not that I don't want people to know what we dealt with, it's just that it's 2:30 and I'm starving. I need lunch.

SATURDAY, JUNE 5, 2010

Oxymoron

Every morning I wake up and take a birth control pill and a prenatal vitamin. Hmmm...

Today I would have been 21 weeks pregnant. I would have passed the halfway point in my pregnancy. I envision myself with a bowling ball belly in cute tank tops and sundresses. I always wanted to be a bikini pregnant girl. I think about the baby that would have been growing inside of me. I think about how wonderful it would be to throw up and want pickles and ice cream at 2:00 in the morning. I think about how our baby would be just a month old on Christmas. I can just see us walking into our family Christmas party and handing the baby off to be cradled in Santa's arms. Humph...

I guess now is a good time to talk about losing the baby. After you have your doubling beta at 48 hours (which is 14 days past transfer), you don't have to go back for another week. I went in for blood work around at 8:00 am on February 16th. Usually, I get my results from the nurses around 3:00. I knew something was wrong when 4:30 came around and I still hadn't heard anything. Finally at 4:53 (yes, I remember the exact time), they called..."Your beta was 1091. It's rising but it's not as high as it should be. Low rising Betas are signs of an ectopic pregnancy. Dr. P wants you to come in on Friday for an ultrasound and blood work." Not good. I immediately started researching Beta numbers on the internet. I found a handful of success stories with low rising Betas. I was going to beat the odds. Friday the 19th, I went in for my blood work in the morning. Our appointment was scheduled for 3:00. B is pacing the small exam room and I am sitting on the paper covered table half naked. Dr. P walks in, puts her hand on my knee and says, "Your Beta dropped to 700. It may be too early to see anything but let's take a look at your uterus." The amazing thing about Dr. P is that she makes you feel okay. Although my body was reacting to the news...I was sweating, my heart was pounding...I felt okay. She's a mother. She gives off the maternal vibe that makes you feel like everything will be just fine. I'm talking like she's 60. I have no idea how old she is. My guess is she's around the same age as us. Anyway... During the ultrasound, I just looked at B. I didn't want to see what I had in there. My head was pounding. My heart felt like it was beating in my ear drums. I heard Dr. P say things like, sack and yolk. I saw B trying his hardest to not break down. I just wanted to get out of there. After the ultrasound, Dr. P told me that I would most likely start bleeding any day. I had a few options: 1) I could take a pill that would dissolve the pregnancy. 2) I could wait it out and naturally pass the baby. 3) I could schedule a D&C and have it surgically removed. The pill wasn't an option for me. The baby was still a living being inside of me. I couldn't just take a pill knowing that it was still living. When we left the exam room, Barbara (my favorite nurse) was waiting with Dr. P. As soon as I saw Barbara, I broke down. I was sobbing on Barbara's shoulder while Dr. P was rubbing my back. I couldn't even look at B. I felt like such a failure of a woman. We're meant to carry children and I can't even do that for two months. After my two minutes of feeling sorry for myself, I said I wanted to pass the baby naturally and schedule a D&C just in case I don't pass it fully. We scheduled the D&C for Friday, February 26th. We went home and cried. We cried on the kitchen floor. We cried in the living room. We cried when we showered. All we did was cry. The next few days were torture. Every time I went to the bathroom, I checked the toilet for blood. I was inspecting every piece of toilet paper...I just wanted it to happen. Finally, on Monday afternoon (while I was shopping with a friend), I started bleeding. We stopped at CVS and got the most awful pads. They were like mattresses. I still make fun of my friend for those darn things. At first it wasn't bad. Just like a period. After a few hours of "not bad," it got ugly. I was buckled over in pain. It was excruciating. I had NEVER had pain that like. The next 24-36 hours were complete hell. On Wednesday, February 24, I went in for my D&C pre-op. I was alone. I didn't think it was necessary for B to be there while they told me how much of the baby had passed. After Dr. P and Barbara asked me how I was doing, Dr. P started the ultrasound. I should mention, that when I talk about having all these ultrasounds, they're not the over the belly kind. Every single ultrasound is a vaginal one. Most people freak out when they find out they are going to have them. Getting one done is like eating breakfast for me. It's just something I do nearly every day. During the ultrasound, Dr. P starts pressing all these buttons, looking really closely at the screen. She's turning the sound on; she's taking pictures... what is going on? Dr. P takes out the wand and says "Ugh, nothing is easy. I'm not done, but why don't you sit up so we can talk." Great, I have an effing tumor or she's going to tell me she has to take out my uterus. What she says next is not what I was expecting.

Dr. P: "Since Friday, the baby has developed a fetal pole and a heartbeat."

OMG!!!!!!!!!!! This is going either be a miracle or it is going to break me down when I just got up. Aye.

With hesitation and excitement, I laid back down on the table. When Dr. P showed me the most incredible flicker of a heartbeat, my heart just melted. Hearing it was incredible, but seeing it was even more amazing. The baby was measuring perfect for six weeks and the heartbeat was a strong 90 bpm...again perfect for six weeks. Dr. P wanted me to have blood drawn to see what was going on with my Beta. She told me to remain cautiously optimistic. Cautiously optimistic, I can do that. We cancelled the D&C and I left with a picture of our baby in my hands. I just sat in the parking lot, trying to get a hold of B, looking at Baby L. B was freaking out. He kept saying "This is unbelievable." Later in the day, she emailed me to tell me my Beta jumped up from 700 to 1200.

Around 3:30, I had severe, severe cramps. I buckled over on the toilet...sweating and praying that everything was going to be okay. This will be graphic...

After a MASSIVE cramp, I felt something pass. It felt like I passed a #2 through my vajayjay. I looked down and saw what looked like a bubble gum bubble the size of a golf ball. Although I knew what it was, I wouldn't allow myself to believe it. I just flushed the toilet and pretending it was nothing. As the night passed the cramping got worse. All I could think of was the baby with a heartbeat. If I was in that much pain, how could a baby the size of a grain of rice be okay?

The next day, I emailed Dr. P with concerns about the intensity of my cramps. She wanted me to go to the hospital to rule out ectopic. We transferred three embryos so there was a chance that one of them got stuck in my tubes. As soon as the tech started the ultrasound, I knew what had happened. I have seen my uterus hundreds of times throughout our many rounds of treatment. My uterus was empty. There wasn't even a sac in there. Baby L was gone and my pregnancy was over.

Misconception #2

Miscarriage is just like a period.

SUNDAY, JUNE 6, 2010

What Defines Me

My strength has been tested for 2.5 years. In the past three months, my confidence has been over shadowed by doubt. Many people feel that what we're going through is a weakness. They look at us and feel bad. It drives me absolutely bonkers (did I really say bonkers?!?!). My heart just breaks for those who feel the need to constantly judge others. What a miserable way to live. Walk a mile in my shoes...never mind a mile...walk ten feet in my shoes...

I knew I was Courageous when my fear of needles became a reality as I became a pin cushion.

I knew I was Brave when I made the decision to come home and watch our baby shed out of me.

I knew I was Defiant when I didn't allow infertility to break me down.

I knew I was Bold when I started having daily exams.

I knew I was Selfless when I didn't think twice about attending a baby shower.

I knew I was Determined when I didn't stop trying.

I knew I was Purposeful when I shared my story.

I knew I was Resilient when the drugs took over my body.

I knew I was Devoted when I kept standing as my world was crumbling.

I knew I was Proud when I gained 20 lbs from drugs.

Walk a mile in my shoes and rethink your judgment of me. From where I stand, I'm in a pretty amazing place.

Misconception #3:

You're thinking about it too much. If you stop trying, you'll get pregnant.

MONDAY, JUNE 7, 2010

Craft Room

Today I spent the morning creating a craft room. Before I begin, let me say that I had ankle surgery 20 days ago. I normally do not have time to create rooms. Normally, I spend my day working. Anyway...I went to IKEA yesterday, bought some organization items, textiles, and a couple of chairs. This morning I spent a few hours making the most AMAZING craft room. We live in a four bedroom house with two humans and three domesticated animal occupants. We bought this house thinking we'll have children to occupy the square footage. I have always wanted four children. B has always wanted two. I like to say "we'll compromise with four." So instead of making a nursery, or a playroom, I made a craft room. I kept thinking about how cute the room would make for a toddler. Sections of the ceiling are angled from exterior dormers, which make the room feel small and childlike. I know one day we will have children. I know one day a child will occupy that room. For now, it will be my play room and when the time comes, it will be our children's play room. How many kids get to have an entire room full of crafts?!?! I'll be the cool mom on the block (probably the only one too...half our neighborhood is verging on retirement).

I'm only two days away from becoming a pin cushion again. I'm excited, nervous, anxious, and slighted. I'm excited to get started again. I'm excited for the possibility of a BFP. I'm excited for the chance to become pregnant. I'm nervous that I have too high of expectations. I'm nervous that I'll be let down. I'm nervous that a BFP will end in another miscarriage. I'm anxious because I HATE needles. I'm anxious because I end up looking like a junky with bruised veins. I'm nervous because I get night sweats, headaches, and MOODY on the drugs. I feel slighted because I have to go through hell to get pregnant. I feel slighted because I am a good person. I feel slighted because I have a big heart and I don't deserve this nightmare. I don't have an illness. I am not in financial trouble. I am not angry. I am not greedy. I have amazing friends, both my parents, both my in-laws, two grandmothers, one grandfather, two grandmother-in-laws, one grandfather-in-law, two brothers, one sister, two sister-in-laws, three nieces, one great niece, six aunts, five uncles, four aunt-in-laws, five uncle-in-laws and many, many cousins. I know that a lot of people have it much worse than I do. I am blessed in many ways. However, that does not take away from my right to feel nervous, anxious, or slighted.

Misconception #4

If you have a miscarriage it means you need a surrogate.

TUESDAY, JUNE 8, 2010

Carnivore

I have always waivered on becoming a vegetarian. I have even stopped eating meat, but something would always bring me back (i.e. Thanksgiving). six weeks ago, B and I watched Food, Inc. I was disturbed, disgusted, and horrified at how the animals are raised and killed. Although this is MY blog and do have a right to get on a meat free soap box, I will not. My purpose for telling the story is not to convert a bunch of carnivores into herbivores. My purpose is this... I stopped eating meat six weeks ago because I couldn't stomach eating chicken knowing how they were terrified when they were about to be slaughtered. I couldn't eat bacon knowing that the pig was killed by a metal plate falling on him. I stopped eating meat for personal reasons....humane reasons. Last night, I forced myself to start eating it again. I made a turkey meat pasta sauce. I make it as sauce heavy as possible. I figured it was a good way to trick my body into eating it...ease my way back. It took everything I had to swallow the damn sauce. I was gagging to the point of causing tears to run down my face. Why am I writing about forcing myself to eat meat on a fertility blog? This is just another thing that infertility has taken from me...free will. I stopped eating meat for six weeks and loved it. It was a choice that I made for me. I felt great physically and more importantly, I felt great mentally. I was doing something that I felt was right. As my start date approaches, I started questioning my protein intake. What if I'm not getting enough protein? What if I miscarry, will I blame my new diet? So, rather than play the "what if" game, I chose to eat meat. I gagged, I cried, and I hated it.

Last night, I started getting a migraine. I usually do not do the birth control protocol for that reason. My first IVF I did the birth control protocol and ended up in the hospital with a migraine so severe, they thought I was having a stroke. Since my period decided to take three months to arrive after the miscarriage and since my body decided not to ovulate in a timely manner, I ended up on the BCP protocol. The migraine started last night and came on full force this morning. I woke up at 7:00, took some Vicodin (had some left over from the miscarriage) and went back to bed. I then slept until 2:00. My migraine is still here but has lessened from the intake of early morning narcotics (only one... I'm not a junky). This is a terrible reminder of what the next month or so will be like.

A friend from high school sent me a really nice message about the blog along with her personal story. In her message she said something that I love; "...there is a baby out there for you, he/she is just having trouble finding you." Tomorrow I start my journey with Lupron. I pray that our baby starts its journey to find us.

Misconception #5

Infertile means we do not know when and how to have sex.

WEDNESDAY, JUNE 9, 2010

7:18

I grew up at house #718. It seems like every time I look at the clock, its 7:18. 7:18 has turned into a joke in our house. I once told B that I thought it was weird that I'm always looking at the clock at 7:18. He made fun of me and jokingly ran around the house saying "Oh my Gosh, it's 7:18. I can't believe it!!" Geesh. I'm superstitious...so what?!?!

I am probably the BIGGEST Michael Jackson fan in history. I'm no joke. When he died on my 30th birthday, I was not only a mess but I also became a little bit obsessed. I guess I've always been obsessed but that's beside the point. My last cycle (when we did get pregnant) we had our embryo transfer on January 26, 2010. That date may not mean anything to the average folk. However, to a Michael Jackson fan, that date means something. January 26, 2010, Michael Jackson's movie "This Is It" was released. The movie is called THIS IS IT...not a coincidence.

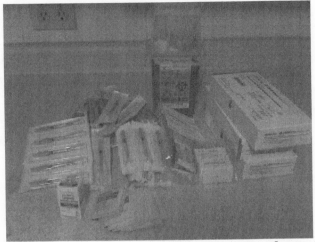

And so it begins today. Today is the start of my Lupron phase of my cycle. Bring on the needles. I have fresh skin, free of bruises and tenderness. So, my shot wasn't so bad. It left a small red rash with a raised center (just like a bee sting). I actually sent a picture via text to a friend of my belly with the caption "Just a little bee sting." She replied "WTF!?!??!?!?" I then had to clarify then I wasn't being literal and that the mark was from my shot. When I finished my shot, I turned around to throw away the alcohol swab and looked at the clock. In bright green, the stove was glowing "7:18." And so it begins...

Misconception #6

It's not meant to be. It will happen when the time is right.

THURSDAY, JUNE 10, 2010

Sleeping with Needles

Last cycle, I started seeing an acupuncturist. My doctor's office is on the first floor of a three story building. The second floor holds the lab and an oncology clinic. The third floor is the chemo floor. Every doctor's appointment, I check in on the first floor, I sign a few papers, then I get a lab slip to have blood work done. One day, I was sitting in the second floor waiting room and I noticed a sign for alternative therapies. There was information on Yoga, Reiki, Acupuncture, massage, and some other treatments. I was hesitant to call due to my fear of needles. However, I figured if the clinic is promoting it, they must believe in it. I called the number and scheduled an appointment. As I was lying on the table with needles sticking out of my body, I was amazed at how my body was responding. My stomach was making crazy noises, I was incredibly relaxed, and at one point, I could just feel the heat coming off my body. I know it sounds crazy. I'm sure all of those things can be explained by something I ate or the temperature of the room. What I do know is this, since doing acupuncture, I sleep better, my migraines have lessened, and our egg/embryo quality has significantly improved. Can I say for sure it's the acupuncture? No. I'm not going to take the risk by stopping treatment just to see if things change.

Yesterday was the first time I slept through a session. My acupuncturist, Alice, put the needles in and within a few seconds of her leaving the room, I was out. I kept dreaming that I was pregnant with twins. The twins were not in the same belly. I had two bellies. They split right where the belly button would be. At one point in my dream, I was sewing two maternity shirts together for my twin-holding double belly. Yesterday, I was saying that I'm superstitious and I believe in signs...What the heck kind of sign is that?? I left acupuncture well rested and relaxed. I quickly forgot about the bizarre double belly dream until this morning.

The Lupron package insert has many side effects listed. One it does not list, although it should, is vivid dreams. Fertility treatments take up your entire life. Although every aspect of your life is affected, once the cycle is over, you very quickly forgot what you went through and dealt with. Once the cycle is over you are either focusing on the fact that you are pregnant or you are focusing on the "what's next." When I had the crazy belly dream yesterday, I didn't make the connection to Lupron. Last night, my dreams got even crazier. I was dreaming that I had a few pet pigs. One of them was very upset with me (yes, it could talk) because I was eating bacon. Let me just say, it has only been two days of eating meat again and I am BARELY eating it. I'm still easing my way in. Back to Charlotte (I know. It's a dream; I can't control the naming of pigs. If only creativity was a side effect of Lupron). Charlotte was distraught and crying over my decision to eat meat again. She asked me to leave the house and think about what I was doing. I ended up meeting my mother at a field. There was a brown horse tied up to a tree. The horse seemed a little skittish. We didn't want to startle it, so we walked around it. After we walked around it, I felt bad. I kept saying to my mother "I rescue animals. That's what I do. We can't just walk away." Just as I finished telling my mother that I wanted to save the horse, a boy comes riding over on a tricycle. He was screaming "That's the horse that killed Michael. Stay away." As soon as the boy got close to me, I recognized who he was. He was D, my brother-in-law. He was D as a 6 year old. He jumped off his tricycle and started running towards us. As he was running, the horse stared lashing out. D wanted us to leave, but I couldn't. I kept yelling "I rescue animals." Then I woke up.

If crazy, vivid dreams were the only side effects I got from Lupron, I wouldn't mind. I know a few people who have been on it for a few days longer than I have. They have yet had any side effects. I'm jealous, envious, and more jealous. I take one dose and I'm a mess. Aside from the vivid dreams, I am having really bad night sweats. I woke up several times last night, completely drenched. There is zero fun sleeping in a pool of your own bodily fluids (that sounds gross). Welcome back Night Sweats, welcome back.

I also get really bloated from Lupron. I'm only on day two of it, so I'm still enjoying having shapely shoulders and a jaw line. Let's see how quickly that changes.

Misconception #7

Undergoing fertility treatments means you'll end up Octomom

FRIDAY, JUNE 11, 2010

Hot Mess

Only three doses of Lupron and I'm a hot mess. Last night I was watching So You Think You Can Dance and I was a mess. You would have thought I was mourning over a death. No, I was crying at a dance show. Not only was I crying my eyes out, I was also a complete bitch. One minute I'm crying, the next minute I'm snapping at B and then I start laughing. Is this honestly what it is like to go through Menopause? Can't menopause last years? How does one deal with that? I slept in just underwear last night. I still had the night sweats but due to the lack of clothing sticking to my body, they were easier to deal with. Night sweats, check! Mood swings, Check! I am dreading what is coming next...fat face Aprill.

Today I went to pick up my prenatal refill. While handing me the prescription, the pharmacy technician asks me, "You're still trying?" When I respond with a VERY short "yes," she then proceeds to say, "It has been a while, Huh. Well, I'll cross my fingers for you." Menopause induced psychosis kicked in. I nearly leaped over the counter to take her down. Even in my bitchiest mood, I could not yell at her. I just don't have that in me...Lupron or not. I figure the best way to handle this situation is to make a list of statements and questions that you should never ask.

1. You're not getting younger. You should really start thinking about having children.

2. What is wrong with you anyway? Can't you just have sex?

3. Are the doctors concerned yet? You must be worried.

4. You knew what you were getting into when you decided to do fertility treatments.

5. Are you having sex during ovulation?

6. They make kits. Have you tried those?

7. You can always adopt.

8. Have you thought about a surrogate?

9. Can you get donor egg/sperm?

10. You don't look well.

11. Are you tired?

12. What if you end up with eight babies?

13. I hate being pregnant.

14. Don't have kids.

15. Life sucks after kids.

16. Are you pregnant yet?

17. Is the problem with you or your husband?

18. Maybe your husband isn't getting excited enough.

19. You should have sex more.

20. I can just look at my husband and I end up pregnant.

21. I don't understand because I easily get pregnant.

22. When you have kids, you'll understand.

23. You must be sad.

24. I feel bad for you.

25. You can take my kids anytime.

26. You're thinking about it too much.

27. If you stop trying you'll get pregnant.

28. Try relaxing.

29. It will happen when the time is right.

30. It's just not meant to be.

I could keep going but this list is getting long and I'm not getting any younger. I guess I should get off the computer and think about starting a family.

Misconception #8

If you're infertile there must be a "problem" with either you or your spouse.

SATURDAY, JUNE 12, 2010

Bye Bye Birth Control

Today is my last day of Birth Control Pills! It felt so good to throw them away! It is also Day one of my period (although the pill is preventing it coming in its fullest form). I just took two steps further in the process.

I lost my shoulders to bloat. Although I knew this was going to happen, I'm still bummed. I was hoping to escape the side effect of bloat. I still have definition between my face and neck...that's good I guess. The longer I have with my face, the better. My stomach is also not doing well. It's very upset. I read in the package insert that upset stomach after injection is very common. If my stomach as any sort of pressure, it makes me want to vomit. Awesome. I have to keep reminding myself that this means that my body is responding.

I got a message on the fertility forum that I take part in. I thought I would share it with you. What I said resonated with her and what she said resonated with me. The sentence in bold really hit home with me.

I just finished catching up on your blog and have to say how amazing it is. It is like you are eloquently stating everything that has been swimming around my brain for years.

*Yesterday was the one year anniversary of the horrible day we lost our little girl. It has been a tough week. 17 weeks of hard, hard work growing that little darling, and then she had to go. Your comment about not looking at the u/s screen really resonated with me. I still get a little sick looking at it - **it's so hard to stomach the sight of an empty uterus after you've been blessed enough to see a full one before...***

Anyway, sorry to be a Debbie-Downer! This has been taking over my mind this week and DH (bless his heart) is starting to look a little weary of my down-trodden heart. Hopefully the weekend will re-energize, revitalize, and redirect.

Many people do not consider losing a child through miscarriage as a death. If you have ever been pregnant, no matter how long you were pregnant for, you understand what it is like to have a baby growing inside of you. That baby's life becomes a part of you. That baby's life becomes more important than your own. If you don't understand that, then you may be missing the maternal gene or like one of my friends calls it, the sensitivity gene. June 10th will never be the same for her just like February 25th won't be the same for me. I will always remember how I was feeling and what I was doing on that day.

Every October 16th I will think of our baby. I will think of the full-term delivery that never happened. I will think of milestones that Baby L will never cross. Every other day I will get an ultrasound during this cycle. Every one of those ultrasounds will remind me of Baby L. I will remember how I was feeling when I saw and heard the heartbeat. I will remember the confusion on the hospital's face when my uterus was empty. I will remember how I felt when all hope was lost. There will always be a date or an event that will make us think of BL. The mourning of Baby L will go on as long as we live.

Misconception #9

The loss of an unborn child is not a big deal.

SUNDAY, JUNE 13, 2010

Common Sense

Yesterday was torture. I was out running errands and had to return early due to an excruciating migraine and KILLER cramps. I came home around 3:00, laid myself down on the couch, and didn't get up again. The only time I got up was to walk myself to my bedroom. Thank God I woke up feeling much better. Other than mild cramps and a dull headache, I feel great.

Yesterday, I received a request for a list of things that are okay to say in my presence. I never want anyone to feel like they are walking on eggshells near me. I never want people to feel like they have to avoid conversation because of what we're going through. I just ask that you use common sense when we're in conversation (A.W., I can assure you, you have common sense). You would never ask someone with an infection on their leg "Have you thought of amputation?" You would never say to someone about to undergo a double mastectomy "You can always get implants." You would never say to someone with Alzheimer's "I wish I couldn't remember my life." You would never to say to anyone with any type of health illness "stop thinking about it and you'll be fine." Imagine if you or a family member was placed in the hospital for an anxiety attack. You are conversing with a group of friends and one of them says to you "What's wrong with you anyway, can't you just be happy like everyone else?" Not only would you be hurt, you'd be pissed. If you have common sense, you would never say those things anyway. I think common sense doesn't just come with age it also comes with life experiences. If you have been blessed with a life full of ease, then for obvious reasons, you wouldn't understand what it is like to deal with any type of struggle. The common sense of what not to say therefore is not there. If I'm ever in a conversation that I'm uncomfortable with, I'll excuse myself. If anyone makes a comment that I feel is inappropriate, I'll tell them. I don't expect anyone to know what will upset me and what won't. I do expect people to use common sense and not say things they wouldn't want said to them.

The Celtics are on so this is going to be a short one today.

Misconception #10

Infertility is uncommon.

Intuition

Since my miscarriage my cycles have been all screwed up. My levels were back to normal the week of March 7th. Normally it takes four to six weeks from the time your levels go back to normal to get your period. My period decided not to come again until May 8th. I woke up on May 8th to severe thunderstorms. I was running a 5k with a friend that day. I text her to see if she thought it would be still on. I checked the webpage for the race for any phone numbers or contact information. We decided to take the risk and drive the 30 minutes to the race. The race was a Fallen Hero Honor Run. It wasn't just a run. My friend said she'd be devastated if they didn't cancel the run and we didn't go. We went thinking it wouldn't actually go on. On our drive there we were making jokes about how my period will decide to show up during the race. I made joking references to Uta Pippig (Boston Marathon winner that crossed the finish line with diarrhea and blood dripping down her legs). As soon as we got there the rain stopped. Well, it stopped until about five minutes before the race. Right when the race started, the weather turned from bad to ugly. It was POURING. We were hit with a huge thunderstorm. Needless to say every single runner was soaked from head to toe. I could barely see with all the rain in my face and I had a slight shiver from the chill. Right around the mile and a half mark I started to get a cramp. I thought I was running too fast so I slightly slowed my pace down. I was keeping pace with a guy in a yellow running shirt. As he crossed the Mile 2 mark, he yelled "Mile 2!" Immediately after that I felt a gush of something warm. Of Course my period decides to come now. I ran the last 1.1 miles as fast as I could. When I crossed the finish line, I looked at my friend and yelled "Uta Pippig!" She replied with "Are you kidding me?!?!" I ran right past her and to the porta-potty. The rain ended up being a blessing in disguise. Had it not rained and had every runner not be soaked, I would have crossed the finish line just like Uta Pippig. Due to the rain you could not tell that I was extra oozy. Awesome.

The plan I follow for IVF is a fairly standard plan. On day 21 of your cycle you start Lupron. About a week after you start Lupron you get a period. On day one of your period, you call the nurses line. They then schedule you for a baseline ultrasound and blood work. If all goes well, you start your stim drugs a few days after that. Day 21 of my cycle was May 28th. On May 28th, I started Lupron. My cycle has not been normal since my pregnancy and miscarriage. At one point I ovulated twice before my period arrived at the race. Then I had this feeling that I didn't ovulate before starting the Lupron. I wasn't sure if that mattered but to make sure, I decided to email Dr. P. She emailed me back and told me to come in for blood work to check my progesterone level. The levels came back negative which meant I had in fact not ovulated. Since I was on day two of Lupron they had to put me on birth control pills to induce a period. If you take Lupron before ovulation it can cause a flare effect on your ovaries. It can stim your ovaries instead of suppress them. I stopped the Lupron, started the pill and here I am today. Since the start of this cycle I have had this strange feeling like it's not right. I know I can't expect my last cycle to be the same as this one. Every cycle is different. However, my last one worked. Since it worked, I'm getting nervous at every little detail that is different this time. Usually your egg transfer is two weeks after your period. This time around, my transfer will be four weeks after my period. You need to be on Lupron for two weeks before starting stim drugs. My baseline is not for another week. I have had this uneasy feeling since my period's arrival in May. Maybe it's my expectations are high so I'm nervous to be let down. Or maybe, it's my intuition telling me to hold off. I again ended up emailing Dr. P with my concerns about transferring a month after my period. She said we SHOULD (yes, she capitalized the word) be okay as the Lupron should prevent any hormonal production from my ovaries...which is what affects the lining. The concern of the "flare effect" is still there since I got my period only a couple days into the Lupron treatment. She told me we could stop now or we could continue moving forward and see how everything goes at the baseline ultrasound. Since I already opened and started the Lupron injections, I opted to keep going. If we have to cancel the cycle on the 21st, then so be it. So the waiting begins....

Misconception #11

Normal is not a miracle.

TUESDAY, JUNE 15, 2010

Good News/Bad News

Yesterday I received good news from one friend and bad news from another. What do you want first? The good news or the bad? I'll start with the bad. My friend's fifth IVF resulted in a BFN. Although she was somewhat prepared for the bad news, she was still devastated. The negative results do not get easier. They only get harder. Each failed attempt breaks down your confidence. After each failed attempt, you feel like you have achieved success in one area...failure statistics. Once you fail, you have hoped that it won't happen again. When I miscarried, I was told that close to 50% of first pregnancies end in miscarriage. As sad as I was, it gave me hope that I crossed that statistic. I am no longer in the first pregnancy category, so the next time it happens, it will work. Again, I'm setting myself up for disappointment. I'm living in the now. If believing that I've crossed the miscarriage barrier comforts me right now, then so be it. I'll deal with the disappointment later. Now, for the good news. My other friend found out yesterday that she had a 100% fertilization rate. What does that mean? Of all her eggs retrieved, every single one of them fertilized. 100% fertilization rate is AMAZING.

Today I'm feeling really dizzy. I think I have a migraine coming on. Booo to drug induced migraines. I do not like them. My skin also feels like its crawling. It's so sensitive to touch...which means, my injections hurt like a mother bleeper. It took me a few seconds just to get the needle to break my skin this morning. It hurt so badly. It actually drew blood. Drew blood made me think of True Blood. I can't wait for the new season! ADD moment... sorry. I know I don't give myself the injections correctly. You're supposed to just stab yourself. I can't do that due to my fear of needles. Stabbing is very difficult for me. After I alcohol swab my belly, I place the needle on my skin then slowly push it through. I know this method is more painful than the stabbing method. It may be more painful physically but it is much less painful mentally.

I'm only seven days away from my Baseline Ultrasound and blood work. seven days...can't pass quickly enough.

Misconception #12

Fertility is hereditary.

WEDNESDAY, JUNE 16, 2010

Blue Whale

I feel like a blue whale today. My face is so incredibly bloated that I bet if you put me next to a blue whale you wouldn't be able to tell the difference. Have you ever seen a blue whale? It has the largest head of any animal to ever exist. A blue whale's head is so big that you can fit an entire professional football team, yes 50 huge men, on its tongue. Did you know that the largest blue whale to date is a female that weighed 389,760 pounds? I'm sure she was on Lupron. If you have not seen a blue whale, you can get a good idea of what they look like by looking at me. My face is huge. Nah, it is gigantic. Gigantic doesn't do it justice. It's monstrous...it's freaking MAMMOTH. For the Love of God it's colossal!! I'm hoping that this means the Lupron is working. If the Lupron is working then we should be good to continue treatment after my baseline on Monday. I'm glad the blue whale exists. If it didn't, they (the animal creators/namers) would have to create a new species because I sure the hell do not look human.

I'm going to go spend my day scaring children. Never mind children, I'm going to scare adults, dogs, spiders... I am going to scare anything that looks at me. I'm going to scare more people than Sloth (Goonies: "Hey you guys" and "Baby Ruth") did.

Misconception #13

If you want it badly enough, you'll get pregnant

THURSDAY, JUNE 17, 2010

T-5

Last night I was debating having a bowl (one scoop...so it was a small bowl) of Ben & Jerry's (Boston Crème Pie... mmmmmmm). Before I continue my story, I would like to disclose that B and I eat very well. We avoid processed foods as much as possible, we eat fresh fruits and veggies with every meal, we very rarely eat anything outside of the whole grain family and we don't eat high fat meats, we stick to the lean proteins. So If I have a bowl of ice cream here and there, I think I'll be okay. I know I just needed to say that to make myself feel better. Anyway, I was debating if I should have the ice cream. I try my very best not to eat past 7:30... of course if we're out with friends or having people over, that doesn't apply. So my deciding factor with the ice cream was the time. Can you guess what time it was? It was 7:18. Of course, it was a sign that I should eat the darn ice cream. So I did.

I had a terrible night's sleep. I had crazy Lupron dreams. I woke up several times completely drenched in sweat. I'm also feeling a little "full." This fullness is making me a little nervous. I have a similar feeling to how I feel on the stim drugs. I'm hoping that this doesn't mean I'm having the "flare" effect with the Lupron. We'll find out on Monday. T-5 days. Not a bad wait. On top of the Lupron side effects I forgot to put on my ankle brace. My poor ankle that is trying to heal from surgery was getting tossed around with my dreams (I was running after a tractor that had my cat Henry hanging off the front). Needless to say, I'm tired.

I am one of those people who very rarely will feel bad for themselves. I take things as they come and accept the good and the bad. It is very easy to remain positive when you remind yourself that there is always someone else who has it worse. I was reading a post on the fertility forum I take part in. The girl lives in the Middle East and found out yesterday that the United Arab Emirates government passed a law making it illegal to freeze embryos. To us, that may make us angry but not seem so bad. However, it is against the Muslim religion to do so. So after they transferred two embryos, they threw the remaining embryos in the trash...against her will and religion. That's not cool. I may hate what I have to go through but at least every part of it is my decision. Well sort of, the insurance company makes you jump through hoops to get where you need to be but still, in comparison, it's not bad.

No matter what happens Monday. Cancelled cycle or not, I do not have it that bad. There is always someone has it worse.

Misconception #14

Fertility treatments make getting pregnant easy.

FRIDAY, JUNE 18, 2010

A whole lot of Fun

I only have four more days until my baseline. I have a feeling my cycle may get cancelled but you never know. I could be wrong. I have only been wrong once in my 30 years of living.

I'm exhausted. I sleep so poorly due to all the side effects. I end up getting out of bed feeling like I never got a chance to close my eyes. It's really great. Lying in bed and feeling like complete shit. Luckily my acupuncturist was able to give me some extra love today. Hopefully I notice a difference tonight.

I went to drugs.com and copied all the side effects of Lupron. I have highlighted in BOLD all the side effects that I have. I didn't highlight anything that had to do with joints, bones and feeling in legs/feet since I had ankle surgery just a couple of weeks ago. I didn't realize how many side effects I had until I did this. 27 out of 42. More than 50% (64% to be exact)... No wonder I feel like shit.

- bone pain;
- swelling, rapid weight gain;
- pain, burning, stinging, bruising, or redness where the medication was injected;
- feeling like you might pass out;
- painful or difficult urination;
- urinating more often than usual; or
- sudden headache with vision problems, vomiting, confusion, slow heart rate, weak pulse, fainting, or slow breathing.

Rare but serious side effects may include:
- pain or unusual sensations in your back;
- numbness, weakness, or tingly feeling in your legs or feet;
- muscle weakness or loss of use; and
- loss of bowel or bladder control.

Less serious Lupron side effects may include:
- acne, increased growth of facial hair;
- dizziness, weakness, tired feeling;
- hot flashes, night sweats, chills, clammy skin;
- nausea, diarrhea, constipation, stomach pain;
- skin redness, itching, or scaling;
- joint or muscle pain; vaginal itching or discharge
- breast swelling or tenderness; testicle pain;
- impotence, loss of interest in sex;
- depression, sleep problems (insomnia), memory problems; or
- redness, burning, itching, or swelling where the shot was given

Misconception #15

It's all psychological. Most people need to just relax and they'll get pregnant.

SATURDAY, JUNE 19, 2010

Gender Reveal

One of my best friends had her gender scan on Wednesday. Her (D) and her husband (T) decided they wanted to find out while they were surrounded by family and close friends. D printed out a piece of paper that said "IT'S A _____." She had the ultrasound tech fill it in, seal it up in an envelope that also included the picture of the baby's genital area (sounds absurd saying that but I don't know how else to word that part of the baby). D then took the envelope to our (I say 'our' because she works at our favorite coffee shop... well; my favorite coffee shop is in San Diego. I'll rephrase that; our favorite LOCAL coffee shop) baker and told her she wanted a vanilla cake with chocolate frosting. If the paper in the envelope said "boy" D wanted the cake dyed blue. If it said "girl," she wanted it dyed pink. D & T then had family and close friends over for a gender reveal party. The cake was just sitting on the counter while we waited for the time to come to cut it. I was going bonkers. I must have asked a million times if we could cut the cake first. I know you're all wondering... how the heck I was there to begin with. Remember the post I had a couple weeks ago that listed all the things "I knew?" I knew I was strong...I knew I was brave...I knew I was selfless...and so on. I didn't just list those things for the sake of a blog. I honestly and truly know I am those things. I am strong. I am brave. I am selfless. I would never allow my personal struggle get in the way of another's joy...especially one of my best friend's joy. I know B feels the same way. So, without hesitation we were there and taking part in every way possible. I even made a toast without falling apart. That doesn't mean I didn't feel like I was going to puke all over myself. However, I would have if need be. Taking part of D & T's excitement isn't about me, B, Baby L or what we are going through. It's about D & T and Baby H. Of course sadness ran through me. I was sad that we would never get to celebrate Baby L's life. I was sad that Baby L would never meet Baby H. I was sad that we don't have the option of having a baby whenever we want. Yes, I shed tears for that sadness and that's okay. Crying for me, for B and for Baby L, surrounded by friends is a good thing. I wouldn't miss taking part of Baby H's gender reveal or any part of Baby H's life, for anything. I don't care if I had to breathe in a paper bag to get through it. I'd sit there with a bag over my mouth with tears of joy streaming down my face. Life isn't always about what we want and what we need. Life is about celebrating the joys and happiness that we're surrounded by. If we were to dwell on the things we do not have, we'd live a miserable existence. Needless to say, we were there. We were attentive. We were happy. We were excited. We were friends and not victims. We love D &T and would never miss this moment with them. Back to the reveal...The emotion in the room was intense. There was anxiety, excitement, happiness, love....it was pretty cool. Right before cutting the cake, there seemed to be a million different distractions coming up. The knife would hit the cake then something would happen where D would stop. Then the knife would hit the cake again and something would happen where D would stop. Finally (after I said, will you just cut the cake already!), the cake was cut and we all saw the BRIGHT BLUE inside. It was such an exciting moment. We all toasted our red Solo cups to Baby Boy Hogan and celebrated his Gender. Hahahaha... that sounds funny. D & T couldn't have been happier. I have never seen such a glow on anyone. T kept looking at the ultrasound that was in the envelope (may I add, the ultrasound tech did a VERY good job zooming in on Baby H's boyhood...darn thing looked like an extra arm) and smiling. At one point T went to the refrigerator and I heard him giggling to himself "It's a boy." That's what life is about. That's why and how I know I have the strength to endure the pains, physical and emotional, to keep going.

As for the side effects, they're still here. My daily migraine didn't hit until we were at D & T's last night. It was probably around nine or so when it came. Two Tylenol and some extra water and it went away. It only bothered me for an hour or so. Not bad. Only three days until my baseline. Yay!

You may notice a link above the "about us" section. It says "The BFP July IVF Club." We have a list going on the fertility forum of all our big dates. One of the members made a calendar on a site that we can look at daily. Since most of the girls follow my blog, I figured I would post it on here.

Misconception #16

Struggling to get pregnant means you will be bitter and angry towards those who don't struggle.

SUNDAY, JUNE 20, 2010

Canine Weight Gain

Sorry for the late post today. I don't really have anything going on. I'm anxious for my appointment tomorrow morning. If my cycle cancels, then we just have to wait another month or two before we start again. It's really not that big of a deal. However, when you have been waiting 2.5 years to get pregnant any delay can seem like a lifetime in length.

My dog seems to be bloating in the abdomen area just as I am. Is it possible for Canines to have sympathy weight gain? If so, Cappy is sympathizing. I hope he is not getting my killer headaches too. Although, since acupuncture on Friday, my headaches have lessened A TON. I still have a constant dull headache all day but I am no longer getting the debilitating 2:00 migraines. I heart acupuncture.

This is what will happen tomorrow:

I will arrive at 8:30 am. When I check in, the receptionist will have me fill out a few forms then hand me a lab slip. I will then go upstairs to the lab, have my blood drawn and then go back down to the fertility clinic. I will be greeted by one of the nurses who will take my baseline form, put it on a clipboard, and walk me to an exam room. Once we get to the room, the nurse will instruct me to empty my bladder. I will then go back to the exam room, undress from the waist down (minus my socks if I have them on. It's always cold in there). I then sit my half naked body on the paper covered exam table with my clipboard and wait for a nurse. While I wait, I will fill out my baseline form. The information is basic: Name, date, date of first day of last menses, list medications taken and cycle day number. When the nurse arrives, she will put on gloves, open a condom, squeeze some lube into the condom and then she will put it on the ultrasound wand. During all of this she will ask me two questions; "Do you have a latex allergy" and "Have you had a period since starting Lupron?" Once she has achieved her goal of putting the lubed up condom (they're always Trojans) on the ultrasound wand, I will lay back with my clipboard in hand and put my feet in the stirrups. Since the nurse has one hand on the wand and the other hand is needed for the computer. She will measure my uterus, my stripe, and ovaries. As she measures them, she will be yelling out numbers and I will be writing them down on my baseline form. That's it. I will then leave and wait for a call from the nurse. Although I am very familiar with my ovary size and what the lining should look like at baseline, I will not know if my cycle will continue or get cancelled until I get the phone call. My hormones could be reading the complete opposite of my ultrasound. They both have to be in a perfect state in order for me to move forward. I most likely won't post tomorrow until after I get the call. They usually call around 3:00ish. I very much dislike waiting...

Misconception #17
Methods like acupuncture don't help with infertility

MONDAY, JUNE 21, 2010

Results are in

Sorry for the late post today. I'm getting texts, emails, and Facebook messages like crazy. I didn't realize people were waiting on my results. Sorry!!!

I got to the office this morning a little before 8:30. After I checked in, I went upstairs to have my blood drawn. I was so freaking nervous. I forgot how much I hate needles. You get used to the needles in the belly but you don't get used to the ones in the arm. Those gosh darn things hurt. Your veins start to develop scar tissue from being stabbed so many times. When that happens, it is so painful to get a needle in. After having my blood drawn I went downstairs. As soon as I walked through the double door I saw Barbara, my favorite nurse. I haven't seen her since my miscarriage. We chatted for a bit...said a lot of "Miss you" comments and then I walked over to the nurses' station. After giving the nurse my baseline paper she told me to empty my bladder. "Already did," I replied (I'm a pro at this). She then put me in a room told me to do my thing and left. I sat my naked bum on the paper covered exam table. I placed a white sheet over my lap and waited. As I was waiting, I filled out my baseline from. A couple minutes later, there was a knock on the door and in came Barbara. She said "I had to fight for you. Three of us wanted you. "Hahahaha...I didn't know my vagina, uterus and ovaries were so wanted. I had a strange feeling of pride when she said that. Fight over me all you want ladies! While Barbara was filling the Trojan with ultrasound gel, I was telling her that I was nervous of the flare effect. She understood my worries and said that your body does wacky things after a miscarriage. No kidding! First she measured my left ovary. It measured at 32x28mm (exactly how it always measures during baseline). My left ovary had multiple follicles under 12mm (exactly what you want for a baseline). My Right ovary measured 22x28mm (again, right where it usually is) and had five follicles under 12. She then measured my stripe which she said was "perfect." During all of this we were talking about 4th of July plans. I was telling her that I really didn't have any since my tentative retrieval date was July 6th. Barbara suggested that we try to start stim drugs earlier so we can avoid a 4th of July egg retrieval. I left the ultrasound feeling good. All I had to do was wait for the blood work results.

Barbara called me around 2:30 to give me my plan. When you hear those words, you know everything looks good. To avoid 4th of July, we will start stims tomorrow. I will drop my Lupron from 10 units in the morning to 5 units. Then between 7:00 and 9:00 pm I will take 225 units of Gonal-F (stim injection). I will do that, Tuesday, Wednesday, Thursday, and Friday. Saturday morning, I will have my first ultrasound to see how those wonderful follies are growing. Here we go...let's go follies!

I'm skipping the misconception for today. I'm excited and don't feel like bringing myself down.

TUESDAY, JUNE 22, 2010

Separation Anxiety

Today I am spending the day filing all our bill statements, insurance statements, tax papers. It's a very boring job but I have to do it. We have an orange storage box that we keep throwing the papers in. If I don't file them soon, the box will be full and I'll be annoyed. I also bleached down the master bath. I guess this is my pre-egg retrieval/transfer nesting. Plus, I'm getting really bored not working. My surgeon said he would clear me for work in a few weeks. I have already created a spare bedroom, created a craft room, weeded and mulched our yard (which is a lot of mulching), washed down our deck, caught up on ALL of my DVR'd shows, played on Facebook way too much, cleaned out/refilled our bird feeders. I'm running out of things to do. I can only drive short distances so I've already tackled all the surrounding stores. B probably has a heart attack every time he comes home and sees a new purchase. I can't complain. The timing of my ankle recovery is perfect for my cycle. I didn't plan it (I planned on my cycle going back to normal months ago) but it worked out perfectly.

My 31st birthday is only a few days away (Friday the 25th) and I can't help but stress about my age. I realize that 31 is NOT old. I do not think that it is old. However, pregnancy complications and risks rise each year I age. The risks are higher once you hit 35. I don't think it will take until then for us to have a baby. Although the risk of conceiving a baby with chromosomal problems rise each year I get older, I'm not worried about the first baby, I'm worried about the babies after that. We'll have to worry about Down syndrome, premature delivery, still birth, maternal delivery death...not to mention the worry about getting pregnant since the fertility rates decline. As if we need a lower chance of conceiving. There's no reason for me to worry about that now. Easier said than done.

I went to a cookout on Saturday that was full of babies, children, and pregnant ladies. At first I wasn't going to go because I wasn't in a place mentally to be surrounded by that. After feeling guilty for not going and after D talked me into it (she told me that she would hang out with me in a corner if need be), we decided to go. It wasn't bad. I wasn't social like I usually am. I stuck to who I knew I'd be most comfortable with. I purposely didn't say hi to a few people that I should have acknowledged. They were pregnant and I wasn't in the mood for pregnancy talk. Attending parties and only taking part in what you can handle is perfectly healthy. I wasn't anti-social, I wasn't holed up in my house, and I wasn't rude. I did what I had to do for me. So I stuck to B, my close girlfriends and their husbands and that's it. If anyone there thought I was rude, oh well. I'm too old (I know, I just said 31 isn't old) to deal with worrying about what people will think of me.

I took the half dose Lupron this morning. I oddly felt like I didn't do the injection correctly. I have gotten so used to the feel of the syringe in my stomach and how long it takes to inject the 10 units. Today's injection felt too short. After pushing the plunger part of the needle all the way down, I sat there wondering if I remembered to put the medicine in. From the small rash I got around the injection site, I know I did it properly. Even with the rash, I'm having doubts about how much I actually injected. I guess I'm having Lupron separation anxiety. I wonder if this is how a child feels when they are dropped off at daycare. Strange analogy, I know.

Tonight I will take my Gonal-F injection around 7:30ish. Gonal-F is in a prefilled pen. All I have to do is turn the dial to 225 units, put a needle on the pen and inject. This differs from the Lupron as the Lupron is in a vile. I draw up the Lupron on my own. I can't remember if I did 225 units last time. I'm sure I did. I respond very well to the drugs so I can't imagine the protocol changing.

Misconception #18

Avoiding situations is unhealthy. You should face them all head on.

WEDNESDAY, JUNE 23, 2010

Waiting Room

My first stim injection went well. Nothing major to report... just another needle in my belly. Other than flatulence (a lot of flatulence), no new side effects to report. That's not true, I am starting to get really dizzy. After I got out of bed this morning, I had to brace myself on the wall until I got my vision back. I sort of black out but not really...my vision blacks out but the rest of me does not. It only lasts for a few seconds so it's not bad.

One of my fertility forum buddies mentioned how the OBGYN office should have two separate waiting rooms, one for pregnant people, and one for non-pregnant people. This is what she said:

Every month when I'd go in for my follicle check I had to spend hours in the waiting room surrounded by pregnant ladies finding out the sex of their child. They would bring the whole family - DH, mom, other kids, etc. Then they'd spent the 30 minutes waiting to see the doctor calling everyone they know, posting the ultrasound photo on fb, etc. Reading material? Take your pick: Pregnancy Today; Fit Pregnancy; American Family; Parenthood; etc. Lol, I finally found a People magazine one day and freaked out with excitement only to see the cover story: "Celine Dion's Fertility Struggles" hahahaha.

I had a similar experience. It went like this...

Right after my first failed IVF, I had my annual pap scheduled. I thought I would be able to cancel it since I had someone (not just any someone, a trained medical professional) up my hooha on a daily basis. I called my OBGYN and they said I still had to go. The day of my appointment, I was already in a bad mood. I don't remember why exactly, I just remember being annoyed. I walked up to the check-in window, gave my insurance card and license, and waited for them to call me. As I was waiting a VERY pregnant girl walks in...a very young girl. She started complaining at the window that her free insurance had too high of a co-pay. She didn't understand how she could qualify for state assisted insurance and still have a co-payment of ten dollars. I just wanted to jump and yell at her. How the heck did she think she was going to afford food, diapers, formula, wipes, and all the other expenses that come along with an infant when she couldn't pay for her free visit? Of course, I didn't yell at her, I just sat there and continued reading Parent magazine. Shortly after the young girl incident, a couple walks in. The wife didn't look pregnant but you know when you see a man in the hooha doctor's office, he's not there on his own. They sat down directly next to me. The entire time the wife was giddy and giggly about the baby they would soon see on a sonogram. She was excited to see the baby move and was hoping they would be able to tell the gender of the baby. The husband was not happy. He wanted to go to work. He didn't want to be there and he clearly was not excited about this pregnancy. At one point he said that if she really thought this through, she wouldn't be excited either. REALLY...I wanted to punch him in the face. Who says that to his wife? Maybe they were financially struggling, maybe she tricked him into marriage by pregnancy, maybe he didn't want children and she did... who knows. All I knew was she was pregnant and I wasn't. My husband wouldn't say those things to me, my husband wouldn't make me feel like it was my "problem," and my husband would be excited. I just sat there pretending to read and thinking about how unfair it was that they were expecting and we were not. Yes, there was one more miserable lady. This lady came in right before I was called into the exam room. She looked very unhealthy. She was wheezing and sweating as she walked into the office. As soon as she walked in, she slid open the waiting room window. Let me just say, the window has a sign on it that says "Do not open the window. We will be with you shortly." She slid open the window and said "I need a bathroom. Do you know how miserable it is to be pregnant and to have to pee?" No "Good morning." No "May I use the restroom?" No "Jane Smith for Dr. So and So. Do you mind if I use the restroom quickly." Nothing came out of her mouth except rudeness. I was pissed. I wanted to shout at her. I wanted to talk to her about gestational diabetes. I wanted talk to her about being kind to people. I wanted to tell her that I would appreciate having to pee so badly due to pregnancy...it's not like her pelvic floor was falling out. I wanted to tell her to be kind because Karma may come back and bite her in the ass...if she didn't start being nice, the karma Gods were going to rip her pelvic floor out during labor. Then she'd really have to pee all the time. I wanted what she had so badly that I would have pissed all over myself with pride. I realize now that I was bitter and angry. At that point we had been trying for a very long time. We had already had three failed IUIs and one failed IVF. Back then it was very easy for me to expect people to want what I couldn't have. Now I appreciate the fact that everyone has problems. What may seem like a problem to them may not seem like a problem to me. Of course that works the other way too. I may really want something they have and they may not understand why I want it. Who am I to judge their marriage, health, personality, or financial situation? I'm normally not the judging type. I happened to be in a place mentally that made me someone who I do not like being. I'm not ashamed of the judgment. At the time, it was what I needed to feel better about my situation. I'm not ashamed but I'm surly not proud of it either. I had a moment of weakness...I like to fault the OBGYN for accommodating the pregnant people and not accommodating the non-pregnant people.

Misconception #19

Marriages rarely survive infertility. Having children makes a marriage stronger.

THURSDAY, JUNE 24, 2010

Aging Requests

Today is officially my last day in my 30th year. 30 was kind. 31 better be generous. My 30th year started off with the death of my obsession, Michael Jackson. I spent the first half of my day riding around in my car (I'm in sales) with my boss. He left me after lunch. I came home to the news that MJ had a heart attack. I sat on the couch crying until they pronounced him dead. I spent the rest of the day in hysterics. I should have known my 30th year was going to be filled with heartache. How else could my year have turned out after starting out like that? I can't complain about the entire year. We went on a hot air balloon ride. We went to Vegas, Vermont, Washington State, DC, Mexico, and Philly. We spent time in Newport and the Cape. We made our home even more beautiful with some renovations. We celebrated the birth of many babies...one being my Great Niece. We made new friends. We got new toys...Dishwasher, Dyson, Weber, iMac, Flip Camera, Keurig, and a vacuum sealer. All of that was/is wonderful. However, it is clouded by the eight months straight of negatives, one month of a positive and three months of waiting. We not only cried for us but we cried for friends who also felt our pain. We dealt with the death of not only our baby but also of friends and family. All good things seem to come with bad things. I also got wrinkles and sloppy teets. Due to medication and treatments, my weight was a rollercoaster...it was up, it was down, it was up, it was down. I would trade in all the material things if it meant I could have a healthy life and healthy baby. So as good as 30 was to me, I would like 31 to be better. Although my birthday will always start with the mourning of my beloved MJ (please do not laugh, I am serious), I pray that it will be the only day of mourning. For my 31st year, I ask the Birthday Goddesses (yes, they are female) for the following things:

*Good health

*A womb heavy with a healthy baby for ten months

*A sub pump and commercial grade dehumidifier (this is really for B not the birthday goddesses)

*Good heath for my friends and family

*Perseverance

*Michael Jackson to be brought back to life

*Many happy moments

*Year full of things that mean the most to me; friends, family and fur babies

*Strength

*Courage

31, please be generous.....

My Fertility Forum Buddies and I were laughing about the ads on the forum. LDC (the girl who brought up the waiting room) pointed out the adoption ads all over the forum. Here we are, gathering on a forum so we can chat about something we all have in common. While we are pouring our hearts out and discussing our ever so annoying drug induced flatulence, we are also reading ads for adoption and egg donors. Today there are two ads that I'm sure have been there the whole time but I'm just noticing. One says "IGNORE ME...I'm used to it" and the other says "ALONE IN THE WORLD. A child dreams of a family." Yes, this is the support the fertility forum gives us. We find it funny. We laughed and joked about it. One girl even gave it a "Bwahahahaha." This is where my brain goes from here...

Often times, people tell me that if I adopt, I'll get pregnant. There is always a story that goes along with it. A friend tried for a hundred years to get pregnant. They decided to give up and adopt. Once they adopted they found out they were pregnant and ended up with two infants. I understand why the story is told. It has a happy ending. I do appreciate the happy ending stories. However, they didn't get pregnant because they gave up. No one ever gives up. You may say you gave up. You may say you're not trying. Unless you stop having relations, you have not stopped trying. The adoption didn't make the pregnancy occur. Time made the pregnancy occur. So here is my misconception of the day...

Misconception #20

After people adopt, they usually get pregnant.

FRIDAY, JUNE 25, 2010

Birthday Suit

First let's have a moment of silence for Michael Jackson. One whole year without the greatest Icon in history....

I am the big 3-1. Thirty-one. In the thirties the human body's major organs start to decline. Miscarriage rates for rise to 20%. The decline in fertility for a woman in her thirties is about 15% per month. Sweet.

Outside of knowing all that, I feel great. I didn't wake up feeling great. I had such a severe migraine that I could barely open my eyes. My husband's "Happy Birthday" caused a pounding in my head. Most people get migraines like that stay in bed. Not I, I have to get up, feeling like I may vomit all over the place and stick a needle in my belly. Don't forget, the needle contains the cause of the migraines. Booo to that. On a positive note, I have the sweet pains of my follicles growing. It feels like little twinges and cramps in my ovaries. Tomorrow I have my first check-in u/s. If I follow the same pattern as the last couple of times it will go like this...

Tomorrow's u/s will show 8-12 follicles. My estradiol levels will be elevated but not by much. If I remember correctly, after my first u/s they start to taper the Gonal-f. Then I'll go back in two days.

Sorry for the short post today. My head is killing me and the computer screen is not helping. I'll try to post more later on today.

SATURDAY, JUNE 26, 2010

Phlebotomist

Sorry for my short post yesterday. I felt like complete crap. Not only was my head killing me, I also had really bad cramps. I was a little nervous about OHSS (ovarian hyperstimulation syndrome). I don't remember ever feeling this bloated, full and crampy. I knew I had my appointment this morning so I wasn't going to worry about it yesterday. Plus, it was my birthday. I wanted to celebrate and not worry about anything.

I left a little early today because my clinic moved and I wasn't sure how long it would take me to get there. Thank goodness that I decided to leave early. The route to the clinic is full of unmarked roads. I drove around the hospitals and surrounding old factories like a mad woman before finally landing at my destination. The building is gorgeous. It's very hi-tech and modern. You don't feel like you're sitting in a doctor's office. You feel like you in the lobby of a trendy hotel. The floors are dark like espresso. The walls are light beige with accenting texture walls. There are some chairs with cushions the colors of the wall trimmed with wood the color of the floors. There are also chairs with cushions covered in symmetrical squares in all shades of purple (plum, magenta, violet, and indigo). When I came up the elevator I was struck with the overwhelming scent of new. I love that smell...New walls, new flooring, new furniture. Since it's a Saturday, there wasn't a lot of staff working. However, I did notice a lot more woman checking in. I wonder if it had to do with the move. Since they can manipulate cycles, I am assuming they avoided having a lot of patients during the move. When I checked in, the routine was the same. I had to provide contact information that they can reach me at later to give me the results of my blood work and the next steps of my plan. I was then sent around the corner and through the door. I then signed in with the lab. The lab sign-in used to just require your name. I signed my name and then went to sit down. The lab girl came out and scolded me for filling it in incorrectly. New building, new rules. Not only did I have to write my name down, I also had to check off boxes with what I was having done. So I checked of ultrasound and blood work. Geesh...excuse me. I was sitting in one of the purple chairs looking at the wall. I noticed the texture of one wall, so I got up and started feeling the wall. Of course I did. I'm obsessed with wallpaper. I want to wallpaper our foyer so badly. However, every Tom, Dick, and Harry has advised me not to. I just love the look of it. Anyway, as I was feeling up the wall (which was in fact wallpapered), I got called into the lab. After stating my name and birth date (which no one noticed was yesterday) the phlebotomist wrapped the blue latex strap around my right arm (I chose this arm because my left one has so much scarring from repeat draws), felt my vein and stabbed me. I always jump when the needle goes in. I never get used to it. After I was done there, I went back to the purple chair and waited. I was called into an exam room shortly after. After emptying my bladder, I got naked from the waist down and plopped my naked bum on the exam table. The new beds are nice. They match the floors. All the cabinets are espresso with stainless trim. I love the look. Anyway, I got the young nurse that I have only had in the OR. I have never had her for checkup appointments. She first measured my stripe. Then she went to my left ovary and then to my right (I had to tell her it was up high and behind my uterus...otherwise she would have been poking around in there forever). Here are the results...

My stripe measured at 7 (Monday it was a 5).

My Left ovary had multiple (about 14) follicles measuring under 12mm (12 is mature)

My Right ovary had ten follicles measuring less than 12mm

No freaking wonder why I feel so crampy, full, and bloated. My ovaries are packed with follies! This is the most I have had at this point. Usually I have around seven or so on each ovary. As far as the ultrasound goes, everything is right where is should be. I'm now waiting on the call to see if the blood work matches up with the ultra sound. I will update you all once I get the call.

There are usually two phlebotomists that always work together. They are both brunettes, petite, vocal, and nice. One of the girls is out on maternity leave. I have been under treatment for so long that during my time there, she got pregnant, had a baby, and is out on leave. She had the most perfect pregnant body. She basically had a basketball sticking out of her scrubs. That's it. Never did I see a bloated face, hands, or feet. She didn't get a big butt. Just a belly. It sort of just popped out too. When I noticed she was pregnant, she was REALLY pregnant. Her scrubs hid her belly very well. The day I saw it, I said "Someone is trying to smuggle a beach ball in here." She said that she had been trying to hide it and told me that if I was offended by it the other girl could draw my blood. WHAT!?!? I told her of course I wasn't offended and I'd like her to draw my blood. She went on to tell me that many of the reproductive patients complained about it. They felt that it was unfair for them to have to look at her. At one point, she was asked to leave her job. Of course, if she left she wouldn't get paid but the job would be waiting for her when she got back. If I asked her questions about her pregnancy, she would whisper or she would say she couldn't answer based on who was waiting for their blood to be drawn. I felt so bad for her. When I see a pregnant woman, I am envious. I'll wish the basketball belly was on me. However, I would never be angry that they are living their life. I would never complain saying she shouldn't have her job. I would never say that it's unfair to have to look at it. I was so mad at my fellow fertility patients. I think it is perfectly normal to be jealous, envious, and even angry. However, it's completely selfish and bratty to be jealous, envious, and angry at someone just because they are pregnant. Yes, we may want what they have but these were the cards we were dealt. The poor phlebotomist didn't deal us these cards. She shouldn't be faulted. At the same time, don't assume because a couple of people complained that I am one of those people who can't handle it. Everyone, fertile or infertile, deserves the right to be defined individually. I am me and you are you. It's that easy.

SATURDAY, JUNE 26, 2010

Update From Earlier Post

The nurse called around 2:30 with my updated plan. The plan is exactly what I expected. My estradiol came in at 400. They want me to lower my dose of Gonal-f. Take the lower dose tonight and tomorrow night. Then I have an ultrasound and blood work on Monday morning. With my estradiol being at 400, that gives us plenty of time for the follicles to mature. Go Follies!

SUNDAY, JUNE 27, 2010

POAS

Many people think the hardest part about fertility treatments are the fertility treatments themselves. Taking multiple injections a day, having ultra sounds and blood work done on a daily basis, dealing with weight gain, bruises, headaches, nausea, bloating, cramping and being incredibly emotional from the hormones...sure those are all things that suck in every way possible. However, they're not as hard as the let down when you get the "Do you have a minute to talk. I'm sorry, the results of your beta came back negative" call. There is nothing worse than that let down. The entire cycle you believe, with all your heart that this time it's going to work. Everything seems to be lining up perfectly. Your blood work is right on target, your follicles are growing strong, and you end up with a bunch of eggs....end result, negative. The letdown is crushing. The letdown is the only reason I would decide to stop doing treatments. It's a hard blow to recover from. That's why I'm a firm believer in POAS (Peeing on a stick). A lot of people believe POAS can make you a little obsessed. I agree with that. Once I start, I can't stop. I'll do ten a day if need be. It's a crazy little addiction. However, there is nothing better than being prepared for the letdown call. Knowing that a POAS is negative makes the gut punching negative a little easier to stomach. I also want to find out like everyone else that I'm pregnant via a POAS. Finding out through a phone call with a nurse is not all that exciting. Seeing the PREGNANT on the digital POAS or the double line on the standard POAS is incredibly exciting. However, a positive POAS can also be stressful. After the excitement, you start to worry about the actual Beta number. What the Doctor likes to see is a first Beta between 50-100. Due to testing much earlier than those who test after conceiving conventionally, you can get a low Beta (below 50). Most likely, a pregnancy with a Beta that low is a Chemical Pregnancy. Which means you are pregnant but the chances of it surviving is low. Many women have chemical pregnancies but have no idea. The pregnancy only lasts a short while. Most women just think their period was a few days late. Even with the cons of POAS, breaking the fall of the letdown is so worth it to me.

One of my friends bought me the BEST pajamas for my birthday. It's basically a long t-shirt (from Victoria's Secret). The material is so incredibly thin and light. I wore one of them last night. You have no idea how great it was to sleep in it. My night sweats barely affected me. It was awesome! If you are dealing with night sweats, I highly recommend buying some of these night gown/shirt things.

Misconception #22

Infertility is not an issue until people hit their late 30's

MONDAY, JUNE 28, 2010

Our Turn

I'm starting to feel like a water balloon about to explode. My ultrasound today was so uncomfortable. I am so freaking full and bloated. I have more follicles than I have ever had. I had six follicles measuring between 12-14mm and 22 measuring under 12mm. Holy schamoly! Here's my prediction, the nurse will call today, tell me to take the same dose of my medicine tonight, tomorrow, and then return Wednesday for an ultrasound and additional blood work. Grow Follies Grow!

This cycle, I am hoping that I can finally be the one to say I'm pregnant. Nearly everyone I know that wanted to get pregnant did get pregnant. I only have a few friends that are currently trying. Since we have been trying, some of our friends have been pregnant, delivered and are now pregnant again. We have friends that started trying months and years after us that are pregnant. I just want it to be my turn. Not just my turn, I want it to be our turn. Yesterday we had friends over for dinner. I loved watching B throw the kids over his shoulder, spin them around, and make them belly laugh. People tend to think you don't know anything about kids and being around them since you don't have them. You get left out of conversation and gatherings.

I cannot wait for the day for people to stop saying to me "One day you'll learn..." and "When you have kids, I'll teach you..." My mother ran a daycare out of our home most of my life. I worked in a daycare in high school. I was a nanny all through college. I was even a nanny for a short while after college. I was always the cousin that babysat for family. My best friend and I started a babysitting club when we were 13 called Elm Street Sitters. My grandmother and several aunts are teachers. I was a big sister through Big Brother Big Sister for eight years (until fertility treatments took over my free time). For years I was a volunteer at camps. Parenting, raising, mentoring, playing, and teaching children is who I am. It's in my blood. When I get the "when you have kids I'll teach you..." comments, I want to jump out of my seat. Even with all the knowledge I have, I would never tell anyone how they should raise their children. I would never say how I do something is the way it should be done. I would never give unsolicited parenting advice. So why is it okay to tell me that I can be taught a thing to two just because I have not carried a child? You know how many children I have taught ABCs to? You know how many bottoms have been potty trained under my reign? You know how many binkies and bottles I have gotten rid of? You know how many times I nurtured a cold, flu or a teething child? You know how many boogie monsters and bad men I have scared away? So please, don't tell me that I will learn. I know. If I wasn't so polite, I would just say back "actually, let me teach you a thing or two." Since I'm nice and would never do that, I only think it and look forward to the day when all those comments stop. This is my time. So Grow Follies Grow!

Misconception #22

Only mothers know how to parent.

TUESDAY, JUNE 29, 2010

Let's Talk About Sex

I can't have a blog entry title like that and not drop some Salt 'N' Pepa lyrics...so here they are...

Let's talk about sex for now to the people at home or in the crowd

It keeps coming up anyhow

Don't decoy, avoid, or make void the topic

Cuz that ain't gonna stop it

In my opinion (this is my blog, I guess technically, everything I say is in my opinion), there are three stages of Baby Making:

1. Practice Stage
2. Timed Stage
3. Treatment Stage

We all know what the practice stage is. It's when you're trying to have a baby but you don't want anyone to know yet. So you tell them that you're practicing. You say practicing but you really mean "trying." During the Practice Stage, you have sex whenever you want as often as you want. After "practicing" you feel confident enough to tell people that you are trying. This is when you're in the Timed Stage. You may not know when you ovulate so you have sex every other day. You may know when you ovulate, so you have sex a few days before, during, and after ovulation. Depending on how long you have been trying or how serious you are about baby making, you may use ovulation kits to dictate when you have sex. After you have exhausted both the Practice Stage and the Timed Stage, this is when you seek out the advice of a specialist or what I call the Treatment Stage. Most people think the Treatment Stage is the most difficult stage. They think it's strenuous on your sex life. They think that you can't have sex when you want to. I disagree. The most exhausting stage is the Timed Stage. You are checking your temperature, you're tracking ovulation. Sex in this stage is no longer Love Making, it is Baby Making. Once you make it into the Treatment Stage, you can go back to Love Making. A lot of people think the two are interchangeable. They're not. Love making means you can have sex when you want. You can have it for fun and for pleasure. Sex no longer has a purpose (other than intimacy) that has to be met. In my opinion, the third stage is a mighty fine stage to be in.

Yo, Pep, I don't think they're gonna play this on the radio

And why not? Everybody has sex...

I mean, everybody should be makin' love

Yesterday Dr. P dropped my dose of Gonal-f to 150. The nurse instructed me to take it last night and tonight and then return tomorrow for an ultrasound and blood work. Ahh...tomorrow I get to meet up with my lovely friend the vaginal ultrasound. They normally don't bother me but as my ovaries are filling up with follicles, the ultrasounds get uncomfortable. At least I get to make love and have sex for pleasure.

I bet my mother just puked in her mouth. Sorry Mom.

Misconception #23

Fertility treatments put a strain on your sex life

WEDNESDAY, JUNE 30, 2010

Patience

Something Infertility should have taught me is patience. Seriously, most of this process involves waiting. I wait for appointments, I wait for results, I wait for calls, I wait to start, I wait to get pregnant...I wait. You would think, after months and months of waiting, I would be a more patient person. Today, I prove that to not be the case. I had my ultrasound and blood work done at 8:30 this morning. I had 11 follicles measuring between 12-16.5mm and 10 measuring under 12mm. So far so good. Usually, the nurses will call around 2:00 or 2:30 if everything looks good and there isn't much of a change. If the news is bad, they tend to not call until after 3:30. It's now 4:41. Now my mind is racing with all the negative possibilities. What if my estradiol levels are too high? What if my hormones are pointing towards triggering but my follicles aren't ready? What if my cycle gets cancelled? All the what ifs are driving me crazy! Hurry up and call already!!!

WEDNESDAY, JUNE 30, 2010

UPDATE

It's now 5:15. I decided to call them at 5:00. I didn't speak to anyone because they are closed. I left a message with the answering service and I emailed Dr. P. I'm now waiting for direction...

I just got a call from the on call dr. I am to decrease my dose of Gonal-f tonight and return in the morning for another (yes, another) ultrasound and blood work. Now do you understand why my arms look like I'm a junky??

Waiting Room

My ultrasound today showed 15 follicles measuring between 12-20mm. I'm not sure what my next steps will be. Only six of those follicles are above 15mm. I can see them having me take a shot tonight and have me come back tomorrow for more blood work and an ultrasound. I can also see them having me trigger tonight because my lead follicle is measuring at 20mm. So again, here I am waiting for the call.

Today while I was in the waiting room, a girl that was waiting for blood work started asking me questions. She wanted to know what I was doing, how long we've been trying, etc. I never ask anyone what their deal is. I know why they are there; it's really none of my business to hear the details. I have no problem answering if people ask me and no problem listening if they bring up them. So, after I answered her questions, she offered her story. She has tried several IUIs and just finished her first IVF. She said she as there for a "check point." Since I had never heard that term, I asked her what she meant. She said that she started bleeding two days ago and they wanted her to come in to make sure the baby is okay. I asked her how far along she is. Her reply, "Five weeks." Since I have been through it so many times, I knew exactly where she stood in the process. She has had two positive betas. She has yet had her third. As if she was reading my mind, she said "next week will be my third beta." She then went on to tell me how her bleeding is heavy but not clotty. She read online that a miscarriage should be clotty. I didn't get clots until a few days in. I wasn't surprised by what she was telling me. It didn't even faze me. Inwardly, I didn't even flinch. However, on the outside, I was sympathetic and understanding. I gave her some of my wisdom and wished her luck. What I learned from that conversation is that Infertility has left me damaged. I am not surprised by bad news. I am only temporarily saddened by it. The constant let down, needles, fear, anxiety, miscarriage... all of those things left me damaged. So I'm not patient and I'm damaged. From damage came strength. I am stronger than I ever thought I could be. I'm facing fears on a daily basis. I keep fighting after constant losing. I tackle every road block head on. I never give up.

Misconception #24
Infertility causes weakness

THURSDAY, JULY 1, 2010

Results are in

I just got the call...

I will not be going back tomorrow morning. I will take my hCG trigger shot tonight at 7:30 and my egg retrieval surgery is scheduled for Saturday morning at 7:30. I'm taking all prayers for lots of mature eggs!

FRIDAY, JULY 2, 2010

Day Before Retrieval

Sorry, I'm not posting today. My ovaries are the size of watermelons right now. I am so incredibly uncomfortable. I can barely walk, sit, or stand. I actually look pregnant. I'll try to post a picture of how swollen and bloated my belly is. It's gross.

My surgery is at 8:30 tomorrow morning. I should be home by 11:00. I'll do my best to post the retrieval results as soon as I get home.

Here we go...

Eggies

I'm back from the retrieval. We got 15 eggs. We got 15 the first round, 18 the second round and now 15 the third round. I'm very happy with that number. I need all fingers crossed and prayers that they're all mature. I'll give the details of the retrieval later. Right now, I am focusing on not puking all over my couch. Once the effects of anesthesia wear off, I'll post details.

SATURDAY, JULY 3, 2010

Updated Retrieval Details

We arrived at the clinic at 8:00 this morning. When we checked in, the receptionist put an ID bracelet on B, handed him a sheet of labels (for his "donation") and then sent us to the waiting area. While B was reading with my head rested on his arm, the OR nurse called me in. Once inside, I was instructed to empty my bladder, get undressed, and put on two gowns, one with opening in the front and the other with opening in the back. While I was getting ready, I was thinking, they really should make gowns cuter. I'm sure cute material costs the same. Having a cute outfit on would make you feel good. You may even forget that you will have a wand up your vagina while an entire room full of people are observing. Having a dulled off white gown on, is not cute. Back to the details of the retrieval...

After a LOT medical history questions, the Anesthesiologist came by to do his thing. He tried inserting the catheter in two spots in my arm. My veins are so damaged from all the needles; he decided to use a vein in my hand. Fortunately, he numbed my arm before attempting to stick me several times. During all of this, we were discussing the medications he would be administering. I told him that I usually fall asleep before being wheeled off to the operating table. He said that they never give medication that makes you sleep until you're hooked up to machines in the OR. Apparently, I have been awake every time, I just don't remember. However, this time, I remember being wheeled into the OR. I remember the doctor saying the ultra sound machine wasn't working. I remember the nurse saying she would call to get some answers. After that, I don't remember anything. About an hour later, I woke up in the recovery area. When I woke up, the nurse said "they got 15 eggs." I felt a huge wave of nausea. I kept willing myself back to sleep. I thought if I didn't fall asleep, I was going to puke all over the place. I think I fell asleep for another ten minutes. Upon waking up, I was given some water and saltines. I knew that I needed to have very little pain and no nausea to be sent home. When I was asked what my pain level was, I lied. I said I had no more pain than what I walked in with. I was then allowed to go home.

I'm sure a lot of you are wondering what the heck do they do during retrieval. It's kind of brutal. All those follicles that we have been developing for weeks need to be aspirated. If there are eggs, they will be inside the follicles. During retrieval, the doctor places a needle through the vagina and into the ovaries. One by one (guided by a vaginal ultrasound) she aspirates the follicles and collects the eggs. 15 eggs may not seem like a huge number, but it is. A "normal" female will produce one, if any, egg a month. The ovaries are built to hold one egg. I have been harvesting 15. Hence, the gigantic belly.

The lab will immediately ICSI (intracytoplasmic sperm injection; directly inject one sperm into the egg) the eggs today. The lab will call us tomorrow to let us know how many of the 15 eggs were mature and how many of the mature eggs fertilized.

No more needles for a while! Right now, I'm only on prednisone and progesterone suppositories. Wahoooo!

Misconception #25

Most fertility issues are due to faulty eggs or egg production.

4th of July

When I talk about 4th of July, I'm not talking about the band or the Beach Boys song, I'm talking about the National holiday; Independence Day. A day before the Declaration of Independence was signed; John Adams sent his wife a letter:

The second day of July, 1776, will be the most memorable epoch in the history of America. I am apt to believe that it will be celebrated by succeeding generations as the great anniversary festival. It ought to be commemorated as the day of deliverance, by solemn acts of devotion to God Almighty. It ought to be solemnized with pomp and parade, with shows, games, sports, guns, bells, bonfires, and illuminations, from one end of this continent to the other, from this time forward forever more.

We celebrate the holiday just as he predicted. We celebrate with family, friends, BBQs, fireworks and parades. You go to a BBQ and see kids running around in red, white, and blue outfits. You go to fireworks and you see families all snuggled up together on a blanket. You go a parade and you see Dads walking around with children on their shoulders and Moms pushing strollers. 4th of July throws in the face of those struggling with infertility, exactly what they are striving for. Someone recently asked me if I would ever use donor eggs. There is always the assumption that something is wrong with the egg or that there is a problem at all. Although there is nothing wrong with my eggs, I answered the question. I replied with "My goal is to be a mother. I will go to the end of the earth to make that happen." B and I will one day adopt, regardless if we conceive or not. Adoption is something that we both want to do. However, I also want to be a mother to a child that I carried in my womb for ten months. I want the feeling of a fetus being nurtured with my blood. I want to feel the butterflies of kicks and somersaults. I want to experience delivery. Yesterday was a constant reminder of what we don't have. (I'm not forgetting about all the things we do have). After having a needle inserted into my hooha, my follicles aspirated, and my eggs retrieved, I sat at a cookout surrounded by babies and pregnant bellies. I had 15 months (assuming I would have shed one egg a month) worth of eggs removed from me. I was in pain. However, I wanted to be with friends. I didn't want to spend the day on the couch by myself. I opted to sit on a lounge chair and enjoy the day (I only made it a couple of hours before needing B to bring me home). I had to feel the pain from my surgery while being surrounded by my biggest struggle. Today will be no different. Today I will have to face it all over again. I will hold babies, I will play games with kids and I will have pregnancy talk with expectant mothers. I will do all those things with an ache in my soul. I will do it while worrying about when the embryologist will call me about our embryos. I will do it while I have pain in my reproductive system from surgery. I know people will look at me with sad eyes. I know people will feel bad for me. Some of you can relate and some of you can't. If you can relate, I'm so sorry. I don't wish this on my worst enemy. If you can't relate, try to understand the strength it takes for us to be there. Our strength doesn't carry us just on holidays, it carries us year round. Don't feel bad or look at us like we're sick puppies. Just understand the kind of people we must be to be able to handle ourselves well. We're strong, brave, selfless people that will persevere.

I started the progesterone vaginal inserts today. I am not looking forward to wearing a freaking mattress pad in between my legs to catch the leaking caused from the insert. Awesome. Today is another day of waiting. Normally, it is my responsibility to call the lab after 2:00 pm to get the details of how many eggs were mature, how many fertilized, and how they are developing. Since today is Sunday, I cannot call. I have to wait for the embryologist to call me. All this waiting...aye!

Misconception #26

Those dealing with infertility will be house ridden and anti-social.

SUNDAY, JULY 4, 2010

Update From Earlier Post

The lab just called. They attempted to fertilize 13 eggs (two must not have been mature). All 13 fertilized! 100% fertilization rate! Woot! Tomorrow I have to call the lab after 2:00 to see how they are developing. Tomorrow's call is usually the call when I find out that they're not looking great. Fingers crossed for great development.

Waiting Game

Why is it that we wait for all the major events in our lives? We wait to go to school. We wait to get our license. We wait to graduate from high school. We wait to go to College. We wait for our first job. We wait to get engaged. We wait to get married. We wait to buy a house. We wait to have babies. I very much dislike waiting. Call me an instant gratification seeker. Call me impatient. Call me whatever you would like. I know I'm this way. Waiting is not fun. Waiting is stressful. Waiting causes anxiety. Not only am I waiting, I'm also worrying about the 13 embryos we have sitting in a lab. They may not be in my womb but they still are 13 babies made up of our genes. They are our babies. Worrying about 13 babies is draining. I'm tired. I woke up a million times last night pondering all the what ifs...

What if they don't develop normally?

What if they don't make it to transfer?

What if the lab forgets to call me?

What if they look great but they don't implant?

What if they do implant and I miscarry?

What if all this doesn't work out?

What if the lab blows up and we lose the embryos?

What if the embryologist had too much fun on the 4th and is sloppy?

What if I am let down?

The lab called at 10:46 yesterday. I'm hoping they call early again. I'm actually not sure if they will call me or if I am to call them after 2:00. Today is the national holiday, correct? I guess that means the lab is officially closed. So they will call me.

Misconception #27

Once a sperm meets the egg, the difficult part of conception is over.

MONDAY, JULY 5, 2010

Transfer

The lab called me around 11:30 this morning. So far so good. All 13 embryos are progressing as they should. They are all between 2-4 cells. Some are fragmented (not great) and some are not. We really won't know how good the quality is until we show up tomorrow. Our transfer time is 10:20 tomorrow morning. Yikes!

The side effects of the progesterone are in full force. My boobs are gigantic and I'm leaking out the vaginal insert goo. Big boobs are a bonus. Vaginal leakage, not so much.

Big Day

Between having to urinate every two hours and my mind racing, I barely slept. I went to bed at 10:00. I was up at 11:30, 1:00, 2:45, 4:00, and now it's 5:20 and I'm up for good. Every time I got up, I had to go to the bathroom. Tossing and turning is manageable. You wake up, you toss, you turn, and fall asleep. Having to go to the bathroom means, you wake up, have full bladder cramps, walk to the bathroom (which involves a light turning on), go to the bathroom, flush the toilet, wash your hands, and walk back to bed. By the time you get back to bed, you're fully awake. I figure since I already have many pregnancy symptoms (from all the hormones) I'd list them out...

Swollen boobs (not sore yet)

Bloat

Cramps

Insomnia

Night peeing

All day peeing

Headaches

Most people will suspect they are pregnant by having a missed period and one or more of those symptoms. The progesterone that is disgustingly leaking out of me prevents a period from coming and has side effects similar to pregnancy symptoms. The only way for me to know if today's transfer works, will be by POAS and blood test. My blood test will be scheduled for 12 days from today. I'm not sure if anyone has noticed that today is the 6th. 12 days from today is the 18th. Picking up what I'm dropping?? My Beta test will be 7/18. If you don't remember reading about it, read my post on June 9th. Crazy!!!!!

I'm still five hours away from my transfer. Seriously, why am I awake??

TUESDAY, JULY 6, 2010

PUPO

I'm officially PUPO (Pregnant until proven otherwise) with triplets. The decision to put three embryos in was a tough one. We waivered back and forth between putting two or three in. I asked if the other embryos would make it to freeze. The doctor said there is no way to know that right now. My thought was, if they may not freeze; why not just put it in? We ended up choosing to put two back in. After the doctor left to talk to the lab, I turned to B and said "we will feel really bad if this doesn't work. We'll keep thinking we should have put the third one in." Shortly after that, the doctor came back from the lab. He sat down on the spin stool and said "Okay, now I'm on the fence." Our embryos look good but don't look as good then our previous cycle. He said based on that, he thinks we should be put three in. He asked us "What would be worse, not getting pregnant or getting pregnant with triplets." So we went with three. The chances of all three taking, is less than 7%.

After deciding to put three in, we were walked down to the OR. For a transfer, they have to take all your clothes off from the waist down. You wrap yourself in a sheet and walk around like that. So as I was walking down the hall in my sheet, B was behind me with his hand on my back. We get to the room, they have B sit in a stool next to the exam table and have me drop the sheet and get on the table. Well, you don't drop the sheet; you sort of just show the entire staff your ass as you get on the table. After sitting down they have me put my legs up on the stirrups. You're probably picturing the standard stirrups with the horseshoe shaped foot holders. OR stirrups are much different than that. You put the back of your knees on these massive pads. Unlike standard stirrups, your legs just hang from the knee down. It's VERY awkward. Anyway, once I was in position, the embryologist asked me for my name and birth date. Once we confirmed that I am in fact me, she went to get the embryos. While she was getting the embryos, the doctor, placed the speculum in and cleaned out my cervix. He actually said "I'm just going to clean out the mucus." I was laughing because he wasn't cleaning out mucus; he was cleaning out the darn progesterone suppository junk that keeps leaking out of me. The embryologist brought in the catheter with the embryos in. While the doctor has his face in my Hooha, a nurse is holding an ultrasound wand on my stomach. Since the uterus is not visible from the outside, the ultrasound is used to guide the catheter into place. My cervix is like a maze. Usually it takes a little bit to get through it and into the uterus. Not today. The doctor was in very quickly. Once he was inside he placed the catheter right next to my uterine lining (where the baby should implant). He counted to three and released the embryos. On an ultrasound, the embryos look like tiny little white dots. He also froze the screen so we could see them sitting there, right where they should be. After we were done, I turned to B and said "Was it as good for you as it was for me?" Hahahaha...

So now we're in the 2ww (two week wait). Ahhhhhh.....

Misconception #28

Just having a sperm and egg meet creates a pregnancy.

WEDNESDAY, JULY 7, 2010

Science Lesson

I figured that today I would give a little science lesson on what is happening to the 3 maybe babies inside of me. I got this off the NYU website:

Days Past Transfer (DPT)/Embryo Development:

One/The embryo continues to grow and develop, turning from a 6-8 cell embryo into a morula

Two/The cells of the morula continue to divide, developing into a blastocyst

Three/The blastocyst begins to hatch out of its shell

Four/The blastocyst continues to hatch out of its shell and begins to attach itself to the uterus

Five/The blastocyst attaches deeper into the uterine lining, beginning implantation

Six/Implantation continues

Seven/Implantation is complete; cells that will eventually become the placenta and fetus have begun to develop

Eight/Human chorionic gonadotropin (hCG) starts to enter the blood stream

Nine/Fetal development continues and hCG continues to be secreted

Ten/Fetal development continues and hCG continues to be secreted

Eleven/Levels of hCG are now high enough to detect a pregnancy

If I end up pregnant, I will be pregnant around Monday or Tuesday. Right now, I'm just an incubator for three babies. Many people do all sorts of crazy things while they are in the 2ww. When you get to the point of where we (the fertility strugglers) are, you will do anything to make it work. Outside of healthy eating habits (which are not for fertility purposes) I don't really do any of the herbs and pills. I do go to acupuncture and I will eat a lot of pineapple. Pineapple contains bromelain. Among many uses, bromelain has been used as an anti-inflammatory. Theory is that bromelain will help reduce inflammation from ovary stimulation and retrieval. First off, I was on prednisone, so that took care of the inflammation. Second, I am a woman of science. I need proof that something works before I will try it. However, with pineapple, I don't really need proof. I'll eat it because I enjoy it. If it helps, it helps. If not, I'll have a nice and clean digestive system.

I'm sure you're all wondering when I'll start POAS. I will test at some point this weekend, probably Sunday to make sure the trigger shot (which is 10,000 units of hCG) is out of my system. If it is, I will get a negative test result. I will then test every day until my Beta. Last cycle, I got my first positive nine days past the transfer (which will be next Thursday).

I'm going to hold off on the misconceptions while I'm in the 2ww. Fingers crossed and prayers accepted that at least one of these babies implant!

THURSDAY, JULY 8, 2010

Time for Human Babies

A couple of months ago, while I was outside weeding, an ambulance with its sirens blaring, sped by. I turned to Cappy (our dog) and said "Oh no. Did you see the ambulance Bud? Is it an emergency Cappy?" You know it's time for a human baby when you start talking to your animals like they are children. I ask our fur babies if they want to dance. Half the time, I don't ask them, I force them to dance with me. I discuss the weather with them. I ask them if I look fat. I turn to them for comfort. Yesterday, I held ice packs to their heads to cool them down. It's time for a human baby. Don't get me wrong, the fur babies will still get treated like humans, however, it's time for a human baby in this house.

Today I'm feeling blah. I have LOTS of cramps. I almost feel like my period is coming. That would be a real big kick in the gut. I know it's not baby cramps...it's far too early for that. There a few things it could be. My ovaries still have to shrink back to their normal size. I'm sure the retrieval causes a lot of gas. Bloating, cramping, nausea are all side effects of the Progesterone. So, who knows why I feel terrible today.

I cannot wait to start POAS. It's so addicting. A lot of people are saddened with the see a negative result so they choose not to test. I will think about whether or not this cycle is working all day and night if I don't test. Testing in the morning helps me get on with my day. I see the result, positive or negative, and I don't think about it again (until the next morning).

Two week waits suck. My brother, his wife, and their kids are coming to town (they live 3,000 miles away) tonight. They will be my pleasant distraction throughout this wait. I cannot wait to see my nieces.

Not sure if it's the heat, stress of waiting or the meds...I need a nap.

FRIDAY, JULY 9, 2010

Double Yolk- 3dpt

Last night, I came home from book club and took a pregnancy test. I had the urge! I told you, it's an addiction. I had one digital test left from when my period went missing after my miscarriage. The digital test came back positive. Usually the trigger shot is out of my system by now. So...what do you think I did first thing this morning?? I bought $70 worth of tests. I'm insane. I know. I just took another digital one and it came back "not pregnant." Yay! The drugs have left my body! I will do my best to wait until next week to test. I have heard of people getting positives 5dpt. I've heard of it but it is rare. I'm assuming if I do end up pregnant, I'll get the positive around the same time as last cycle (9dpt).

I got a call from the lab today. Three of our embryos made it to freeze! I'm so excited. We have never had any make it to freeze. The other seven degenerated and were discarded. Having three "snowbabies" also makes me confident of the ones in me. Hopefully they are doing well in there...implant embryos, implant!!

Every morning I eat egg white with my breakfast. Sometimes I scramble them. Mainly, I hard boil them, and pop the yolks out. Yesterday one of my eggs had two yolks. It wasn't one yolk broken in two. The egg actually had whites running through the two yolks. There were two separate yolk sacs. As you know, I'm a true believer in signs. Do you think that means two of the maybe babies in me will stick? When I was little and I got two pieces of cereal stuck together in my bowl, I used to say "I'm going to have twins." Maybe fate was telling me (since I was 5) that I am destined to have twins. That would RULE! After all we've been through to get pregnant, I'll take as many as God wants to put in my womb. Bring it on!

SUNDAY, JULY 11, 2010

5dpt- Debbie Downer

Sorry for not posting yesterday. I spent the day with my nieces then we went out to celebrate my sister's birthday. By the time I came home, I was exhausted. I haven't been feeling great. My stomach has been all sorts of upset. I have been having really bad cramps...the kind that make you buckle over. They come quick, hit hard and leave fast. I remember this happening to me when I got pregnant in January. However, it happened right before my beta. I called the emergency line on a Wednesday (8dpt) thinking I could be having an ectopic. They told me the pains were too high and it was probably GI related. Then the next day I got my faint positive. I also woke up last night with a nasty cold. My throat is KILLING me. This is where the Debbie Downer comes in. In February, I got a really bad cold. Two days later, I started miscarrying. Obviously, I don't think I'm miscarrying...that's impossible since I'm not pregnant. However, being sick while a baby is trying to develop, doesn't work out for me. So I'm not feeling so hopeful right now. If this cycle doesn't work out, at least we have three snowbabies that we can try again with. I did take a test this morning (I wanted to wait until tomorrow) and it was negative (as expected). If this doesn't work out I may finally get pissed off. Normally, I am ready to try again. I think this time, I may be angry at the world. One girl on the fertility forum told a story about how her cousin walked into the ER with severe stomach pains. It turns out that she was in labor. She carried full term and had no idea she was pregnant. REALLY?!?! There are people who are popping out kids by the handful. They don't appreciate their kids. They don't care for their kids. Why is it fair for them to have kids? Teenagers are popping out kids more than ever. Come on, you don't know how to get pregnant? Anytime a penis goes into the vagina, you're at risk for pregnancy. Get some freaking birth control and use a damn condom. There are women who smoke, drink and do drugs while they are pregnant. Tell me, on what universe, is that fair?

People who deal with fertility treatments never have an easy pregnancy. We are surrounded by heartbreak. We sit in waiting rooms surrounded by people who have had struggled for years to get pregnant. We sit in waiting rooms next to woman who are waiting to hear the details about the baby they are losing. When is it safe for us to be excited and hopeful? I have friends who have miscarried in the second trimester. I have a friend who miscarried in the third trimester. When is it safe for them to enjoy their pregnancy? Ultrasounds turn into anxiety ridden events. We worry that we won't see a heartbeat any longer. Anything we do, we feel like is a jinx. Of course the fertile community worries as well. However, the level of worrying is different. Those who have never shown up to an ultrasound to see a deceased baby; those who have never lost a baby; those who were never told the details of their embryo don't have a history of being let down. Getting congratulated, registering for baby items, setting up a nursery...we make every move like it will be our last. Every positive thing feels like it will soon come to an end. How on earth is that enjoyable? I want to be excited over bedding and wall paint. I want to spend hours registering for binkies and blankies. I want to buy onesies and bibs. Ah, I'm in a bad mood.

MONDAY, JULY 12, 2010

6dpt- Borders

I'm out of my funky mood today. I wish I felt better. I am sick...very sick. I'm congested, can't stop sneezing and my throat is on fire. I slept for a couple of hours this afternoon. I was hoping that napping with cure my summertime cold. Maybe I'll wake up cold free.

I went to Border's today to grab my next book for book club (Heart of the Matter by Emily Giffin). While I was in line, there was a woman who I wanted to punch in the face. She was with her son who I am guessing is around 5 years old. As she was getting in line behind me, she was yelling "You are on my only nerve. You either stand here and shut up or I will shut you up myself." In the two minutes we were in line, I heard her call her son an idiot, stupid, jackass, dummy and useless. Right before I was called to the next available register, she said told him that she never should have had him. Okay...Maybe I am overly aware of kids. My uterus does hurt every time I see a baby or hear a baby cry. When I see children in stores, I can't help but stare at them. No, I'm not a creep. I want children so badly that I can't help but look at them and think of what my life would be like with them in it. Needless to say, I always notice when children are being treated poorly. I get angry every time I see an infant in a stroller without an adult next to it. I do not understand why parents think it's perfectly safe to leave a baby next to cucumbers while they are near the onions. I get angry every time I see a child running through a parking lot. Just the other day, B and I were leaving a restaurant when I noticed that this couple left their toddler (definitely less than two) next to their car unattended. The mom was somewhere behind the car and the dad was in the backseat doing something. The toddler ran onto the median. All that little boy needed was two seconds to get hit by a car. Anyway, I either notice more than the average person or there are a lot of really bad parents out there. Back to the lady at Borders. Why the heck does she get to have a child? That poor boy is going to have, if he does not already, so many emotional issues. I highly doubt that woman reads to her son. I highly doubt she soothes him when he's sick. I highly doubt she does crafts or colors with him. So not only is she emotionally abusing him, she is stunting his development. I guarantee he has learning disabilities. Seriously, how does that make sense? People always say, "If it's meant to be, it will work out." Why is that woman meant to be a parent and B and I are not?

POAS resulted in a negative today. My days of negatives are running out. Positives should start showing any day now. Come on embryos...burrow!!

TUESDAY, JULY 13, 2010

7dpt- Early Morning

What does one do at 3:30 am when they can't sleep? Pee on a stick. Again, negative. There is a reason why they don't do your blood test until 12 days past the transfer. So I know that it's still early to get a positive. However, many people start seeing positives 6dpt. I don't consider myself out of the running just yet. If I get a negative on Thursday, then I will assume that it didn't work. Yikes...only one more day for that pretty extra pink line to show up before I get nervous. I only have digital tests left. Those tests are harsh. Missing a pink line isn't a big deal. With the digitals, you either get a "PREGNANT" or a "NOT PREGNANT"....harsh.

There is no way to tell (physically) if it is working. Due to the amount of progesterone I'm on, my body thinks it's pregnant. So I have uterine cramping, sore swollen boobs (my nipples KILL), and a belly that looks pregnant. So, I have no idea if it's working. I hope and pray that it is. This is our time. Well, it should be our time. If it doesn't work, at least we have the three snowbabies. At least I'll get a little break from the hormones and surgeries. For that, I am grateful. We had ten embryos that they watched for freezing. 3/10 made it to freeze and 7/10 degenerated. That means one third of them are of excellent quality. If those stats go along with the three in me, then one of them has a good chance of taking. Please, please, please take! Last night at B's softball game, someone asked what day it was. I replied "Day 6." It's our time....

WEDNESDAY, JULY 14, 2010

8dpt- IVF Pregnancy Tanks

Yesterday, a friend mentioned that she saw a tank top that said "Pregnant is the new skinny." I thought it would be fun to post what Infertility tank tops would say...

Pigs Flew
Made in a dish
One night in a lab
I cost thousands
I was worth the wait
I kicked infertility's ass
FINALLY
One tough Mommy
three years in the making
Made by an Embryologist
Retrieved, Fertilized and Transferred

Today's POAS result...NOT PREGNANT. Sweet. Today is the last day I would expect to see a negative. I'm not officially worried yet...just slightly worried. I will be really worried tomorrow. Not only will I be worried, I'll have a really bad day. I really thought this cycle would work. If it doesn't work, then the whole "positive thinking" thing is a sham.

THURSDAY, JULY 15, 2010

9dpt- Round Three Let Down

So...yesterday I was going POAS crazy. I went to Walgreens and purchased many tests. I wanted a few different brands. I came home and took one of the inexpensive Walgreens brand tests. Low and behold, there was a faint line. It was faint but clearly visible. We've been doing this far too long to be excited over a line. I wasn't excited but I did get some hope back. We decided to wait until the morning and test again. This morning I took the same brand test and a digital test. I got a big fat white screen and a "NOT PREGNANT." B thinks it can still happen. I however, am a woman of science. I'm going with science and history and not banking on a miracle. Game Over. Two and a half years of negatives and it still sucks. I'm not angry like I thought I would be. I'm not as sad as I thought I would be. I didn't cry at the results. I didn't feel bad for myself or for B. I did cry when a friend said she cried all the way to work because she was really hoping this time would be different for us. It is what it is. For some reason, this is the life we were given. Of course I was hoping to not have to go through this let down. This is the worst part. I just put my body through hell. We just spent thousands and thousands of dollars. We just worried and prayed all for nothing. It's sad. It sucks. It's unfair. It's also our life. I can't live my life in worry and sadness. We do have those three embryos sitting in a freezer. For that, I am grateful. I am also realistic. I know that the survival rate of embryos coming out of freezing is low. The success rate of a frozen embryo transfer is also low. So, yes we have them waiting for us, but I also understand the odds of them becoming the babies I carry to term. Grateful but not hopeful.

I have a bridal shower and bachelorette party on Saturday. Dr. P is allowing me to do my Beta on Saturday morning to confirm the negative. Being able to have a glass of wine on Saturday will be nice.

FRIDAY, JULY 16, 2010

10dpt- Getting Life Back

People keep telling me that it's not over yet, miracles do happen. Although I appreciate the optimism, I do not think anything will change. I gave up on miracles a long time ago. I work with science now. I know petri dishes, estradiol, progesterone, motility, morphology, follicles, cells, fragmentation and so much more. All of those things make a baby. None of those things include miracles. I have had a 24 hour migraine that is kicking my ass. My head feels like it is going to explode. I asked Dr. P if I could stop my progesterone so my period can come and this headache will go away. She said no. I didn't think she would say yes. Until the blood work comes back, I still have to treat my body like it is pregnant. I'm very much looking forward to getting my life back. I'm looking forward to getting a good workout in. I'm looking forward to being hormone free. I'm looking forward to having a real coffee. I'm looking forward to having a martini. I want to lift heavy things. I want to swim for hours. I can't wait to foil my hair. I'll even clean the cat litter again. I look forward to not having to wake up to needles. I look forward to not having vaginal ultrasounds every other day. I VERY MUCH look forward to ending progesterone. I know that I'll only get to do these things for a short while because I will be back to being a science project in a short while. So even if I get my life back only for a few days, I am very much excited for it.

SUNDAY, JULY 18, 2010

Pregnancy Test Shame

Today is 7/18. Two weeks ago, I was excited for this day to come. Today, it's just another day. Dr. P allowed me to do my beta on Friday so we could confirm the negative and I could stop the progesterone. I got the call that it was negative around 2:30. I wasn't surprised. I wasn't upset. I just was. This is our life. This is all we know. We don't know any other way. I'm used to negatives.

Over the past couple of days, many people have asked me if we have thought about a surrogate. The answer is yes, I have. Although I have thought of it, it's not an option for us. Our issue is not with my body. The issue is with embryo quality. Our embryos wouldn't survive in another uterus either. They would also die in a surrogate. A surrogate is for someone with an issue with their blood or uterus. A surrogate is for someone who cannot carry children. That is not me.

Dr. P is going to do an endometrial biopsy. She said it's probably "TOTALLY overkill" but wants to make sure that there is no underlying infection that has gone undetected. This is pretty much the last thing we can do. Not that I want something wrong, however, it would be nice to have something to fix. Although, something to fix would be nice, I have a feeling the biopsy is going to be fine. She also said that most embryos at her clinic survive the thawing process (that's double the national average. I'm thinking it's due to the strict freezing criteria). Dr. P said frozen embryos have half the success rate of fresh ones. Either way, I'm psyched to get going again.

When I was being a POAS fanatic (which I think is why I was so prepared for the results of the beta) I couldn't believe how embarrassed I was to be buying them. What is with the feeling of guilt and shame that comes along with buying pregnancy tests? I'm 31 years old. I'm married (not that that matters). Why is it that I felt so trashy buying them? It is the strangest thing. I mentioned it to one of the AGC girls and she said she feels the same way. I normally don't care about judgment. How one feels about me is no reflection of who I am. So why on earth do I care what about the cashier at the pharmacy thinks? When I mentioned it to B, he said he used to feel the same way buying condoms. So strange.

MONDAY, JULY 19, 2010

Sugar Coating

Today, my period came with a vengeance. Periods after a negative should be light and pain free. I should be spared from the cramps and super-sized tampons. On the bright side, the start of my period means the start of a FET (Frozen Embryo Transfer) cycle. At this point, I have no idea what that entails. Still, I'm looking forward to it. Since 7/10 of the embryos degenerated and three made it to freeze, I'm hoping that means the frozen ones are of great quality and will work. I know the stats and understand the chances of it actually working. I hope it does but I don't have my hopes up. I had to go in for another Beta today. It's just policy since we did my other one early. When they call with the results, I should get some direction on what my next steps are. Fun Fun...

One of the benefits of not being pregnant is the ability to enjoy the ever so sweet taste of Advil. Oh how I missed it. The reason it tastes so sweet is because the coating is lightly sugared. There is nothing like NSAIDs for period cramps. You forget about all the great things you're missing while you are under treatment. NSAIDs are one of them. Yummm.....

Today is my first day back to working out. I had a decent workout this morning. It's not as good as it usually is but I'm still recovering from ankle surgery. It was good to get my heart pumping and blood flowing. Breaking a sweat feels good. Not only does it help with stress, it may also help with the booty I developed this cycle. I love when people say "wait until you have kids." Believe me, I cannot wait! I'll take six extra asses if it means I get to have a kid. I will not complain about how I look after children. My body changing for a purpose is well worth it to me. My body changing for a period with a vengeance, not worth it (and worthy of complaint).

TUESDAY, JULY 20, 2010

Would have been...

I am so over this waiting thing. I have realized that I am happiest when I am under treatment. I guess it makes me feel like we are working towards something. Waiting seems like a waste to me. Whatever, I'm so over this. Everyone keeps telling me to stay positive. Seriously, positivity means nothing to me. Yes, I am positive but that's not getting me pregnant. B and I completely disprove the whole "being positive" helps theory. We have been positive and upbeat for 32 months and are still childless. I hate to say it but I'm so over all this nonsense. Enough is enough. We're good people. We deserve this. I try not to judge others. I try to avoid gossip. I give more than I have. I volunteer. I put myself in situations that make me uncomfortable because I am selfless. I care about making other people happy regardless of how it makes me feel. There is the thought that you are only given what you can handle. Maybe I should stop being a good person and start freaking out and being selfish. Maybe if I start showing signs of not being able to handle this anymore, it will work out. Maybe my good nature is harmful to my future as a parent.

This would be my last week in my second trimester. Saturday would be the start of my 28th week. Awesome. So not only do I get to enjoy the feeling of a failed cycle, not only do I get wait to try again, I also get to think about what would have been. I get to think about all the milestones I will not cross. I get to think about how I would only have 12 weeks left in my pregnancy. I get to think about Baby L and how I won't get to meet him/her. This is a great week. I'm so happy that it's happening. Please, give me more hell to bear. Apparently my load isn't heavy enough. It looks like I will never break so you might as well give me more. Why the hell not?

WEDNESDAY, JULY 21, 2010

One Nighters

After cooking dinner, I was waiting for B to get home from work. I decided to watch a little Teen Mom while I waited. One of the girls thought she was pregnant again. She kept saying "we only forgot the condom once this month." The really frustrating part for me is that we will never be in that position. They already had one "mistake" and now they're thinking they're on their second (she ended up not being pregnant). We can't even plan to have a baby never mind mistakenly have one. I just don't get how so many people can get pregnant from one night. With all the information I know about what goes into conception and pregnancy, I do not understand how people get pregnant in the first place. I was talking to a friend yesterday who just had her 5th failed IVF. She has a 3 year old daughter that was the result of a one nighter. I should add it was with her husband of many years!! The way I said that sounded like it was a one night stand. Anyway, her daughter is a pure miracle. Yesterday during our conversation she said "I knew she was a miracle baby when we first found out I was pregnant. However, it wasn't until recently that I really appreciated the miracle." I don't want to go into the details but medically, she and her husband were not supposed to be able to conceive naturally. One night that month they had sex...one night. I can't believe that can actually happen. Believe me; I am so happy it did happen....I just don't get how!

The biggest struggle during an off cycle is the actual waiting. Most couples try to conceive, when their cycle ends up with a period, they try again next month. Unlike most couples, we don't get to remain active in the trying category; we are completely controlled by science. It doesn't matter how much we are intimate, we will never end up pregnant on our own. We have to have someone else make our babies. That blows

THURSDAY, JULY 22, 2010

Chemistry Set

Tomorrow we have our WTF appointment. There really isn't anything to learn or hear about the cycle that just failed. I am anxious to hear the details of the FET we will be doing next cycle. I have no idea what drugs I will be on or how long I will be on them. I have no idea how long the process is from start to finish.

I am a planner. Having a plan will make me more at ease. We'll also talk about the endometrial biopsy. I have no idea what they will be testing for and looking for. I am a science project. I get poked, prodded, stuck with needles, injected with drugs, eggs removed, ovaries vacuumed and overdosed with hormones. It makes me think of the chemistry sets we used to play with as kids. I'll post the results of the WTF appointment as soon as I get home tomorrow.

SATURDAY, JULY 24, 2010

WTF Appointment

So the appointment came and went. It went very well. I guess it's hard for it to go poorly. Not only did we discuss the cycle and what we will do next time, we also did an endometrial biopsy and a sonohystogram.

When we first got there, I couldn't help but stare at a very pregnant woman. Once you are eight weeks pregnant, you are released to your OB. Seeing a woman with a big belly (I'm guessing she was around seven months) is very unusual. I couldn't for the life of me figure out why the heck she was there. Anyway, when we saw Dr. P she asked us "Talk first or torture first?" We chose talk first. I know I have mentioned it before but I'm going to say it again...Dr. P is so incredibly sweet. She is by far the best physician I have ever had (including Dr. H, my pediatrician). She was sitting across from us at her desk, after a big sigh, she asked "How are you both?" I said to her what I've been saying all along "We're used to it. This is normal for us." She replied with "I don't want it to be your norm. Let's change that." These details may seem silly to some of you. However, these are the details I remember. I remember how I am treated more than what was discussed. I'm a cancer. Cancers are emotional people. We relate to emotion more than anything. As far as the failed cycle goes, there really isn't anything we could do differently or have done differently. The embryologist suggested changing the protocol for me. Dr. P isn't all that comfortable with that. I respond very well on the protocol that we used. Every cycle has been consistent. There really is no reason to risk the consistency. I asked a million silly questions and Dr. P answered every single one. I went as far as asking if we could buy donor eggs and sperm and experiment with them. Use other sperm with my eggs and other eggs with B's sperm to see if we get better quality. Buying sperm and eggs for experimental purposes is so incredibly pricey. Hey, it's a WTF appointment. Anything goes during these things. Stupid questions are allowed. Once I was done asking insane questions, we discussed the frozen embryo cycle. The embryologist told Dr. P that of our three snowbabies "one was really good, the second that was pretty good and the third is not as good as the other two." My clinic has a very strict freezing criteria, even if the third isn't as good as the other two, I'm confident that it is still good. The process of the FET is this: On Day one of my period, I will start taking oral estrogen three times a day. On day 12 of my cycle, I will go in for an ultrasound. If my lining looks good, then I will start progesterone and they will schedule the thawing and transfer of the snowbabies. Dr. P had two concerns. The first is that I will be on a very high dose of estrogen. She is concerned about my migraines. So she gave us two options. Start with the estrogen and if I start getting symptoms we can cancel the cycle. Since the embryos are frozen, we won't be losing anything (other than time). The second option is to go with a natural cycle. No estrogen and follow the cycle very carefully. I would get monitored for ovulation and all that fun stuff. My cycles have been messed up since my miscarriage. I'm ovulating at strange times and my period is coming whenever it wants. For that reason, I opted to go with the estrogen based cycle. The second concern...sort of...she wasn't concerned but felt that it should be addressed, is she wants me to take the injected form of progesterone. During a FET cycle, progesterone is not being produced naturally. Injected progesterone is better when there is no other progesterone. The injected progesterone is called PIO: Progesterone in Oil. Yep, in oil... peanut oil to be exact. PIO hurts like a mother effer. As soon as she said she wanted to talk about progesterone, I knew where she was going. I said "oh no. I heard they kill." Dr. P didn't even try to sugar coat it. She said they are very painful. PIO is an intramuscular injection. It has to be injected in my hiney by someone other than me. I have to seriously think about whether or not I want B doing them. He's not great at giving injections. She said we could still do the vaginal suppositories if I didn't think I could handle the shots. I don't care if my ass falls off from pain, I will do whatever gives us the best chance of success. PIO it is.

After we were done talking, we walked down to the exam room. As soon as we walked in, I saw all the tools needed for the Endometrial Biopsy and the Sonohystogram. Yikes! Ignorance is the way to go in this situation. I say that but an hour before the appointment I sat in a coffee shop with two friends watching an endometrial biopsy online. Once I was in the room, I undressed from the waist down, wrapped a lovely white starchy sheet around me, and waited for Dr. P. I kept saying to B "I am so nervous." I had butterflies and knots in my stomach. I'm sure watching the video online didn't help. Once Dr. P came into the room, I laid back, put my legs in the stirrups, and tried to go to a happy place. First Dr. P put the speculum in. I always think of the most random questions while I'm going through this stuff. I asked her if the speculums are sterilized and repackaged or do they get thrown away...sterilized and repackaged is what happens with them. So while I'm asking this, she gets the speculum set up and gets the catheter thingy majigy ready. The catheter is very long and thin. As the catheter is being put into my cervix she said "You will have a little cramping." HOLY MOTHER OF GOD! A little!?!?!?!? I thought I was going to pass out. Once the catheter passed my cervix and entered my uterus, the cramping shot through my entire body. Once she was in there, she counted to ten. With every count, she pushed the end of the catheter into the back of my uterine wall. The catheter works with suction. So every push onto the uterus collected some tissue. At this point, I'm sweating and feeling light headed. I just laid there staring at the brand new ceiling tiles (much better than the water stained ones at the old office). Dr. P put the tissue into a specimen cup and then said "We need to do one more." For the Love of God! This time, I squeeze B's hand. Dr. P has the catheter in there for quite some time. I'm telling myself that we're almost done. Then she says "Okay, count to ten." I replied with "Holy crap, you haven't started counting yet?" The second time, she counted MUCH faster. After the biopsy was done, Dr. P said that the biopsy is worse than labor. I went from thinking I was going to pass out to feeling proud that I didn't pass out.

I have already done two sonohystograms. They are fairly painless. You do get slightly crampy but it's manageable. The negative side of a sonohystogram is that it is messy. Saline pours out of you as you're lying there. A catheter is placed into the uterus. Once the catheter is in place, a vaginal ultrasound is placed into the cervix. Once the doctor gets a good image of the uterus, saline is injected through the uterus. The purpose of the sonohystogram is to see if the uterus fills normally. The normal fill shape of a uterus is triangle. As soon as the saline was injected I saw that it filled like a heart. I asked right away if there was a polyp. Dr. P said that she was 99% sure that it was not a polyp but tissue from the biopsy. The only way to be 100% sure is to do a hysteroscopy (a scope is put into the uterus to see what's in there). So...I have a hysteroscopy on Tuesday. Joyous.

As we were signing our consent forms for the FET, I asked if the insurance company considers an FET an IVF cycle. If it does, we may want to consider keeping the embryos frozen until our insurance coverage runs out. The out of pocket costs for an FET are much less ($15k) than a fresh cycle. We are still trying to figure out the logistics of it all. I'll find out more on Tuesday. I think what will happen, is we will pay out of pocket for the FET and save the insurance coverage for future fresh cycles

SUNDAY, JULY 25, 2010

28 Weeks

Yesterday would have been my first day in the third trimester. I'm surprisingly okay with it. A few times yesterday, I thought about it but for the most part, it was just like any other day. When I saw pregnant bellies, I thought about how I would look. When I saw babies, I thought about the life Baby L will never have. I think the days will get harder when Baby L's due date approaches. For now, I'm happy with my small belly, somewhat skinny hips and little boobs. I'm enjoying having a glass of wine with dinner. I am loving the ability to work out. I especially am enjoying a needle free life. I am focusing on me. Of course, I would trade all those things in for a healthy baby in my womb or in my arms. However, I'm realistic; I know I can't trade things in. If we could, we would all have what we want. So for now, I'll enjoy the life I have.

MONDAY, JULY 26, 2010

Slight Change of Plans

Well, I guess I shouldn't say slight change of plans yet. There may be a slight change of plans. Dr. P told me today that she wants B and I to do Karyotype testing (we talked about it during WTF appointment). Karyotype is a picture of a person's chromosomes. Normally you don't do karyotype testing until you have had three...yes, three...miscarriages. This is why Dr. P rules. She wants to leave no stone left unturned. She said that if we find any abnormalities in either B or I, we will move forward will a fresh cycle (yes...the whole shebang again). The difference in doing a fresh vs. frozen cycle would be that we would genetically screen the embryos before transferring them. The way that is done is through a process called PGD: Preimplantation Genetic Diagnosis. Basically on day three of fertilization, the embryologist takes a biopsy of one cell per embryo. That biopsy screens the embryos at risk for any disease. B is in a meeting out of town all day tomorrow. So he'll get his Karyotype done on Wednesday. I'll do mine before my hysteroscopy tomorrow. I'm still shedding tissue from the biopsy and I'm already on to another test. I just ate some Chunky Monkey Ice cream...so I can't complain! Hopefully I'll get the biopsy results tomorrow while I'm at the office. I'll post the results of both the biopsy and hysteroscopy tomorrow.

TUESDAY, JULY 27, 2010

Stoic

After my biopsy post, a friend sent me an email to tell me that I was bad ass. At the time, I found it cute and funny. Today, I am going to agree ONE HUNDRED PERCENT with her. I am bad ass. This is how the hysteroscopy went today...

I walked into the exam room and the nurse told me that she needed a urine sample "only five drops." I can't control urine drops, so I gave her whatever came out. When I came back from the bathroom, I looked at the exam table and thought to myself "what on earth?!?!?" On top of the table paper there was an absorbent pad (sort of like what you keep around your house for potty training puppies and kittens). Underneath the pad there was a clear trash bag. The bag was in between the stirrups. Once I got undressed from the waist down, I sat on the absorbent pad and the doctor went over the risks with me....infection, perforation of uterus, bowels and some other things. Ya ya ya...let's just get this over with. The doctor asked me if I wanted any sort of numbing agent. I declined it. We put my body through the ringer and we give it crazy amounts of drugs. Anytime we can, I try to avoid drugs. I can handle pain. The doctor puts in the speculum and starts dilating my cervix with saline. After lots of water pouring out of me, she starts to put the scope in. Maybe I should explain what the scope looks like. The scope is about a foot and a half long. It's metal and tube-like. Unlike a catheter, it's hard and unyielding. My cervix is not a perfect straight path. My cervix has a nice bend. A firm scope without any flexibility can be quite tricky and painful to get through. Anyway, I was watching the monitor, I'd see the opening of my cervix, then I'd feel sharp, sharp, SHARP pain....then I would see the scope passing through the speculum. Ahhh....she didn't get in. I then would see and feel it all over again. After a few attempts, she asked me if I was sure I didn't want any numbing agents. Again, I declined. The doctor then took a tool that looked like massive tweezers. She said, "I am going to pinch your cervix so I can move it. You will feel a little pinch. A little pinch?!?!?! Are you pinching or removing my cervix all together?? I'm pretty sure it feels like my cervix was just ripped out! Yes, I'm screaming inside. I'm sweating, I'm screaming and I'm in agonizing pain. However, I do not say a word. I just laid there and took it. I'm not going to yell "ouch" or say it hurts. What good would that do? The goal is to get the scope into my uterus and make sure everything looks good. To reach that goal, I just have to suck it up. So I did. The doctor kept saying "You're so stoic...you're so stoic." After a few more attempts, the doctor asks me again if I want Lidocaine injected into the cervix (I think that's where she said it would go). She also said that she needs to try to manipulate the cervix to get the scope in and it will hurt a lot more. Holy Moly...what could possibly hurt more than this? Anyway, I again decline the Lidocaine. After three minutes or so of pain so bad that I thought I was going pass out (and I did almost pass out...my blood pressure dropped to the high 80s) the nurse suggests we page another doctor. I'm assuming this would be why a hysteroscopy is normally a surgery that you get put under for. It was SO much more painful than the biopsy. The other doctor came, took the speculum out, and miraculously got the scope through my cervix and into my uterus. I'm not saying that it was any less painful...it was just much quicker. The inside of the uterus is flesh colored. It has red specs in various places (I'm assuming its blood). There were all sorts of white webby looking stuff. I asked if that was endometriosis...it wasn't, it was mucous (gross, I know). Then I asked if you could see endometriosis and they said not from the inside. Then the doctor moved left to right to see the opening to my tubes. From the inside, they just look like little black holes. It's pretty cool. He then moved to the top of my uterus. At 2:30, there was a ridge. It actually looked like the inside of a peach (with the pit taken out). Oddly enough, I'm eating a peach right now. A peach really does look like a vagina. Strange. Anyway, there was a little ridge. He said that he could "bump" it out. He took the scope, whacked the ridge. A good portion of the ridge fell right off. I asked if we should be concerned about it and he said no. He said the inside of the uterus is not smooth. It has bumps and ridges. He said that my uterus looked perfect. I clarified with "Would you say that you are 100% sure that my uterus is good." He said "Yes. I'm 100% sure." I have had many tests done on my uterus and tubes in the past. Every time I have been told they look perfect. I just wanted to hear that nothing has changed after the miscarriage. Yes, we are putting my body through the ringer but I don't care. I'd rather know that everything we can possibly test is tested. Once we were done, I went to sit up, at the same time both doctors and the nurse asked me if I was okay. I said I felt fine. They then told me to lay down. The nurse took my blood pressure and again, it fell below 90. I felt okay so for them to all say something to me must mean that I looked terrible. While the nurse cleaned the room, I had to lay there. It took about 15 minutes or so for my blood pressure to climb back up (she let me get up once it hit 115). I was shaky and wobbly for about an hour after. That's that. After today, I will agree, I am bad ass and stoic.

The biopsy results are not in yet. Hopefully we'll get those soon. The karyotype results will take ten days. We should get those at the end of next week.

Now all I can think of are vaginas and peaches.

WEDNESDAY, JULY 28, 2010

B Period

Two nights ago, I had a dream that B got his period. I was so excited for his period because it meant that we could start our next cycle. I'm not on Lupron so I can't use that as an excuse for my bizarre dream. I guess I'm just a weirdo.

My biopsy came back normal. When I talked to Dr. P last night, she said I can stop questioning my body and whether we should look into a surrogate. I'm passing all tests with flying colors. I knew I was fine based on previous tests. However, when people are constantly asking you if you have thought about surrogacy/donor uterus, it's very easy to start doubting yourself. We put my body through the ringer but I needed it. I needed to be reminded that it's not my body. My body is capable of carrying a child. Phew to that...

Late afternoon (yesterday), I got an email from Dr. P asking if she could call me. She wanted to talk about the protocol for the frozen embryo transfer. During our WTF appointment, Dr. P said that after four failed cycles, she would present us to the board. When presented, the board will then have a round table (basically brainstorm) on what to do next. During our conversation yesterday, Dr. P said that she was losing sleep over us. She is very concerned about the amount of estrogen required for the frozen embryo transfer and my migraines. She ended up presenting us to the board yesterday. The board unanimously agreed that I should not be doing an estrogen based cycle. Obviously migraines are a concern but the more serious concern is clotting. This is why most women with migraines can't take birth control pills. With that being said, we have agreed to do a natural cycle. Dr. P said the success rate is the same. The only difference is that the natural cycle is less convenient for both the clinic and me. I will have to monitor my ovulation through at home ovulation kits. Once ovulation is detected, I will go have an ultrasound and blood work done. The blood work will confirm ovulation and the ultrasound will show if my lining is ready for implantation. Now we are trying to decide if we should thaw out all three embryos. We only know failed cycles. Dr. P however, has seen and sees both sides. She said many times she has seen failed cycle, failed cycle, failed cycle, triplets. Of course, we would take triplets but there are so many risks to take into consideration. So now we wait and think....

THURSDAY, JULY 29, 2010

Sperm Mix Up

The first step in fertility treatments (after testing) is IUI (insemination). Once your body is ready for insemination, you make an appointment with the urologist for the sperm donation. The morning of the IUI, B would go into the urologist, do his thing in a cup and leave. I would then come two hours later and pick up the sperm (it's literally in a vile that's in a paper bag that says your last name on it). During the two hours in between B's "donation" and my pick up, the urologist spins the sperm (cleans out seminal fluid and separates good swimmers from bad). One of my IUIs I got the urologist before the sperm was ready. I was in the waiting room with a guy who was also waiting for his sperm (his wife was already at the doctor's office waiting for him). He was clearly unhealthy and didn't take care of himself. He was very over weight (not that weight matters but health does). He smelled like smoke and was hacking up his lung. As I was sitting there, all I could think of were all the television shows where they had embryo/sperm mix ups. I sat in the waiting room, with my hands folded on my lap and my head bowed. I sat there and prayed over and over again that I not get this man's sperm. I was so worried that we would be one of those unfortunate couples that ended up with someone else's child. I just kept saying "dear God, please do not let me get pregnant by this man. Please let me get B's sperm." Hahahaha...I now laugh that my worries were about getting some random gross guy's sperm. My prayers now are much different!

I'm still torn on what to do about the embryos. Since our history is constant failed cycles, I want to transfer three embryos. My goal is to carry and deliver a child. My goal is to be a mother. I want a healthy child...that's it. I'm afraid that we'll be putting ourselves in too much risk by thawing and transferring three. For two of our fresh cycles, we have transferred three and ended up not pregnant. However, since the snowbabies are frozen, we know that these embryos are good quality. Also, on top of that, we have to think about money. I hate to put a monetary value on this but it's hard not to. Our insurance covers a certain amount of cycles. A cycle is a cycle, regardless if it's fresh or frozen. A fresh cycle costs between $18k-$20k. A frozen cycle costs $2k. If we put two in now and it doesn't work then we use the third later...we used up two covered cycles (that only cost the insurance $4k as opposed to $40k). If a cycle is a cycle, I feel like we should put them all in at once and only use up one covered cycle. Aye Aye...I do not know what to do.

FRIDAY, JULY 30, 2010

I Know

I was talking with a friend yesterday about how people think that just because I am open with our fertility struggles it gives them the right to say whatever they want. Don't get me wrong, being open is so well worth it. I don't have to hide anything. I don't have to sneak out and take shots. I can be a bitch and no one asks why. It does come with some downsides. The main one being, unsolicited advice. I know I will one day have children. I don't need anyone to constantly remind me of that (unless I ask). I know that you can have a glass of wine and get pregnant (you don't think I've tried that??). I know that many people end up pregnant after adopting. As I was talking to my friend she shared a story with me that I thought I would pass along...

Her sister was in Wal-Mart with her four children. As she walked in, the greeter asked her "What's wrong with your daughter? Is the heat doing that to her eyes?" Okay, let me start by saying this. Her daughter (who we will call 'L') was born legally blind. She knows that L looks different. She knows that L is disabled. She is open to discussing L's vision and treatment. That however, does not give people the right to point it out to her. She ended up calling Wal-Mart. She told the manager that she did not want anyone being reprimanded. She was only calling to bring to the manager's attention that she knows her daughter is disabled and she knows that she looks different. She told the manager that it doesn't mean that anyone has the right to point it out. It's painful enough as it is. You have no idea how much I can relate to that.

TUESDAY, AUGUST 3, 2010

A whole lot of nothing

Sorry I've been MIA. I haven't much to report on these days. I have no tests, no appointments, no changes. The only thing we're waiting on is my period. Actually, we had the Karyotype testing done last week. Those results should be in the end of this week/early next. They said it would be 10-15 days.

B and I have decided to move forward with adoption. No, this doesn't mean we have given up. Adoption is something we both wanted to do long before we started traveling down the infertile road. Moving forward with the adoption process doesn't mean we don't think we will get pregnant. It doesn't mean that we won't try anymore. Wanting to adopt was a dating prerequisite for me. If you had no interested in adopting, then we would never see a second date. If I were single, I would already have a house full of foster kids. I would also have a house full of animals. I have always wanted to save those deemed unadoptable... humans and animals. One of our fur babies (Ralph) was left in a box outside of a grocery store (called Ralph's). Our second fur baby (Henry) was smuggled over the border from Tijuana. Lastly, our Dog Cappy was a severely abused dog that was abandoned (he was thrown out of a moving vehicle) at a shopping plaza. He was male aggressive, dog aggressive and severely sick. I cannot walk away from an animal or a human in need. I give more than I have. I would adopt or take in every child with disabilities (physical or mental) and/or behavioral issues. I realize that it takes a special person to be willing to do that. I would never force the issue with B because he would do it just for me. I would never want that. Anyway, we are moving forward with adoption. The adoption process takes years. You have to complete home study classes; you have to fill out an insane amount of paperwork. It will be a year before we are out of the paperwork phase.

Although I'm talking about it on the blog, I am not yet comfortable talking about it in person. So if you know me, please don't ask me about it. It took me and still is taking me a few years to break through the infertility misconceptions. I don't have it in me to battle another one. For years I heard insensitive comments about trying to conceive. I have been learning as well as educating on fertility treatments. It has taken us a very long time to get to the point of being able to talk anytime, anywhere with people about infertility. For years I have been defending my body as well as B's body. I'm not yet ready to battle nor defend another aspect of my life.

WEDNESDAY, AUGUST 4, 2010

Nose Job

My Karyotype results came back yesterday. Normal. I'm actually surprised by it. My grandfather had early onset Alzheimer's. My mother has Multiple Sclerosis. My sister had epilepsy most of her life (she grew out of it). I wouldn't have been surprised with an abnormality. I'm can now say I am 100% okay.

So what's with people telling me I'm fat lately? I realize I have gained weight. I've been on drugs/hormones for nearly two years. I'm also 31 years old. I'm not in my teens or my 20's. I'm THIRTY ONE. Not a kid, not a young woman... I'm a woman. Plus, I'm 5'8" and 135 lbs. I'm not breaking the scale by any means. I am healthy; I eat a clean and fresh diet, I exercise regularly, I do not smoke nor do I drink caffeine (mainly for migraine purposes). No, I'm not the 110 pounds I once was. Again, I'm 31. Yesterday, someone at work told me that I had huge hips. Seriously?? You think I'm not aware of the size of my hips? My response... these hips were made to birth children! Another person in the conversation then asked me if I had good news. Really? I was just told that I have huge hips and you think I have good news? No, I do not have good news. My news is this... what the heck happened to common courtesy? Imagine if I walked into work and said "hey Sally! Beautiful day. Have you thought about pinning your ears back?" or "Hey Bill, looking like you need some Botox" or "Yikes Barbara, time for a nose job." With that being said... I am going to take my wide ass and hips and go to work.

THURSDAY, AUGUST 5, 2010

Baby Love

So it seems like I am bumping into pregnant ladies that are due in mid-October a lot more lately. I'm sure it's because they are further along and nearing the end of their pregnancy... so it's more noticeable to me. B's cousin is due ten days before I was due. Being around her is hard. I can talk to her about anything; I just can't look at her belly. No biggie. Yesterday, I was talking to the receptionist at one of my doctor's offices. She stood up to walk to the printer and I noticed her belly. It was huge. Not huge, huge... but huge. I asked her how she was feeling... how the weather has been for her. Then I asked the question I shouldn't have... "When are you due?" She is due mid-October. I didn't want to ask for a specific date. Even if I wanted to, I couldn't speak. For the first time, I felt overwhelmed by a belly. I was light headed, I was at a loss for words, I was nervous. I just wanted to get the hell out of there. It was taking everything I had not to cry. The lump in my throat was so huge, I could barely mutter a word. I just gave a half ass smile, turned around and sat in the waiting room. Of course, the only reading material was Parent Magazine. I did my best not to stare at her. I did my best to pretend that it didn't bother me. It sucked. I hated every second of it. I have a feeling that the next ten weeks is going to be torture. Awesome.

You should see the reactions I'm getting from people will I tell them all the tests came back normal. I have been saying for months and months and months, that my body is okay. I couldn't be more blunt. I have said things like, "The babies would die in you too." I guess I'm realizing no one has believed me. When they ask about the test results, and I tell them everything is normal, they look at me like I just told them they are dying. Many people have gone as far as responding with "Really...are they sure?" What can I say or do? The only thing I can do is laugh about it. If I wasn't so Awesome (yes, I am going to praise myself here), I would punch them in the face. People look at me with sad eyes. They look at me and feel bad for me. In all honesty, I feel bad for them. I feel bad that they are not strong nor will never be as strong as me. I do not walk around bitter and angry. I do not look down on others. I do not pity others for their struggles. I feel compassion and empathy for others. I feel bad that others don't have the capacity to feel those emotions. They can only feel bad for me because they think their life is better and/or easier. Of course, this doesn't apply to everyone. I may be jealous and envious but it only lasts for a short while. I have the most incredible life and wouldn't trade it in for the world. This is my life. I love all of it...the good and the bad. This is who I am and without it, I wouldn't be me.

FRIDAY, AUGUST 6, 2010

Science Mumbo Jumbo

B's Karyotypes came back... normal. We are officially Normal. Hahahah... I can't believe the amount of relief that comes with knowing your chromosomes are normal. Dr. P sent a blurb from the report. I cannot tell you how impossible it is to read. Honestly, I have no idea how anyone can understand that language.

Since we're officially Normal, we will definitely be moving forward with the natural FET. We also decided to only put two back in. I am not comfortable with two and I'm not comfortable with three. To be safe, we'll stick with two. I don't mind the idea of triplets. I'd actually love it. Why not get as many as you can at once? Having triplets (when we could have prevented it) would be a selfish thing. I don't want to be the reason for our children spending the first few months of their life in the NICU. I don't want to risk losing one and putting the others in danger. As much as I want the highest chances of success, I also want the best possible outcome. My goal is to deliver healthy babies. So... two it is. Now we just need my lovely period to come (it's not due for another two weeks) so we can get this show on the road.

SATURDAY, AUGUST 7, 2010

Okay Okay Okay

I know I'm driving you all crazy with my indecisiveness. Well, there has been another change. I'm not all that comfortable with our decisions about a frozen transfer. I do think a change of pace by transferring two blastocysts would be nice... however; all I can think about is the money. Our insurance covers six cycles. We only have five cycles left. I am sure you're wondering how we have so many cycles left after all the cycles we have done. We have two insurances. Our primary insurance is through my work. We have already used up the lifetime cap for fertility treatments on that plan. We pay out of pocket for a second plan (B's work plan had minimal fertility coverage). Our secondary plan is the one that covers six cycles. They paid for half the cycle we just did (even though it wasn't a full cycle it counts as one). So, that leaves us with five chances. Using a Frozen transfer as one of those chances seems like a waste to me. I wouldn't be on meds... which saves the insurance company $8,000 or so. I would only cost the insurance company a couple thousand dollars for the thawing process and the transfer. On top of that, we would only have four chances left. So, with all that being said, we have decided to go through with another fresh cycle. I KNOW!! I was looking forward to being needle free. I was looking forward to a change. However, I want as many chances as possible. Frozen embryos can stay frozen forever. So, when we run out of insurance coverage, we will turn to the snowbabies. Right now, Dr. P is trying to figure out the logistics to make this work. I will have to go in for blood work to make sure I have ovulated. I also will have to start Lupron (I am so not looking forward to the hot flashes and bizarre dreams) in the next day or two. I have to get my hands on some fast. As far as scheduling goes. I will be transferring at almost the exact same time as I would for the frozen transfer. So we're not losing any time. I know... I can't stop changing my mind. I wish our decisions weren't this hard. I wish our decisions could be more about if we feel like having sex or not. Booo Hoo.

SUNDAY, AUGUST 8, 2010

Montauk Daisy

I went for my blood work today. My first fertility doctor was the doctor working. When he called with my results he told me that my progesterone was 1.01... basically that means I have not ovulated yet. I asked him if I was about to ovulate, would my levels be any different. He replied with "I don't see you starting a period in the near future." I was very confused. I am not expecting a period for another two weeks. So I agree, I don't see one in my near future either. He then said that he suggests I go on Provera to induce a period. Huh!??! Why should I force my body to bleed when it's not ready. We have put my body through hell and back. If it needs a few extra days, then so be it. He then said he will suggest to Dr. P that instead of going on Lupron on day 21 of the next cycle that I do an antagonist protocol. Uh Uh, I am so not messing my body up to try something new. I emailed Dr. P and said that if it's okay with her, I am vetoing the Provera. I want my body to do what it needs to do on its own time. Dr. P agreed and said that she wants to give it a few days and retest. I go back on Wednesday to see if the levels increase (I'm 99% sure they will... I can feel something going on in there today). I'm back to being a pin cushion... right where I belong (or at least feel comfortable).

We want to have some sort of memorial for Baby L. We went out today and bought two Montauk daisy bushes. They are in full bloom in October. Right now, we're trying to decide where to plant them. They need full sun... which isn't a problem. I want to be able to look at it anytime I'm home. I want to be able to look out the window and see the flowers. So, we have to find the perfect spot for them. Today's post will be short (and of course, sweet) because B and I are going on a Montauk planting hunt.

TUESDAY, AUGUST 10, 2010

Father of the Year

Last night, I had dinner with the AGC girls. Normally, there is a ton of traffic. As always, I planned ahead and left a little early. Well, for some reason, there was no traffic at all. There was barely anyone on the road. I ended up getting to the restaurant 45 minutes early. What does one do when they have 45 minutes to spare... shop! I'm more of a window shopper these days. I just do not like the styles out. Anyway, I was walking through the maze of clothes at Macy's when I heard a little girl SCREAMING. This wasn't a standard tantrum scream. This was an ear piercing, I'm being kidnapped scream. Instantly, my stomach drops. I rushed over to the direction of the screams. Around the corner came a guy (Jesse James kind of guy... tattoos, soul patch, baseball cap, t-shirt and jeans) and his daughter. She was throwing the biggest fit I have ever seen. She was screaming at the top of her lungs "Why can't I stay with Mommy. I want to shop with Mommy." She was about 4 years old. She was wearing a cute pink dress with sparkly pink flip flops. Her hair was pulled back in a ponytail. Cute girl with a bright red face, booger bubbles coming out of her nose and tears streaming down her face. Cute girl with a blood curdling scream. Her father kept his hand on her wrist, his mouth shut and just kept walking. Whenever he passed a shopper, they would smile. In the midst of psycho child tantrums, he stayed calm. Right after they passed the perfume counter, the little girl, threw her body on the ground and believe it or not, started screaming louder. The guy just picked her up, threw her over her shoulder, and kept walking. He stayed calm (at least he looked calm) and he didn't let her win. All the woman who witnessed it were whispering to each other "Poor guy." I however, thought, now that is a man who should reproduce! Everyone else kept feeling bad for him. All I could think of was "finally a good parent!!!!!" Mr. Dad of tantrum girl, I salute you!

I planted the daisies yesterday. I wanted to plant them outside of the nursery window. However, I have a future plan for our kitchen. When we remodel the kitchen, I'd like to bump out one of the walls for a little extra space. With the kitchen and the nursery being so close together, I'm not sure what will happen with the landscaping. I didn't want to plant the daisies only to have to pull them up. So, I planted them near our front door. When they are in bloom, I will send a picture.

I bought ovulation tests yesterday. I like to be in control. Not knowing if I ovulated will drive me crazy. As of this morning, I have yet ovulated. I read online that Lupron can cause you to miss ovulation. I hope this isn't the case. I do not want to take medication to fix what another medication did. So, I will wait until I ovulate naturally... even if that means I have to wait another month.

THURSDAY, AUGUST 12, 2010

Seesaw

True Story...

Yesterday I went in for blood work to see if I have ovulated yet (I have not). When I got there, there was a couple checking in and a couple in the waiting area. The couple checking in was an older couple... well, at least the guy looked older. The other couple was a younger couple. The guy was gross (wait to you hear what he said before you get mad at me for calling him gross). After the older couple was checked in, I checked in. I got my paper work, walked through the doors and into the lab. My blood work only took two minutes. In the two minutes, the two women who were waiting had left. They weren't near the lab and they didn't walk through the lab into the exam rooms. They must have been either in the bathroom or meeting with their doctor. As I was walking towards the elevator, the gross guy said to the old guy "Now if that was my wife, I'd have no problem getting her pregnant." I was bullshit. BULLSHIT. Not for me but for his wife. I was so angry that his poor wife, who, for at least a year has been dealing with the letdown of infertility, was married to him. I then had to stand at the elevator and listen to him chuckle at his own insensitive, gross, violating comment. Vomit.

So, I bet you're wondering where the Seesaw title comes from?!? Well, here it is... We're now doing a frozen cycle instead of a Fresh. I know we keep flip flopping in our decision. Yesterday, Dr. P called me to tell me that she found out that I was misinformed about our insurance coverage. We get six covered cycles with our insurance. The financial department told me that frozen cycles count as one of those six cycles. Dr. P found out, that it doesn't count. If you do a frozen cycle before your six cycles are up, you're basically getting free coverage. Well, it's not free... but you know what I mean. She also found out that after the six cycles, they will not cover anything that has to do with fertility. No Betas, no lab work, no ultrasounds... nothing. With all that being said, it makes sense for us to make sure we use all our snowbabies before we use up the six cycles. Even though I haven't ovulated and nearly a month has passed since the biopsy and all the fun tests we did, we are still going to wait until next cycle. Clearly, my cycle this month is all screwed up from being poked and prodded. We'll wait until I ovulate, get a period then we'll thaw out and transfer the snowbabies... only two of them.

SUNDAY, AUGUST 15, 2010

Negative Nancy

I am used to people making judgments about infertility. I'm used to people minimizing what I'm going through. I'm used to the insensitive comments and belittling remarks. It happens on a daily basis. Last week, I was with some friends. There was one person that managed to minimize the most sensitive subject for nearly every person in the room. One friend that was part of the conversation recently lost her best friend in war. He was killed in Afghanistan this past October. Everyone (within our community) knows about his death. They also know about how close he was with my friend. The insensitive person talked about people in war in a negative way. I don't want to go into the details because my friend reads this blog and I don't need her to be reminded of how insensitive some people can be. Everyone in the room was uncomfortable with the comments. I was cringing. I kept looking at my friend out of the corner of my eye to see how she was doing. When I saw her eyes fill up with tears, I wanted to put the negative Nancy in her place. Right as I was about to say something to her the subject changed. I cannot tell you how uncomfortable it was. My stomach was in knots. I was so angry at the girl and so sad for my friend. I am so used to being the person who is getting attacked or judged. It's part of my everyday routine. Witnessing another person deal with it was very difficult. I was horrified for everyone in the room. I was horrified for the person speaking. For the first time, in a very long time, I was not the person being judged (My time came...

Infertility comments came within a few minutes of the anti "hero" kick). It made me think of all the times people have made rude comments to me in public. Do others feel how I did the other night? Do they get knots in their stomachs and get uncomfortable? Do they feel as bad for me as I did for my friend? It is incredibly hard for me to understand people like that. I just cannot comprehend being insensitive. There are certain subjects that you should always approach with sensitivity. Being an adult, you should know that.

I still have not ovulated. I'm a medical mystery. Doing the biopsy could have thrown my body off. I'm going to be 60 by the time I get pregnant. At least I can work towards breaking a world record.

MONDAY, AUGUST 16, 2010

Smiley Face

My routine every morning for the past couple of weeks has not changed. I wake up, pee on a digital ovulation test, wait for the result then go back to bed for a little longer. With the digital tests, you get an "empty circle" if ovulation is not detected and a "smiley face" if it is detected. Every morning, including this morning, I got an "empty circle." I went in for my progesterone test at 8:45. Dr. P emailed me around 3:00. Still no ovulation. Of course, I knew this, since I've been testing every day. Dr. P told me she was going to check my TSH, prolactin, FSH, and estradiol levels to make sure nothing hormonal is causing me not to ovulate. She was able to add the tests on to the blood they took this morning. There's always a blessing somewhere... today's blessing is that I don't need to get poked again for the additional tests. I have been feeling aches, dull cramps and a fullness in my uterus for the past few days. Last week I had the egg white mucus that comes along with ovulation (normally I would apologize for TMI but this is a fertility blog... all modesty went away a long time ago). I thought for sure something was going on in there. When I got home from work, I took another test. Finally a smiley face! I'm so relieved that I'm not crazy and I don't have some sort of alien baby growing inside of me. I'm glad that what I was feeling was ovulation. Normally, ovulating on day 29 of a cycle would be very abnormal. However, I have been on fertility drugs for well over a year and a half. I'm sure my body has no idea what it is doing right now. With the smiley face, comes a period (in two weeks). We're looking at a frozen transfer around the end of September. The joys of infertility. You would have thought I saw a positive pregnancy test. I was jumping for joy... I sent texts to friends and an email to Dr. P. Geesh... When we finally get pregnant, I'll be sending the president a letter requesting it be a national holiday!

THURSDAY, AUGUST 19, 2010

Proud Mama

Our dog Cappy was severely abused (I may have mentioned this in previous posts). We have spent a lot of money and time on his rehabilitation. When we first got him, he bit two people. We could barely walk him down the street. He was terrified of his own shadow. Although we don't know his full history, it is assumed that he was the bait dog in dog fighting. It's very common for bait dogs to have their teeth kicked out and legs broken (so they can't bite back and they can't run away). Since he has had both of those things happen and he has severe dog aggression, the vet assumed he was the bait dog. B couldn't even hug me without Cappy jumping between us and barking at B. We think he was not only in a dog on dog abuse situation, he was also witness to domestic violence. Cappy is a Great Dane/Lab mix. He's as cute as can be. Since we've had him, he's been under strict training. The main thing we have been working on is his self-confidence. His behavioral specialist (yes, he has a therapist) explained to us that abused dogs have two responses, fight or flight. He has only known how to fight. We have been working very hard on teaching Cappy that he doesn't have to be in every situation. If he is uncomfortable all he has to do is walk away. One of his fears is men. When we first got him, he couldn't be near them. If we had a cookout, we'd kennel him. If we had a man or many men over, we'd put him in another room. Now, he can be near men. When he gets uncomfortable, he walks away (he's comfort spot is behind the couch). As great as he is doing, I will never trust him with children. That doesn't mean he is unsafe to be around. It just means, I will never allow him to be alone with them. You never know what would trigger him to snap. I will not take that risk around children... obviously. Although, he is very paternal around babies. If a baby cries, he sits right next to it to make sure it's okay. If it doesn't stop, he walks around until he finds the baby's mother. Toddlers still scare him. First off, they are eye level which is threatening to all dogs not just abused ones. They are erratic and hard to predict. When we have toddlers in our house, we usually have Cappy outside. Last night, I had a couple of friends over for dinner. One of them has a 16 month old. She's very mobile... in fact she runs around. Cappy was definitely freaked out by her. I put him outside so she could run around and play inside. When we were out on the deck, I had Cappy come in. The trainer taught us to introduce children to dogs by first letting the dog smell the child through you. Usually, I hold the child's hand in mine and let Cappy smell my hand. Babies, I usually have Cappy smell their feet. Yesterday, I had Cappy smell her foot. As I was holding her I wrapped my hand around her foot. He kept running up to me and smelling her. Then at one point, I squatted (still holding her) and had Cappy come up to us. He was very hesitant. He would slowly approach us and then quickly run away. All the while, R kept saying "HI, HI, HI" (she thinks animals will speak back). Anyway, after a couple of minutes, Cappy came up to us, turned his body around, and backed into us. He wanted so badly to allow R to pet him but he just wasn't comfortable facing her yet. So he did the only thing he could think of... he turned around so he couldn't see her, put his butt in her face, and let her pet him. After he did it once, he couldn't stop. He kept coming back for more. He was so proud that he figured out a way to let her do what she wanted to do and still not have to put in a situation he wasn't comfortable with. I couldn't have been a happier Mom. That was a really long story for me to get to that one point. Oh well.

I forgot to mention that all the tests Dr. P ran on Monday came back normal. There's nothing abnormal about this girl!

FRIDAY, AUGUST 20, 2010

Knowledge

One of my college roommates called me last week to tell me she is pregnant. After many "congratulations" and "This is so exciting for you," she told me the story of finding out. She missed her period a few months in a row. Each month, she kept taking pregnancy tests. Each test was coming back negative. She called her doctor and requested to be tested. They did a urine test, which also came back negative. She then requested a blood test which came back positive. A few days later, she fell. When she went to the doctor, she asked that they do an ultrasound to make sure the baby was okay. The baby was fine and perfect... in fact the baby was so perfect, that it was measuring 12 weeks. TWELVE WEEKS! She had been pregnant the entire time and didn't know. I should say, she did know. She felt pregnant. She was getting really sick. However, tests were telling her she wasn't. Ahh... this drives me nuts. Not her being pregnant. I am extremely happy for them. Both K and her boyfriend will be wonderful parents. So when I say that this drives me crazy, I don't want to take away from the excitement and joy of their pregnancy. What drives me crazy is because of infertility, I know way more than the average person about what it takes to become pregnant. I know many details involving cells in an embryo. I know about embryo development. I know that a sperm meeting an egg is not all it takes. I know when a placenta is being formed. I know how much hCG should be secreted into the blood stream. I know far too much. So the entire time K was telling me the story, all I could think about was her hCG and how it should have been detected. I kept thinking that she is that .1% that pregnancy tests do not work for. I kept thinking about how crazy it is that she does not fit into the 99.9% accurate statistic. It drives me crazy that I know so much. I wish I didn't. I wish I was clueless about it. I wish I thought all it took was a glass of wine. I wish I thought that if you stop thinking about it, it will work out. I wish I didn't know so much. It drives me crazy.

Problems

Yesterday, B and I sat on the couch and watched Grey's Anatomy ALL day. Our plan for the day was to clean out the nursery and prime the walls. We started working on it when I was pregnant and stopped after I miscarried. All the tools need to be removed from the room and the walls need to be primed. It was a beautiful day out. We should have been sitting on the beach. The last thing I wanted to do was to organize and clean out the nursery. So I convinced B that we should watch an episode of Grey's. Before a few months ago, we never saw one episode of Grey's. We were told it was a really good show so we started getting it on Netflix. We started with Season One and watched it through each season thereafter. Yesterday, we watched Season 5. At one point, B said, "Everyone has problems on this show." I replied with "Everyone has problems. That's true in real life too." There are those people who walk around thinking that they have everything. They think that their life is the best life you could possibly have. They don't have everything. Every single person walking on this earth has a problem. It may be a problem in their marriage. It may be a problem at work. They may be battling something from their past. They may be struggling with finances. Their roof may need to be replaced or their brakes are wearing down. It doesn't matter how big or small the problem is... everyone has one. I know I have said it before but I think it needs to be said again... People look down at me/us, because they think that we have it worse than anyone else. What they don't realize, is that they have some sort of problem/struggle of their own. We're all broken in some way... whether we want to admit it or not. People can be so quick to judge and criticize. No one should judge another person's struggle or brokenness. Who is to say my struggle is worse or less worse than another person's struggle? We have all struggled. What may seem bad to one person may not seem bad to another and vice versa. Life is complex. It's not meant to be judged.

Last night, I had this bizarre dream. I was in a coffee shop. It didn't look like a coffee shop. It had ladders all over the place and torn up couches. I just knew it was a coffee shop (dreams are good like that). Anyway, I kept having to go to the bathroom. One of the times I walked into the stall (which was made up of fabric covered headboards), pulled down my pants and started to pee. All of a sudden, my abdomen started to swell. In a wave motion, the swelling traveled down to my hooha. Once the swelling reached my hooha, my uterus started to fall out. My uterus did not look like a uterus. It had long stringy things (like a close up of a wart). A couple of days ago, I was looking at medical images of warts at work) and it had white lining that kept turning into blood. I kept calling Dr. P asking her what to do. I don't remember what she said or if I even talked to her. All I kept thinking was "My Uterus is falling out." Bizarre.

Tomorrow morning I have another progesterone test. Since I got the "smiley face" on the ovulation kit, we should expect to see high levels of progesterone. Fingers crossed...

SUNDAY, AUGUST 22, 2010

Birthday Blog from B

Part of my birthday gift this year from B was a posting on his blog. Although it's been a couple of months since my birthday, I thought I would post it. It's hard for people to understand that I can be happy. It's hard for people to understand that Infertility doesn't define me. I define me. We define each other. We're incredibly happy. Life is about appreciating the blessings and not dwelling on the broken pieces.

(THE ACTUAL BLOG POST FROM B)

25 JUNE 2010

An Instant

He walked right in the door. Same as every day. It had been a long one, this day. Stress and worries and not much time for the quick phone calls, two to five minutes each, they usually had during the workday, three or four times a day, where she updated him on the minute details of exactly what she was doing or had been doing or was thinking of doing next and why or how she planned to do it. He loved those calls for all their nothingness and triviality that meant so much because it was between the two of them - like the one this week where she called only to say that the roses that she planted in their garden had bloomed. "B, did you see the roses?" "No" "They bloomed, like 20 of them, they look *so* good." "Really?" "Yeah. That's all." "Okay, bye." "Bye."

And she was there. There she was, as she was most nights, sitting on the couch with her 'fur babies'. She called the pets 'fur babies'. This particular night was stifling hot. And she was less sitting as she was poured onto the couch in the manner one employs so as to not have any two pieces of the body touching, anywhere. Fingers even spread apart. Seeing her induced a smile and memories of how he would come home to her back when they lived in an apartment, with a roommate, in a different place. He would come home later in the evening from work than she. She would wait up for him, sitting on the couch, this one more a love seat, in this exact poured manner - keeping cool and lazily looking at some television show with the remote hanging in her hand hanging off her arm hanging off the side of the couch. And he would, before even placing down his bag, climb onto the love seat, opposite her, and grab her feet or legs or some other nearby body part and squeeze. That's all. Just squeeze. And she would smile, before even looking up to acknowledge that he had come in and before even saying hello. And but this would be communication enough.

This was home for him. Just as it had been back in the apartment. A catharsis. Immediate and total. Home. No, Home! Really, a purifying of emotion. Like coming to the surface of the sea after a near drowning. And it wasn't so much that he was home - like this was his house - as it was that she was there and that she meant 'home' to him. Comfort. Stupid pet names. Subtle knowing smiles. Nighttime laughter. 17 on a scale of 1 - 10. Spooning (when it wasn't so hot). Telling her about nightmares and vice versa. Throwing a leg over hers in the middle of the night. Being late for work because being in bed with her sure beats anything the day can bring. And remembering that time, the exact time, that they realized they wanted to grow disgusting and old together. This 'home', this feeling, could get him through anything, he was sure of it. He lived for it, I guess you could say.

And so he looked at her, wryly, out of the side of his head. And smiled. A satisfaction all over his face. And she knew, he thought, and she smiled back, he thought. Nothing more. Nothing more needed. And 'thank god for this' he thought to himself.

And says..."*Happy Birthday, Bushkies.*" And they'll talk more later, I'm sure, but it won't match this instant - like meeting her again for the first time. He started dancing around the room. Dancing and sort of strutting. He had totally forgotten about the day, about everything. He's moving like James Brown - sort of. An idiot. She made him do this. Not like forcing him to do it, the 'dancing', but something about her turned him into a child. Like seeing her triggered this trick the back of the brain liked to play on the front, it always had, whatever it was. An idiot child with one pursuit, a single objective...to get her to laugh. However brief and fleeting - so long as it was a true laugh. That laugh, so pure, all the reward he needs.

"Stop it Lovey."...laughing

MONDAY, AUGUST 23, 2010

Best ovulater ever

My progesterone levels came in yesterday at 13.6... basically this means that I rule and I am the best ovulater ever. Since we're doing a natural FET, I'm comforted knowing that I have high ovulatory progesterone levels. Say that three times...

My brother came over today and primed our foyer and the nursery. I'm psyched about that. I just couldn't walk into that room to even clean it out. It's now stark white. With new paint, comes new direction. Hopefully only good things will happen from now on. How life changing paint can be...

THURSDAY, AUGUST 26, 2010

Benefit Cut

Okay... I hate to complain about a benefit... but I am going to. I realize that a benefit is just that... a benefit. However, when you are job hunting, you don't look at just job responsibilities and/or salary, you also look at the benefits package. five years ago when I was applying for jobs, I had a couple of offers. I ended up choosing one company over another because of its benefits. I found out today that they are significantly cutting some of our benefits. One of them being Maternity Leave. They are dropping leave from 18 weeks to 6 weeks. I realize most people only get six weeks to begin with. However, over the past five years, I have stayed loyal to my company. There have been layoffs and restructures. I have gone through handfuls of managers and partners. I have had to go through training after training for new products. Through all of this, I have stayed with my company for one sole reason, 18 weeks of maternity leave. I've even dealt with some HR issues that would have made any sane person leave. I, however, chose to deal with it all head on just for that darn 18 weeks of bonding time with my baby. The icing on the cake... freaking infertility. Had we not been dealing with this for so long, I would have been able to take advantage of the 18 week leave package. Had my pregnancy not ended in a miscarriage, I would have been able to stay home with Baby L. Freaking infertility. It takes so much from us. Isn't the "not getting pregnant" thing enough?

To make my day even better...

I'm Italian. I have thick gross eyebrows. I have to wax my brows just about every ten days or I look like Einstein. It's extremely difficult for me to find a salon that knows how to deal with my crazy brows. Last year, I finally found one. My brows always looked perfect when I walked out the door. Randomly (about three weeks ago) the salon closed. So, I tried out a new waxing lady today. She basically waxed ALL of my brows off. When I walked in the door, B asked "Why did she do it like the people who pencil their brows in?" Seriously!?!?! Take away the one benefit that makes me stay with my company and my eyebrows on the same day? I must have been a murderer in my past life...

FRIDAY, AUGUST 27, 2010

Babies R Us Meltdown

You won't even believe this story. I can hardly believe it...

Yesterday, I was talking to my friend D, she had mentioned that the only big item left on her registry was the crib mattress. Around 7:00, I drove to Babies R Us to grab the mattress for the shower tomorrow. If you have never been to Babies R Us on a Friday night, consider yourself lucky! It is pure chaos. There are people everywhere. Couples registering. Kids getting pictures taken. It's crazy. After waiting in line for a few minutes, I print out D's registry. Once I get to the mattress aisle, I notice that the mattress is not on the registry. As I'm flipping through the pages, I am pacing the aisle. I walk over to the crib section to ask a store employee if there could be any reason, other than it already being purchased, for the mattress to be off the registry. As I'm talking to him, there is a group of young girls playing a game. My guess is that they are in their teens/late teens. Not only were they young, they were also loud and obnoxious. The game they were playing went like this... A female walks by them, pregnant or not pregnant, they judge how they will be as a parent. While I'm talking to the store employee about the mattress, I hear one of the girls say "Oh that bitch, she's going to be a bad mom. You can tell she's just bitchy." The store employee and I roll our eyes and continue our conversation. The next thing the girls say (this is the part I freak out at) is "That bitch, in the purple and white striped shirt. She's definitely not going to be a mom. She's too stiff. She's not meant to have kids." Yes, I was and still am, wearing a purple and white striped shirt. I tried so hard to focus on the store employees purple shirt. I couldn't make eye contact with him because I knew I was going to freak out. As soon as I heard my shirt being described, my pulse started racing. I could feel a lump in my throat. The purple shirt didn't help me. I just started hysterically crying. I put everything I had in my hands on the floor at the employee's feet and I walked out of the store. At this point, I am beyond hysterical. I couldn't catch my breath. I could barely see through my tears. As I was stepping off the curb and into the parking lot I hear "Excuse me. Excuse me." Are you flipping kidding me?? Someone wants to ask me something now??? Right in the middle of a nervous breakdown?? I turn around and see this cute pregnant girl wearing a purple empire waist dress running at me. "Yes?" I say. She says, "My husband is going to kill me. I left him in there alone in that chaos but I had to come out and say I'm really sorry those girls were so rude." I attempted to say thank you but it just came out as deep, hysterical breaths. I managed to say "I've been going through a lot lately and I probably am more sensitive than usual. I guess I took it too personally." At this point, I was doing the "only inhale talking." You know when you have cried so hard, the only way to talk is while you're trying to catch your breath. That's how I sounded. She said that she hasn't gone through a lot and she found it offensive and she again apologized for having to hear it. I asked her when she was due (November), said congratulations and walked to my car. I sat in my car for several minutes bawling my eyes out. First of all, that should never happen. Those freaking brats should be smacked. One of those freaking brats is going to be a mother! For the love of God. Not only should that not have happened - it happened to me. It happened to a person who has been trying for years to have a baby. It happened to me when I'm six weeks away from my due date to a baby that I lost. It happened to me when I'm weak and sad. Those brats get to reproduce and I do not. Seriously... did that just happen??

SATURDAY, AUGUST 28, 2010

Stiff

I was thinking about it this morning... I definitely DO NOT look stiff! I look nice and friendly. I look happy and cheery. Maybe I had I serious look on my face while I was looking for the mattress... one thing is for sure... I do not look stiff!

Today marks six weeks from my due date. Aye! I can't believe it.

On a happier note... my blog has had over 11,000 hits! Whoop!

I have to hurry up and wrap my presents for the shower. I'll type more later.

Love,
Stiffy

MONDAY, AUGUST 30, 2010

Clarification

I was corrected about my due date. Yes, I was corrected about MY due date. However, I was wrong. Saturday, I would have been 33 weeks which means I would be 7 weeks from being due. However, in my mind... Saturday was 7 weeks... now I'd be 6 weeks and a few days away. So whatever.

Here's a little something that drives me bonkers...

Somehow, when you become pregnant, your name gets put on list for all the baby vendors to send you stuff. I have no idea how it happens... I can't imagine the clinic sells your information. I never signed up on any of the baby websites or anything. A few weeks after I miscarried, I got a "Congratulations! You are now entering your second trimester" card in the mail. It was from a cord blood banking company. Today, I got one in the mail (from the same company) that said "You are only a few weeks away from meeting your baby. Now is the time to consider storing cord blood" card from them. If we can mysteriously get on a list then we should be able to get off it. Really... I don't need the reminders of what I will not have.

A friend that I met through a friend sent me a packet of baby dust in the mail. When she was having a hard time getting pregnant, a blog friend sent it to her. Since she had her daughter (nine months ago) and is now pregnant again, she decided to pass the dust along to me. It's sitting on my night stand next to my Fertility Buddha and St. Gerard novena. In my living room I have a Willow Angel of Hope that I got from a friend. Next to her, I have a lucky feather (that my friend gave me this weekend). Next to that I have a Poem of hope that my Sister-in-law gave me on Christmas. I have Christianity, Buddhism, ornaments, poems, and Mystical dust working for me. If this cycle doesn't work, I don't know what else I can do!

THURSDAY, SEPTEMBER 2, 2010

Aunt Flo

Normally my period goes like this... I'll have insane cramps and a migraine then my period will come the next day. Yesterday I had zero cramps and zero hints of a migraine. Today, I had my boss with me (I'm in sales. When I have my boss with me, he literally sits in my passenger seat and meets with all my Doctors with me... ALL DAY). I was actually relieved that my period wouldn't be coming. Well, sure enough, I wake up at 5:30 to pee and what comes? Yep, my period. I was just psyched that I bypassed the cramps and migraine. When I woke up at 6:45 I felt like I was hit with a sledge hammer all night. I had a killer migraine and killer cramps (four delicious Advil didn't do a darn thing). Needless to say, I should have been miserable all day. However, I was nothing but excited. Day one of my period means we are one step closer to thawing out those wonderful embryos!

My sister-in-law just got engaged this past weekend. We are beyond excited! A & C are a fantastic couple... plus, we need a family wedding! In our fantastic world of Infertility. This engagement puts more pressure on this FET (Frozen Embryo Transfer) cycle. If this cycle doesn't work, then that means we will have to stop trying until March. I am okay being pregnant at her wedding but I do not want to be due near her wedding. We can't risk missing the wedding. So... that means, waiting for a LONG time. I'll go crazy before then. So let's hope that this one works.

SUNDAY, SEPTEMBER 5, 2010

Wahhhhh

Yes... wahhhh... that's me feeling bad for myself. Yesterday, I spent the day with a friend doing wedding stuff (for another friend). We had a great lunch on the water... although; my salad did have a lot of dead fruit flies on it. I, however, did not care. I was enjoying it. Plus, who couldn't use a little extra protein. Anyway, after lunch we went back to the hotel. Met up with the Bride and Groom for a bit then we went out for dinner and drinks with some friends. I got carded... YES!!!! I love when that happens. Then I was told my license had expired in June. I have been carded many, many times and not one person noticed... not even I noticed. Fortunately, I had left my passport in my car from our last trip (which was in December). I'm glad I'm a slow poke at putting things away. B had my car with his friends so he came to meet us. On the way home, I asked B how everyone was doing. He went through the list of people. Everyone is doing well. Then he said, "I told you Joe Schmoe is having a baby right?" Uhm, no. This Joe Schmoe that B speaks of is on the bottom of my living creature list. He is down there with spiders and cockroaches. I do not like this guy. He's scummy. Needless to say... I cried all the way home because I felt bad for myself. I felt bad that a person that I think is a jerky, scumbaggy piece of poop gets to reproduce and we do not. Seriously... Wahhhhhhhhh

WEDNESDAY, SEPTEMBER 8, 2010

Day 7

I am on day 7 of my cycle which means... we're just about two weeks away from a transfer! "Normal" people get to try to conceive by having sex. We however, try by injections in my belly, hormones, ultrasounds, blood work, petri dishes, embryologists... so these past two months of NOTHING (although I'm very happy for the lack of needles) have been torture for me. I need something to do. I want to feel like I am trying. I want to feel like I'm doing something to help us achieve our goal. Being on day 7 may seem boring to some but for me, it means I can start peeing on sticks! Yay!! A friend of mine got this fancy schmancy ovulation monitor for when she was trying. Basically, you set the monitor to day 1 of your cycle. Every morning, you turn it on and it will tell you where you are in your cycle (fertile wise). It will tell you when to pee on a stick so it can check your hormones. It will tell you if your fertile window is low or if it is at its peak. Since I have to test for ovulation, I have to get use this handy dandy monitor. Exciting stuff.

I know the past couple of months have been slow with my posts. Taking two months off makes it hard to always have something to say. I promise you, it will start picking up now. Now that I am looking for ovulation and will start peeing on sticks, I will have daily updates again.

I have recently decided that I am not going to care about other's feelings when they say things to me about babies and fertility. Usually, I take the advice or listen when people tell me that I should start trying soon or it will be too late. Lately, I have been saying exactly what's on my mind. For example in the past few days I have two things really annoy me. First, we met a couple that got married a couple of months before us. They mentioned that their anniversary will be before ours. After a few giggles and "how nice" comments, one of them said "Yep, three kids in three years." Then the husband asked us if we had children. When we said that we did not, his reply was "What are you waiting for? You better hurry up." Deep breaths Aprill... Deep breaths. Then today, I had a nurse practitioner tell me that she knows exactly how I can get pregnant. You ready for this?? All I need to do is add a serving of fat a day to my diet! What!!! That's it... then I'll get pregnant! I have found that instead of letting people tell me what I need to do or when I need to do it, telling them that they said something rude or asinine makes me feel so much better. Here's a list of responses I have used lately (I say it in a calm, nonchalant voice... with a slight hint of sarcasm and matter of fact tone):

Really? All I need to do is add one WHOLE serving to my diet a day? Why have we been spending so much money on seeing some of the best reproductive specialists in the area when all I have to do is eat fat! I'm going to eat ice cream every night!

You're right, I should start trying to have children soon. God forbid I suffer another three years of fertility treatments because I waited too long.

I actually find that question rude. I've learned over the years to never ask if/when someone would like to have children. You never know if they can have children.

All you did was not think about it and you got pregnant? Why haven't I thought of that? I guess I have been using all my thinking time on how to get pregnant and didn't have any time to think about anything else.

Do we know how to have sex? We should have sex during ovulation? You put the penis where? You mean it doesn't go in my ear? I thought your eggs traveled through your inner ear?? (I have never said that but that would be funny).

THURSDAY, SEPTEMBER 9, 2010

Day 8

Day 8 of my FET has been nothing short of boring. However, the fancy schmancy fertility monitor did have me pee on a stick today. That was very exciting! I'm not used to doing nothing. Don't get me wrong, I love the needle free cycle (well, not 100% needle free but close enough). However, not doing anything is boring. Sooo boring. My excitement is waking up and pressing the "on" button on the fertility monitor. I'm not expecting it to tell me anything other than that I'm in low fertility stage. If my cycle is normal (which at this point, I don't know what normal is), I won't start to see changes in my hormones/ovulation until day 17 or so. That's only nine days from now. Hopefully the monitor has me pee on a stick every day until then... otherwise I'll go crazy with boredom!

For the first time since February, I went into the nursery. I have gone in it briefly... to pass through it or to grab something. Yesterday I spent about an hour or so in there. We were renovating it before and then just left all the tools and supplies in there. I cleaned most of it out yesterday. Now all that is in there is paint supplies. I finally picked a color for it. I picked a teal color. If we have a baby boy, teal goes well with light blues and greens. If we have a baby girl, teal goes well with orange, red, and lilac. If we don't have a baby, teal makes a great library/office color. My brother is going to paint it for us this weekend. I want its history to be replaced with the future before October 16th gets here. October 16th... yikes! That's only five weeks and one day away! In 36 days, we would have been welcoming a baby into our lives. Vomit.

FRIDAY, SEPTEMBER 10, 2010

Day 9

Day 9 brings us the same results as day 8... nadda. Even without ovulation, I enjoy having to test. Peeing on a stick brings me so much satisfaction.

I was talking with one of my fertility buddies today. Our conversation goes along with my previous posts about being brutally honest to shut people up. I was dying laughing when she said this...I'd thought you'd all find it humorous as well. She was mentioning that she will be attending a family reunion this weekend. She's bracing herself for the "when will you have kids" questions. She said although she is going to refrain from being a smart ass, she would love to say... "Well, you see, we'd love to have a slew of kids, but for some reason my body is rejecting your precious family genes and killing the embryo every time it tries to make a home in my uterus."

Today, I have indulged in some serious retail therapy. Actually, the last 24 hours have been costly. I bought myself a ring yesterday (I ordered it last week but didn't pay for it until it came in yesterday). Today I bought a new chandelier for the dining room. I also bought a new chandelier and wall sconce for the foyer. If this is how I'm going to get through the next five weeks, I better start saving my money! It's going to be an expensive five weeks!

SUNDAY, SEPTEMBER 12, 2010

Day 11

Days 10 and 11 are the same as the others. Still nothing. I am expecting a change sometime at the end of this week.

My nightmares have been horrendous. I have been having them for a while now. Usually, I am being chased or witnessing some hideous crime. Last night, for the first time, I had a baby nightmare. It went like this...

I was having a lunch/play date with a friend and her two kids (real friend and real kids). We were on a boat; however, we stayed in the cabin. After our lunch was over, we decided to leave the boat and go shopping. She took her two year old and asked me to take the baby (she's around 4/5 months). So I grabbed the baby and the diaper bag and made my way off the boat. The only way off the boat was to walk, waist deep in the water. I held the baby up over my head and walked towards the dock. Once I got to the dock, my friend asked where the baby was. All of a sudden, I couldn't remember if I took her off the boat. I kept saying "I swear I lifted her over my head." Neither of us remembered. My friend swam to the boat to see if we left the baby in there. She screamed from the boat "She's not here." At this point, I'm hysterical. I keep spinning around yelling for the baby. At one point, I look down and I see the baby's boot at the bottom of the ocean. I wanted so badly to dive under and grab it. I just couldn't. I was paralyzed with fear. I kept saying, "I can't swim. I can't swim." A bystander jumped in the water and started looking for the baby. After a while, the police came and told us there was nothing left to do. They told us to go home and wait for them to call. My friend disappeared (My awake self is assuming she started to head home. My nightmare self just thought it was normal). After my friend had disappeared, I called B to tell him what happened. He said "that's impossible, the kids are with Ben" (their Dad). I started screaming at him because he was wrong and not helping. I hung up to call Ben and Ben's Dad answered. When I told him what happened he said "Aprill, I was with Ben all day. He has been watching the kids." I kept crying and crying. I kept saying "then how did I lose the baby? How could I have a baby one minute and not the next?" His response was, "You are making this up. This didn't happen. Ben and the kids are home. You have convinced yourself that since you lost your baby, you will lose every baby... including your friends' babies." I then asked, "Does Allison know that the girls are safe?" Then I woke up.

The next four weeks and six days better go by quickly. If I keep having dreams like that, I'll be a walking zombie.

MONDAY, SEPTEMBER 13, 2010

Day 12

I still only have one bar on the fertility monitor. However, I can feel my body going through some changes. I bet we'll start to see changes on the fertility monitor soon. I took a picture of fancy monitor on Saturday so you could see what I'm talking about. In the upper right hand corner you will see a "10." That number represents the cycle day. On the left side, you will see a bar graph. The graph has three bars. The first (lowest) bar means low fertility. Once your hormones start changing, the second bar will fill in. This is when you have high fertility. Then the day ovulation is detected (when the LH surge happens) the third bar is filled in and an egg appears on the bar. When that happens, you are considered to have peak fertility. Your LH surges 24-36 hours before ovulation... so it doesn't tell you the day you're ovulating but tells you that ovulation will occur. We're getting close to thawing out the snowbabies! It can't get here soon enough.

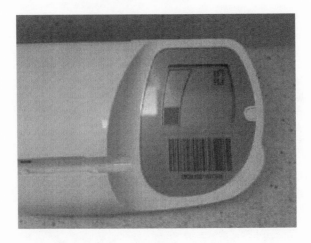

WEDNESDAY, SEPTEMBER 15, 2010

Day 14

Day 14 still nothing! I have a whirlwind of a week/weekend coming up. Tomorrow I'll be traveling to NYC for a meeting. I'll be returning around 1:00 am on Friday morning. B and I are taking 7am flight to PA for a weekend. We'll be in PA until Sunday... then back home late Sunday night. It's going to super busy.

I had a weird day today. First, I was told I look terrible (this actually happened yesterday but I'm going to complain like it happened today). Today, I was asked by an employee of one of my offices when I was due. She wasn't asking because I look pregnant (I'm back into a size 4 pant and a small top... I better not look pregnant). She was asking because she partially heard my conversation with another staff member. I was talking about my friend D who was pregnant. Then, I went shopping for a new suit. I wear a suit every day to work. I don't think I have purchased a new suit in five years. I figured if my retail therapy is going to keep going, I might as well use it towards things I don't like buying either... like suits. After shopping and leaving empty handed, I was stopped by security. They claimed they had good suspicions that I had unpaid merchandise in my bags. I then had to act really annoyed (I was only slightly annoyed... but slightly annoyed is boring) while they searched my bags and pockets. I figure, this is a good time to list the things I'm appreciative for...

My Husband/Marriage
Our Home

Our three fur babies
Family
Friends
No needles
Being a size 4
Perseverance
Being a size small
Our snowbabies
Dr. P
New Chandeliers
My new fertility friends
Retail Therapy
Strength
This Blog
Patriot's season tickets
My cousin Buddy being able to drive me home after drinking too much at a game
Vacations
Pain Free Ankle (only one)
Stackable Rings
Burritos
Indian Food
Pandora Bracelets
four weeks two days

FRIDAY, SEPTEMBER 17, 2010

Day 16

I got home from NYC around midnight last night/this morning. After taking a shower and packing my bags for PA, I went to bed around 1:00 am. My alarm went off at 4:30 and we were on our way to the airport at 5:15. I am exhausted! We have finally arrived in Erie, PA. I cannot wait to see our friends. I especially can't wait to dance all night at their wedding. This wedding will be the last wedding that I wear my orange dress. I'm sad that I will be retiring it. It has provided way for many compliments and many borrows. Awesome Orange Dress, you will be missed.

Day 16 and still NO change with the fertility monitor. I normally don't test positive on ovulation kits until days 17-20 or so. So, it's still early for me.

Four weeks

SATURDAY, SEPTEMBER 18, 2010

Day 17: Orange Dress Retirement

Day 17 and the fancy schmancy fertility monitor is still giving me one bar. Dr. P sent me an email yesterday. It only said this one sentence: "Your ovaries like to keep us waiting with baited breathe!" She couldn't be any more right!

Last night, after dinner, B and I had a couple of drinks at the hotel bar. During our conversation, I mentioned that if this cycle doesn't work, I don't know if I could do it again. I can do the shots, the appointments, the waiting, the commitment. I can do everything involved. I just am not sure if I can go through the letdown... again. How many let downs can one go through? When my fertility friends say they don't think they can do it again, I always respond with "You never know how strong you are until you have to be. You can do it again." Here I am, not taking my own advice. This morning I went for a run through Erie. I passed a cancer center that had a sign that said "Life is not a problem that needs to be solved. It's a reality that needs to be experienced." That can't be any more true. How many times I have said, "This is our life" or "This is what we know." I have never looked at our struggles as being a problem. I have never felt bad for what we're going through. I have accepted it. This is our life and our experience. I couldn't have run past that sign at a more perfect time. Instead of feeling like I can't do it again, I'm feeling motivated to keep trying. I'm also motivated to celebrate my last wearing of my orange dress. Tonight, I will celebrate the marriage of L & B with my orange dress!

MONDAY, SEPTEMBER 20, 2010

Day 19

I'm starting to get annoyed. Day 19 and still no change. I thought last month my cycle as abnormally long because of all the treatments. I figured it would go back to normal this month. I guess I was wrong. My body has been on drugs for two years so I don't blame it for being confused. Still, I would have liked for it to be somewhat normal. Wahhhhh. I guess we'll just keep waiting.

On the trip home last night, I started to feel sick. My throat was scratchy, I had a dry cough, my stomach didn't feel right, and I had the aches. Well, I was up all night with the most persistent (and annoying) dry cough. I woke up this morning feeling like my throat would burst into flames any second. I'm slightly congested but not nearly as bad as I thought I would be. Now I am not only waiting for ovulation, I am also waiting to be hit by a cold.

Three weeks five days

WEDNESDAY, SEPTEMBER 22, 2010

Day 21

I have the flu. My body has decided to replace ovulation with aches, chills, vomiting and some other nasty stuff. I should be very upset with my body. If we transfer on or around the 5th of October (which at this rate, is very likely), my beta will be on or around Baby L's due date. That's crazy. I would write more but I can't seem to sit up for longer than ten minutes without puking. Today, I will sit by the TV and drink clear fluids. Fun!

Three weeks three days

THURSDAY, SEPTEMBER 23, 2010

Day 22

After feeling like I was hit by a truck and throwing up everything in me, I feel great. I must have had a 24/48 hour bug. Last night I had a killer headache. I kept waking up throughout the night from it. I figured it was from throwing up so much. This morning I found out that it is because there has been a rise in my estrogen! Woot! Finally, movement with the monitor. I have moved up to the second bar. Estrogen starts to rise right before the LH Surge (ovulation)... which means, I'm only a handful of days away from ovulation. I'm very happy about this because I thought I was going to have long cycles forever. This will make me only a week off from my normal cycle. Slowly, my cycle is going back to normal. I can NOT wait to eat breakfast. Yesterday my diet consisted of toast and soup. I have never been happier to eat egg whites!

Day 23

Last night I took a digital ovulation test (the smiley face one). The results... a smiley face! I figured, since LH surge was detected, the fancy schmancy ovulation monitor would show at least three bars if not the egg today. However, the results showed only two bars again. I wasn't sure what to expect for my blood work results today. Surprisingly, the smiley face was correct and the super expensive monitor was wrong! My LH was high (I forget the number) and my progesterone was 1.6. Basically that means, I surged recently. I'll give the fertility monitor a chance to redeem itself tomorrow morning. If it doesn't show improvement, I'll... well, I won't do anything. We'll just know it's not all that accurate. Dr. P is having me come in on Sunday to see how my levels are rising. We are getting close to a transfer!

Yesterday I worked a conference in the morning. There was a pregnant girl working the display next to me. During one of the breaks, we talked briefly. I made the ever so awesome mistake of asking her when her due date is. Her response?? October 17th. One day after mine. For the rest of the conference, I could not stop staring at her. I had knots in my stomach. I was sweaty. AND, I was being a creep by staring at her belly. I couldn't believe how big she was and how small I am. I kept trying to imagine myself, standing at the conference, with a big swollen belly. I tried to picture the conversations I would be having. "Oh, aren't you sweet. I feel huge so I love hearing that I look great." "We don't know what we're having. We want it to be a surprise." "Only three weeks left. I can't believe it." "The summer was so easy. I stayed in the AC and ate ice cream to stay cool." Nope, instead, I sat there feeling like I would puke all over myself.

Three weeks one day

FRIDAY, SEPTEMBER 24, 2010

Day 24

The fancy fertility monitor finally gave me my egg. I got the third bar and the egg all on the same day. I'm curious as to why the cheap pee on a stick test detected it earlier. I think the sticks give you the best 24-48 hours to conceive and the monitor gives you the best day. I'm not sure. I took a picture of it so you can all see it. It's kind of funny... the egg even has a little yolk...

I just thought of a funny story from our travels to PA...

I read the book The Second Life of Bree Tanner on our way to PA. During our layover, we were sitting at our gate, waiting for our plane to be fixed. If you don't anything about the book, it's a short story about one of the characters from the Twilight Saga. There are vampires, werewolves, and what not. Anyway, I put the book down and started people watching. A girl wearing jeans and a tan button down shirt caught my attention. She had light brown hair that was frizzy and wild. I thought to myself "werewolf." I said "werewolf" with a creepy, scary movie voice... Weeeeeeerrreeeewoooooolf. Right after I said that to myself, B said "What?" I looked over at him and just started cracking up. I was laughing so hard that I had tears pouring down my face. I was laughing so much I could barely breathe. I was trying to tell him that I meant to think "werewolf" in my head but I accidentally said it out loud. I couldn't get out one word because I was laughing so hard. Once B figured out what happened and why I was crying, he started cracking up. We were literally buckled over laughing for about five minutes. I wonder if anyone heard me?!?!

I was miserably sick last night. My congestion was so bad that even Sudafed wasn't helping. I woke up feeling zero percent better so I didn't end up going to the baby shower. I guess my cold is a blessing in disguise.

Three weeks... that's it. three weeks

SUNDAY, SEPTEMBER 26, 2010

Day 25

My morning has been filled with cleaning, organizing, picking out paint colors and waiting. I finally just got the call from the nurse. My Progesterone increased from 1.6 to 2.6. I go back tomorrow morning for more blood work. If my progesterone rises above 5, my transfer will be on Thursday. I have work obligations Tuesday and Friday. I have all the time in the world every other day... of course it all works out to be this one week with conflicts. Hopefully, it rises and we can avoid a Friday transfer. If it comes down to it, I will skip the work thing.

Last night I kept having dreams about chandelier shopping. I was in a shop that had a MASSIVE chandelier. It filled up a space about half the size of a football field. I kept saying "I wish I had a house that we could put this in." At one point, B said "Even if we did, I bet this thing costs a fortune." I walked over to the price tag (that was the size of me), flipped it over and saw in big red numbers $1,600. "It's the same amount I've already spent on chandeliers. Can I buy it?" I yelled. "Retail therapy is getting expensive," said B. Then my dream turned bizarre. We were at an Olympic size pool having a dance contest... it was weird. Needless to say, even in my dreams chandeliers and retail therapy consume me.

Two weeks six days

MONDAY, SEPTEMBER 27, 2010

Day 26

Ready for the buzz kill?? My progesterone was only 3.8 today. This means two things. 1) If it is not above 5 tomorrow, my cycle will be cancelled (yep!). 2) If it is above 5 tomorrow, we will transfer on Friday. Friday is terrible for both B and me. If it comes down to it, I will have to back out of my work obligations (not cool) and B will not be there for the transfer. What the (insert F word here)!??! Is it not enough that we have to go through this bologna to get pregnant? Conception is already an obstacle... why the eff do we have to have obstacles on top of the obstacle?

Our consent form went missing for this cycle. Dr. P emailed me and told me to double check with financial that our approval and consents were all set. While I was speaking with the financial lady, she had to run to grab my file. She came back with a manila folder about 2 inches thick. My heart just sank when I saw it. I can't believe we are one of those couples with a fertility history that makes our file so thick. Who would have thought we would be here? Who would have thought this hell would never end?

Two weeks five days

TUESDAY, SEPTEMBER 28, 2010

Day 27

I will be heading in for my progesterone check in a few minutes. I'll update once I know something. This could end up being a bad day. Ugh...

TUESDAY, SEPTEMBER 28, 2010

Progesterone Results

It was a long day of waiting. My progesterone levels were at 5.25 this morning. Above 5! Which means, we will be thawing out and transferring two embryos on Friday!

WEDNESDAY, SEPTEMBER 29, 2010

Day 28

Two weeks three days. That's all I have today.

THURSDAY, SEPTEMBER 30, 2010

Day before transfer

I can't believe we're finally transferring. I was excited all yesterday and today, I have been nervous. I usually go back and forth between excitement and anxiety. So at least I know I'm on track with my emotions. I'm excited because we get to finally do something towards our goal. I'm nervous because I'm realistic. The two embryos we transfer tomorrow will be numbers nine and ten. Eight Embryos have been put in my uterus and we still don't have a baby. I found out today that the doctor that is doing the transfers tomorrow is the guy that I do not like. B and I had a terrible experience with him our first IVF. Argh...

At my bridal shower, my bridesmaids made an "Advice for the Bride" book. Each guest got their own page to give words of wisdom and marital advice. The first year we were married I looked at it all the time. Yesterday was the first time in a couple of years that I picked it up. I couldn't believe how wise our friends and family are. I thought I would list some of them...

Love each other more through the hard times...

Remember to keep love alive. It will carry you through any storm...

Love conquers all. No matter how great the obstacles, when two hearts are united in love, problems will be solved...

Patience will prevail...

I got nothing. I'm 18! (Hahaha... That was from B's cousin. I thought I'd throw that one in there because it's funny).

Two weeks two days

FRIDAY, OCTOBER 1, 2010

Transfer Day

Yikes! I barely slept. I'm so anxious for today. I am not sure how I will be after another negative. At this point, a negative is not an option. I refuse to let it fail. Usually I go to acupuncture before and after my transfer. However, today I have a work obligation that I cannot miss (Dr. P and the lab have been beyond flexible with my changing schedule). I will have to go directly from work to the transfer. Which means, I will not have time for acupuncture before the transfer. My acupuncturist told me to come as soon as I'm done. I usually lay on the bed for an hour. I'm guessing I'll be home around 2:00. I'll post the details of the transfer then...

FRIDAY, OCTOBER 1, 2010

Transfer

I just spent the afternoon on the couch being lazy. It was nice! So the transfer went well. It took a LONG time. We were in the procedure room around 11:00. While I was sitting with the white sheet over my lap I couldn't stop bouncing around. First off, you have to have a full bladder for the procedure (the bladder is above the uterus and when it's full it makes it easier to access the uterus). My bladder was so full it hurt! Secondly, I was nervous. I have never been this nervous for a transfer before. It seemed like they were taking forever to come to the room. While we were waiting, there was a knock on the door. Normally when the staff/doctor wants to come in, they knock and walk right in. This time, there was a knock and a pause. After we yelled "come in," the door opens and there was Dr. P! I was so relieved to see her. She said that she overheard someone say they needed saline downstairs. She immediately offered to run up to get it so she could see me. She was standing there with her bottle of saline and a cute outfit! She looked very spiffy today. She had on a cute black pencil skirt with a purple satin blouse... very Addison (Private Practice) like. Anyway, she came in and gave us a hug and wished us luck. Instantly, I felt better. While we were talking, I asked if all the embryos survived the thaw. She informed us that one of them died during the thawing but they thawed the third one and it did wonderfully. She also told us that the doctor working was Dr. Old Pants and not Dr. Jerk face. After she left ("they're going to kill me if I don't get this saline to them") the doctor came in. Normally during the procedure, the doctor will explain what he/she is doing in a vague manor. They will say "you will feel my hands" or "I am going to clean you so it will be cold." Dr. Old Pants was VERY descriptive. At one point he said "Okay April, it's going to feel cold. That's because I will be cleaning the inside of your vagina." Hahahah... for some reason, I wanted to burst out laughing. As you may remember from some of my previous posts, the path to my uterus is a tricky one.

The doctor couldn't get the catheter in. He tried for 40 minutes. FORTY! Let's not forget, my bladder is the size of a basketball just waiting to explode. After 30 minutes or so, I finally said I can't do it anymore. The entire time, I held B's hand (more like squeezed the heck out of it) and prayed that I didn't pee all over the doctor. He then took the speculum out and told me to let some urine out. Once I was going, it was hard for me to stop. I am pretty sure I peed for ten minutes straight. When I got back to the room, I was worried that I let too much out. My fear was very quickly set straight when the ultrasound wand was back on my pelvic area. My bladder didn't even change size. It was still as full as ever. I can't believe how much urine I had. Anyway, after about 45 minutes or so, the nurse suggested we call in the doctor who got the scope in for my hysteroscopy. She came back to the room with... guess who... Dr. Jerk face. AHHH! I turned to B and said "How ironic." He was very professional and polite. Oh I forgot to mention this part... embryos are light sensitive and you can see the ultrasound better in the dark... so the procedure is done in a dark room. The doctor wears a head light... you know, the ones you can buy at sporting goods stores for hiking. It's fairly comical to see that light all up in your hooha. Anyway, he put on the head light, sat down and all of a sudden he says "I'm in." I had no idea he was even trying. He got in immediately. He went from our enemy to our savior (Dr. P's words)! The catheter has a sheath and an inner part. They put the sheath in first. Once the sheath is where they want it (on the lining of the uterus), the embryologist gets the embryos out of storage, puts them in the inner part of the catheter and CAREFULLY passes it to the doctor (the new procedure room has a mirror on the wall. It is actually a pass through. When the doctor needs the embryologist, he/she knocks on the wall and the embryologist pushes the mirror open. It's pretty cool). The doctor then puts the inner part into the sheath and injects the embryos. Since these embryos were more developed and in the blastocyst stage, we could see them very clearly on the ultrasound. They were perfectly placed on/next to the lining. So now we just need them to hatch and implant!

I had B take a couple of pictures. We could only take before and after pictures because we couldn't take pics during the procedure. I actually didn't even ask. I did however, ask for pictures of the embryos for the blog. Once I get them I will post them.

This is when I was antsy pants waiting for the doctor to
come in (before Dr. P's surprise visit).

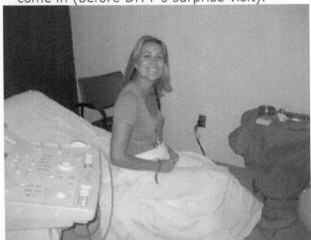

All the instruments used for procedure.

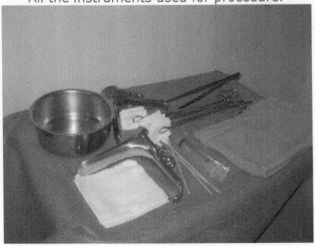

After the procedure, you have to lay flat for 15 minutes.
I'm lying flat!

SATURDAY, OCTOBER 2, 2010

1dp5dt

1dp5dt... I'm sure most of you are wondering what the heck that means. It stands for one day past five day transfer... aka, today. I feel pretty good today. I had a crazy busy and stressful week. After the transfer yesterday, I came home and crashed on the couch. Not just for an hour. I crashed all day and night. I woke up with really bad nausea (I think it was the late night bowl of ice cream B and I had) at about 2:30am. I've been having some off and on cramps all morning. I'm sure the cramping is from the 45 minutes of constant poking by a catheter. Dr. P emailed me last night and told me the policy for taking home pictures of embryos has changed. I have to fill out a release form before they can give them to me. Hopefully I'll get to that on Monday so you all can see what they looked like. Last cycle, I posted what happens after a 3dt. It's pretty much the same for a 5dt... here it is:

1dpt... Blastocyst hatches out of shell on this day

2dpt... Blastocyst attaches to a site on the uterine lining

3dpt... Implantation begins, as the blastocyst begins to bury in the lining

4dpt... Implantation process continues and morula buries deeper in the lining

5dpt... Morula is completely implanted in the lining and has placenta cells & fetal cells

6dpt... Placenta cells begin to secret hCG in the blood
7dpt... More hCG is produced as fetus develops
8dpt... More hCG is produced as fetus develops
9dpt... hCG levels are now high enough to be immediately detected on HPT
Hopefully our blasts are hatching today!
Two weeks

MONDAY, OCTOBER 4, 2010

3dp5dt

Sorry for not posting yesterday. My day was spent in the ER with B. He dislocated and fractured his elbow playing softball. He claims it was a fluke thing but I can't help remind him that he plays for the YMCA not MLB. The ER doctor and B's nurse were both pregnant. Guess when the nurse is due? Yep... same weekend as me! There are 365 days in a year, why do I keep meeting the women due the day I was?

Saturday night, I woke up with sharp and intense cramps. I cannot tell you how bad they were. They only lasted ten minutes and then I was fine. I woke up yesterday feeling 100% normal and today I feel 100% normal. I hope the cramping was a good thing and not a bad. I guess we'll know in a few days.

I started testing today. I know it is far too early but I can't help it. If this cycle worked, I should see a positive result around Thursday. I am labeling and taking pictures of the tests so you call can see them. I'll also call the lab today to get the pictures of the embryos.

One week five days

TUESDAY, OCTOBER 5, 2010

4dp5dt

We're getting close to the time where I should see a positive. Only a day or two away. Today's test was stark white negative. Aye. Last night, B and I were lounging on the couch and I had this overwhelming feeling that this cycle didn't work. B kept telling me that it did work. Normally, along with my period, I get a migraine. I get one a week before and one a day or two before my period comes. I got my week before Migraine last night. Dr. P thinks that I got one the cycle that worked too. I don't remember if that's the case. I ended up hysterically crying while I lying in bed. Every night since I was in my teens, I pray before I go to sleep. I pray for things like strength, health, perseverance. I pray for family and friends. Last night during my prayers, I broke down. My prayer sounded like this "I pray for strength for whatever the outcome of this cycle may be. Forget that, I pray that it works because I can't do this anymore. I can't deal with the loss of a baby and the loss of another cycle at the same time. Please don't make me do this again, I just don't have it in me." My hysteria and prayer lasted only a minute. It started when B was brushing his teeth and ended before he was done (however, he brushes forEVER). Anyway, I cried, I moved on and here I am. We'll see what the end of this week brings. Right now, my optimism level is at a zero.

The Baby L Daisy bush has started to bloom. One of the bushes died... the other looks great. I'll take pics when it stops raining.

One week four days

WEDNESDAY, OCTOBER 6, 2010

5dp5dt

Ahhh... My posts are starting to become all too familiar. I started testing with two tests in the morning. I use a test one of my doctors gave me and a First Response Early Result test. The ones I took this morning could not be any more negative. The control line is dark and thick. The test line is so nonexistent that it looks like someone spilled bleach on the test. I will be hopeful for one more day. If I don't get a faint line tomorrow, I'm waiving my white flag (just on this cycle).

When I go to acupuncture, I usually focus on one thing. If it's while I'm waiting for my period, I focus on my period. If it's after a transfer, I focus on the embryos hatching. Yesterday, I focused on the embryo development. While I was in my meditative state, I decided to talk to the embryos. B said "they don't have ears yet." No kidding... I was talking out loud, I'm not a wacko. I was thinking to them. Anyway, this is what I said...

I know you're both in there all hatched and attached. I just need you to focus on implanting and growing. You have a Mommy and Daddy that will love you more than you can imagine. You have friends and family that have been waiting to meet you and will spoil you rotten. You will have two cats to play with and a dog to protect you. I will give you sugar. If you want to play football, I will let you. Even though I think it causes brain damage. You can get a puppy. We will laugh, sing, and dance.

We'll play games and read books. We'll watch movies. Please, please, please try your hardest to survive in there. If you can make it ten months in there, you'll have so much to enjoy out here.

I hope they found my pleading inspirational and my bribes worth fighting for!

One week three days

The most Negative test results possible (from today)

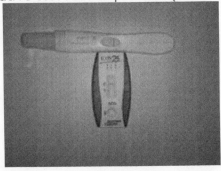

THURSDAY, OCTOBER 7, 2010

6dp5dt

Well, today brought us a nice bright and shiny negative. I'm surprisingly okay. Of course I'm disappointed and sad but I'm okay. The one thing that I ask of you all is to not feel bad for me. It really pisses me off. It's one thing to feel bad or sad that this didn't work. Just don't feel bad for me. I hate the pity and "Poor April" looks I get. Our society has made us believe that if you cannot have children or do not have children, there is something majorly wrong with you. Yet, we can be in financial ruin and no one would pity you. You can have a horrible marriage and no one will say "poor you." Just because people have children or do not struggle having them, doesn't mean that they have a perfect life... one worth envying. We have an incredible marriage (one so strong that when we went to a therapist after the miscarriage, we got kicked out). We have a beautiful home. We are both successful with our careers. We have wonderful family and friends. We travel often. We have three fur babies that we share an unconditional love with. We are happy. If this is our life struggle, then so be it. I'm not going to battle our reality. It is what it is. It doesn't make us, break us or define us. It's not something to be pitied over or looked down on.

One week two days

FRIDAY, OCTOBER 8, 2010

7dp5dt

Even though my blood test isn't until Monday, I have already discussed the plans for our next cycle with my doctor. She agreed with me, that if it worked, I would have seen a positive test result by now. I'll give the details of the next cycle tomorrow. Honestly, I don't think it will ever work.

I got the pictures of our embryos today. I wish they took so I could say "this is what our babies looked like five days after conception." Instead, all I can say is "They're pretty cool looking..."

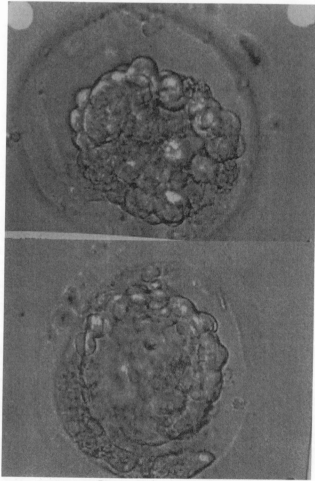

One week one day

SATURDAY, OCTOBER 9, 2010

Day 1

As predicted, my period came first thing this morning. Everyone kept telling me it was too early for period symptoms. One thing that I can talk proudly of is how well I know my body. The good news is, today is day 1 of a new cycle. I talked to Dr. P about going on Birth Control this cycle. Usually, I do not do a BCP cycle because of my history of migraines. However, from all the years of being on drugs, my cycles are starting to be long and annoying. I don't have the patience for my body to figure itself out right now. Being on BCP for the first three weeks will regulate my body and then I don't have to deal with waiting. You all know how much I hate waiting! The only other change this cycle will be at the embryo transfer. Dr. P wants to try doing the transfer under anesthesia. Since I have that tough angle in my cervix, she is wondering if we are stressing my uterus out too much. A transfer should only take a few minutes. If you remember my transfer post, mine took close to an hour. The severe cramping I am getting every cycle after the Transfer is not normal. Dull/light cramping is normal. The cramping I have been getting is the "buckled over, drenched in sweat" kind of pain. Being under for the transfer is only a theory. We don't know if it will really help but it's worth a try. If all goes as planned, I will be on BCP for 21 days, Lupron for 14 days, stim drugs for 10 days or so... which means, six or so weeks from now, I will be having my egg retrieval and a few days after that, another transfer. This is one subject I do not want to be an expert on. Sadly, I am.

One week. Ugh.

SUNDAY, OCTOBER 10, 2010

Apple Picking

I can't believe I would have either already delivered or would be delivering in the next six days. Ahhhh! If you asked me a few years ago if I thought I would be here, I'd say no. If you asked me a few years ago if I could handle what we've dealt with, I'd say no. I still cannot believe this is our life. I used to think, this will happen... given time. Now we're both starting to realize that this may not be in our cards. On paper, there is no reason for it to not work for us. I wish there was something to fix. I wish I could blame it on something either of us has done in the past.

We are both healthy and young individuals. We don't have a history of smoking. We eat well and are active. We are extremely happy people. Clearly, staying positive does not help. So I may just become a Negative Nelly. Well, not really... it's not in my personality to be that way. Although, I wish I could. If I were to be negative all the time, then I couldn't be let down.

I started my BCP yesterday. Even though I have my period and I've started my next cycle, I still have to go to the office tomorrow for my BETA. I'll still cry when I get the "Do you have a minute? I'm sorry" call. That call never gets easy... no matter how many times you have heard it.

Yesterday, we went apple picking. If I could survive the mesa of pregnant people, I can survive anything! All day I was face to face with big bellies. I had the opportunity to fall apart. I had the chance to feel sorry for myself and B. I could have been a mess. But I wasn't. Infertility may have control of my body but it will not have control of my emotions. I will not let it break me down. I will fight it and eventually, I will win.

Six days

MONDAY, OCTOBER 11, 2010

Beta Day

Yes, I still had to go in for my beta today... even though I started my period and started the meds for my next cycle. I just got the "I'm sorry" call from the nurse. I laughed at her... then I felt bad so I went into this long winded story about having my period. She probably thinks I'm a lunatic. Ahh well.

One of the things I hate about infertility is how much it takes control of your life. Those who don't deal with it have no idea how much of our life has to change or be put aside from it. I'm going to list all the things that the fertile may take for granted and the infertile may miss...

Buying Jeans
Buying any clothes
Going to the gym
Drinking Coffee
Eating sushi
Planning vacations
Appointmentless days
Drinking Wine
Drinking any alcohol
Having a period on my own
Ovulating on my own

Watching movies with babies without crying
Sleeping through the night without night sweats
Eating whatever I want, when I want
Boxing
Enjoying a baby shower

Five days

TUESDAY, OCTOBER 12, 2010

With bad comes good

October 1st was the day of my transfer. It was also the day I had my final interview for a promotion. I'm sure you remember talking about the work conflicts I had with the transfer. The interviews were the conflicts. Anyway, the transfer and interview were on the same day. The results day was also the same. Yesterday was my beta. Yesterday was also the day they were making the offer for the position. With my negative beta came a promotion! I'm very excited about it. My last day in my current role is Friday. I'm jumping right into my new role on Monday. I'll be traveling to DC for a national meeting. YIKES! Talk about throwing me right in! B and I went out to dinner last night to celebrate. While we were eating Sushi (of course, I want Sushi anytime I'm not in cycle) we were discussing the timing of it all. My thoughts are this... what if all of this infertility hell we've been dealing with was all so I would be working when this opportunity opened up? If we weren't dealing with negative after negative, I'd be out on maternity leave right now. I wouldn't have had the opportunity to post for this position. Maybe now that I have established myself in the new role, we will finally get pregnant. I'm really counting on the "everything happens for a reason" bologna.

Four days. HOLY CRAP.

THURSDAY, OCTOBER 14, 2010

Not every day can be my day

Today is not my day. Yesterday, I woke up with a bruise running through a vein in my leg. It goes from my inner knee, all the way up my inner thigh. Dr. P sent me to the hospital today to have an ultrasound on it. After nearly two hours of waiting at the hospital, I walked up to the receptionist and asked how much longer she thought it would be. Mind you, I was not at the ER, I was at a scheduled radiology wing. Well, I must not have been the first person to ask because the charge nurse nearly lost her mind on me. "The reason why you are waiting so long is because we are doing your doctor a favor. We are squeezing you into an already booked schedule. We have to take all the scheduled appointments before you. Didn't they explain this to you." said super grumpy nurse. I simply replied with "Yes, I was told I had to wait. I didn't think it would be this long. "Then I walked away. At the radiology department, there are about ten ultrasound rooms and a few CAT/MRI rooms. The sonographer brought me to the changing area. She told me to undress from the waist down and put the robe on with the opening in the front. As she was telling me this, I started to feel sick to my stomach. I wasn't sick because of the bruising, I was sick due to the fact that we passed the ultrasound room that I was in when I found out that I passed Baby L. After I got dressed, I sat in the waiting area with my clothes in my hand. I just kept praying that they did not bring me into that room. After a few minutes, the sonographer came to get me. Sure enough, she brought me into the empty uterus room. I started crying instantly. No sobs, no noise, just tears. She kept asking me if I was in pain. "No," was all I could muster. I couldn't tell her why I was crying. I was afraid it would make me worse. I just laid there, staring at the psychedelic painted drop ceiling tile above my head. The red and blue paints brought me right back to where I was on February 26th. I cried the entire ultrasound. I'm sure she thought I was a lunatic, crying over a bruised leg. I don't care. I still can't believe that in two days, TWO, we would be taking home a baby. Most likely, we would have already taken home a baby. Baby L is missing out on a good life. B and I are missing out on being good parents. There is nothing about this day that I like. Nothing.

Two days.

FRIDAY, OCTOBER 15, 2010

Bad day gets worse

So my day didn't improve after my post yesterday. Right after I wrote the post, I went outside and grabbed the mail. In the mail was a massive package of Enfamil formula with a card from the company saying "congratulations, your baby's arrival will be any moment." FANTASTIC. On top of that, I woke up at 1:00 in the morning with severe cramping on my left side. I could barely take a step without collapsing. I tried to sweat it out. Finally at 2:00, I woke B up and said we needed to go to the hospital. Not only did B have to dress me, he also had to escort me out. Every step I took sent shooting pains throughout my body. After a couple of hours in the ER, the doctor drugged me up. I quickly became loopy. I didn't know my arse from my elbow. After a painful pelvic exam and ultrasound, they discharged me and told me that most likely it's GI related. What they meant was "you probably have to poop." I'm sorry, do you think that I don't know what constipation feels like? Uhm, ya, I know when I have to POOP! I had my WTF appointment with Dr. P at 9:20 this morning. She said that I had an ovarian cyst that ruptured. So I'm not crazy... phew. The pain from that is insane. I guess it's a good thing when they rupture. The pain is intense but quick (mine lasted 24 hours or so... but the severe parts only a few hours). If they leak, then you're in pain for a long time. If they don't rupture, they can twist your ovary (which is not good. If your ovary twists, it dies). Wait, there is more! With my new job, comes training. Training was originally supposed to be the week of November 8th. Dr. P, B, and I discussed our plans to work around it. Of course, what happens? The training was just moved to the week of the 15th which means, cycle canceled. Argh. I can't catch a break.

The GOOD news is we're in Portland at a super cute Bed and Breakfast.

Tomorrow.

SATURDAY, OCTOBER 16, 2010

Dear Baby L

Baby L,

Today is the day that we were supposed to meet you. We were supposed to wake up with fear and fall asleep with pride. We'll never get to swaddle you or hold you. I'll never get to see your Daddy put on your diaper backwards. I want so badly to touch your soft skin. I want to hear your sweet cooing. I want to smell your new skin. I want to teach you how to be kind. I want to help you with your homework. I want to put band aids on all your boo boos. I'm really good at scaring boogie monsters. You'll never get to try adult food for the first time. You'll never take your first steps. We never get to argue who will wake up for a night time feeding. I imagine watching you sitting next to your Daddy while he plays his guitar and sings you a song. You'll never get to meet your fur brothers. I want to sing with you. I want to dance like a crazy people in the living room. I want to drop you off at school and give you a big hug and kiss... to the point where your cheeks are flushed with embarrassment and you say "Not here Mom!" You'll never get to see San Diego, where Mommy and Daddy fell in love. I want you to be able to love your aunts and uncles as much as we do. I want to yell at your aunts for spoiling you. I want to drop you off at your grandparents and come back to find out they fed you something I would never allow you to have. I want you to go to College or open a business or do whatever it is you want to do. I want to yell at you for being late. I want to cry when you tell me that you don't need me. We're sad that you'll never experience love but know, even without you here, you're loved more than anyone could ever love you. I know you're being taken care of by Papa. I'm sure he's blowing your mind with his golf ball trick. I'm sure Nana is making you pizzelles and Gramp is teaching you about grapes. I'm sure Dwyane is teaching you the ins and outs of football and telling you embarrassing stories about our college days. I know that Rusty is playing with you and making you laugh with his doggie smile trick. It's comforting to know that you are being taken care of.

I love you,
Mommy

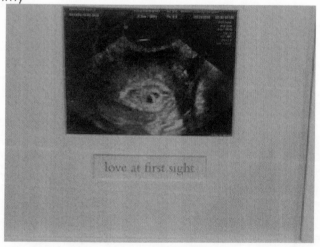

love at first sight

SATURDAY, OCTOBER 23, 2010

I'm back

I'm sorry for the lack of posts this week. Once we got back from Portland, I had to leave for a four day work trip. B had his elbow surgery the day I returned...it has been a little hectic since I got back. I haven't had a chance to sit down and post.

Portland was great. There's nothing like the soothing effects of blueberries and friendly people. We walked around, watched some Grey's on Netflix, went to the Art Museum, and had fantastic meals. The Bed and Breakfast made phenomenal breakfasts. I think I gained 10 pounds last weekend.

At the art museum, there was a painting called "Adriana Hannaford." I tried calling the museum to get the name of the artist so I could try to find a copy of it online for you all to see. I wish I wrote the artist's name down. For the life of me, I cannot remember it. Anyway... the painting was of an 8 month old baby. She was dressed in a white gown, holding wilted flowers and wearing a white gown. The background was gloomy. There were dark trees (almost dead looking) and dark clouds. There was a flower bush next to her that was covered in twigs and dead flowers. The four flowers she held in her hands were colored (rose) yet wilted. The caption said the painting was made in tribute of Adriana Hannaford. She died when she was 8 months old. The gloomy background was meant to represent death. The white gown was to represent innocence and life. The four wilted flowers were in reference to her four siblings that also died at a very young age. I just stood there and cried. I was sad for

Adriana Hannaford but my tears were not for her. My tears were for her poor mother, who lost five children. I can't imagine the strength she must have had. To have a tribute painting made that was so dark and honest, she must have been made of steel. I can't imagine the courage and strength she had. It's amazing to me that women have been dealing with infertility and loss for centuries and we are just now getting to a point where it is culturally acceptable to discuss it (it's still taboo just not as much as it used to be).

THURSDAY, OCTOBER 28, 2010

Baby Blues

Ahh... I know. I haven't been around lately. I pretty much lost my caring drive. It seems like everyone and their mother gets pregnant so easily and we can't even create embryos in a lab that work. I'm starting to be more realistic about this whole process. It's probably not going to work out. While we still have insurance coverage, we'll keep trying (even though I'm at the point of not caring).

Dr. P has made a couple of changes to my plan. Since my transfers take a long time due to a curve or bend in my cervix, they are going to put a stitch in after my retrieval. The doctor will pull the stitch down during the transfer to straighten out my cervix and make the transfer easier (and less stressful on my uterus). They will also do the transfer under anesthesia.

Right now, I'm supposed to be tracking my ovulation. I'm not. I'm sick of being a lab rat. I will know when I ovulate. If my body decides to be somewhat normal this cycle, we should be transferring mid-December.

I promise to write more... I was just in a funk for a couple of weeks.

SATURDAY, OCTOBER 30, 2010

Even the best fall down sometimes

Today I was out with girlfriends getting a pedicure. While we were walking to the car, it was mentioned that it will soon be November. Ahhh... Life is moving forward for everyone. Yet, even with time passing, my life is staying the same. Sweet! I'm sure I sound like a Debbie Downer. I'm not. I'm not moping around. I'm not walking around with a pout on my face like Eeyore. I'm just being realistic. My brush with having a child passed. We will be parents. Motherhood is not something I am doubting. I am coming to terms with the fact that our children may not look like us. Our children may not be the same ethnicity. They may not carry our traits and talents. Every day I go to bed praying that it will happen for us. Every day I wake up and look at the sonogram of a baby we will never meet. Infertility has controlled our lives for far too long. We stopped planning vacations. My body has been put through the ringer. It doesn't even look the same. We have to back out of plans to accommodate appointments and surgeries. I have a needle phobia that I have to ignore (which is NOT easy). I used to believe in miracles... I used to pray for them. Now I believe in science and pray that modern medicine brings us a baby. I'm sure this post is going to cause a lot of "you must stay positive" comments. Believe me, if positivity created miracles, then I wouldn't have had to flush our baby down the toilet. Okay... so I just sat here wondering if I should delete that comment. I decided not to because it's the truth; it's real. With all that being said, I'm not nearly as hopeful as I once was. Even with hope aside, we will keep trying. I will continue to pump my body with hormones. I will continue to allow the drugs to make me gain weight and be uncomfortable. I will shake and get dizzy every time I need to stick myself with a needle. I will allow my veins to collapse from the daily blood tests. I will freely open my legs so nurse after nurse can give me vaginal ultrasounds. I will vomit after every surgery. I will allow my eggs to be removed by the dozens. I will let my guard down after a transfer. I/we are knowingly putting ourselves out there to be let down, once again. Even the best fall down sometimes...

MONDAY, NOVEMBER 1, 2010

Disappointing Halloween

One of my favorite things to do is give out candy to trick or treaters. This year, we had not one knock on our door. ZERO trick or treaters. I was so bummed. We live on a road without a sidewalk. I don't blame parents for not coming around... but come on! Don't they know how much I love giving out candy?!?!? I even buy big bars.

Maybe next year I'll dress up as a petri dish. Even better, B can be a super sperm and I can be a high quality egg. It would be awesome (and totally inappropriate) if I dressed up as a cervix and B as a vaginal ultrasound. Maybe I'll be a needle and B can be the swollen bruised belly. Ahhh... fertility costumes.

THURSDAY, NOVEMBER 4, 2010

Pap Smear Flattery

I think every woman dreads her yearly Pap. Who likes to have their breasts examined by cold hands and their cervix scraped with a jagged brush? I nearly forgot about my appointment. I booked it while I was checking out from my appointment last year. For some strange (yet strangely intuitive) reason, yesterday, I thought I may have an appointment coming up. I checked my calendar and I didn't see anything in the near future. Then I asked B if we had any missed calls on our house phone (generally, I check the messages daily but since B has been working from home I stopped checking them). Sure enough, when I checked the messages, there was one confirming my appointment for today. My hooha can't escape medicine.

I arrived to my appointment slightly early today. I walked into the office and got into line to check in. As I was waiting, I noticed (well, I couldn't help but glance over at them because they were so loud) two very young mothers with their children (one an infant and one a toddler). One mother kept yelling at her daughter for being a baby. "Don't whine"; "Oh you think you can have everything. You think you'll be spoiled just like your sister." She would smack her hands and yell at her not to touch her new shirt. She was not only obnoxious; she was verbally abusive to her toddler. I wanted so badly to take that poor little girl away from her and smack her damn mother across the face. After I check in, I sit down to fill out the patient update forms. I end up sitting in between two very pregnant people. I'm sure I've mentioned this in previous posts...I am okay with babies and pregnancy talk. The one thing I can't handle is bellies. I can't look at them. Even with my pregnant friends, I look at their faces. Anyway, being sandwiched between two protruding bellies is not ideal. Midway through my paperwork, another pregnant girl walks in. She chooses the seat across from me. At this point, I'm staring. I have thoughts running through my mind that are very unlike me. I kept looking at them and trying to find something "wrong" or what I perceived at the time as "wrong." I kept thinking things like "she's overweight. How come she can get pregnant and I can't" or "Her boyfriend is irritated to be here. He probably doesn't even want the baby." While I'm being crazy, TWO more pregnant girls walk in. My twenty minutes of waiting was done with two young mothers (one of which was a terrible mother) and FIVE pregnant women. By the time I get called in, I'm shaking and on the verge of tears. Once I am in my room...which was insanely cold...the nurse weighs me. Her response to my 133 pounds was "Wow, you've had a wonderful year. You have lost 7 pounds." Uhm, I would not call this year wonderful, it was far from it. The reason I am down 7 pounds, you ask? During last year's appointment, I was full force into the Lupron stage of my cycle. I have lost some weight but most of the 7 pounds she was praising came from not being in a cycle. Dr. D (who I love...not as much as Dr. P but a good amount) knocked on the door and entered looking somber. With a breathless voice she said "This has been a very tough year." Amen to that Dr. D! She started asking me where we stand in our cycles....what our next steps are. As I'm responding to her questions, my voice is cracking and getting shakier and shakier. She mentioned that she was very impressed with my weight. I replied jokingly saying that Lupron was giving me a lot of weight loss credit today. The conversation that came about after was very flattering and not expected. She mentioned that nearly all of her IVF patients come in gaining significant amounts of weight (10-20 lbs in year). She also said that very few IVF patients maintain their weight throughout treatments. The fact that I have lost weight and have been able to maintain good health was very impressive to her. Who would have thought my aging adult body would be impressive. Praise the Lord for some flattery during this time! Who knew it would come during an annual Pap Smear.

Unexpected Facial

I went on vacation last week to San Diego. I seemed to have packed and over packed everything... minus one thing; my computer cord. So I wasn't able to post all week/weekend.

San Diego was very much needed. VERY much needed. I was getting to the point of not giving a shit about trying. Everyone and their mother was/has been getting pregnant. The only ones not getting pregnant are the ones already pregnant. Don't get me wrong, I think it's great that it comes so easily for most people. I don't wish this nightmare on anyone. With that being said, as great as it is for others not to go through this, it isn't easy for me to see. It seems like fall was the time to have a babies. I needed to get away from it all. There is only so much you can take. B and I used to live in San Diego. We have a really great (incredible, really) group of friends out there. I (not we because B didn't go) spent the week sitting on the beach, hanging out with friends and sitting at our favorite coffee shop. The thing about San Diego is this... the beach towns are full of college students and surfers. You don't see babies and pregnant women walking around. In fact, while I was in the beach towns, I didn't see one (outside of my friend's daughter). I didn't see one belly. I didn't see one baby. Fertility wasn't shoved in my face the entire week. While I was downtown, I definitely saw a stroller here and there... maybe five total. Being separated from the world of conception was much needed mentally. I feel more positive about trying again and more hopeful for it working.

I started testing using the fancy schmancy fertility monitor late last week. I got the two bars this morning which means, I will start Lupron very soon. Dr. P wants me to do a progesterone check a week after surge is detected. However, next week is the week that I had work conflicts. I emailed her this morning to see if it would be okay for the test to be on Sunday. I'm sure its fine. If all goes as planned, we'll be transferring Mid-December.

TUESDAY, NOVEMBER 9, 2010

Unexpected Facial (for real)

After posting yesterday, I realized that I titled the post "Unexpected Facial" but I forgot to talk about the facial. hahahahaha! I blame jet lag!

My friend owns a Spa in Solana Beach, CA. I called her to see if she had any availability for a facial while I was in San Diego. She's so awesome, she took me on her day off. I'm not sure if it's the hormone fluctuation or age... either way, my face needed a serious scrubbing. I was expecting to catch up with my friend during my facial. What I wasn't expecting, was for her to snap me out of my funk. She reminded me repeatedly that I have control of my body. During the past couple of years, I have let go of the control and allowed my body to control me. She stood over me and started telling my body what to do. As crazy as it sounds, I felt a wave of relief. It was almost as if all my negativity left me. I realized she was right. I have allowed my body to control me. I have allowed it to control my thoughts, my life, and my plans. I will no longer allow it to do that. She also talked to me about negativity of others around me. She mentioned that gossip about me sends negative vibes my way. Even if I'm not hearing the gossip. She advised that I cut out all the people in my life that may add to that negativity. She's right. You all know (since I've said it many times) all the pity and "poor Aprills" drive me crazy. I can't stand it. Not only have I allowed infertility to consume me, I have allowed others to bring negativity to me. So, all that is over. From now on, I'm in control. My first command... I command my body to make a freaking baby!

SUNDAY, NOVEMBER 14, 2010

Day 24 Still two bars

This is starting to feel familiar. I'm on day 24 and I still have only two bars on the fertility monitor. I'm not in a rush so I don't mind. I just want my body to do its thing when it feels ready. I go away this week for work (this was the conflict I had with the last cycle... which is why I cancelled it). I'm sure, as luck would have it, I will ovulate while I'm away and I'll have to find a lab that opens early enough to draw my blood.

I was at a work function a few nights ago. The discussion was about Multiple Sclerosis. There was a panel of four speakers. One of the speakers was asked a question comparing friends that have the same form of MS. The speaker said something that stuck with me... "I like to think of MS patients like fingerprints. We all have fingerprints, yet, no two prints are exactly the same. Our fingerprints are unique to us. Just because I have a fingerprint and you have a fingerprint that doesn't mean they are comparable." That analogy is so true for many instances in our lives. It is especially true for those struggling with loss and/or infertility. I have had so many people reach out to me about what they're going through. Every single one has mentioned that they realize it's not as bad as what I'm going through. That's so untrue. Just because I've gone through A, B and C, that doesn't mean their experience with X, Y and Z are less or more difficult. Everyone has a story and no two stories are alike. I'm very grateful that so many people are sharing their fingerprints with me.

TUESDAY, NOVEMBER 16, 2010

Two bars, one bar, zero bars... shoot!

Yep, my body is officially messed up! I hate this for many reasons. The main one being, that infertility already has control over us and our plans. Now it has control over my cycles. My cycles were like clockwork every single month. They were normal beyond normal (if that's possible). Then we started pumping drugs into my system and now, here I am, all messed up. Either I'm messed up or the fancy schmancy monitor is messed up. I had two bars on the monitor for six days. Then yesterday it dropped to one bar. Today, I turned it on and it had one bar with a flashing "m." I had never seen this before so I went to the Clearblue website... this is what it says:

What does a flashing "m" mean?

A flashing "m" symbol on the display screen indicates that the end of your cycle is near and your period may begin within a few days. If your period starts set your Fertility Monitor for the next cycle. Do not worry if the "m" symbol is not flashing and your period starts: the "m" button can still be set. If the "m" symbol flashes for several days and you think that your period is late, then you may have conceived and we recommend you use a home pregnancy test such as Clearblue Easy®.

Uhm... what?!?! I'm on day 26 and now I'm getting my period?? What the hell? Since I'm out of town for work, I had to find a lab near here. Dr. P faxed a lab slip over so I can have my progesterone checked tomorrow morning. We'll see what it looks like. If I get my freaking period and I have to wait out another cycle, I'm going to scream. I'm not in a rush... seriously, at this point, what's the difference of a couple of months when you've been waiting years?? However, if I want to get that fantastic maternity leave benefit, then I have to "conceive" by the end of 2010. Waiting out another cycle would totally ruin that. What is going on? Maybe I'm just meant to wait. Maybe that's my calling. Some people find their calling in volunteer work, careers, hobbies, family life... I find mine in waiting.

Posting has been hard while I'm away because the internet is terribly slow in the hotel. I'm not sure I'll get answers tomorrow or Thursday. Once I do, I'll post them. Fingers, toes (everything but legs) crossed that the monitor failed and it's not my body failing.

WEDNESDAY, NOVEMBER 17, 2010

Honestly... WTF

First of all... the lab here is terrible! It was a nightmare for me just to get some blood drawn. I'd give you the details but it's honestly just going to annoy you. I left there annoyed and bruised. Anyway, my progesterone came back at 0.4. It has dropped. Dr. P wants me to come in on Saturday to check it again. I think my period is coming. I am crampy, I have been fighting off a migraine, and I'm exhausted. The exhaustion could be from sitting in a room for 9 hours a day while I'm in training. But still, I feel like my good old friend is coming.

Before I start to get all negative and down for having another cycle get pushed back a month or two, I'm going to list all the benefits of not doing this cycle...

We usually go on vacation (usually Caribbean) for our Anniversary. We were putting off planning this year's trip because of our cycle. Now, we can go.

I'll be able to have some really good workouts over the next couple of months (I have really missed that).

WINE during the holidays... need I say more?!?!

I won't be bloated and fat on our Holiday card.

I can possibly... POSSIBLY... wear a bikini on vacation... that's still a POSSIBLY though.

I can use my remaining vacation days on fun things and not for retrievals or transfers.

Another off cycle means I have another excuse for retail therapy! I do need a hall table that will look nice with our new chandelier.

I'll be needle free for an additional 30 days or so.

Am I missing anything? There's always a light at the end of the tunnel... right??

MONDAY, NOVEMBER 22, 2010

Strangle Hold

There are many things in life that I have yet experienced. Some of them I look forward to and some of them I hope to never come in contact with. I unfortunately came in contact with one yesterday. I could count on one hand the amount of times I have become embarrassed. I am open with my life and my emotions... therefore; the most common embarrassment triggers mean nothing to me. I also very rarely get anxious. I think the two go hand in hand (in most situations). Yesterday, I came face to face with not just anxiety but a full blown anxiety attack. I'm not sure if any of you have ever had one (I hope and pray that you never do)... if I had to describe in one word, it would be SCARY.

One of my best friends had her baby Saturday evening. Yesterday, B and I went to the hospital to spend a few hours with the new family. At first, it was just the five of us (two couples and the baby). After about an hour or so, another couple came in. At one point, the boys were on one side of the room talking and the girls were on the other (yes, like in 5th grade). I looked over at B and I saw him blankly starring at the other two guys. The guys (minus B) were sharing delivery stories. I know how much those conversations make you feel like an outsider. I know how lonely they can make you feel. When I was watching B, I started to get nervous for him. I started to get sweaty and my heart started racing. I took a couple of deep breaths and my heart went back to normal. The boys then left to go to the waiting room (children weren't allowed on maternity floor. Our friend had to leave her daughter in waiting room) to relieve another friend from watching the baby. The boys left and the third friend came up to the room. During our conversations, I kept getting shortness of breath and light headed so I decided to sit down. The three girls were sharing stories about delivery and baby things. When I could feel my body temperature rising, I realized it was a good time for me to go. At this point, I thought I was on the verge of tears. I've never had any experience with anxiety; therefore, it didn't even cross my mind. The three of us left at the same time. As we were walking down the hall, the two girls were talking about how much has changed since they delivered a year ago. I just went right for the elevator. No slow walking or talking for me. I didn't want them to see me cry. I didn't want D to feel bad in any way. The day was about her, her husband and her new baby. I didn't want to put a damper on it. As we were in the elevator, my legs started feeling weak and my hands were shaking like a leaf. I kept telling myself "Just make it to the car before you start crying." As we got off the elevator, I saw B, P and the baby (technically, she's not a baby... she's a toddler... but I still say baby) sitting there. When I saw them, I started to feel like I couldn't breathe. I walked right passed them and headed towards the front door. No, I didn't say anything. I was afraid if I spoke I would break down. I heard B ask "Ape, where are you going?" I turned around, waved him to leave. As soon as I turned the corner, I started hyperventilating. It felt as if someone was squeezing my throat closed. My legs kept buckling and my arms were shaking. I honestly thought I was having a heart attack. It only lasted about two minutes (that might even be stretching it). I'm hoping none of you know how it feels to be strangled... it's not good. It's scary. Not just scary, it's frightening. The feeling of not being able to breathe is one thing. The feeling of not being able to breathe due to being strangled is another. You fight it and it only gets worse. The anxiety attack all happened in the hospital lobby. After it was over, we walked to the car. I cried for about 15 minutes then I was fine. Today however, is another story. I feel like I was hit by a bus. It took everything out of me. I'm exhausted and weak. I feel like I ran a marathon. I am actually sore. Anxiety attacks are not cool. I pray that this was a onetime thing. ONE time... I will NOT do that again. I refuse.

A friend of mine said today, she can't handle baby conversations. It makes her feel left out and lonely. My response "Apparently, I don't like it either! Makes me choke on air!" All kidding aside, it's another reminder of how infertility takes over... even when you don't want it to. I do feel like the baby/pregnancy world has become overwhelming. Everyone seems to be sharing news of pregnancy. I can't go a day without a text or an email with an update. I get pictures of babies and details of pregnancies every day, if not a few times a day. I couldn't be happier for those who are lucky enough to enjoy it however, it has become increasingly difficult. As difficult as it may be, it would be more difficult if people hid it from me. So I do what I have to, I get the details, I send my congrats and I cry my eyes out. What else can we do? There is the saying "You're only given as much as you can handle." I don't know who defines "handle" but clearly, they need to shorten the criteria. I think I can speak for B when I say, we're at our low. This is as low as we can get. I'm not sure how much more we can handle.

I'm very fortunate for so many blessings in my life. One of them being my new job. It gives me something to focus on. I can dive into my work and hide from everything else. Maybe the benefit of all this crap is that I'll be able to put so much into my work, I'll have some good bonus dollars coming my way. We'll see how that goes.

I had my progesterone checked again today. It was 1.4 on Saturday and 1.4 today. I feel sort of gooey (yes, sorry) which is usually my first sign of ovulation. So hopefully it's coming. Who knows. That's another frustration that I don't want to get into right now. Maybe tomorrow.

TUESDAY, NOVEMBER 23, 2010

Rewind

Back in June, I listed 30 comments that I find offensive and annoying. With all that is going on right now, I think now is a good time to rewind my posts and repost them. So here they are...

1. You're not getting younger. You should really start thinking about having children.
2. What is wrong with you anyway? Can't you just have sex?
3. Are the doctors concerned yet? You must be worried.

4. You knew what you were getting into when you decided to do fertility treatments.
5. Are you having sex during ovulation?
6. They make kits. Have you tried those?
7. You can always adopt.
8. Have you thought about a surrogate?
9. Can you get donor egg/sperm?
10. You don't look well.
11. Are you tired?
12. What if you end up with eight babies?
13. I hate being pregnant.
14. Don't have kids.
15. Life sucks after kids.
16. Are you pregnant yet?
17. Is the problem with you or your husband?
18. Maybe your husband isn't getting excited enough.
19. You should have sex more.
20. I can just look at my husband and I end up pregnant.
21. I don't understand because I easily get pregnant.
22. When you have kids, you'll understand.
23. You must be sad.
24. I feel bad for you.
25. You can take my kids anytime.
26. You're thinking about it too much.
27. If you stop trying you'll get pregnant.
28. Try relaxing.
29. It will happen when the time is right.
30. It's just not meant to be.

WEDNESDAY, NOVEMBER 24, 2010

Babies, Babies, Babies!

We have another friend who was due a day after D (friend that delivered on Saturday). She actually had her baby two weeks ago. She was bringing the baby over to D's house last night so I decided to visit. I hadn't seen the other baby since he was born. I know what you're all thinking... WHY WOULD YOU DO THAT?? I'm normally very good with babies. My friend's call me the baby whisperer. You have a crying baby, I'll get it to stop. You have a potty training issue, I'll solve it in a day. You have questions about caring for a baby, I can answer it. My mother ran a daycare through our home. I am the second oldest of four children. My younger brother is five years younger than me and my sister is seven years younger than me. When I was 12, my best friend and I opened a babysitting company called "Elm Street Sitters." I nannied my way through college (I nannied for four children all under the age of 8). When I first moved to San Diego and I was looking for work, I nannied (for five children). I can handle not one, not two, not three, but many children at the same time. I do not get flustered. I do not get nervous. I can sit in a room full of new mothers and fully engage in child rearing conversations. I can give advice because I have more knowledge and experience than most mothers. We go to cookouts and I'm the one crawling around the lawn with the kids. So normally, I am fine near babies and baby talk. I don't know what happened on Sunday. Well, I do know... my body started reacting to biological changes caused by anxiety... What I don't know, is why all of a sudden a baby, hospital and/or discussion would trigger that. So, yes, I know it sounds crazy to go over there and hang out with two newborns and their parents but I knew I'd be fine. Sunday was an anomaly.

As we were sitting there talking, I kept thinking about how it's such an injustice that I have all this knowledge and natural abilities to care for a child yet, we can't have one. Here we are, already pros and we can't freaking get pregnant. I should take that back, we can get pregnant, we just can't create an embryo healthy enough to survive. Seriously, how does that happen? We're good people with good hearts. We give more than we have. We constantly put ourselves in situations that are difficult (obviously, I nearly passed out in a hospital lobby) because we put other people's joys in front of our pain. Is this a cruel joke? Is this really happening? I don't get it. I don't. I can't stand the "Everything happens for a reason" response... when I hear it, I just want to shout "What the eff could the reason be?" What am I supposed to be learning here? That I can cry daily and still function normally? I can have my windpipe squeezed by my sympathetic nervous system and still walk out of a hospital? I can witness every Tom, Dick and Harry (or Jane, Pam, Patty) enjoy child rearing and child bearing and still enjoy my life. What's the lesson? If everything happens for a reason, I think the reason should have come out by now. It's been three years for goodness sake. Reason... come out, come out where ever you are!

Well, that was a rant I wasn't expecting to have.

FRIDAY, NOVEMBER 26, 2010

Full circle on Thanksgiving

Yesterday, I woke up and said "Screw Infertility." I have been putting myself aside in the name of medicine. When I work out, I work out hard. There is no easy workout for me. I work out like I'm training for the Olympics. Since my last cycle, I have barely been working out because I was afraid I would mess up my cycle (ovulation). I woke up yesterday and said screw it. My sister-in-law and I went to the boxing gym and got our butts kicked. It felt so good. I have missed that feeling. I have missed feeling like I was in control. I loved every second of it. I'm definitely paying for it today. I had to have blood work again this morning. I could barely walk DOWN the four flights of stairs. DOWN... not up. I'm sore. We agreed we'll go back tomorrow no matter how sore we are. I can't wait.

Yep, went to the lab again today. And again, they missed my vein. Awesome. There is nothing like having someone fish around under your skin with a needle. I have every physical symptom of ovulation (cramps, egg white mucous) so let's see what the blood tells us.

Yesterday, we had a lot of time (mainly driving time) to reflect on this past year. Our first transfer was one year ago, on Thanksgiving morning. In one year, we had two failed IVFs, one successful IVF, one miserable miscarriage, one failed FET. That's insane! As insane as it is, it's also a good reminder of how strong of a couple we are... both individually and together. Although that year may seem like a terrible year for most people, we see it as something to be thankful for. We have overcome so much. We have endured and persevered. We have learned so much about our strengths and weaknesses. Most importantly, we didn't grow apart, we became closer than ever. Plus, with all that, how can you go down? We can only go up from here!

SATURDAY, NOVEMBER 27, 2010

I'm sneaky

When I went in for blood work yesterday, I decided to check off some other lab tests. I knew I had all the physical symptoms of ovulating and just checking progesterone wouldn't give us any answers (progesterone rises a couple days after ovulation). I checked off a couple of other tests (I'm sneaky, I know) on my lab slip. When the nurse called in the afternoon with the results she said "Your LH (this is the test I checked off) was ovulatory. The Dr. wants you to come in on Monday to check your progesterone." Hahahaha... see! We (or I) needed to know that! At least I am still in tune with my body. There were a couple of days that I was questioning that. If my progesterone rises, as it should, I'll start Lupron next week. Bring on the night sweats and vivid dreams... and 20 extra pounds, why not?!?!

I had curtains made for our dining room. They were installed while I was away at training. I love the curtains, hate them with the wall color. Even though we painted the dining room less than a year ago, I decided to paint it again. Let me remind you, that I can barely move from the Thanksgiving boxing workout. I spent a few hours yesterday prepping and painting the room. My back and biceps felt like they were going to fall off. As painful as it is, I love it. I love the feeling of a good butt whooping. Anyway, coat two has to go on today. I have been doing it for hours and still only have 1.5 walls done. I'm taking my sweet time. I like painting rooms when we pay my brother to do it.

Ugh... Back to breaking my sore limbs off.

Rescued by Pillows

My progesterone levels were 2.6 today (they have to be above 3 to start Lupron). It usually takes a few days for progesterone to rise after ovulation. If I just ovulated on Friday, I'm right on track. Dr. P wants me to come in on Wednesday to repeat the test. If it's above 3 (which it will be) I will most likely start Lupron on Wednesday. The most likely has nothing to do with me or my body. The clinic only closes one time a year... that's on Christmas. When the IVF coordinator plans out my cycle, she will have to make sure any major procedures (Ultrasounds, retrieval, transfer) do not end up near or on Christmas. Hopefully I can start Lupron on Wednesday and get this show on the road.

Since we did a natural FET, the last time I stuck myself with needles was for my last fresh cycle which was in July. It has been nearly five months. I can't believe it. My nemesis and my best friend, the needle, has been gone for quite some time.

I have complained about my sleeping habits a million times on here... I finally decided to do something about it. B and I went on a pillow hunt. I promised myself that I would not look at prices and just buy the pillow that I found most comfortable. 99% of the time, I'm waking up because I'm uncomfortable. A good night's sleep shouldn't have a price tag on it. We went to the store and starting pulling pillows down one by one. After trying about 15 or so out, I picked the one I liked best (I actually purchased two of them). Well, let me say... I have EXPENSIVE taste. Who would have thought a pillow could cost $160?? Not I! Of course, I did not pay that much. Black weekend sales were going on so I got 60% off plus an additional 20%. I still paid a fortune ($50 each) for them but it was worth it. For the first time, since I can remember, I slept for five hours straight. I am normally up every hour or so. I felt like a million bucks (as I should since the pillows cost nearly that much) all day today. I am forever grateful for those two pillows.

MONDAY, NOVEMBER 29, 2010

Tangled

On Sunday, B and I took B's cousin to see Tangled. Am I the only one that didn't know the full story of Rapunzel? The Brothers Grimm version is slightly different than the animated version. For the sake of time, I'll just tell the version we watched on Sunday.

Once upon a time, there was a childless King and Queen. They tried and tried to have children. They finally conceived only for the Queen's body to not take to pregnancy well. As she was on bed rest (not just any bed rest... she was dying) they heard about a magical flower that could save her life. There was an enchantress that had been keeping the flower hidden. She had been using it for years (hundreds of them) to maintain her youth. Eventually, the King's people found the flower. They made a healing potion for the Queen... she was healed and delivered a healthy baby girl. Since the Queen ingested the potion during pregnancy, the baby was born with the power of the flower. The enchantress heard of this, so she broke into the palace and stole the baby. She locked her in a hidden tower that was without windows and doors. The King and Queen never stopped looking for her. Every year, they released floating lanterns into the sky with hopes that she could see them. She could. When she turned 18, she asked the enchantress (whom she thought was her mother) if she could leave... before I give the movie away (which it may seem as if I have. I haven't. This all happens in the first two minutes), I'll stop. Needless to say, I cried a lot. I cried when the King cried on the baby's birthday. I cried when they released the lanterns. I cried when they were reunited. I cried for the Queen who struggled for so long to have a child to only have it taken away from her. I related to a damn animated movie. Awesome.

While my acupuncturist was removing the needles from me yesterday, I asked her if I am the longest IVF patient she has. She said, "No. I had one patient that I couldn't believe how many times she tried IVF. She did six before stopping. She never produced a lot of eggs so she never had a lot of embryos. They did genetic testing on the embryos and never had any normal ones to transfer. After six tries, she stopped." I then said, "Well, I'm about to start cycle #5. I'm getting close." Aye. I can't believe how much we have gone through.

I'm anxious to find out if we start tomorrow. I'm feeling good about this one...which could be a bad thing. Feeling good about it can result in a huge let down if it doesn't work.

WEDNESDAY, DECEMBER 1, 2010

One step forward, two steps back

I waited for the call all day. Every time the phone rang, I got excited. I couldn't wait for the call with my plan. At 4:44, the call finally came in. Cycle Cancelled. My progesterone dropped. I didn't ask what that meant or how that could happen. I just said "thanks" and hung up the phone. I don't have it in me today. I just don't.

"Waiting for the fish to bite or waiting for wind to fly a kite. Or waiting around for Friday night or waiting perhaps for their Uncle Jake or a pot to boil or a better break or a string of pearls or a pair of pants or a wig with curls or another chance. Everyone is just waiting." ~Dr. Seuss

THURSDAY, DECEMBER 2, 2010

Here's to...

Dr. P called me on her drive home yesterday (not to worry, she has Bluetooth). We talked for about an hour (because she rules). I promise I will share everything we discussed... just not today. I still don't have it in me.

One of my friends sent me an "I'm sorry" text. My response was "it could be worse." Our conversation then turned into this...

Friend: I tell myself that daily. Here's to not having cancer.

Me: Here's to not having MS

F: Here's to not being limbless

Me: Here's to not being flat chested

F: Here's to not having our faces burned off with poison

Me: or Acid

F: Here's to not being blind

Me: Here's to not having a beard

F: Here's to not having IBS

Me: Here's to not having chronic yeast infections

F: Here's to not being eligible to be on the biggest loser

Me: Here's to not having diarrhea (I guess that's the same as IBS). Here's to not having unmanageable nostril hair

I know some of those things are shallow...but they made me laugh.

As I was typing this post, Dr. P messaged me "I'm going to make getting you pregnant my life's work!" My response, "You're an over achiever!!" Here's to Dr. P fulfilling her life's work!

EDIT: We just booked our trip! Yay! Punta Cana, here we come!

SATURDAY, DECEMBER 4, 2010

Conversation with Dr. P

This is what Dr. P and I discussed on Wednesday.

What happened this cycle: Basically, we have no idea. Dr. P said it's very common for cycles to get messed up from drug confusion. Sometimes your body gives all the signals of moving forward but your brain isn't responding. She said I could have easily had the physical symptoms but my brain wasn't giving the signals to my hormones. With that being said, she has never seen anyone surge without ovulating. AH HA! Of course, until now. She had me come in today for repeat progesterone to see if it was just being slow to rise (it wasn't, it's still dropping).

What's next: Dr. P would like to try changing our protocol for this next cycle. The only reason she wants to change it, is for the sake of time. To do the current protocol (Lupron/Gonal-F), we would have to wait or induce a period, wait for ovulation (at this point, who knows how long that will be) and then start Lupron. So we'd be looking at another few months. With the antagonist protocol, we would induce a period with Provera, then start meds the first day of my period. The cycle is much shorter (because there is no Lupron phase). She mentioned that the antagonist cycles generally produce less eggs. Since I produce 15-20 eggs a cycle, she's not worried. She said even if we got half the amount of eggs, it's still plenty. I don't like the idea of not having 20 embryo options but if she's not worried, I'm not worried. The glitch with the next cycle is the lab. As I mentioned in previous posts, the lab closes for a week around the holidays. During the week that they are closed, the lab gets cleaned. Once it's cleaned, they bring in mouse embryos. They need to ensure that none of the chemicals used in the cleaning, kills the mouse embryos... which I find very cool. After the mouse embryo test, the lab reopens. If we started Provera right now, my cycle would fall in that "cleaning" week. So the IVF coordinator is coming up with a schedule so I can start my next cycle as soon as possible, without falling into that week. I should know the details of that on Monday. The worst thing that could happen is for my period to show up on its own. For the first time, I'm hoping my body stays messed up.

Donor Eggs/Sperm/Embryo/Uterus: I asked Dr. P if or when will we start discussing some sort of donor something. If she said to get donor anything, I would do it in a second (minus sperm... I'll explain why I don't want donor sperm in a future post). Dr. P said that getting donor anything is always on the back of her mind for all her patients. With us, she said that it's really buried in the back of her mind. She said, "If we were to look up Unexplained in the dictionary, you and B would be there. You're the true definition of unexplained infertility." She mentioned that most of her "unexplained" patients, become explained over time. With us, there isn't one thing that is slightly off to direct her towards a solution. On paper we should have no problem conceiving. She also said, "We achieved a clinical pregnancy with you. Unfortunately, it didn't result in a live birth. However, we achieved a true, clinical pregnancy. With you two, I wouldn't know what to suggest for a donor. There isn't a part of the equation that needs to be fixed. I wouldn't be able to tell you to get donor sperm, donor egg, embryo, or even donor uterus. All of those things are fine with the two of you." She's right, we don't and wouldn't know what form of donation would be needed. So I guess, that's that.

PGD- Preimplantation Genetic Diagnosis: I asked if we could do PGD. In fact, I have asked many, many times in the past. I know there are rules and there is a process that needs to happen before you get approved for PGD. We do not qualify for it. Some of the criteria are genetic abnormalities, recurrent miscarriages, advanced maternal age. Yep, again, not us. I just feel like we have tested everything else within our bodies. The only thing left is the embryo. She agreed to allow us to do PGD after this cycle. Since we don't fit the diagnostic criteria for PGD, we would have to pay out of pocket for it.

We also talked about some other things but they're not really worth posting. She did send me a funny email today. I sent her

an email that said "Day 1 of bikini workout. Can't I just watch TV and drink coffee instead???" I Love her response:
1. You'll be skinny and look great. Even if you do nothing.
2. You have a great husband who loves you unconditionally and will think you're gorgeous at any weight.
3. Everyone else will be drunk.
Hahahaha... Love her!

SUNDAY, DECEMBER 5, 2010

My life is comical

I am on my way to a baby shower (No, I was not joking when I said I am surrounded by pregnancy) so I don't have time to post. I just wanted to let you all know how insanely humorous my fertility life is. After my post yesterday (when I told you that all we needed was for me to NOT get my period) my body did a funny thing. I got my period at Midnight. Yep, the exact thing we did not want it to do. The exact thing we needed it to do to cancel yet ANOTHER cycle. Awesome, right!??!

WEDNESDAY, DECEMBER 8, 2010

Back On The Saddle

I'm finally back in a cycle. Dr. P gave me a few options for this cycle/next cycle.
Long-term options for next cycle:
1. Try to see if you get back on track and ovulate and start Lupron the way we'd planned (I really think you'll ovulate this month)
2. If you don't ovulate, do an antagonist protocol with your next period.
3. We could try Clomid this month. It would increase the likelihood that you would ovulate in a predictable fashion so that we could truly do a luteal phase Lupron start.
After much debate, B and I decided to go with option #3. We're not sure why my body has been funky lately... if I were a betting woman, I'd bet that my body has no idea what it is doing without the meds. We have been controlling it for years with meds... Why wouldn't it be confused? We figure, let's try the Clomid plan... why not? I am on Clomid for five days (cycle days 3-7). Once I surge, I go in for progesterone check 5-7 days later. If my levels are above 3, I'll start the Lupron Protocol. Needless

to say, I'm happy we have some sort of plan. Waiting until February was not going to fly with me.

I was on the wrestling team in high school. No, not a girls team... a boys team. I'm not talking about some wimpy wrestling. I'm talking about true Greco Roman wrestling. I had a boyfriend that wrestled and thought it was the end all and be all of sports. Once I was making fun of him... I was basically poking fun at him for being such a "tough guy." He responded to my taunting with, "A girl would never make it through a season." One thing you will learn (if you have not already learned) is that you should never say never to me. If you tell me I can't do something or that it can never happen, I will do everything in my power to prove you wrong. After that conversation, I went on to join the wrestling team. Before the season started, there was an informational meeting. I went unnoticed throughout the meeting until the Q&A session. During the session, I raised my hand and said to the coach (who turned out to be incredibly awesome) "What are the rules about females wrestling on the team?" He paused for a moment, then responded with "there would be some logistics to work out but if she wants to wrestle, she can wrestle." Guys in the room made jokes and said a lot of "ya right." I walked in the first day of practice like I belonged there. After a couple of weeks of proving myself to the boys, they were great. They never looked at me or treated me any different than the other team members. I was on the wrestling team. Gender didn't matter to them (other teams/towns, that's another story). The way wrestling works is, every week before a match, you compete against your own teammates in a "wrestle off." The person who wins is the one that wrestles in the match. I wrestled in every match. I wasn't State Champion, but I was decent. The most important part is that I was able to prove my boyfriend wrong. In fact, his town wouldn't wrestle me. The coached forced his players to forfeit. I actually had some choice words about this (I got suspended from two wrestling matches because of it). I don't remember exactly what I said to the coach. The only line that I can remember is "The only reason you won't wrestle me is because I don't have a dick." Ya, real nice April. In hindsight, I would have worded that a little differently. In the end, I found a sport that I fell in love with. I made friends with some incredible guys. I even got national exposure (MTV flew me into Key West to be a guest on one of their shows). The icing on the cake, I proved that if you want something badly enough, you can make it happen.

There has been nothing... not one thing... that I have aspired to do or have wanted and not been able to accomplish it.

Not one thing until now. This whole infertility thing has thrown me through a loop. If I want control, I take it. If I want it to happen, I make it happen. If you tell me no, I prove you wrong. No matter how much determination I have; No matter how much positivity I have; No Matter how badly I want to kick this "unexplained infertility" in the ass, I can't do it. I think this is (partially) why I am having such a hard time with this struggle. I have never been in this position before. Infertility has taken one of my strongest attributes and made it into a struggle. I know it will happen. It will. I just don't like losing control. I want it to happen now. Not later. Not someday. Now.

TUESDAY, DECEMBER 14, 2010

Miss me?

I know, I know. I have been missing in action. I haven't really had anything to update you all on. I should change the title of this blog to "Always waiting to ovulate." It seems like every post for the past few months has been about waiting for ovulation. I took my last Clomid pill on Saturday. Dr. P said that I should expect to ovulate within a couple of weeks. So, I just wait. I'll think of something (other than waiting) to write about tomorrow.

WEDNESDAY, DECEMBER 15, 2010

Holiday Cheer

Every year at Christmas time, I used to "adopt" a family and buy gifts for them. At some point (after College), I stopped. I am not sure why I stopped. I loved doing it. A friend of mine did it this year. When she mentioned it, I thought "why on earth did I stop doing that." My siblings and I (and sibling-in-laws) decided to adopt a family rather than exchanging gifts. I called a few local shelters until I found one with families (with children). We have been buying gifts for those two families. My brother doesn't want us to talk about it with people because he thinks it defeats the purpose of doing it. He believes good deeds should go unrecognized. I agree with him, however, I can't help but talk about how fun it has been to fulfill people's holiday wishes. I love walking into the toy store to buy the one thing a child has asked for. One child asked for a game that is on this years "hot list." I had to call around and drive to three stores before I found it. I actually got the last one. I can only imagine the excitement on the boy's face when he opens it. It makes me look forward to not only having our own children to buy presents for but it also makes me look forward to sharing the adopt a family tradition with our children. It also gives me a good excuse to peruse the baby/children aisles.

On the fertility side, I am still waiting. I am super crampy. I'm hoping that means the Clomid is stirring up a good ovulation. I have to have my progesterone checked 5-7 days after surge is detected. The only conflict we may have is our trip to Punta Cana. To avoid this conflict, I have to either surge before the 20th or after the 25th. How much do you want to bet, I surge between the 20th and 25th?? Other than waiting, I'm in a good place. This time off has given me some time to accept the situation for what it is. Do I like it? No. Do I wish it was different? Yes. However, I am okay with it. Maybe my acceptance is highly influenced by the holiday cheer. Acceptance is the first step to any type of recovery, right? Maybe I am recovering from infertility denial. Either way, I am happy.

FRIDAY, DECEMBER 17, 2010

Words of Wisdom

I know people mean well when they give you their "words of wisdom." I do my best to listen, say thank you and move on. However, the one that I can't wrap my head around. The one that I can't make sense of. The one that I can't rationalize as being true is "Everything happens for a reason." I just don't get it. I understand that there is significance in every part of our life. Every event, whether good, bad or just, unjust, there are lessons to be learned. Do these events really have to happen? Aren't there other opportunities available to teach us these life lessons? I feel that we have created this thought of everything happening for a reason because all unfair events must present us with some sort of life changing meaning. We can't just chalk it up to bad luck. Is it because believing that everything happens for a reason gives our hard times a purpose? My friend's husband passed away when she was 9.5 months pregnant. She's now a widow with two toddlers. What's the reasoning behind that? Has her loss added value to her life or her children's life? What about my friend who suffered five miscarriages? How about my friend who lost her twins at ten weeks? Or what about children suffering with terminal illness? If you want to find a reason, you will. I have created reasons for our loss and struggle many times. At one point, I told myself that my promotion wouldn't have happened had I not lost Baby L. When the position opened up, I would have been on maternity leave. I have told myself that if we didn't go through the fertility struggles, I wouldn't have been able to help so many other women with their struggles. You can find a reason for everything. You can find a purpose in every struggle. You can learn a lesson from hardships. You can find a reason but that doesn't mean that everything happens for a reason.

MONDAY, DECEMBER 20, 2010

Christmas Wish

Today is the 20th. I still have not ovulated. Now I can't ovulate until Christmas day. If I ovulate before then, I'll be away when we have to do our lab work. How much do you want to bet I ovulate in the next five days? I have ALL the time in the world to ovulate and only 5 days I can't. The way my body has been playing tricks on me, I wouldn't be surprised if I happen to ovulate on those five days.

I was at a work event last week and someone asked me if I was pregnant because I wasn't drinking. Okay, call me a b*#@^ but HELLO, what the heck is wrong with you?!?! You NEVER ask a woman if she is pregnant. NEVER. My response was "why, do I look fat?" The last thing a non-pregnant person wants to be asked is "Are you pregnant?" If you have been trying and are asked that, the question is a dagger right through your gut... or heart or lungs. If you haven't been trying, the question is a dagger through your ego. It may induce a crash diet or an eating disorder. You might as well say "Oh, you look fat. If you're not with child, then you need a serious trainer." Never, ever, ever ask a woman if she is pregnant. NEVER.

We had B's family holiday party on Saturday. B's cousin (who was pregnant the same time I was; we were ten days apart) was there with her two boys. Although I held the baby a lot, it was really hard for me to see him. Every time he was in my arms I kept thinking about Baby L. Baby L would have been that size. Baby L would have been that age. I kept imagining the clothes I would have put on Baby L and all the "oohs and ahhhs" Baby L would get. I kept thinking about how I would be handing off my baby so I could have a break.

Santa (B's uncle dresses as Santa and gives out gifts to everyone. Usually the young kids scream with excitement and the older kids sit on Santa's lap and crack jokes. It's a good time) brought me the new Michael Jackson CD, Michael Jackson pins and a Michael Jackson picture book. Santa really does know exactly what you want! I usually don't make Santa requests... however, this year, I'm requesting a baby or two or three. Dear Santa, please bless us with a Christmas miracle.

TUESDAY, DECEMBER 21, 2010

Reality TV

One of my favorite shows is a Reality show. I have been watching it for a couple years. Recently, they started airing their fertility struggles. Last night's episode showed the struggles of their second IVF (the first ended in miscarriage). The woman ended up with OHSS (Ovarian Hyperstimulation Syndrome) after her retrieval (15 eggs). OHSS is very painful. VERY painful. Thankfully, I have never had to deal with it. Anyway, they ended up freezing all their embryos because they couldn't do a transfer until she healed from the OHSS. About a month later, they transferred two on day 5, hatching blastocysts. The couple was so excited. They kept saying that they knew it worked. During the episode, I couldn't help but yell at the TV and say "You're getting too excited." I'm a veteran at this. I know what excitement can do to you... it make the letdown unbearable. Over and over again, they both talked about it working. Then the beta call came in. When the phone rang, the woman was jumping with joy. She called her husband into the room and they excitedly said hello to the doctor. As soon as the doctor said "Hi," I knew it didn't work. There is a tone that the giver of negative beta results has. Seeing their faces was heartbreaking. Hearing them talk about it was devastating. When you're going through a cycle you have a million emotions running through you. You're excited. You're scared. You're hopeful. You're guarded. You're nervous. You're stoic. You're all over the place. Although you always want to be excited and hopeful, you keep your guard up. You want to do everything in your power to protect yourself from heartbreak. If there is going to be a letdown, you want to prevent it from knocking you off your feet. Even though we have been (several times) where this couple just came from, it was very difficult to witness. Witnessing it crushed me. I never realized how awful the scene is. I have always been in it. I have always been guarded and protected. To actually see what it is like to get the news saddened me. It saddened me to know that we have become pros at it. It saddened me to know that we repeatedly experience that. It saddened me to know that there is a good chance we will be there many more times.

The husband told his wife that it was okay to be sad but they will not be sad forever. He mentioned how wonderful their life is. They have a beautiful home (I'd call it a McMansion), a wonderful marriage, successful careers, great friends and family. They have so many incredible things that this one thing will not define their happiness. Their incredible life together will define their happiness. When he said that, I wondered if he reads my blog. Is he quoting me??

Dr. P is having me go in tomorrow morning for an ultrasound and blood work. She wants to see if she can get an idea of what is going on in there. Awesome, I went from a normal girl to a medical mystery.

WEDNESDAY, DECEMBER 22, 2010

Fertile Mertile

We now know why I am so uncomfortable. My ovaries are gigantic. They are full of a bajillion follicles. The nurse said "Holy Crap! I've never seen anyone as fertile as this. You have more follicles from low dose Clomid than most women get during an IVF cycle." Ha... I'm a childless fertile mertile. Is that not an oxymoron or what!??!

As great as a bajillion follicles are, they pose a little problem. Even though the chances of us getting pregnant naturally are slim to none, there is still a chance. If I was doing an IUI cycle, it would be cancelled due to the large amount of follicles (because millions of sperm swimming around in there could result in a multiple pregnancy). Since we don't know exactly when I would ovulate (we know it will be soon), we decided to do a trigger shot so I won't become the next Octomom. I will ovulate 36 hours after the trigger shot. Now we have a time frame to abstain from intercourse. Abstain from intercourse... definitely not my words!

It seems like every cycle we have some sort of bad timing. This time, the timing couldn't be more perfect. I took the trigger shot around 5:00 this evening. Which means, I will ovulate at 5:00 am Christmas Eve morning. I will start Lupron one week after ovulating... which is the 31st. We get back from Punta Cana on the 30th. I don't have to travel with drugs and needles! Okay, scratch that. B just called me and I told him that the timing is perfect and he said "uhm, no that's wrong. We fly home on the 31st." hahahaha... So, I will be traveling with a cooler, meds, and needles all for one shot!

I started my second cycle (the cycle that worked) on the 29th of December last year. I'm starting this cycle on the 31st. If this cycle works, I will have practically (plus or minus a day or two) the same due date. Weird, right?

FRIDAY, DECEMBER 24, 2010

Twas the Night Before Christmas

Twas the Night Before Christmas (IVF Style): By Whitney (one of my fertility friends)
www.whitneyanderick.com
Twas the day of the transfer and out the door we went,
My hormones were raging and I felt emotionally spent.
The stockings were hung by the stirrups with care,
In hopes that a baby soon would be there.
The nurse was prepping and readying the bed,
While visions of implantation danced in my head.
Me in my paper gown, and my husband in his cap,
I was getting ready to settle down for my Valium nap.
When out in the waiting room there arose such a clatter,
My husband sprang from the OR to see what was the matter.
Down the hall he flew like a flash,
Ran into the receptionist and gave her the cash.
The florescent light beamed down from the ceiling above,
Giving the luster of paleness to my true love.
When, what to our wondering eyes should appear,
A man in a white coat and I felt nothing but fear.
With a look in his eye that said nothing was missed,
I knew in a moment it must be my reproductive endocrinologist.
More rapid than pregnancy news, his assistants they came,
And he whistled, and shouted, and called them by name!
"Now Betty! Now, Alice! Now, Sally and Sue!"
"On Donna! On Margaret! On Kelly and Drew!"
"Get the embryologist in here. Get her right away."
"We're ready to do this! I hope this will be your lucky day!"
As we said a prayer and everyone got ready,
The doctor pulled the catheter trigger and held it real steady.
So, up to the uterine lining it flew,
With a shot full of embryos and culture solution, too.
And then, in a twinkling, I knew I desperately needed to pee,
I said, "My bladder is about to explode, don't you see?"
As I wiggled and squirmed and looked for my man,
I turned just in time to see him coming with a bed pan.

He was dressed in paper footies and was as handsome as ever.

I sighed in relief and immediately felt better.

I laid still for 20 minutes while he watched the clock,

Then, in someone came. "You can get up," said the doc.

But his eyes, they were serious,

He said, "There's something we need to discuss."

"Lay still for three days, before you get up and go."

"You must give those embryos time to burrow in and grow."

So off we went as my husband wheeled me away,

Back to car and we were on our way.

I laid in the backseat and looked at the embryo picture,

And, hoped with all my might that God might hear my whisper.

I felt chubby and plump, from all the hormones,

And, then thought of tomorrow's injections with a groan.

With a wink of my eye and a twist of my head,

I knew the two-week-wait would be something to dread.

When we arrived back home, my mom went straight to her work,

She made a great lunch, then turned with a jerk.

She said, "You just lay there to relax and rest."

"Leave everything to me and don't you stress."

With two weeks to wait and Lovenox to endure,

We readied ourselves for heartache some more.

I stressed about my symptoms and missed drinking wine,

Then we prepared for the big test and we hoped for two lines.

TUESDAY, JANUARY 4, 2011

Happy New Year

We're back! Sun kissed, relaxed and ready for a new year! 2010 was a rough year. 2011 is our year. I can feel it.

Although our trip started off rocky, I can't complain. Most people weren't as lucky as we were. We just made it out before the storm. Thank goodness! We really needed some time away. We had a few days of rain in Punta Cana. It didn't stop us from sitting on the beach. Punta Cana rain comes with 80 degree weather. So we would park it under a cabana and read while listening to rain and waves. It was quite relaxing. I drank about 50 virgin Banana Mama's. We enjoyed some incredible meals. We played lots of Scrabble (which I did not win one game). I read four books. We had a blast. Now back to reality...

I'm on day 5 of Lupron. So far, the side effects are mild (knock on wood). I have mild night sweats and that's it. No crazy dreams. No headaches. I am having trouble with the shots. It's taken me two or three tries before I can get the needle into my stomach. I'm not quite sure why this is. One of my friends thought maybe it could be from weight loss. I haven't lost much weight. Since we had five months off from the drugs, I definitely thinned out. Maybe my muscle is closer to the surface? I don't know but it stinks. We have our baseline ultrasound on the 13th. If all goes well, we'll start stims on the 14th.

Speaking of weight loss. For the first time in two years, I wore a bikini! I was terrified! I have not shown the skin of this belly since we started the injections. Well, I did it. Not only did I wear a bikini, I also walked around without a cover up on. If I can tackle the bikini, I can overcome infertility. The bikini was just one of many obstacles we will overcome in 2011.

FRIDAY, JANUARY 7, 2011

Watch your mouth!

I was away at a two day meeting on Tuesday and Wednesday. There were a couple of people at the meeting that were new. One of them (who was insanely sick and should have stayed home) said a few things to me that made me want to scream. While we were sitting a table (at dinner) with about 15 people she asks me if I have children.

1. This question drives me crazy.
2. It's none of your business!

Anyway, I'm sure smoke was coming out of my ears but I politely answered her with a simple answer of "no, we do not." One would think that would be the end of the conversation. One would think. She then replied with "Well, why not?" The rest of the conversation went as follows...

Me: *Ignoring her like I didn't hear her*

Rude Girl: How old are you?

Me: *Ignore*

RG: How old are you?

Me: 31

RG: 31? You're not getting younger.

Me: *Blank stare*

RG: Do you guys talk about it? You must talk about having children.

Me: Whether or not my husband and I want children is for discussion between the two of us and the two of us only.

RG: People wait too long these days. If you keep waiting, there could be problems.

Me: *I stood up and left the table*

Seriously? What is wrong with people? Did she not think for one minute it was none of her business? Does it not cross some people's minds that it could be a sensitive topic? I wanted to say to her "I'm not getting younger, really? For your information, I have been sticking needles in my belly for years. I have had more vaginal ultrasounds than one human should have in a lifetime. I have had over 60 eggs removed from my body by aspirating follicles (which cause my ovaries to be the size of watermelons) with a vacuum sucking needle. My body has been through several cycles of induced menopause. It has been tricked into being pregnant several times. It has been pregnant once. I have sat over a toilet for days while I passed our baby. I went from a size 2 to a size 8 from years of pumping my body with hormones. No shit, the longer you wait, the harder it can be. Maybe you should think before you speak or learn to watch your mouth." Yes, but of course I didn't and never say those things. Although, I should.

On a happy note, today, I am wearing a size 2 again! There is a benefit to having five months off of treatment. I'm a little over a week into Lupron. If my baseline ultrasound looks good next Thursday, I'll start my stim drugs... so, the size 2 won't last, but it is nice!

SUNDAY, JANUARY 9, 2011

Easy Cycle

I am a little hesitant to say that this cycle has been very easy for me. I was afraid if I talked about it, I would jinx it. I barely have night sweats... I had a few when I first started Lupron and have none since. I haven't gained weight... YET. I have a headache today but that could be from my period. My period came today which is perfectly timed. You need it to come after the start of Lupron and before your baseline ultrasound. My baseline ultrasound is Thursday. I cannot wait for that appointment. The baseline is what will make this cycle feel real. If we get the okay, we'll start stims on Friday. Yay! As of right now, I'm very calm about this cycle. I'm not worried about it not working. I'm not worried about the number of eggs or embryos. Maybe this calmness means I'm an official veteran to IVF. Whatever it means, I like it.

WEDNESDAY, JANUARY 12, 2011

Snowman Blues

We woke up this morning to a foot of snow and it's only the beginning of the storm. As soon as I got up I went outside with Cappy. Well, I took my shot then we went outside. All I wanted to do was build a snowman. Well, building a snowman with a fur baby is not that easy. Every time I got a good ball of snow going, Cappy would come running over to dig at my ball. He would dig at it, bite it, then look at me like "do it again Mom!" After the snowman attempt, I tried making a snow angel. Cappy thought it was time to sprint circles around me and to dig at my feet and arms. It is time for a human child.

Tomorrow is my baseline ultrasound. I can't wait. I can't imagine anything holding up the cycle. Hopefully I'm correct.

I came home from our AGC dinner last night to a very unexpected comment on my Facebook page. This is from a high school friend and classmate.

This is going to sound totally random cause I'm not a huge commenter but I was behind in my blog feed readings and I caught up on yours today. So here is my comment, I have decided that out of everyone I know (yes, really everyone) you deserve to have all the happiness in the world in 2011. Okay maybe not all of it but at least a big big chunk! I mean it, from how open you are to how amazing you are graciously moving forward with whatever comes your way you are a huge inspiration to me and I imagine too many others as well. I may not struggle with what you struggle with but your journey is an inspiration to me in other areas of my life. So that is my wish today on 1-11-11 that you find your happiness in 2011!

I love it. I love it for its unexpectedness. I love it for its kindness. I love it for its candor. I love it because infertility inspires even those who are not dealing with it. My favorite poet is Emily Dickinson. One of my favorite quotes by her is "Not knowing when the dawn will come, I open every door." I don't know when we'll have a baby. I don't know when this chapter of our life will be over. All I know is that we will have a family and this nightmare will be over. I won't close my mind to the possibility of it happening. It's just a matter of when it will happen. Until then, my heart, my mind and my spirit remains happy and ready.

THURSDAY, JANUARY 13, 2011

Here we go...

Walking into the clinic this morning I felt a little nostalgic. I hadn't been there in a few weeks. A few weeks may seem minimal to most people. However, the clinic has been my second home for a couple of years now. A few weeks away feels like a lifetime. I'm glad to be back.

My blood work and ultrasound was pretty uneventful today. The lab tech who always misses my vein was working again. I guess I have grimaced and winced enough for her to realize she shouldn't draw my blood anymore. When I walked in she didn't even get off her seat. She said "You prefer Paula to draw you, correct." Yes, Ma'am. That is correct sister. I'm all set with needles floating around in my arm. Anyway, Paula drew my blood and it was seamless.

The ultrasound looked good. My lining was nice and thin (which is how it should be and why you need to get your period before starting). My left and right ovaries were clear of any cysts (which are a common side effect of the drugs). I had a baseline of over 12 follicles on each ovary. They are small and ready to be stimulated.

Usually the lab calls after 2:00 with your results and next steps. I got a message from Dr. P a little before 3:00 that said "Finally Starting!! Very Exciting!!" About an hour later, the nurse called me with my plan. Here it is:

Drop Lupron from 10 units to 5 units in the morning.

Take stim drug (Gonal-F) between 7:00 and 9:00 pm starting tomorrow night.

Follow that plan Friday, Saturday, and Sunday. Then Monday I have an appointment at 9:00 am for blood work.

We're about ten days away from egg retrieval. Here we go...

SATURDAY, JANUARY 15, 2011

Mind over Body

I was talking with a friend last night about where this "I feel good" attitude has come from. When your body fails you, your mind automatically tries to compensate. We all want complete control over our bodies and our lives. When we lose that, our minds take over. Many different thoughts and emotions start to kick in. We become "Mind over Body" beings. For so long, I wanted this to work out. I wanted to know every detail about fertility because I thought I could find something to fix. I wanted it so badly that it consumed me. Don't get me wrong, I still want it very badly. My 'want' is in a different way. I know that we will be parents. I have no doubts about that. One way or another, we will have children. Babies/pregnancy are not the end all/be all to life. There is so much more to life than babies/pregnancy. I know I have said it a million times over... we have a wonderful life. This is just one portion that isn't going as we thought it would. In the big scheme of things... this is minuscule. For so long we went through emotions (that I know are/were healthy at the time) that don't fit our life anymore. We constantly wondered "why us." Why do we deserve this? Are we being punished for something? What's the lesson we're supposed to be learning?

On top of those thoughts, I found myself maintaining a strong front in order to protect B. Women tend to be the caregivers in families. We are maternal by nature. We want to protect those around us. We want to shield them from harm. Although B and I have been very open with each other throughout this process, I know a part of me was holding back because I wanted to keep him safe. He doesn't need that. We don't need that.

I think all the emotions we have gone through are a normal and healthy part of the acceptance process. Without those thoughts and emotions, I wouldn't be in the place I am now. The place being one of acceptance. I have faith that God has a plan for us. It may not be the one I originally hoped for but so be it. I trust that we are doing all we can and should. I trust that whatever the plan is for us, it is one that we will love. I feel good about this because I accept whatever comes our way. I get it now. I am not being punished. I am not a failure of a woman. I am not contagious. I am not strong. I just am. I physically feel good. I mentally feel good. I have faith and trust. I have the most amazing husband around. I have my fur babies that I love more than you could ever imagine. I am She-Ra. Hahahaha... I wasn't planning on comparing myself to She-Ra but it's true, I am She-Ra. I remember watching the cartoon when I was growing up (it was one of my favorites, next to Strawberry Shortcake). She-Ra was the princess of power and strength. Every episode she was overcoming feats that were deemed impossible by other characters. I am She-Ra. I like it.

My first night of stimming was uneventful. I did instantly bruise... boooo! I am bruising a lot more this cycle because I am taking baby aspirin. Other than that, I still feel great. Oh, I almost forgot, I will be going to the Patriots vs. Jets game this weekend (I definitely did NOT almost forget that... I almost forgot to mention the meds). The game is at 4:30 which means I'll have to take one of my shots at the stadium. At first I thought I would just leave the meds in the car and I'd leave the game early to take it. Then (mainly after all the press conferences of the Jets talking so much smack and me wanting to see every minute of the Patriots winning) I decided to call Gillette to see what the process is to bring a cooler, needles and meds into the stadium. It's actually quite easy. Security emailed me a letter that I have to bring with me through the security line. That's that. The only bummer is that I have to shoot up in the bathroom of the Stadium. Kind of gross but worth it.

MONDAY, JANUARY 17, 2011

Preparations and Lessons

During three separate conversations today, the topic of life lessons and life preparations came up. If it comes up three times in a day, it's worthy of a blog post.

This morning I was talking to a friend about Colicky babies. I told her a story about a friend whose baby had Colic for eight months straight. Poor guy screamed for hours and hours a day for the first eight months of his life. It took my friend five years (of trying naturally) to get pregnant and her delivery was a near death experience. She literally almost died. In fact, she saw herself on the table... yes, a true out of body experience. Scary (and cool... now that she's safe and healthy). Due to her struggles conceiving and almost dying during delivery, the Colic was a piece of cake. Don't get me wrong, it was hard on both her and her husband... I'm not saying it wasn't. I'm just saying that her appreciation level for her health and a healthy baby made the obstacles in parenthood seem minuscule. Like I said to my friend earlier... it's incredible how life prepares you in crazy ways.

I have another friend who was suggested by her fertility doctor to use donor eggs during her next cycle. Since October(ish) she has been going through the process of being matched with a donor and the process of grieving the loss of having a biological child. She also went through a roller coaster with potential donors. A couple of weeks ago, her first choice donor agreed to do another cycle (she had already done two cycles for another couple). The donor cycle was in place and all she had to do was start birth control pills with her period to get the cycle going. Her period never showed. So last night, after being a couple of days late, she took a pregnancy test. Low and behold, she's pregnant... naturally and unexpectedly. She went to the doctor this morning and they confirmed it. I was talking to her today about this wonderful miracle and she said "You know the best part? Going through the donor process makes this that much sweeter. Funny how things work out." I then told her the story about my friend and her Colicky baby. I told her the same thing I told my other friend... it's incredible how life prepares you in crazy ways. She replied with "Infertility has given me many hidden blessings."

Life throws us curve balls. Life often makes us wonder "why." Life comes with so much uncertainty. One thing is for sure, with every obstacle, every struggle and every ounce of doubt comes a lesson that eventually prepares us for the future. It may prepare us to be stronger for a future struggle. It may prepare us to relish in a moment. It may open our eyes up to a miracle that would have gone unseen otherwise. Although we don't know it at the time, life gives us struggle to make our lives better. That is partly why I feel so good this cycle. A while back I realized this (along with many other realizations) and I am ready for whatever life may bring.

I had my blood work this morning. Today will be day 4 of stims and they are already dropping my dose down. When the nurse called with the results and steps of my plan, I wasn't surprised. I woke up this morning with a KILLER migraine. I knew it meant that I'm strongly responding to the stim drugs. I will take the new dose (187.5) tonight and tomorrow. I will then go in on Wednesday morning for blood work and an ultrasound. Egg Retrieval is getting close!

WEDNESDAY, JANUARY 19, 2011

All most there

I woke up today feeling crappy and a little full. I know crappy and full are good things. I made it this far without any side effects. With only a week left, I shouldn't complain but I am going to... I feel like CRAP! I have a killer migraine and my belly is so sore!

I knew going into my ultrasound that I wasn't going to have any mature follicles... as tonight's shot will only be my sixth one. My right ovary is measuring 31x32mm (that's normal for this stage in the game) and it has 15 follicles; all measuring around 9mm (over 12 is mature). My left ovary is measuring 31x28mm and has about nine follicles. One of those nine is measuring at 13mm and the rest are around 10mm. I'm right on track. The nurse just called with my plan. She instructed me to take the same dose of Gonal-f tonight (187.5) and return in the morning for only blood work. My guess will be they will have me return Friday for an ultrasound.

My clinic is doing a clinical trial. I actually think they are doing two IVF trials right now. I'm waiting for a call back from the research department for the details of the second one. I have included the inclusion/exclusion information for one of the trials. If accepted, you will get a free cycle... I figured it is worth posting. Their number is 401.453.7500

Ages Eligible for Study: 35 Years to 42 Years
Genders Eligible for Study: Female
Criteria

Inclusion Criteria:

Willing and able to provide written informed consent for trial P06029 as well as for the Frozen-Thawed Embryo Transfer (FTET) follow-up trial P06031, and for the pharmacogenetic analysis (if applicable).

Female and >=35 to <=42 years of age with indication for COS and IVF/ICSI. Body weight ≥50.0 kg, BMI >=18.0 to <=32.0 kg/m2. Regular spontaneous menstrual cycle with variation not outside the 24-35 days. Ejaculatory sperm must be available (donated and/or cryopreserved sperm is allowed). Results of clinical laboratory tests, cervical smear, physical examination within normal limits or clinically acceptable to the investigator. Adhere to trial schedule.

Exclusion Criteria:

A recent history of/or any current endocrine abnormality.

A history of ovarian hyper-response or ovarian hyperstimulation syndrome.

A history of/or current polycystic ovary syndrome.

More than 20 basal antral follicles <11>15.0 IU/L or LH >12.0 IU/L during the early follicular phase.

Positive for HIV or Hepatitis B.

Contraindications for the use of gonadotropins or GnRH antagonists.

A recent history of/or current epilepsy, thrombophilia, diabetes, cardiovascular, gastro-intestinal, hepatic, renal or pulmonary or auto-immune disease requiring regular treatment.

Smoking or recently stopped smoking (i.e., within the last 3 months prior to signing informed consent).

A recent history or presence of alcohol or drug abuse.

The subject or the sperm donor has known gene defects, genetic abnormalities, or abnormal karyotyping, relevant for the current indication or for the health of the offspring.

Prior or concomitant medications disallowed by protocol.

THURSDAY, JANUARY 20, 2011

Estradiol High

Well, we got the answer to my killer headaches. My e2 levels doubled over night. Yesterday, my e2 was somewhere around 700. Today's blood work showed e2 levels of 1358. Dr. P sent me an email that said "Your estrogen is flying... just warning you that I have to drop your dose again. AND you're stuck seeing us pretty much every day until you get triggered!" For the amount of follicles I had in there yesterday, this makes sense. The only thing that makes me nervous is that it doubled over night AND the follicles weren't mature yet. I just hope the follicles are growing at the right pace (alongside the e2 levels). If the e2 gets too high, it can be dangerous because it puts you at risk for hyperstimulation. I found this on the Internet (if Dr. P reads this post, she'll kill me. She's always scolding me for looking things up).

A level of 1,500 pg/ml on day eleven might be considered acceptable in a stimulated cycle, as reflecting the presence of a reasonable number of mature follicles. However, if this level were present on day eight, it would be considered unacceptably high. It would almost certainly reflect the presence of an excess of follicles. At this stage (day eight) they would still be immature ones. Their quantity, however, would suggest that continued stimulation would carry an unacceptable risk of developing OHSS-- ovarian hyperstimulation syndrome.

Before we continue, one important point: levels of estradiol are not the same from person to person. They cannot simply be compared from one to another. People vary-- everyone is slightly different, and everyone responds to a different degree. Some more so than others. A level that is dangerously high in one person-- or dangerously low in a second-- might be normal and healthy for a third. This is why blood levels can't just simply be compared. It's also why blood levels can't always be interpreted with complete certainty in the first cycles. Without prior cycles to 'calibrate' the levels, the meaning of a level can only be determined as to what it usually means-- what it 'probably' or perhaps even 'almost certainly' means.

Those levels reflect seven days of stim. According to the above statement, I'm in dangerous zone. Dr. P is very VERY conservative. If she thought I was at risk, she would have either lowered my dose more or told me not to take it at all tonight. I shouldn't be worried...but of course, I am. I have an ultrasound and blood work tomorrow morning (yes, I'll have to brave the storm to get there). We'll know more then. Until then, here's to being crampy and full!

FRIDAY, JANUARY 21, 2011

Cool, Calm, and Collected

I drove through a snow storm (we literally have close to three feet of snow here. It's from four different storms) this morning to have my ultrasound and blood work. It usually takes me 25 minutes to get to the clinic. Today, it took me just under four hours round trip. During that time, B sent me an email that said "Man. Please be safe. I like having you as a wife." Hahahaha... Thanks Lovey!

My e2 was 1,736. Dr. P emailed me this afternoon saying, "so happy! Estrogen is slowing down... 1,736 today. Same dose, back tomorrow, but act surprised when the nurses call you)." Phew! I have been cool, calm and collected this entire cycle... until today. When my dose was dropped yesterday because of my e2 doubling, I was expecting to have a lot of mature follicles. Today, I didn't. I had nine mature follicles (measuring between 12-17) and 15 that were still immature. Even the mature ones are on the small side of maturity. So all of them, mature and immature, need more time. After I got Dr. P's email, I relaxed. Having my e2 slow down, gives us time to continue stimming.

We have absolutely nothing planned (thanks to the Patriots losing) this weekend. I really have to clean since I won't be cleaning after the transfer. Speaking of the Patriot's. I never had to take my shot at the stadium. We sucked so bad that the game ended earlier than expected. I did however; have to take the shot in the car. It actually hurt badly. I think the pain was from the meds being so cold.

I do have one new side effect. Body pimples. Yep, I have them on my back and my boobs. Not my chest, my actual boob. Sexy right!?! I only have a few on my boobs but still... gross! My back is a different story. It's covered like a pubescent teen's face. I don't mind temporary side effects. As long as they go away after the cycle.

The plan for tonight is for me to take the same dose (112.5) tonight and return in the morning for blood work and an ultrasound. Come on follies, grow!

SATURDAY, JANUARY 22, 2011

Hello Auntie Cindi :)

While I was sitting in the waiting room for my blood work/ultrasound today, I read an article about infertility in the United States. It was only a few sentences long (in Conceive Magazine) and basically just said that it's on the rise. It was a short and vague article so I decided to do some of my own research. The CIA has reports out on all countries and their fertility rates. The United States is sadly, listed at 125. The top, most fertile countries are:
1. Niger (Africa)
2. Uganda (Africa)

3. Mali (Africa)
4. Somalia (Africa)
5. Burundi (Africa)
6. Burkina Faso (Africa)
7. Democratic Republic of the Congo (Africa)
8. Ethiopia (Africa)
9. Zambia (Africa)
10. Angola (Africa)
11. Republic of the Congo (Africa)
12. Malawi (Africa)

I intended to only share the top five. Once I saw that the top five were all African Nations, I decided to keep going down list. Afghanistan breaks the trend coming in at #12. What is the African culture doing differently than we are here in the United States? I read some studies that mentioned developing countries limiting themselves to less children to prevent over population. I'm sure that plays a slight role (or a major role in countries like China that have a one child limit law) in the fertility rate. However, the average woman in Niger will carry and deliver seven (the average for the other regions were all six) children. I guarantee you will not now nor ever see a fertility clinic in Africa. Infertility affects 6.1 million people in the United States. What are we doing here, that is causing such high infertility numbers? Is it an age thing? Are we waiting too long to have children? Is it our highly processed foods? Is it all the technologies we surround ourselves with? Do we focus too much on work? I don't know. I like to think 31 is not old. We eat a very clean, healthy diet consisting of fresh (organic) fruits and vegetables. We only eat Organic, free range/wild caught meats. I work to live and not live to work. Although, until recently, I did have a stressful work place. I don't know. We're definitely doing something that is effecting our reproduction. I just don't know what it is. Maybe I should take a trip to Africa and do some research.

Today's results:
e2- 2,700
14 follicles measuring 12-17
17 follicles under 12

Dr. P messaged me and said that the on call doctor called her and they agreed to "be greedy" and push me one more day. She said "we truly could have triggered you today but we decided to be greedy." I will take the lowest dose possible (75) of Gonal-f tonight and return in the morning for more blood work and another ultrasound. Those are just routine. I definitely will not go another day. I'll trigger tomorrow night and have egg retrieval on Tuesday. Almost there!

SUNDAY, JANUARY 23, 2011

I'm a machine

I'm a machine. Being a machine comes with consequences. Today I had 16 follicles measuring between 13-23mm. I'm INSANELY nauseous. I keep eating because it temporarily soothes the nausea. My estrogen jumped from 2,700 yesterday to 4,700 today. YIKES! I'm now in danger zone. Dr. P called in a drug (oral, not injection) that I have to start immediately and continue for eight days. We also had to buy a scale to monitor my weight. One of the initial signs of OHSS is rapid weight gain (two or more pounds a day). As I was drafting this post, the on call doctor called me. He wanted to make sure that I fully understood that situation that I'm in. First, I asked him about my nausea. He said that there is no doubt in his mind that my nausea level is through the roof. I took some notes during our conversation...

1. Half dose of hCG

hCG makes OHSS worse so they want me to take only have my dose of hCG (trigger medicine) tonight. I take the shot at 7:30 tonight. Retrieval surgery is scheduled for 7:30 am Tuesday.

2. Retrieval is going to be longer than normal

Since they are fairly sure I am going to have OHSS, they expect my time in recovery to be longer. Normally they only rupture the mature follicles. The follicles contain granulose cells (which increase the severity of OHSS).

3. Granulose Cells

A granulose cell or follicular cell is a somatic cell of the sex cord that is closely associated with the developing female gamete (called an oocyte or egg) in the ovary of mammals.

4. Long term issues

OHSS is generally made worse by pregnancy. The doctor said "We highly anticipate you getting pregnant. Pregnancy makes hyperstimulation worse. You will then have a very sick and uncomfortable first trimester. You will also have to be monitored very closely."

5. Initial OHSS Discomfort

The initial discomfort that I will experience will all stem from bloat. With OHSS your blood gets thicker due to losing fluid. Your body responds to this with pain and bloat. He also said I will have difficulty urinating.

6. Transfer

If we can keep this at the mild or moderate stage (they're taking all the precautions to do so), then we will continue with a transfer on Friday. If the OHSS gets severe, then we will have to freeze our embryos and not do a transfer this cycle. We'll cross that bridge if we have to.

I guess I should be freaking out but I'm just grateful that everything else has gone so well. So, it is what it is. I'm preparing for a rough recovery and hoping it all leads to a baby... or two.

Here's a link if you want to learn more about OHSS... http://www.ivf.com/ohss.html

MONDAY, JANUARY 24, 2011

Day Before Retrieval

It's nice to not have any injections today. I woke up, opened the medicine cabinet, and realized "I'm needle free." Wahoo!

We have to check in for pre-op at 7:00 am tomorrow. We know, due to the hyperstim, that surgery and recovery is going to take longer than usual. Normally, we'd be home around 10:30. I'm not sure what time we'll be home tomorrow.

I'll update you all on egg number and how I'm doing as soon as I get home.

TUESDAY, JANUARY 25, 2011

Retrieval

Now that I'm done puking my brains out, I can finally update you all.

The retrieval went well. They got 19 eggs. Since they had to rupture all the follicles (including the small ones) some of the 19 eggs were small which means they'll be no good.

I'm in some pain but it's nothing Vicodin can't fix.

All in all, I'm happy.

WEDNESDAY, JANUARY 26, 2011

Fertilization Report

I mentioned before, that I am a wreck from the retrieval through the transfer. There are just so many things that could go wrong. The eggs could be immature, they may not fertilize, they may fertilize but not develop well. Needless to say, I'm always incredibly nervous.

So far, we have good news. Of the 19 eggs, 17 were mature. They ICSI'd (injected the sperm directly into the egg) all 17 of the mature eggs and 16 fertilized normally. So far, so good. I have to call the lab tomorrow, between 2:00 and 4:00, to see how they are dividing and to get my transfer plan.

I know this all sounds wonderful... which it is. Don't get me wrong. I'm very happy to have such great numbers. To have that many fertilize, is incredible. However, we always have great numbers at this point. Our embryos tend to slow down in development or start to develop poorly. We just need a handful of those 16 to be superstars. All it takes is one... but I'm going to be greedy and say I want three to transfer and a few to freeze. Heck, I've put my body through hell over the past couple of years. I deserve to be greedy.

I feel decent today. I had a working lunch today. I thought I felt great all morning then as I was sitting at the lunch, it took everything I had not to puke on the table. Fortunately, I just had bad nausea and not actual vomit came out of my mouth. I'm not in pain today. I'm sore... like I had a tough ab workout. I'm nauseous but otherwise I feel great.

I was actually bragging to Dr. P... well, not bragging... more being confident with how great I feel. I thought since I felt so great, the OHSS is remaining mild and not getting worse. She told me that it's great for right now but when you get pregnant is when we'll have issues. I'm just happy that she said "WHEN" you get pregnant. I love this new attitude of mine. I only see the bright side. I wonder how long this will last.

Come on maybe babies... divide, grow, divide!

THURSDAY, JANUARY 27, 2011

Day 2 Report

Okay... I'll do this in bullet format because that's how I took my notes:

1. All 16 embryos have divided and are continuing to develop. None of the embryos have a presence of multinucleation (more than one nucleus). Multinucleation is a sign of chromosomal abnormalities.
2. We have five high quality 4-cell embryos. At day 2, they like to see 2-cells. We also have a couple of 6-cells, a couple of 5-cells, three (more) 4-cells and one 3-cell.

When the embryologist told me that the best ones we have are the 4-celled embryos, I questioned the quality of the rest. She said that they're all good. They rate the embryos on several different parameters. The five that got rated "high quality" aced the criteria in those parameters. Confusing, I know. Her exact words were "This Cohort of embryos are on the high end. I don't want you to think otherwise. We like to see 2 cells at this stage in the game. All of your embryos are much further developed than 2 cells." That made me feel better.

3. As far as transferring. Normally, we transfer on day 3 (tomorrow) but because we have so many embryos doing well, they want to push me to a day 5 (Sunday) transfer. However, there is a criterion that needs to be met for that to happen. We are borderline with that criterion. The Lab director, Dr. P, and the doctor working procedures tomorrow all discussed what we should do. They agreed to schedule me for a transfer tomorrow at 9:00 am. The embryologist will look at the embryos in the morning and make a decision if I should come in or if they should cancel tomorrow's transfer and push it to Sunday. She said there is an 80% chance of it getting cancelled tomorrow.

4. What's the difference between a 3-day vs. 5-day transfer? On day 3, the embryos are still in the early stages of development. An embryo that may look good on day 3 could end up being a poor embryo. An embryo on day 3 that is slower to develop may end up being a high quality embryo on day 5. Basically, if you wait until day 5, you have more information on embryo quality therefore; you have a better chance of choosing the embryos with the highest chances of implantation. I'm sure you're wondering, why everyone doesn't always do a 5-day transfer. Dr. P always says "your uterus is the best incubator for the embryos." A petri dish is not a natural environment for embryos to develop in. Some embryos may do poorly in a dish but thrive in the uterus. The lab requires you have a certain number of embryos doing well in order to do a 5-day transfer. If you only have a few good embryos, it's not a smart idea to keep it out of its natural environment longer than necessary.

So, that's that. Right now we're scheduled for a 9:00 am transfer tomorrow. We have to check in at 8:30. The embryologist will be evaluating the embryos at 7:00. They will call after that to let us know what we should do. I go to an acupuncture session before my transfer. This whole "wait for a call" plan makes that tough. I am going to go to acupuncture at 7:15... It may be useless but I'd rather it be useless than miss it.

I can't believe I am going to have anesthesia again tomorrow. I can't wait to puke my guts out.

FRIDAY, JANUARY 28, 2011

Transfer Day

As you can tell by the posting title, we ended up transferring today. Some of the embryos arrested in their development. I'm not surprised by this at all. Normally, they arrest on day 2... They hung on an extra day. Others started to fragment. We had a handful of good ones and three grade 3 (perfect) ones. The embryologist and the doctor said we could have waited until Sunday to transfer but they felt that we would end up transferring the same ones that we would today. Since the uterus is a "safer" more homely place for the embryos, we transferred two of them this morning. One was an 8-cell and one was a 7-cell.

Dr. P called me on her way home last night to discuss how many we will transfer. Normally, we transfer three. We normally transfer three because the quality of the embryos are decent (good enough to transfer and able to implant) but not perfect. OHSS worsens when pregnancy occurs. If by some miracle (after many, many failed cycles) I got pregnant with triplets, it could be very bad. Life threatening. Crazy that infertility made me not even flinch at the words "life threatening." I focused on actually getting pregnant. Who cares if I croak in the process?? Obviously, I do care. They only wanted to transfer one but I pouted and whined and got two.

Since I was under anesthesia for the transfer, B couldn't be in the room. Neither of us would be able to witness the transfer. I asked the doctor if he could take a picture of the transfer. It's a strange request. When you go through infertility treatments, especially as long as we have, you have a sense of losing control. You lose control of your time. You lose control of when you want to "try." You lost control of your body. You lose control of your mind. You lose control of decisions. This cycle we even lost control of our choice for transfer. I wanted to see that the embryos were put in the right spot. It has nothing to do with doubting the doctor. It has everything to do with feeling like I have control of something. I asked, I explained and then we never talked about it again. No one ever gave me a picture so I assumed he couldn't take one (he said if the computer has the capability, he would take one). First thing B said when I walked into the waiting room was "Want to see the picture?" Ahhhhh! The doctor came through!

The image is obviously of my uterus and the surrounding organs. The large spot of black above the red circle is my bladder (nice and full). I put the red circle around my uterus. You can see the triangular shape of the uterus in the center and off to the sides you can see the tubes running into the ovaries. In the center of the uterus there are two white dots. The one on the right is brighter than the one on the left. That my friends, is my control. Our two perfect embryos sitting right where they should be.

Now we just need them to grow, hatch, attach, and implant!

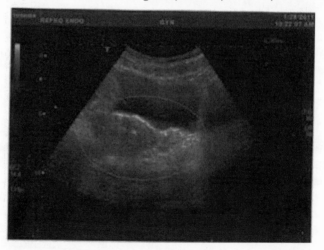

SUNDAY, JANUARY 30, 2011

2dp3dt

Two Days Past 3-Day Transfer and I have zero urges to POAS (pee on a stick). Normally, I start testing right away. Not this time. This time around, I'm not anxious for it to work. Every other cycle, all I wanted was for it to work. I would pray and beg for "this to be our time." God has a plan for me. No matter how much begging or pleading I do, the plan is the plan. If this is our time, I'd be psyched. If not, I know it's just a small part of a bigger plan. I'm sure I'll get the itch to POAS next week. As for right now, I have zero desire to.

The night of the transfer I woke up with severe cramping. SEVERE. I literally just laid in bed for two hours holding my breath and sweating them out. Awesome. There is nothing like terrible cramps early on to make you doubt the cycle. I was bummed about it yesterday morning but quickly got over it.

I have been quite constipated from all the meds. Normally, I'd give you a TMI warning but you're following a fertility blog. Bodily functions and fluids are a common topic of discussion here. Anyway, I've been super constipated so Dr. P told me to take Colace. After a couple of days of Colace, I noticed I was getting really bad cramps from gas. I stopped the Colace because the gas was worse than not going to the bathroom. I was wondering if the pains I had on Friday night were from gas and not my body rejecting embryos (that's what I initially thought). I guess we'll know in ten days. Pooping, gas... Really, this is my life.

I'm done with most of the meds. Now I'm just on baby aspirin, prenatal vitamin and progesterone. For those of you who don't know anything about progesterone... here's a little info. It comes in many forms, the one I take is a vaginal cream. It's in a pre-filled applicator. I take it (I guess it's called taking it???) once a day. It's disgusting. It leaks out of you. It clumps up on your underwear. It's gross. It also makes your body think it's pregnant. My boobs are huge and incredibly sore. My nipples feel like someone is cutting them with razor blades. I'm nauseous and bloated. My uterus even has the "pressure" you get when you're pregnant. Yes, all this joy from a cream that leaks out of you all day. I'm bored with being fake pregnant. I'm ready for real pregnancy... this fake stuff is for the birds! What does that mean anyway? For the birds?

MONDAY, JANUARY 31, 2011

3dp3dt

Well, it's official. I'm an old lady. I have resorted to prune juice. It is absolutely repulsive. I don't know how people regularly drink it. Ugh... I have the chills just thinking about it.

I haven't had any more cramping... which is hopeful.

I still don't have the urge to POAS. We're getting another big snow storm tomorrow through Wednesday. So I definitely will not be buying any before Thursday. Once I have them in my house, I won't be able to resist. Thursday is 6dp3dt and some people get BFPs (big fat positive) that early. The cycle that worked, I didn't get a BFP until 8dp3dt. Only a few more days until we know something.

I caved and called the lab today. Normally, they call you if you have any embryos that made it to freeze. The lab lady first looked in the computer and nothing showed up. She said, "Normally, if there were any that made it to freeze, it would be in the system." I said "Okay, thank you." She said she wanted to check my file before we hung up... "Just in case it just hasn't been put into the computer." When she came back she said "looks like two made it to freeze." Ahhh... snowbabies! Having snowbabies is very exciting but at the same time it's discouraging. We had 16 embryos and only 4 were good. Well, two were definitely good and hopefully the two in me are good. I guess it's not that discouraging. We've never had perfect embryos. Never. We now know we can make them. For so long, we wondered if our body chemistry's will always make a weak embryo. It seems like every cycle, even with a negative result, we end up learning something positive. So even if this cycle doesn't work, we know that it's just a matter of finding that one lucky embryo... and we can make it.

Today is the day the embryos should start attaching themselves to my uterus and begin the implanting process. Attach Embryos!

TUESDAY, FEBRUARY 1, 2011

4dp3dt

Ahhh... the dreaded period cramps came today. I know what you're all thinking "it's way too early." Didn't this happen with my FET? I swore my period was coming a week before my beta and everyone said it was too early... I ended up being correct. I think... I'll go through my October 2010 posts to see if I'm remembering it correctly. Anyway, I have not just period like cramps, I also have lower back cramping (which usually comes with my period).

I also am having crazy food aversions. Every morning, for as long as I can remember, I eat two egg whites (hard boiled form) for breakfast. Yesterday they tasted a little funky but I was able to stomach them. Today, uh ah. No way was that thing being consumed. It was making me gag. I also have a weird metal taste in my mouth. The metal taste could be why I can't eat my favorite foods (minus Girl Scout Cookies... I can ALWAYS eat those). I'm only four days past the transfer so the ONLY thing it can be, is the progesterone.

Speaking of the progesterone. A friend of mine told me that the Cronin will build up in your cervix and you have to remove it with your finger. This morning, I put on a latex glove and dug right in. She was right... that stuff really does build up in there! I made a lot of room for fresh progesterone by getting a lot of yucky clumps out. Maybe now when I laugh or pass gas, it won't leak out.

Today is the last day of implantation (if it's happening). Here's to hoping and praying...

WEDNESDAY, FEBRUARY 2, 2011

5dp3dt

I got the dreaded cramps in the middle of the night. When I got them, I grabbed my journal that I keep in my nightstand and took notes. I documented every detail I could. I always tell Dr. P about them after the fact and have not been able to figure out how to prevent them. I swore up and down it was my body rejecting embryos. The first thing I did this morning was send Dr. P an email with all the details of the cramps. Here's her response:

"It's your bladder! It totally sounds like bladder spasms. Not sure that everything, every cycle was your bladder, but THIS sounds like your bladder. Often with big ovaries people have trouble emptying completely or have more bladder sensitivity/symptoms. The location is right too because it IS RIGHT above your public bone! That's great news!"

This actually makes sense for me. I was in a really bad car accident in college (hit by a drunk driver). I had some serious bladder issues due to trauma from the steering wheel. I had 17... Yes 17 UTIs in one year. I had so much scar tissue around my bladder that would cause my bladder to spasm (which caused the UTIs). I lived on antibiotics. Finally, I had to have surgery to fix it. That was in 1999. I've never had issues with it since. It actually never crossed my mind to ever mention it to anyone, including Dr. P. I'm glad she's so smart and figured it out. That is one of the many reasons we love her so much.

Yesterday, I had to brave the storm (yet again) for acupuncture. I thought it would take me much longer than it did. When I arrived 30 minutes early, I wasted some time at the Pharmacy. I needed some more baby aspirin and of course, I bought some HPTs. When I say some, I mean eight... six FRER (First Response Early Result) and two Clearblue digital.

I did POAS this morning. I can't have the tests in my possession and not obsess with them. I just can't. They're addicting. I took two today. I know... ridiculous. The first one I took this morning at 6:30. When I first looked at the test it was negative. When I looked at it about 20 minutes later, there was a FAINT and I mean FAINT, second line. You're not supposed to look at it after ten minutes because an evaporation line can appear. Normally, I break them apart so I won't keep looking at them. I didn't break this one apart. My intentions, when I went back and grabbed it, were to break it into pieces. That's when I saw the second line. It is VERY early. VERY, VERY, VERY, Early to actually be positive. I'm seven days before a "normal" person would miss a period. VERY Early. I decided to stop my mind from going crazy by taking another one (around 2:30). That one did not have the faint second line. Most likely, the second line this morning was an evaporation line. I doubt I have any hCG left in my system from the trigger. In previous cycles, the trigger was out of my system within a few days. I took half the dose I usually take so the chances of that being what caused the line are slim. I sent the picture of the test to Dr. P and she saw the line too. I'm not crazy or making it up. It was there... we're just not sure why. We'll see what tomorrow brings.

THURSDAY, FEBRUARY 3, 2011

6dp3dt

I have to go to work, so this will be a short post. I figured you were all as anxious as I was this morning so I figured I would update you now instead of after dinner. I took another test... again at 6:30. The line is still there. It's taking about five minutes to show up instead of three. It's strange how it's showing up. It starts of as a white line then turns pink around minute five. It is so faint... soooo faint. I actually tried taking a picture for you all and it doesn't even show up on the camera. If we were a few days before my beta, I'd be nervous. It is so early. Most people would say too early. Since we're a full week away from my beta, I'm not worried. I do have two digital tests. Those things are black and white. PREGNANT or NOT PREGNANT. There are no misinterpretations in those. They are also super-duper expensive. I'd hate to waste them. They're not supposed to be used until four days before a missed period. That would be Sunday for me. Maybe, I'll use it Saturday. It would still be early but not terribly early.

FRIDAY, FEBRUARY 4, 2011

7dp3dt- UPDATED

I've been having a lot of trouble sleeping. I'm sure it's due to my brain being on overdrive. I've been up since 1:30... Fun!

I took another test this morning and it's clear as day negative. Stark white. I'm not sure what the lines were that we were seeing. I'll upload a picture of one of them so you don't think I'm crazy. I think a couple of things could have or could be happening.

1. The hCG trigger was still in my system. Although possible, I find this unlikely since in previous cycles I've taken double the dose. When I've tested in the past, it has been out of my system a couple days after the retrieval.

2. I'm experiencing a chemical pregnancy. A chemical pregnancy is a very early miscarriage. Basically, a pregnancy has occurred and detected but is miscarried before a heartbeat is detected.

Although I was seeing positive tests, I wasn't quite excited. One of the blessings of infertility is that it prepares you for the good, bad and the ugly. This cycle, no matter the outcome, has been a blessing in many ways. For the first time we were able to create "perfect" or what seem to be perfect embryos. Up until this cycle, we were not able to do so and we didn't know if it was possible. We now know that it is possible and it is just a matter of time. We just need to find that one perfect embryo.

A couple/few years ago we were at a friend's house. We were in the two week wait for our first IUI. As we were sitting around the fire pit, we were talking about the IUI... the process, the probabilities, etc. One of the couples that were there had gone through fertility treatments. At one point they mentioned that it took them five years to get pregnant. Later in the evening, as B and I were driving home, we started talking about how sad it was that it took them that long. We even talked about how there was no way it would take us that long. Ahhh... and here we are.

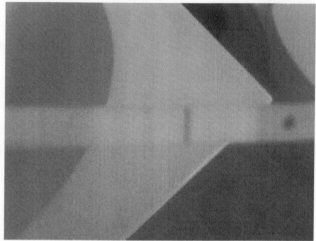

Here is one of the tests from yesterday. I'm not crazy nor was I seeing something that wasn't there... right??!?!

UPDATE:

After several people mentioned the blue dye tests showing evaporation lines, I did my very best to take a picture of the pink tests. Pink dye is very hard to get on camera so I circled all the lines. I promise you, in real life they are visible... no squinting, no special florescent lights needed. The last one... without a line... is one of the ones from today.

SATURDAY, FEBRUARY 5, 2011

8dp3dt

The time has come for us to get ready for round five. The tests (I took three different brands) all came back negative today. I know what you're going to say... It is still early. It could be a late implanter. It's not. Game over. Dr. P has agreed to let me do my blood test on Monday so I can stop all the meds. My plans for Monday are: 1) Wake up 2) Eat Breakfast 3) Go in for Beta 4) Work 5) Run 50 miles 6) Lift weights for 12 hours straight 7) Vacuum my house. I always thought it was weird that "no vacuuming" was on the list of things not to do.

Many of you are going to say sorry or feel bad. Please don't. We're not sad. Frustrated... yes. Sad... no. I know it's hard for people on the outside to understand... especially those with children. This is a thorn in our side. It's a struggle that has gone on for three years too many. However, it's not the end all be all. There is much more to life than having children. Of course we want them... very badly. What woman doesn't want to experience carrying a child? Although we want this to work, we don't live our life consumed by this. This is just a small portion of us. We are not defined by this. Nothing in our lives change by this not working. Nothing. We will still wake up and do the same things that we always do. We will still laugh at the same jokes. We will still have dinner with friends. Nothing changes. Even if your inclination is to feel bad or sad. Don't. It's a waste of emotion.

We have an appointment with Dr. P on Wednesday. It was originally scheduled for the end of February. We changed it so we can have a plan in place before I get my period...which will be as soon as I stop the progesterone. We have two snowbabies. We're going to keep them frozen for a while. I'd rather do another fresh cycle. Fresh cycles have a higher success rate. Frozen embryos tend to be weaker because of the freezing and thawing process. They also don't always survive the thaw. Hopefully we'll have a couple more make it to freeze. If we have more than two frozen, I'll do a FET (Frozen Embryo Transfer).

I may just vacuum like crazy today. I'm so wild!

SUNDAY, FEBRUARY 6, 2011

9dp3dt

I cannot wait for my beta test tomorrow. I'm not looking forward to the results or the awkward call with the nurse. I'm looking forward to being done with Progesterone and preparing to start again.

During our pre-transfer consultation, the doctor said "You have had a success. Not only does that mean you have embryos that can survive, it also tells us all the plumbing works correctly." Yes, I have been pregnant. How can you call it a success when it ended up in the town sewer? Drives us nuts when they say that. NUTS.

It still amazes me that people can just get pregnant. After all we know, how do some people ACCIDENTALLY get pregnant? There is just so much involved and so much that can go wrong. Of course, with only 12%... I shouldn't say only, a few million people is a lot... with 12% of the population being infertile, 88% of the population have no struggles what so ever. A friend said to me the other day "I am amazed nowadays that people get excited when seeing a positive test..." I'm with her. After a positive test, there is so much more involved before you take home a healthy baby. The day I heard Baby L's heartbeat, was the same day I miscarried. Usually hearing the heartbeat puts you into the "safe zone." Reproduction is mysterious... at least to me.

I've said it before and I'll say it again... If anyone HAS to go through this, I'd rather it be me. I don't wish this on my worst enemy. I know I can handle this. It's emotionally and physically grueling but only a select few are capable of handling it. I am one of them. I'm a strongly believe that God only gives you as much as you can handle. I keep telling myself to fall apart and be a mess so He thinks I can't handle it anymore. Haha... maybe I should have a breakdown and then I'll be at my "can't handle anymore" point.

I vacuumed like crazy yesterday. I vacuumed the floors, furniture, curtains. I steam mopped the floors. It's funny how badly you want to do something just because you were told you can't. Yesterday, I said I didn't understand why they say not to vacuum. Well, I understand now. After I was done I was cramping VERY badly. I had to lay down.

Superbowl Sunday. The Patriots aren't playing but to me, they're already Superbowl Champs. I mean, they did beat the Steelers and the Packers this year... right?!?! If anything is going to make me have a breakdown, it will be thinking about that Jets game... aye.

MONDAY, FEBRUARY 7, 2011

Beta Day: UPDATED

Yay! No, that's not sarcasm... I am actually excited to go in for a Beta that I know is negative. I know this sounds deranged. I swear, I'm sane. The fact that I woke up singing "The Time of My Life" (no, not the Black Eyed Peas version... I'm singing old school, Dirty Dancing version) may not help my stance in sanity. Being genuinely happy for a day that would make most woman a basket case is also not helping my case in sanity. Okay... on a side note, I just Googled "basket case" after I typed it. I knew it meant "crazy" but I wasn't sure where it came from. This is what Wikipedia says: Basket Case originally, a British slang for a quadruple amputee during World War I, may also mean: Derogatory slang for a mentally-ill person or a badly run organization. I don't like that. I am not going to use that term any longer. Let me rephrase... Being genuinely happy for a day that would make most women an emotional wreck, is also NOT helping my stance in sanity. Needless to say, I'm excited.

I woke up with a killer migraine and period cramps. I meant to not take the progesterone so my period can come. Taking all my pills and progesterone has been my morning routine for so long. Even though I meant to not take it, habit made me take it anyway. Once that beta call comes in, I'll be eating up lots of Advil to kill these cramps.

Every week when I go to church, I feel like the pastor is speaking to me. Which is why I like my church so much. The sermons are relevant to everyone. The way it goes at my church is like this... the band plays three or four songs, the pastor will do a 30 minute sermon, and then the band closes with another song. The second song the band played yesterday was about all the miracles God performs. There was a line that they kept singing over and over again. It was "He gave a barren woman a house full of kids." No lie. No Joke. I guess that is partly why I am in such a great mood. I know this will happen... it's just a matter of time.

"Remember, happiness doesn't depend upon who you are or what you have; it depends solely upon what you think." - Dale Carnegie -

UPDATE:

Well, we got a beta shocker. I asked for an early beta so I could get some closure... instead, I got some gray. My beta came back positive. It's low... 15. It's low but it's still two days earlier than usual. All night, I kept praying that my beta would come back at 6 (above 5 is positive). Even if the cycle didn't work, I just wanted to regain faith in my uterus. I wanted confirmation that my body can do it. Dr. P keeps telling me/us, over and over again that my body is 100% okay and the issue is our embryo quality. Whether this pregnancy lasts or not, this beta helped me regain confidence in my body. I go back on Wednesday to see if the levels rise. They need to double every 48 hours. We want it to be at least 35 on Wednesday. GROW!

TUESDAY, FEBRUARY 8, 2011

11dp3dt

After I got home from work yesterday, I thought it was a good time to POAS. My beta was 15... Extremely low...but high enough for a pregnancy test to detect it. Sure enough, after days of negatives, the faint pink line arrived. I took another line test today to compare it to yesterdays. If my beta is rising, the line should get darker. And it did. Then I took a digital test. The digitals usually pick up hCG levels around 25. The digital came up "PREGNANT." My beta is definitely rising... fingers crossed that it's rising a lot. We need it to at least double. AT LEAST.

My beta on my previous pregnancy was 86 on 12dp3dt (tomorrow). 86 is right in the middle of what the doctors want to see at that point. They like to see your beta between 50-100. Your levels generally double every 48 hours. Even if mine doubles, that would put me at 30... Well below what they want to see. When I addressed my concerns for the very low number with Dr. P she replied with "The number doesn't necessarily matter. It's the doubling that does." So... double, double, double! Actually, I'm going to be selfish... triple, triple, triple!

I know everyone's reaction is to be excited and send lots of "congratulations." However, we are far from being safe. 15 is very low. The numbers need to double, then double again. Then continue to rise. Then we need to see a heartbeat. After that, we have to get through the first trimester. We're still eight weeks from being safe and we're not even through the first obstacle.

A friend sent me a very sweet (and much needed) email yesterday. There was one line that really struck me. He said, "I find when you're looking for a miracle, you often find out that you had it inside of you all along." I absolutely LOVE this line. It's so true. We constantly are looking for miracles. When we do find them, we realize, we had it in us the entire time.

Here are the pictures. The pink lines are really hard to get on a picture... especially a phone picture. The first one was taken at 4:00 pm yesterday. The second one was taken this morning at 5:30 (I know. I have serious sleeping issues). The digital was also taken this morning.

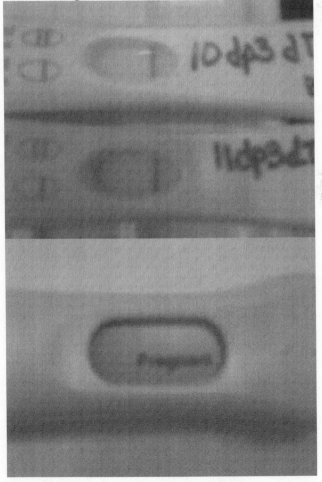

WEDNESDAY, FEBRUARY 9, 2011

12dp3dt: UPDATED

Late afternoon, early evening, I got one of the worst migraines I have ever had. I guess it wasn't the worst but it was one of the most painful. Unfortunately, I know my body all too well. When I get a migraine that severe, it is (generally) due to a major drop in hormones. Although I want to be the one person that defies the odds. Although we've wished for a miracle of all miracles, I know what the beta results are going to be. Since I got the positive digital yesterday, I know that the levels had risen since my beta on Monday. I know, due to the migraine, that my beta has dropped. I'm just not sure how far. It could have gone up initially then dropped. My guess is that it is going to be around what it was on Monday.

We don't allow ourselves to get excited. We know the way this roller coaster works. Our expectations are low. No matter the outcome, I have restored faith in my uterus. We just need to find that one healthy embryo.

When I talked to Dr. P on Monday, we agreed to keep our appointment for this afternoon. If the beta doubled, she would message me and we would cancel the appointment. If it didn't double, we would keep the appointment and discuss the plan for our next cycle. I always get excited for the follow up appointment. I am a planner. I like having a plan. I will update this post as soon as Dr. P messages or calls me.

UPDATE:

My beta came back at 51. It more than tripled. Now, I'm in the normal range. On the first beta (which should have been today) they want the levels to be between 50-100. 51 isn't fantastic but it is trending in the right direction. I guess my migraine was from the increase in hormones... not a decrease. I'm shaking like a leaf... I was a nervous wreck all morning.

FRIDAY, FEBRUARY 11, 2011

4 weeks 3 days: UPDATED

Sorry for not posting yesterday. I was exhausted. If I could have, I would have been in bed by dinner time.

I am very crampy today. Cramping is normal in pregnancy and miscarriage. I can't over think it. All I can do is wait. I went in first thing this morning for another Beta. I think Dr. P is works at the satellite office on Fridays. Since she's not in the main office, I won't get a message with the results. I'll have to wait (like everyone else) for the call after 2:00.

It's strange knowing so much about my levels. Most people find out they're pregnant at home. They then call their OBGYN who will have them come in for blood work. They will receive a call confirming they are pregnant. Then they don't know anything else until they go in for an ultrasound at eight weeks. They never know what their starting Beta is. They never know if their levels are doubling. All they know is that they are pregnant. Having all this information just adds stress and worry to the process. The positive in knowing all the details is that if a miscarriage is going to happen, you know in advance. You can, somewhat, prepare for it. Not that you can prepare all that much for a miscarriage.

I wish it was legal to show a picture of my boobs right now. Actually, I think it is legal... I just wouldn't post them on the Internet... or take pictures of them at all. Anyway, last night we were getting ready for bed and I said to B "Look at these things. I look like a porn star." Seriously, my boobs are gigantic. I never wanted big boobs. I like my little ones. They fit into clothes easily. I can run without them hitting me in the face. However, I am realizing that big boobs make your body look skinnier. Not bad.

I'll update this as soon as I hear something.

UPDATE:

Beta came back at 114. It more than doubled. I'm still really nervous. Every time I go to the bathroom, I inspect the toilet paper expecting to see blood. I'm not being negative. It's just all I know. My history with pregnancy is poor. I took a personal day today so I can worry and not be focused. I'm not sure when my next Beta will be. My guess is either Sunday or Monday. The nurse will call me after 2:00. For now, I am going to watch TV and do nothing.

SATURDAY, FEBRUARY 12, 2011

4 Weeks 4 Days

Yesterday was a rough day. I started the day with moderate cramping. Slowly throughout the day, the cramps progressed to severe. It got to the point where I couldn't walk. At one point, I was laying on the kitchen floor, hysterically crying because I couldn't get to the couch. My poor dog just sat next to me licking my tears. When I did make it to the couch, I was literally rolled up in the fetal position, shivering from the pain. I knew what it all meant, I was starting to miscarry. I talked to Dr. P in the early evening. She said it could be one of two things.

1. Uterine contractions/Start of Miscarriage
2. OHSS getting worse with the pregnancy

She told me to take Vicodin for the pain. I refused "just in case." She reassured me that Vicodin is perfectly safe in pregnancy. She said that there is no evidence that suggests Vicodin causes birth defects. The only worry about Vicodin use in pregnancy is when it is used long term, the baby could develop dependence. Still, I didn't want to take it. She said that if I won't take Vicodin, take extra strength Tylenol. I wouldn't take that either. I ended up taking two regular strength Tylenol. It did absolutely nothing.

Around 8:00 I started spotting. The spotting was very light and remained very light. I never actually saw blood drops. I only saw pink toilet paper when I wiped. Either way, we all know what that means. Once I started spotting, the pain got worse. That's when I was shivering on the couch; writhing with pain. I felt bad for B as he wanted to do something but there was nothing to do. When I started shivering from the pain, I took a Vicodin. It didn't even dull the pain. Not even the slightest. Around midnight, I was finally able to fall asleep and go to bed.

I woke up at 4:00 am and didn't have any cramps. For a few minutes I thought "Maybe it is the OHSS." I was proven wrong when I woke up at 6:30. I got up, went to the bathroom and BOOM... the cramps are back. They are definitely not as severe as last night. However, they are much more severe than how they started yesterday. I think I'm in for another rough day.

SATURDAY, FEBRUARY 12, 2011

Optimism

I love the optimism you all have. One thing you all know by now is that I know my body very well. There is a reason why I wasn't happy to have my beta double. Even with a doubling beta, I was miscarrying. I knew it. I knew it when I woke up Friday. I knew it when I was having my blood drawn. I knew it when my results were in. Women know their bodies incredibly well. I am no exception to the rule.

I am going to warn you that this post is very graphic. I have also included a very graphic photo. Do not read anymore if you don't want to/can't see or hear it. If you want to read it but don't want to see the pictures, I put pictures of me in the hospital up. The graphic photo is after those.

I debated whether or not I should post images of what you pass during a miscarriage. Many of you read my blog because you can relate to it. Many of you read the blog because you cannot relate to it and you want to learn more. The subject has been taboo. Women tend to feel shame and embarrassment when it comes to miscarriage. I want to be as open as possible. I want to hold nothing back. I want others who are dealing with similar situations to know that they're not alone. For that reason, I decided to document the details as much as possible.

Many people believe that miscarriages are just like periods. Some may say "it's like a heavy period." Maybe that is the case for some people. However, that has never been my experience. My miscarriages have been severely painful. If you read my post yesterday, I was shivering from pain and I have a very high pain tolerance. For me to say something is painful, it has to be VERY painful. If anyone gets period cramps like the ones I was experiencing, then there is something seriously wrong with them. The pain you get in a miscarriage isn't just in your uterus (like with a period). It's in your uterine area, ovarian area, side and back. All a miscarriage is, is contractions. If you have had a child, you can relate to that. If you pass masses during your period, like the one in the image below, then you seriously need to see a doctor. A miscarriage is NOT like a period and should never be compared to one.

As the morning progressed yesterday, I started to get lightheaded and dizzy. Anytime I tried to stand up, I would black out. I'm not talking about the kind of blacking out that involves fainting. My vision would go black and then return a few seconds later. Although the pain was all over my abdomen and lower back, it seemed to be more intense on my right side. Having one side hurt more than the other made me nervous. I was afraid (thanks to Google) that my ovary was contorting from the OHSS. I called and left a message at the clinic. At about 9:00 am the on call doctor returned my call. He was concerned that I was losing too much blood which was causing me to black out. At the time, I wasn't bleeding all that much. I had already passed a large clot which I thought (and later was confirmed) was the sac (baby). Other than that, I hadn't been bleeding. He still wanted me to go to the hospital to be examined and to have some levels checked.

We arrived at the hospital sometime around 11:00 am. One very noticeable difference between the fertility clinic and the hospital is the level of sensitivity of the staff. The fertility clinic would NEVER have you repeat why you were in. They would have you say it once and then refer to your chart if they needed to be reminded. Every single person I talked to I had to say "I'm having a miscarriage and my doctor is worried about anemia and OHSS." Not only did I have to say out loud that I was having a miscarriage. I also had to either say myself or hear them say to me "This is your second pregnancy. Zero children." Correct!! Now please, stop rubbing it in.

After having three vials of blood drawn at triage, I was checked into a room. "Get naked, put this gown on with the opening in the back and if needed wedge this pad in between your legs." No thanks sweetheart. If I am going to suffer through a miscarriage in a ugly hospital gown, on a stirrup conversion bed, I am going to bleed all over the sheets. You can clean it up later. I'm not going to sit here, without panties on, holding a massive pad between my legs.

About 45 minutes later, I was brought into an ultrasound room. As the doctor was putting my info into the computer (yes, I had to say, yet again, why I was there and I had to say second pregnancy, zero children) she said "Your doctor ordered a beta and it came back at 89. That's good." I then I had to tell her, the DOCTOR, that I was definitely having another miscarriage. There I was, the patient, telling the doctor what was happening. She said "well, that's what we're trying to rule out." "My beta was 114 yesterday, I'm definitely having another miscarriage." She then says "Oh. I'm sorry." I could feel the let down from B. I didn't even have to look at him. I could just sense it. I didn't reply with "thank you." I replied with "that's okay." I'm not sure who I was trying to convince that it was okay. Her, myself, or B.

Before the ultrasound, the doctor wanted to do an exam. "You will feel my fingers on your thigh." I just wanted to laugh and say "Sweetie, I have random nurse fingers, hands, and ultrasound probes up in there hundreds of times a year. You don't have to warn me about your fingers on my THIGH." Of course, all I said was "Okay." Once she got the speculum in, she asked the nurse for some swabs (I'm not sure if that's what they're called. They're the huge Q-tip thingies). She started cleaning out my cervix. As she was doing so, she said that she was collecting fetal tissue that was sitting in my cervix. They will send the tissue to the lab for tests. Basically, they will be able (if they collected enough) to tell us what was wrong with the baby. It seemed like she collected a lot. I don't know, maybe she just liked the sight of my cervix. After that, she did a PAINFUL exam. She was all up in there. After she left the room, I turned to B and said "She was so rough. I just got fingered by a monster." Finally, it was time for the ultrasound. At first, they couldn't find my uterus. They had me empty my bladder because they thought it was taking up most of the monitor. Sure enough, after I went to the bathroom, they had no problem finding my uterus. My empty uterus. My lining was HUGE. REALLY HUGE. Which, it should be. It was also empty. So the thing I passed in the morning (image below) was the sac. Both miscarriages, I passed the sac whole. This may sound sad or gross but it's actually a very good thing. My body did what it needed to so a D&C is (usually) not necessary. They also looked at my ovaries. My left ovary was normal size. My right ovary was not. It was very enlarged. The extreme pain I was getting on my right size was a combination of the miscarriage and my ovary being big and sore from OHSS.

Then, we were discharged with a big "Sorry" and a $50 co-pay. On our way home, B asked me how I was doing mentally. I'll say to you all what I said to him. I'm okay. I wasn't excited about this pregnancy. My intuition was telling me that something wasn't right. My body was telling me that it wasn't going to last. I was prepared. People tend to pity and feel bad for infertility patients. When in fact, they should be envious of the strength (definitely not of the struggle) we have. We are strong, stoic, brave, spirited, and resilient. We are the most resilient people around. I asked B the same question. His response "defeated." I told him that defeat can only come at an end. We're not at the end. We will beat this thing. We will not end defeated.

I woke up around 5:30 this morning in so much pain. My belly was distended and hard as a rock. I was vomiting from the pain. I decided to take a hot shower to see if that would help. It didn't. Then I decided to act as if I were in labor. I have watched enough labor and delivery shows to know what is soothing during labor. While I was in the shower I was squatting and pushing as hard as I could. I know that makes me sound like a nutcase but I figured if they say miscarriages are the same thing as labor contractions, why not try it. It actually helped a lot. The pushing was very soothing for the cramps. I stayed in there for over an hour. When I first woke up, I took 800mg of Motrin and a Vicodin. That didn't kick in until about 20 minutes ago. Now I feel better. My flow is very heavy today. I'm going through about two pads an hour. It's zero fun.

Now that we have had two miscarriages, we qualify to do PGD (Preimplantation Genetic Diagnosis). With PGD, they biopsy the embryo on day 3 for any abnormalities. Then they will transfer the normal ones on day 5. We have always known our issue is embryo quality. The success rates with PGD are lower because the biopsy can damage the embryo. For us, the benefits outweigh the risks. I rather have nothing to transfer on day 5 than transfer what appears to be a healthy embryo and have another miscarriage.

Yesterday I enjoyed every second of taking Motrin. Last night we had sushi. Today I am going to have coffee... with caffeine. I can always find a positive in a negative. Motrin, Sushi and Coffee... It has been a long time!

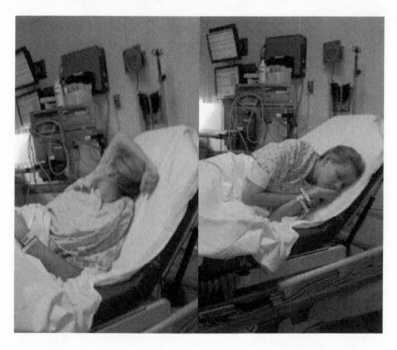

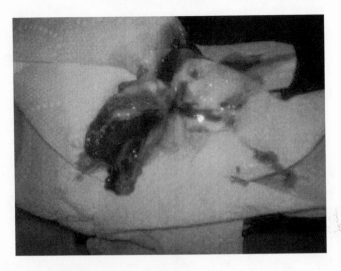

WEDNESDAY, FEBRUARY 16, 2011

WTF Appointment

First off, let me say, I feel great. The miscarriage was fast and furious. It was done as fast as it came. The bleeding only lasted three days. I had a beta today to see what my levels are at. I have a feeling that it's very close to being back to normal... if not already normal. My last miscarriage, it only took five days to go from 1,500 to 11. I'm going to try to remember everything we talked about at the appointment. We were there for three hours so my brain is full of information.

1. Progesterone: I asked about my progesterone levels (thanks to some insight from a friend). My levels have been normal throughout every cycle. However, since there is no harm in doing the progesterone in oil (PIO), Dr. P suggested that we do it the next cycle. We're doing it for no other reason than "why not." The only bummer is that it is an intramuscular injection that goes into your lower back. Not pleasant.

2. Reasons for recurrent miscarriage: We have already exhausted all testing possibilities for my body. After the last miscarriage, I wanted every test under the sun... all for peace of mind. Most, if not all, of the tests are usually done after two or more miscarriages. Dr. P agreed to do them all last year (probably because I'm so annoying). According to all the tests, my body is not the issue. Granted, there may be things wrong that we cannot test with current technology. With what/how science allows us

to test, we have ruled out my body as being a cause for miscarriage. That leads us to genetics.

3. Preimplantation Genetic Diagnosis (PGD): We have known all along that our embryo quality generally leans on the poor side. You may remember, several months ago (sometime after the first miscarriage) I asked Dr. P to run a karyotype testing on both B and me. Karyotype is a profile of a person's chromosomes. The purpose of testing the Karyotypes is to see how the chromosomes look... size, shape, and number of chromosomes. You would think that if there was an abnormality, we would have a genetic problem. You have two sets of chromosomes. One could be abnormal and one could be normal. Since you have a normal one, you are a normal, healthy person. Since an embryo takes half the chromosomes from the egg and half from the sperm, the embryo could end up abnormal. To make a longer story longer, both of our Karyotypes came back normal. Normal Karyotypes does not mean you will only have normal off spring.

PGD searches for 12 chromosomal abnormalities within the embryo. There are more abnormalities that you can test for. However, the 12 abnormalities that they test account for 98% of miscarriages due to chromosomal issues. There are 24 or 26 (I already forget what the PGD doctor said) abnormalities. The reason they don't test for the other ones is because only 2% of miscarriages happen from those abnormalities. She also said that if those other abnormalities are found, those embryos wouldn't even implant. The tests they run make up for 98% of the chromosomal miscarriages... I'm comfortable with that.

The PGD doctor pulled up our lab report from this past cycle. All of our embryos would have been biopsied and sent to the lab. She said even the few that arrested in development would be sent. Obviously, those embryos wouldn't be used in a transfer but it would give us an answer on what happened with them.

We have heard that the success rates are lower with PGD. The PGD doctor said that there was one study that suggested PGD lowered success rates but she discounted that study. It was in a poor journal (not peer reviewed). It was a poorly supported study and it was the only study. She also mentioned that although there is no evidence that supports PGD lowering success rates, there is also no evidence that supports PGD increasing success rates. She told us to look at it like another selection criteria. All IVF embryo cohorts will have abnormal embryos in them. Without PGD, we are trusting the naked eye (well, naked with a scope) to pick which ones "seem" normal. With a fertile person, their embryo could divide slowly. Have some fragmentation and still end up with a normal, healthy live birth. She used our previous embryos as an example. She said "we threw all these away because they didn't look like we think they should look. When in reality, they could have been normal embryos. The ones that were transferred were obviously the best looking but clearly not normal."

The steps in PGD are fairly straight forward.

On day 3 of development: Opening the Zona (the outer layer of the egg/embryo)

Biopsy of one cell. Cell is placed on slide and sent to a lab in NJ for analysis

Transfer of normal embryos on day 5

PGD, although very scientific, is not an exact science. Every cell in an embryo is different. They could biopsy an embryo and take the one cell that ends up abnormal but the embryo itself is normal. They would destroy that embryo because the cell they took showed an abnormality. At the same time, they could take a cell that is normal but the other cells are abnormal. They could transfer an embryo that tested normal but really wasn't. I forget the exact stats on that. It's very low but it is a possibility.

When you have had multiple miscarriages. Two out of four cycles considered a "success" and no live births... PGD is a very good option. The benefits definitely outweigh the risks... at least in our situation.

If our next cycle comes back with zero normal embryos, we will use our frozen ones as back up. That reminds me, she also emphasized that if we have a cycle with zero normal embryos, that doesn't mean we won't ever get one. Her exact words, "you have to remind yourself that this road is going to be long and hard but it will take you to a live birth. I know that is hard to understand when you're going through so much. Just remember, you will get there."

4. Next cycle: I asked Dr. P if it is completely out of the possibility for us to try to get pregnant before the end of March (that's when my good maternity leave plan ends). She said that it's not. It all depends on my levels.

Hopefully, they are nice and low and we can get going again.

5. IMSI (Intracytoplasmic morphology-selected sperm injection): A couple of girls from the AGC group mention IMSI to me. I emailed Dr. P about it yesterday. Today she said, "I wasn't ignoring your email. I was actually in grande rounds when I got your email so I asked the group about it and I put a call into our head embryologist." She said that of everything I Google (I reassured her that this wasn't a Google find... it was a find from friends) and ask her about, this is the only one she finds valid. When doing IMSI, the embryologist uses a microscope with 8000x magnification. It gives a better view of the sperm (size, shape and they can even see inside the sperm's head... crazy, I know). This is a very new technology. When Dr. P mentioned it in grande rounds, they all (doctors, fellows, residents) researched it. They could only find studies in Europe and one other place... I forget where she said. The studies are promising however, until it is studied in the US, most clinics won't invest in a multi-million dollar machine. She did say that in a handful of years, she would expect most labs to have the technology. She said, "with that being said, our goal is to get you pregnant with a healthy baby. I don't want you to ever feel that you have to stay here or can't get a second opinion. If you know of a clinic that has IMSI technology and want to go there, you should." She mentioned that if there are any clinics that have it, she could guess which ones did. She was right, two of the three clinics that she thought would have them, do have them. Those are the only two, we both know of, that do.

Both B and I realize that we could go anywhere else. My group is one of the best groups (based on success rates) in the area (New England). Dr. P always provides me with studies to back up our plan. She never just tells me anything based on her opinion... it's all scientifically proven. She knows I need this. She also is one of the most amazing people I know. She's kind and warm. She puts up with my craziness. My messages and calls. On top of all that, she's cutting edge. We were in a clinical trial for PICSI. We ended up being in the control arm. Even though the trial was not complete, she knew this was something we needed. She fought (whomever it was she had to fight) for us to use the PICSI dish clinically. Sure enough, she won and we were the first couple treated with PISCI clinically. She has fought boards and insurance to run tests and do procedures. I could go elsewhere but I wouldn't get what I'm getting. Although we don't have a baby, I have had 50% of the cycles work. I did get pregnant two times out of four. If she said no to PGD, then I would consider going elsewhere. I have to look at the overall picture, I don't just need science and medicine, I need comfort and peace of mind. She gives us that. AND she has been successful. I know it sucks to say that when we don't have a baby... but it's true. I have been pregnant twice. We now just need to find the right, healthy embryo. I truly believe PGD will get us there.

I think that is everything. Basically everything. We talked about a lot but those were the four major topics. I'm sorry if that was rambled on and if it is hard to read. I had three hours of information in my head... it was hard to sort out and write down. I probably won't update this with the levels of my beta until tomorrow.

OH... I almost forgot. I finally went for a run yesterday! It felt so good! I'm so incredibly sore today. Even my shoulders hurt. I think the shoulder pain is from trying not to croak... I probably tensed up!

SATURDAY, FEBRUARY 19, 2011

Vicodin High

I'm sure you're all wondering how my beta is/was dropping. I said I would post the results on Thursday and never did... sorry. As you all know, they checked my beta while I was there for my WTF appointment with Dr. P. My Beta came back negative. I was pregnant on Sunday and not on Wednesday. Crazy. I have to admit, I am proud of my body for doing what it had to in a timely manner. Many people wait months and months for their betas to drop. Both of my miscarriages dropped back down to zero within a couple of days. Go me.

When they called with my results, they also told me that they were calling in a prescription and I was to start it the next day (Thursday). It just so happens that my WTF appointment and my beta were perfectly timed. If we even waited one more day, I would have had to wait for a period before starting again. I took my third dose of Clomid today. I have an ultrasound scheduled for March 1. If all goes as planned, I will be doing retrieval/transfer around the last week of March. I'm excited and slightly nervous (mainly for the Intramuscular injections).

Funny story...

A few weeks ago B signed up for a class. The class happened to be last Sunday. He was hesitant to go but really, there was no reason for him to stay home. All I was doing was taking Vicodin and Motrin. I was barely functioning. While he was gone, I was on a Vicodin high. I don't really remember what I watched on TV. I know I cleaned out our DVR and that's about it. Thursday afternoon, I got an email from 'Meaningful Beauty'. My 90 day supply of wrinkle cream was being shipped and would arrive within 10 business days. It took me a few minutes to remember ordering it. Sure enough, while I was all doped out on pain meds, I ordered Cindy Crawford's skin care products. I vaguely remember the conversation I had with the sales rep. I remember telling her that I better look meaningful and beautiful. For some reason I think there was a dog barking in the background. Maybe she worked from home? Who knows... all I know is that I will be getting a million dollars' worth of Skin Care thanks to Vicodin.

TUESDAY, FEBRUARY 22, 2011

Up and Up

Today was a day full of surgeries, doctors' appointments, and lots of prayers for my AGC girls. Everything turned out perfectly. Surgeries went well, tests came back normal and betas came back positive. All in all, life is on the up and up for my friends.

I finished the Clomid on Monday. I'm already wishing away weeks. I just want to get to retrieval/transfer time. The waiting can be torture. I think my ultrasound is Monday... or Tuesday. I forget. I should call today and figure that out.

I'm making the best of my "time off." I started back up at the gym. I also started working out with my trainer again. I was in the best shape of my life when I was working out with him. I only stopped because he charges monthly. I would only be able to work out a couple of weeks in the month then stop for my cycle. He kicked my butt even though he took it easy on me. I can't believe how much muscle mass you can lose in a short period of time. I was struggling. Biggest Loser style. I was grunting, yelling, whining... basically, I was a wimp. I made it through. I can't wait to see some results. I'll need my arm strength back so I can carry around twins :)

AGC has its first baby being born in less than a week. I can NOT wait! There won't be a dry eye in the room when he comes out. I'm so excited. I feel like I'm waiting for my own baby to be born!

Other than that, I have nothing going on (besides work). Life is so lame when you're not in a cycle. Maybe my 90 days' worth of beauty products come in soon. I'll at least be able to report on that!

SATURDAY, FEBRUARY 26, 2011

Baby L

Yesterday was the anniversary of us losing Baby L (1). I can't believe we have to start numbering our losses to differentiate between them. I remember every detail of that day. I can tell you what I was wearing (Steve Madden flats, skinny jeans, and a turquoise rain coat), what Dr. P was wearing (black pencil skirt, white button down top and a lab coat), what the weather was like (raining and cold). I can tell you every detail of every conversation I had that day. When you go through something so life changing, you don't forget anything about that day. Not one thing. I still can't believe it has been a year since our first lost. We're one tough couple. When you put our history on paper or say it out loud, you would think that we're crippled with depression. Yet, here we are, happy and living our life to the fullest. I think people expect us to look bad and not be functional. I think people expect us to not be able to handle babies and baby talk. I think people still expect our struggle to define us. It has defined us, just not how others expect it to... it has defined us as persistent, determined, and optimistic. It has made us stronger as a couple. It has made us more appreciative of all the things we have (our home, our careers, our fur babies and our marriage). One of my favorite quotes is: "Strength does not come from winning. Your struggles develop your strengths. When you go through hardships and decide not to surrender, that is strength." Some may allow their struggles to define them but we only allow it to develop us.

In my last post, I mentioned that life was boring. Literally, the next day, so much happened...

First, I got this survey in the mail.

I have no idea how/where they are getting their information from. Clearly, whoever their source is, does not fact check. Just a few days after having another miscarriage, I get a letter congratulating me on the birth of our new baby. Absolutely absurd. I get this stuff all the time. Usually it's from Viacord (who I can't stand) and Enfamil. I sent a nasty letter back. Big idiots.

We do have some exciting news. Our first AGC baby was born! Many people have asked me what AGC is... it's a group of women, all struggling with infertility (all in different forms). We get together every four to six weeks for dinner. Our first baby was born to M, the first (besides me) AGC girl. This baby is a BIG deal. HUGE. After three years, five miscarriages and a lot of persistence, he arrived. I can't think of a more deserving set of parents. They have been through the wringer and back. They have suffered a great deal yet have stayed strong. He's not only the first AGC baby, he's also the first PGD baby (that I know). When I was holding him the other day, I kept saying "I can't believe you were a blastocyst and now you're a human." To think, he was part of a retrieval, PGD biopsy, transfer and now he's a real baby. It's surreal. It's overdue. It's awesome. We were talking about how well he did his first night. He slept well, barely cried... he was a perfect baby. Then B (M's husband) said "the nurse said he'll start crying once he figures out that crying leads to feeding and diaper changes." My response was "He was biopsied and already proven perfect. He'll never cry, ever!". Hahahaha... obviously, I'm being silly but it is still really awesome. Congrats M and B!

So... my Meaningful Beauty came in the mail! Yay! I actually LOVE it. I am so grateful for Vicodin purchases! My skin is so incredibly soft and my eye wrinkles already look better... and it has only been a few days. It really does make your skin glow. The infomercial was telling the truth! Everyone should buy it.

SUNDAY, FEBRUARY 27, 2011

Home Visit

There is one part (adoption) of our journey to parents that we have kept somewhat private. It's not that we are hiding it. We have been in the process of adopting for a year now (since the first miscarriage). During the initial stages of the process we found that people were generally very opinionated about the adoption path we chose. We interviewed private agencies and state agencies. B was comfortable with the private agencies. I was not. There was something about the way they talked about the infants that didn't settle well with me. They inferred them to be "premium" babies... it sort of felt puppy mill-ish to me. I know plenty of people who adopted through private agencies and it worked out just fine. I just knew, that wasn't the right path, at least not for now.

All my life I have given more than I have. If you ask me for a donation, I will donate. If you are struggling financially, I will help you out... even if I don't have the extra money. I can't walk by a box of kittens that were left outside of a store without finding them all a home (usually the home is mine). When we were looking at adopting a dog, I wanted the one that was deemed unadoptable. I couldn't bear the thought of him not being loved. The thought of paying $40,000 for a baby that will get adopted anyway, didn't settle with me. All I could think of were the thousands and thousands of children bouncing from foster home to foster home. Although I think private adoption is a wonderful avenue, it just isn't the one for me. After a lot of research and discussion, we decided to start the process of adopting through DCF (Department of Children and Families).

I didn't want to talk about it because children in the system have a reputation for being troubled and dangerous (I'm sure movies like the Orphan doesn't help). Making a decision as big as this is something that needs to be done without opinion and questions. Deciding to move forward with adoption (no matter what form) also means you have to mourn the possibility of the loss of a biological child. That is a process I wanted to go through with B and only B. I didn't want to go through it with other people's negative outlook on the process. I didn't want to go through it with other people's opinions on the children or type of children. I think it takes a special kind of person(s) to be able to deal with the emotional trauma that many of these children have been through. B and I are those special kind of people.

The system is messed up. Our paperwork got lost in a government restructure. Then we were found but were directed to the wrong agency. For months I kept resending applications and making phone calls to make sure they were received. DCF adoption can be done two ways. 1) You can adopt directly through DCF 2) You can go through a contracted private agency. The pool of children (I really hate saying it like that but that's how the state refers to them) are the same. There really isn't a difference. Initially, we decided to adopt directly through DCF. There is an office close by and it was just convenient. After the whole paperwork debacle, we had an interview with a social worker. I hated her. She was plain rude. She was meeting us for the first time and treated us like criminals. As we walked out of the office I said to B "She was a douche bag. I can't work with her." B agreed. I called B a little while after we left (we took separate cars) because I was so upset about how it went. We talked about how discouraging it is that we have to be treated this way to have children. Yet the true criminals are the biological parents. They have children (many of them have LOTS of children) then neglect them so they can get high. They have children then abuse them. Or, they have children and leave them sitting by a dumpster. Here we are, two stable, loving people and we have to be treated like crap in order to become parents. Needless to say, we decided to start interviewing the contracted agencies.

About six months ago, we settled on an agency. I'm going to fast forward a bit... This past Thursday, we had our first home visit with a social worker. I was nervous all morning. My house has never been cleaner! I was being a crazy woman. I was expecting another d-bag (I know, I have a trucker mouth). The social worker was so incredibly nice. It's a very strange feeling to be sitting with a person, knowing that their intent is to judge you... judge your home, judge your marriage, judge your personality, judge your ability to care for a child. Every time we answered a question, I afraid we said the wrong thing. At one point (during the home inspection part) she said "Wow, it looks like a magazine." In normal circumstances I would take that as a compliment. However, I was so paranoid, instead of saying "Thank you," I said "We just remodeled this ourselves. Everything is from Home Goods." I was hoping what she heard was "KID FRIENDLY. They can break anything they want!" I can't tell you how stressful and anxiety ridden it is to have a person come into your home with the sole purpose of judgment.

The next phase in the process is a 10 week course. The course is run by a social worker and an adoptive parent. The course will cover the different forms of disabilities (they call everything considered outside the norm a disability. A disability can range from a learning disability to sexual abuse) that the children can have. They will discuss the different types of adoptions. By the end of the 10 week course, we will be able to tell the social workers what we can handle and what we can't. A lot of people think that when you adopt through the state you get whatever child they give you. We have a lot of say. Not only can we specify age, gender, and ethnicity. We can also specify which disability we are willing or are able to handle. We were supposed to start that course next weekend. We just found out that they are cancelling it... yet again. They rescheduled the course to begin in April. We will be on the West coast for a wedding one of the weekends, so we cannot take the course. We're hoping that they cancel it again in April and reschedule for May.

We're still about a year away from being matched with a child. It seems like a long way away but we're halfway there.

I have an ultrasound tomorrow to see how my ovaries are doing from the Clomid. Most likely they will have me trigger soon. Once I trigger, I will start Lupron. We're only four weeks or so away from another transfer.

TUESDAY, MARCH 1, 2011

HCG

Yesterday's ultrasound went as expected. I have a bunch of huge follicles that were ready to be triggered. I triggered last night. The hCG trigger is 10,000 units (which is equivalent to having a beta of 10,000). I decided to do an experiment with pregnancy tests. When I get positive pregnancy tests, the lines are never that dark. They're there... just not dark. I have never had a beta reach 10,000. My beta during my first miscarriage was around 2,000 or so. Pregnancy tests detect hCG at 25. So, I figured I would take a couple of tests today to see how dark the line gets. They came up positive right away but they're not nearly as dark as the control line. I have seen tests where the test line is darker than the control line. The chemical combination in my urine must somehow lessen the effects of hCG on a pregnancy test. I have no idea what the experiment proves other than, even with HIGH levels of hCG, pregnancy tests come out with a light/faint positive. Plus, it gave me an excuse to Pee on a Stick.

I have a progesterone check on Monday. If all goes well (which it should) I will start Lupron Monday or maybe Tuesday. Tuesday makes more sense... but we shall see. I did the calculations. If all stays on schedule (following the schedules of my previous cycles) we're looking at retrieval the end of the first week of April. It will also give me a due date of December 28th. Our anniversary. Of course, that's only if I follow the schedule of previous cycles. Cycles can vary so much so you never know.

I was playing around on the website for the lab that will be doing the PGD. I have to get ready for work so I can't go into details now. I'll post either later tonight or tomorrow about it. It's VERY fascinating!

WEDNESDAY, MARCH 2, 2011

PGD

AGC had another miscarriage today. Ahhhh! I thought for sure we were on our way to another AGC baby. IVF miscarriages happen more often than natural conception miscarriages. When we were learning about PGD, the PGD doctor explained to us that most IVF (with ICSI... which is when you directly inject the sperm into the egg) embryos are abnormal. The reason for this is eggs that normally wouldn't be fertilized or sperm that wouldn't normally fertilize an egg are being forced to fertilize the other. In natural conception or as it's called in infertility world, conventional fertilization, the weak egg and/or sperm don't make it to fertilization. If they do make it to fertilization, the embryo is generally of poor quality and won't implant.

The website for the PGD testing lab is quite fascinating. This statement is from their website:

Many IVF embryos are chromosomally abnormal

Multiple studies conducted at different IVF clinics have shown that significant numbers of IVF embryos are chromosomally abnormal. This is true even for embryos with good appearance or "morphology." The number of embryos that have abnormal chromosomes increases as women age. A technique called Preimplantation Genetic Diagnosis or PGD allows selection of chromosomally normal embryos for transfer to the uterus. This can improve the chances of pregnancy and delivery, and can reduce the chances of having a baby with a condition like Down syndrome. It also decreases the chances of early pregnancy loss.

Chromosome abnormalities in embryos as a main reason for infertility

Research over the past several decades indicates that more than half of the embryos produced through IVF are chromosomally abnormal; this includes those with good morphology and from young patients. Embryos with poor morphology and from older women are even more susceptible to chromosome abnormalities. Growing embryos to day-5 of development – or the blastocyst stage – allows for selection of embryos that are more likely to be chromosomally normal since many chromosomally abnormal embryos do not reach this stage of development. However, some 40% of blastocyst stage embryos are still chromosomally abnormal [1].

The vast majority of embryos with chromosome abnormalities will not implant or will miscarry during the first trimester of pregnancy. Thus, implantation failure and loss of abnormal embryos are believed to be the main reasons for a decrease in viable pregnancy rates with advancing maternal age. Aneuploid embryos are mostly indistinguishable morphologically and developmentally from chromosomally normal ones, thus, without genetic screening, embryologists cannot identify abnormal embryos and may transfer such embryos, reducing your chances of achieving a viable pregnancy.

Ahhh... JUST what we need. I'm looking forward to getting some answers. I hope, hope, hope that we get at least one normal embryo. If you're interested in learning more about PGD, their website is full of information:

http://www.reprogenetics.com/

I have the sweet pains of a drug induced ovulation today. My right ovary is a rock star. It has been snap, crackle, and popping all day. I'm looking forward to Monday, when we can start Lupron. AND we can end this week of abstinence!

I called our social worker yesterday. Since we can't attend the class that starts in April, I wanted to see if there were other agencies with classes. The process has been hard and draining. I just want to move forward. As you all know, I hate waiting.

SUNDAY, MARCH 6, 2011

Badonka donk

Tomorrow I start Lupron! Woot! Well, I may be speaking too soon. I have an appointment for blood work in the morning. If my progesterone is high (meaning, I ovulated) then I start Lupron. I don't see why it won't be high... but you never know.

I'm really anxious to get started this time around. I'm anxious to get to the PGD portion of the cycle. I'm interested in finding out more about our embryos.

A million and a half questions run through my mind daily. What if they are all abnormal? What if they all look like crap but are actually normal? What if we carry a gene for some crazy disease? What if this cycle sucks and we don't end up with enough embryos? What if we have normal embryos and I still miscarry? What if they all end up being crappy and don't make it to the biopsy? I have a million questions and zero answers. I have come to terms with our path to being parents. Even with acceptance, patience seems miles away.

We still haven't found a replacement course. It looks like our adoption plans will be on hold... once again... for a few months. It's so frustrating to know that there are children just waiting. Some of them are bouncing from foster home to foster home. Here we are, willing (and sane) to adopt and we can't. The process is frustrating. I keep telling myself that one day, this will all be worth it (and hopefully, we'll forget we even dealt with it). In the meantime, I go on the website and look at the children that are waiting. I read and reread their biographies. I watch their adoption videos. I don't think I will ever be able to choose. When the time comes for us to be matched, I hope they give us one option. I hope they say "this is your child." Otherwise, we're screwed. I can't choose. If they give us four options, I would take them all. I could never choose one over the other. I don't know how we'll do it. I guess it's like everything else... you just do it.

Funny story...

So, if you have never met me in person, you may not know this. I have a huge ass. HUGE. My mom always called it a Ballerina butt. That's the nice version of "gigantic bubble butt." In fact, on Christmas Eve, B's grandmother said "Aprill, you look like one of those Kardashian sisters." Yep, it's that big. Yesterday, B and I went rock climbing at an indoor gym nearby. B saw a bunch of young kids (probably around 12 or so) staring at by badonka donk. After a couple of minutes one of them says "It's a beautiful sight, isn't it?" Bwahahahahahahahahahahahaha! If they only knew that fat asses were NOT beautiful! One day they'll learn...

MONDAY, MARCH 7, 2011

And the Lupron Begins...

I just got the call from the IVF coordinator. My progesterone was nice and high so I can start Lupron tomorrow. Here's the breakdown of my plan:

3/8: Begin Lupron
3/22: Baseline Ultrasound
3/23: Begin Stims (Gonal-f)
4/3: Retrieval
4/6: PGD Biopsy
4/8: Transfer

I pretty much always follow the schedule they give me. It may differ a day or two. However, this cycle, we're starting my stims at a lower dose (due to the OHSS last cycle). It may take a little longer for the follicles to mature. Bring on the Lupron Dreams!

Speaking of dreams...

I had a dream last night (it's a recurring dream) that I was in trouble and needed help. Every time I tried calling for help, my fingers would mess up the number. I had to keep hanging up and redialing. Now that I am typing this, I have a vague memory of a child needing help. I don't know whose child it was or what was wrong with them. I remember trying to call for help and B yelling "just call an ambulance." I wonder why 9-1-1 wasn't what I was dialing. I remember a lot of 3's being in the number. Strange. That's without Lupron!

I saw this quote today. It is perfect for how I feel. I know it's hard for some people to understand that I am okay. I have said it many times... I have a good life. I have a great home, a great marriage. I have wonderful fur babies. I have great friends and family. I have passions and hobbies. I have a job that I love (most of the time). We travel often. I have a wonderful life. This quote sums it up perfectly...

"Be content with what you have, rejoice in the way things are. When you realize there is nothing lacking, the whole world belongs to you." ~ Lao Tzu

No two cycles...

No two cycles are the same. I have to keep reminding myself of that. No two cycles are the same. Last cycle was so easy. I had no side effect (until the OHSS kicked in at the end)... I felt great. I guess I didn't repeat that to myself enough... No two cycles are the same.

Yesterday was day 1 of Lupron. The injection was fine. Unlike last cycle, I had no troubles getting the needle through my wonderful belly. I take the Lupron first thing in the morning. I wake up, feed the fur babies, grab my materials (alcohol swab, needle, Lupron, and sharps container), shoot up, and then make breakfast. By 7:00 last night, I had a KILLER headache. Not quite a migraine but close. Day 1 and Lupron kicked my ass. Not only did I get killer headaches I had night sweats like a menopausal lady. AND I had some of the scariest dreams... SOOO SCARY! At one point, I woke up and wanted to write it all down so I could blog about it. I somehow convinced myself that I would remember the details. I remember nothing. All I remember is that I was terrified. If it happens again tonight, I'll write it down.

I've been working out with a trainer again. Yesterday, I noticed that I was struggling through my session. I ended up talking to him today because I don't think I can continue with him while I am under treatment. Technically, I could but I'd rather save the sessions for when I can get my ass kicked. Lupron is kicking my ass... one ass kicking is enough.

Right now, I'm sitting at a MS support group. The leader opened the group with a joke. What do you think the joke is about...? Infertility. Seriously, you can't escape it! It was cute and funny though...

WEDNESDAY, MARCH 9, 2011

IVF Costs

Sorry for the lack of posts this past week. Like I said in my last post, this cycle is kicking my ass. I feel like complete hell. Curious as to which symptoms I'm getting?? Where should we start? Let's start with the nausea that is so bad that it's making me a complete bitch. Well, maybe moodiness is its own symptom. I have awesome acne on my back... really cute. My head feels like someone is constantly drilling a jack hammer through the back of my skull. I'm exhausted ALL day long. I have hot flashes and chills. Of course, I couldn't escape the wonderful night sweats. Actually, today, I'm feeling slightly better... better as in, instead of feeling like complete hell, I feel like I'm in purgatory. My appreciation for women going through menopause is huge. I can't imagine how women go through this for months and years. At least I know this is temporary for me.

We have been extremely lucky to have had insurance coverage for our cycles. The State we live in is 1 of 14 States that require all insurance policies to have some sort of fertility coverage. However, even with fertility coverage, we have to spend some moola. On top of the insurance we get through my company, we also pay out of pocket for a secondary plan. That plan costs us $316 a month. The secondary plan also has a deductible of $2,000. This is the bill from our last cycle.

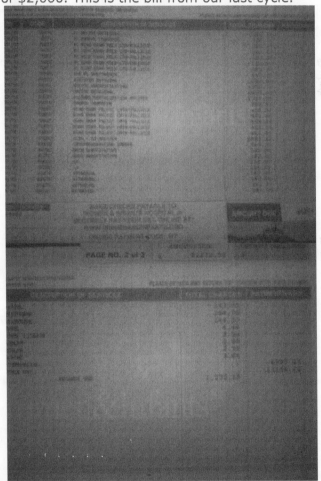

One of our plans paid the clinic $4,400 and the other plan paid $13,000 leaving us with a balance of $1,300. On top of that, we have to pay for the PGD which we are getting at a discounted rate of $4,700. So, this week alone, we are cutting a check for $6,000. That's WITH insurance coverage... TWO insurances. AGC has many girls that live in States without coverage. They are all out of pocket. Yes, it's not cheap to be reproductively challenged.

It's a shame that there aren't laws requiring some sort of coverage. Sure, we'll pay for oxygen and inhaled steroids for your Chronic Obstructive Pulmonary Disease from your smoking habit. Sure, we'll pay for your diabetes (self-induced) medication because you won't change your diet and/or exercise routine. But I'm sorry, you have a medical condition that is completely out of your control and we won't pay for any of the treatments. It's absurd. Don't forget (Yes, we just got our tax forms back from our accountant so I'm a little fired up) you get penalized because you have a dual income with no kids. How about you give us a tax break for TRYING and SPENDING LOADS of moola to have children. OR pass a law that requires ALL states have fertility coverage.

I have had some really bizarre Lupron dreams. Tomorrow I'll tell you about the elephant dream. Right now, I'm going to sit my nauseous, fat ass (oh yeah, I've also already gained 4 pounds) on the couch and catch up on some daytime television.

Elephants

I know... I keep saying I'll be better about posting and I'm not. To be honest, I've had a crazy week with work. I've done a lot more driving than I'd like to.

An update on the costs...

I called the clinic today to verify I had the correct amount for PGD. I didn't. The correct cost is $5,400. Buzz kill. Wahhhhhhhh

I still haven't gotten my period. Why is it that she comes when we DO NOT want her and she doesn't come when we do want her?? She has until Monday night to arrive. She was due two days ago. Hopefully she comes. We are traveling April 14th. Right now our transfer is scheduled for April 8th. We don't have any room for delays. If you all could please do the period dance, I'd greatly appreciate it.

I'm not sure how I'm feeling this cycle. I'm not excited like last cycle. I'm also not negative. I guess I'm indifferent. I just don't really care. I am anxious to see what the PGD results tell us. I guess the lack of enthusiasm is good. I've been excited so many times just to be let down. Maybe this "blah"ness is a good thing.

I have had some CRAZY dreams. OH YA! I forgot to tell you about the elephant dream. Here it is...

I was with my sister (I was my current age and she was a child... 5 or so). We were on vacation at an all-inclusive resort. We decided to walk down the beach to check out the other resorts. As we were walking, the beaches got more crowded and loud. I said to my sister "These must be the kid friendly resorts." Then we got to this one resort that had live elephants everywhere. We walked by a group of tourist that were all attached by a rope. The rope was clipped (the clip was one of those clips that you use in rock climbing. I'll find a pic on the Internet and show you). I couldn't believe that they would have those clips through their nose. I kept saying "That is so unsanitary." As we were walking, my sister starting yelling and pointing. I turned around and saw HUNDREDS of baby elephants lined up. They were in perfect formation. One behind the other... row after row after row. They had on beautiful headpieces. They were bright in color and full of sequence. I pulled her aside because I was worried that we would get trampled. As I moved away, she started yelling and pointing again. I turned and saw that the spot I moved us to also had rows and rows of elephants. Only this group was larger, adult elephants. I looked forward and the ladies that were attached by the nose with dirty, rock climbing clips started chanting some mumbo jumbo. At this point, I'm getting anxious. I knew we were in danger but I couldn't figure out what kind. I wasn't sure if the spooky nose clip people were going to hurt us or if the elephants were going to trample us. I picked up my sister, put her on my hip and started running towards the back... the only place without elephants. As I was running, I had noticed that I ran into a marble foyer. I was yelling "HELP" over and over again. I heard a sound over my shoulder. I turned (still with my sister on my hip) thinking it was someone answering my cries for help. It was not. It was a herd of horses. All dressed with the same head dresses the elephants were wearing. They were coming at us full speed. I kept spinning in circles trying to figure out where to go. To my left were baby elephants. To my right were adult elephants. Straight ahead were the crazy nose ladies. I just folded myself around my sister and dropped to the ground. As the horses were about to run over us, I woke up.

Yep, that's a typical dream from Lupron. Needless to say. I'm not sleeping well. Here's a pic of the clips that I was talking about.

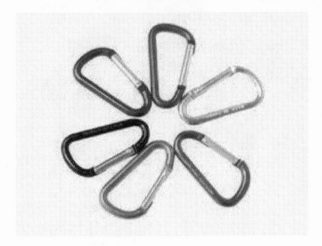

THURSDAY, MARCH 17, 2011

Gauji

Marc Sedaka (comedy script writer and son of singer Neil Sedaka) wrote a book titled: What He Can Expect When She's Not Expecting. I'm going to pick it up today. I'll read it over the weekend and let you know if it's worth buying. I watched the clip below and it sounds like a decent book. I'll report back to you once I'm finished.

http://today.msnbc.msn.com/id/42096898/ns/today-books/

Gayle King also interviewed him. The interview is pretty decent. They talk briefly about "unexplained infertility." Which is the diagnosis we were given. Here's the link: http://gaylekingshow.com/b/What-He-Can-Expect-When-Shes-Not-Expecting/209635377909664894.html

My period still hasn't come. She has three days. I triggered February 28th which means I ovulated March 2. That makes my period due on the 16th... this past Wednesday. I'll give her one more day before I freak out. My boobs are killing me and I had a migraine a couple of days ago. Hopefully that means she's on her way.

My Lupron dream last night was a mixture of scary and funny. I remember being anxious and scared but I don't remember the details. The only part of the dream I remember is this...

B and I were at a factory that made apples. They made apples by combining them with water. We bit into a HUGE green apple. As soon as we pulled the bitten piece away, our faces and neck were covered with water. B's mom came up to us and asked "what kind is that one." I said "It's a Gauji (pronounced Ga-ooo-jee). Gala apple and Fuji water blend." HAHAHAHAHAHHA... I woke up right after that portion of the dream. I didn't want to forget Gauji so I laid there saying "Ga-ooo-jee, Ga-ooo-jee" repeatedly. That's going to be my new favorite word. Gauji.

SATURDAY, MARCH 19, 2011

No love for Infertility

Borders, Barnes & Noble, the Library, and Village Pharmacy (an infertility pharmacy that carries books and DVDs) all DO NOT carry the book I was looking for. Seriously, there is no love for infertility. You can find four bajillion books on pregnancy, how to get pregnant, baby names... and you're lucky if you can find two for infertility. I ended up ordering it on Amazon. I paid the extra $12 to have it delivered today.

During my second IVF cycle, my period didn't come before my baseline. Someone said to me "If you want your period to come, put on white pants, put on a bathing suit, or take a pregnancy test. If you do any of those, your period will come the next day." Well, I don't have white pants that are warm enough for this weather. I am most definitely not walking around in a bathing suit. So, I went out and purchased a pregnancy test. I took it last night. This morning, I woke up with killer cramps and my period. Hahahah! It worked!

Do any of you watch Private Practice? This week's episode??? HOLY MOLY!

We're going to Rock Climbing today. I only have three more days of being able to work out. I'm going to enjoy it while I can!

MONDAY, MARCH 21, 2011

Don't Stop til You Get Enough

I was talking with a friend today about how I'm excited about this cycle. Two days ago, I was over it. I could have cared less if the cycle happened or not. I was indifferent to the entire thing... the process, the results... all of it. Today, I'm excited. She said "You know, you said and did the exact same thing your last cycle." Apparently, I am "blah" until I get to the real heavy duty stuff... STIMS! I can't wait to get my baseline done tomorrow. Maybe I'll even get the Hottie young doctor again. I guess it won't be as cool to have the handsome young fellow doing a vaginal ultrasound when you are on day 3 of your period. Once stim meds start, the cycle flies by. I only stim for ten days or so. We're only two weeks away from retrieval. Yowzers!

Amazon screwed up and didn't send my book this weekend. I did pay an extra $12/15 (I forget exactly how much) for next day delivery. I got my shipping costs back but am still bookless. Once I get it, I'll let you all know.

I tried to be very active this past weekend. While on stim meds, I'll have a couple of weeks of no activity. There's nothing worse than the feeling of wanting to work out. Talk about feeling blah. So I figured I would be as active as I could leading up to the baseline. Saturday, we went rock climbing. Sunday, we did a TON of yard work. Well, B did a lot of work. I put together our chiminea... which was a workout! It is a cast iron chiminea... by the time I was done, my back was killing me. KILLING me. On my way home from work today, I stopped at the gym to get a good run in. I'd prefer to run outside but we got hit with a snow storm today. Welcome to spring in New England! Anyway, I was psycho, crazy, runner girl at the gym. I did just under 2 miles of sprints. When I sprint, I sprint for two minutes (with the treadmill speed between 8.0 and 9.0) then walk (at 3.5) for one minute. I do that several times until I hit 2 miles or so. After I hit two miles, I walked for a few minutes then jogged another mile. It felt great. I'll be able to get one more workout in tomorrow... then it's back to my fat jeans and feeling gross.

Most of you know (and if you don't, you will quickly learn) that I am an INSANE Michael Jackson fan. INSANE. You know, he died on my 30th birthday. Not cool. I cried all afternoon and night. B got a text from his buddy today that said "Sitting in my accountant's office in the waiting room (15 minutes early) so I started reading Aprill's blog and MJ starts playing on the radio (Don't Stop til You Get Enough). Good Sign. "I couldn't agree more Q! We won't stop until we get four babies. FOUR!"

I'll update you all once I get the call after my baseline. Usually they call after 2:00 (EST).

TUESDAY, MARCH 22, 2011

Finally... we begin

Baseline ultrasound was uneventful. The lab didn't kill my arm when they drew my blood. The ultrasound tech didn't rip out my cervix with the vaginal ultrasound. I had multiple follicles less than 12mm on both ovaries... which is what you want to see. My lining was nice and thin... which you also want to see. So we're good to go!

The nurse said "Okay sweetie... I know you're a veteran but I still have to go through the list. Tomorrow morning you are to drop your Lupron dose from 10 units to 5. You are to start Gonal-f tomorrow evening. You need to make sure you take your shot every night at the same time... between 7:00 and 9:00. Whatever time you pick tomorrow, you will need to keep for the rest of the cycle. Your dose will be 187.5iu. Due to your high response last cycle, Dr. P wants to see you earlier than usual for just blood work. We need you to come in on Saturday morning at 8:30. Let me make sure we're on the same page. Did you get your Progesterone in Oil, Medrol, Vicodin, and Motrin? Are you all set with prenatals and Gonal-f? We are doing ICSI, PICSI, Assisted Hatching, PGD, Transfer under anesthesia. Is that all? Are we on the same page?" UHM... is that all?!?! Hahahah... Yes, that's ALL! I'd prefer the all to include having relations with my husband but hey, I'll take this ALL. Geesh! You would think I'm trying to clone myself not reproduce!

We had to pay for the PGD today. We had transferred the money from our savings into our checking account. My account looked nice and big for about three days. Now it's all gone. Let's hope that $5,400 gets us some answers and a couple of babies!

I am dying today. Well, not literally. My headaches are brutal. I know it's the Lupron and I just have to deal with it. The migraine is so bad I can barely turn my head. Boooo. I came home from work today and took a Vicodin. They give you Vicodin after your retrieval so it's the only thing I'm comfortable taking right now. Normally, I try not to take anything. I couldn't hang today.

We finally scheduled our appointment with our wedding photographer to pick out our album photos. Hahahaha! Yes, we've been married for over three years. We're slow! We had other priorities... like starting a family. Making photo albums wasn't on the top of the list. I'm excited to get it done... even though it's 3.5 years later.

I'm going to lay down. Hopefully this migraine leaves before my two day meeting... which starts tomorrow at noon.

WEDNESDAY, MARCH 23, 2011

UPDATED: 5 IVFs and still a novice

Ahhhhh...

Well, I screwed up starting stims. I was supposed to drop my Lupron dose down to 5 units today. By habit, I woke up, fed the animals, and took 10 units of Lupron. Dr. P said she was going to talk to the nurse but most likely we won't start stimming until tomorrow. Boooooo! One day won't kill me. However, we are traveling on the 13th of April. As of right now my transfer is scheduled for the 8th. If my cycle gets pushed, even by a couple days, I won't be able to go on our trip... Which would totally stink.

I'll update this once I hear final word from Dr. P or the nurse.

UPDATE:

I got the green light to start stims anyway. This may mean I'll be stimming for a little longer than usual. So I'm in the same boat as I would be if I start the meds tomorrow. I guess starting relieves some stress so why not??

THURSDAY, MARCH 24, 2011

Insert foot in mouth

I just got back from a two day meeting. I am so ready for pajamas and DVR. Funny story from dinner last night...

We're at dinner with my team, my boss, and our national sales director (big wig). We're all trying to decide which desserts to order. We agreed to order a couple different ones and all just try a bite. The girls on my end of the table wanted banana gelato. The guys all thought it sounded nasty so they ordered pistachio gelato. The desserts came. We're all trying them. Then super smart Aprill yells across the table to a male co-worker "This tastes better than you!" Yes. I said that. I meant to say "this tastes better than yours." The table was in hysterics. For the rest of the meeting, I didn't live it down. Can I blame that on Lupron? What about Gonal-f?

My injection last night was somewhat painful. It's strange. Sometimes I can't get the needle through my skin. I had to try four spots before it went in. I can't figure out what I'm doing differently the times it is like that. Speaking of injections, we have our progesterone injection training tomorrow. I am not looking forward to a 3-inch needle going into the muscle of my butt.

1. I'm a needle phobe.
2. Its peanut oil with progesterone. You can't tell me that won't burn.
3. I'm a needle phobe.

How does a needle phobe get stuck in this situation?

My headaches have not improved. They're killing me. Now that I'm stimming, I won't take anything for it. I know there are things that are safe. I know crack heads have babies all the time. I know that it's not impossible but I just don't want to. I don't want to do anything that I could wonder "what if" later on. If the cycle doesn't work, I don't want to have any doubts about any decisions I made. Which means I'll be suffering with migraines for a couple of weeks.

The book came in the mail today. After I put on pajamas, take my shot, and throw on Days of Our Lives, I'm going to start reading it.

I guess that's all I have for today. They should seriously reconsider doing something else instead of sales meetings. Putting a bunch of sales people in a room with four walls for two days is not a good idea. We're in sales. We are extraverts. We're used to moving around, traveling and conversation. Two days in a conference room = me completely brain dead.

SATURDAY, MARCH 26, 2011

Warrior

I had blood work this morning. Normally, blood work takes all of two minutes... five minutes if they are super busy. As soon as I pulled into the parking lot, I knew I was going to be there a while. I had to drive in and out of the lot twice before finding a spot. I easily could have parked behind the building but that would have required walking in the cold. For some reason, you can't take the stairs up (the clinic is on the 4th floor), you can only take them down. The clinic only has one elevator and it is slow as molasses. Once I finally got to the 4th floor, I was welcomed by a full waiting room and a line of people waiting to check in. I have seen it very busy but never that busy. There was some construction on the highway that caused a lot of delays, I wonder if a lot of people came late and that's what made them get backed up. I don't know. All I know is that I was 15 minutes late and when I finally checked in, they forgot to put me on the schedule. So I had to wait for them to print out my lab slip and all that jazz. An hour and 15 minutes later, I got my blood work done. Nice way to spend my Saturday morning! The meds are making me insanely tired... waking up was pure torture this morning. Anyway, they are dropping my dose down to 150 tonight (from 187.5), tomorrow and then I return on Monday for more blood work. Usually, I'll get an ultrasound too. Although, the nurse didn't mention that when she called.

We had our injection training yesterday. I was so nervous. SOOO nervous. In fact, I had diarrhea all morning. Speaking of diarrhea. I ended up stopping before our appointment to get some Pepto. By the time we got to the appointment, my stomach settled... well, the Pepto kicked in. After the appointment, I went straight to acupuncture. Every appointment starts with Alice (my acupuncturist) checking the color of my tongue and my pulse. While she was checking my pulse she said "Did you skip lunch?" I responded with, "No, my stomach always rumbles when I lay down on the table." She said, "hmm... I always check three pulses. Your GI pulse is always so dull, I barely can feel it. Today, it's the strongest one. Is your stomach upset?" Bahahaha... Uhm yes Alice, I got myself so worked up about injection training that I caused myself to have diarrhea all morning. I thought it was pretty cool that she noticed that from my pulse. Okay... back to the training. The needle wasn't as large as I thought it would be. You draw the medicine from a 2 needle with a wide gauge (I forget the exact number) then you switch the needle out for a 1.5 needle for injection. Still scary as hell but not as bad as I was expecting. The injection goes into the muscle on the upper/outer quadrant of the butt. If you were to divide your right butt cheek into four even quadrants, the injection goes in the muscle on the upper, right side. If you were to put your hands on your hips, where your thumb falls, is where the injection goes in... This doesn't work for me because I have really long legs but works for most people. B did a decent job. He was hesitant (which scares me) but I trust he'll dart that needle right into my muscle. Ahhhhh!

Last year (around when we were pregnant then miscarried) we went through a wave of people getting pregnant around us. It seemed like we were getting "I'm pregnant" calls every day. Then we went through the wave of all the babies being born. Now, we're back at the beginning of the cycle. It seems like we're being told (again almost daily) that someone is expecting. Although we're happy for those people, the announcements are always a kick in the gut. I'm so jealous (and frankly pissed off) when people can get pregnant by having sex. Here I am, a total needle phobe, sticking myself with three needles a day, inducing menopause, stimulating my ovaries to produce a bajillion eggs, feeling like shit almost every day, all for nothing (thus far). What the eff? I allow myself to feel bad, cry, or be jealous for just a few minutes. Then I have to put back on my warrior hat. If I allow myself to wallow in what we don't have, I'll never have the strength to go through another cycle. After crying myself to sleep last night, I woke up ready to take on the rest of this cycle. Now if it could just freaking work.

I started reading the book. I am not impressed. I don't want to make any judgments until I finish it but so far, the author comes across as a dick. He makes a lot of jokes about infertility. He also implies that infertility is the women's problem and the man is just there to say the right things. I don't know... I'll finish it this weekend and give you a full report when I'm done.

My Poor Belly

Normally, I don't get bloated and uncomfortable until trigger/retrieval time. I am only on day 4 (tonight will be the 5th dose) and I'm already huge. Huge and ridiculously uncomfortable. I still have six days (or so) to go. I may explode. Awesome.

It's hard to tell in pictures how bad the bloating is. I took this one last night. Don't mind my sweats! It's like I have a shelf belly. The bloating is literally only where my ovaries are so it's all belly button and below. Mind you, my non-drug size varies from a 2 to a 4.

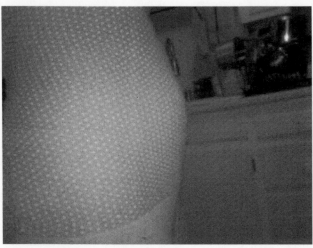

I have clothes in my closet ranging from 2 to 8. So I'm good for work clothes. Outside of work clothes... not so much. I guess I'll be wearing leggings and sweats until retrieval.

Okay... I'm going to try and finish that book now. I'll report back later.

SUNDAY, MARCH 27, 2011

Surprise, We're Expecting!

Ahh... no, not B and myself. Don't we all wish! We're not expecting but it seems like everyone else is. After our miscarriage last year, we were surrounded by pregnancy announcements, baby showers, and eventually births. After the births, things slowed down. Pregnancy announcements, although existent, became scarce. Then miscarriage #2 happens and now it's baby announcement central. This weekend alone, we had three couples tell us they were expecting. I debated whether or not I should post about how to tell an "infertile" couple that you're pregnant. I don't want to hurt any one's feelings. AND I most certainly don't want to take away from any one's excitement. After much debate, I decided I should discuss it (mainly from the feedback from my post last year about what not to say to a person trying to conceive).

I understand that conversation is two way. I know that the person receiving the news is not the only one in the conversation. I know that me getting the news is just as hard as you giving it. I have no doubts that trying to muster up the courage to tell a reproductively challenged person that you're expecting is hard and scary. The point of this post isn't to repel people from sharing exciting baby news. Sharing pregnancy news is exciting. It's one of the few moments in your life that you get to decide when and how to share it. The point of this post is to share what it feels like for me; for us; those who want it so badly.

Email: Nowadays, technology can seem like a conversation killer. We don't call anyone anymore, we text. We don't speak in full terms, we speak in abbreviations. We share news on social websites rather than in person. Although 99% of the time, this can be annoying and somewhat regressive, I think it's a perfectly acceptable form of announcing pregnancy. I know you're scared to have the conversation. I would never be offended to receive the news via email. If it's plastered on Facebook and that's how I'm finding out, then yes, I'd be offended. However, a personal email, announcing the news would actually be wonderful. I want to be excited for you. I want to celebrate with you. However, there will be a moment after you tell me that the wind will be knocked out of me. Having it announced in an email gives you the ability to not feel bad and me the ability to handle my emotions before calling you with excitement.

Social Gatherings: As I mentioned earlier, there will be a moment when I will need to catch my breath. If we're out at a party or a bar, I will have to pretend to be happy and excited. I want the ability to be genuinely happy and excited. I don't want the setting to determine how I feel. 99% of the time, I cry my eyes out after a pregnancy announcement. The tears aren't because I'm not happy for you. They're not because I don't think you deserve a child. The tears are part of my grief. It truly has nothing to do with you. It has everything to do with mourning what I want and don't have. Infertility takes over your life. It takes over your schedule, your travel plans, your hobbies, and lifestyle. Being out, socializing, these are our escape from infertility. We would be forced to continue the night with fake, happy faces when in reality, we feel like we're going to vomit and breakdown in tears. Try to avoid parties, bars or any other forms of social gatherings.

Conception Time: PLEASE, whatever you do, do NOT tell me how long it took you to conceive. I know four months seems like a long time to you but it's not. It takes the average female 7-12 months to conceive. I know they can be torturous and stressful months... believe me, I know. But now is not the time to share with me how much or little time it took for you to conceive.

Infertility: I know you're interested about where I stand in a cycle. I know you care about the process. However, mixing a pregnancy announcement with a conversation about a miscarriage or IVF cycle is not a good idea. Please don't have me go through the grueling details about my cycle and what I'm going through just to have it followed up with an "I'm pregnant" announcement. At the same time, don't announce that you're expecting then ask me where I stand with treatments. The two conversations should never be mixed.

Keep it Simple: I do want to talk about baby showers, morning sickness, and pregnancy excitement. I do want to hear about how you're feeling. I do want to be a part of the pregnancy. As I mentioned before, I need time to process the information. I need time to cry, yell, and bitch at the unfair aspects of life. That time will be needed immediately after the announcement. Try to keep the announcement brief. I will never make you feel like your pregnancy is hurtful to me. I will ALWAYS be excited and happy... even when it's taking me every ounce of strength I have to continue with the conversation. The simpler the conversation, the better. Once I have dealt with my own emotions, I will be able to talk about puking on yourself, swollen ankles, and massive boobs. I DO want to talk about these things. I just need to work it out in my head first. I think I mentioned in my post yesterday, that I feel bad, cry, and move on within minutes. If you keep the announcement brief and simple, I will have the space to deal with my emotions.

I know this seems like a lot of "guidelines." The reality is, there is no formula that calculates the proper way to share exciting news with a friend struggling to conceive. There is no formula that calculates how the infertile should handle other's pregnancies. I wish it were that simple. I know that I am a mother. I may not be one yet but I will be. I may not get there the way I want. It may take methods that I don't want to deal with. It has proven to take years longer than I expected. I don't know how or when we will get there. I just know we will. In the meantime, all I can do is be as happy as I can be until we get there. Even if it means having difficult discussions, like this one.

MONDAY, MARCH 28, 2011

Boring Post

Sorry for this boring post. I feel like crap. Complete crap. I'm going to make this update short and sweet.

I had an ultrasound and blood work this morning. My estrogen levels are around 625 (I forget the exact number). My right ovary had one follicle measuring 13mm. My left ovary had two follicles, one measuring 12mm and the other 13mm. I also had 19 follicles measuring less than 12mm. They dropped my dose down to 112.5 and are having me return tomorrow morning for blood work only... no ultrasound. Normally, my follicles "pop" all at once. I bet a lot more of them will be greater than 12mm on Wednesday.

Okay... I seriously need to lay down. This cycle better end up in a healthy pregnancy because it sure is kicking my ass.

TUESDAY, MARCH 29, 2011

Book Report

First, I'll give you my cycle update. My estrogen is in the 800's today. That's a nice, steady increase. We're down to the last couple of days. B and I just went out for some ice cream. Cake batter ice cream with cookie dough and Oreos make your follicles grow, right?!?!

Finally, the book report...

WHAT HE CAN EXPECT WHEN SHE'S NOT EXPECTING

How to support your wife, save your marriage and conquer infertility!

By: Mark Sedaka

The author's writing style is... well, is one I do not like. Infertility is a sensitive topic. Jokes are okay. I like jokes. I like comedic relief. However, his joking styles make the reader (or at least how I felt) feel like the subject itself is a joke. The sequencing of the chapters brings you start to finish from trying naturally to In Vitro. Without going into too much detail, here's what I did not like about the book.

1. Although he repeatedly states how frustrating and stressful the process is, he jokes far too often about it.
2. He basically faults the female. His purpose in writing the book is how to support the female. "more often than not, we poor schlubs are left to fend for ourselves-not quite sure when to chime in, when to keep quiet, when to take action, when to lay low."
3. He believes that once a woman decides she wants a child sex sucks. He calls it "lousy procreation sex." He gives four suggestions on how to handle the lousy sex.
4. He often says that women NEED children whereas men do not.
5. In the "who are you" chapter, he lists three "universal truths." I disagree with every single one of them.
   Fertility-challenged women hate kids. I love kids. I love babies.
   Fertility-challenged women hate when people talk about their fertility-challenged... ness: I enjoy being a resource for others struggling. I like having others to talk to about it. I love being supportive and being supported
   Fertility-challenged women hate to be compared to other fertility-challenged women: This one... I don't 100% disagree or agree with. I don't like when people say "I know this couple who tried for a bajillion years and once they adopted they got pregnant" or "I know this couple who tried for a bajillion years and once they stopped stressing or thinking about it, they got pregnant." At the same time, I like comparing my cycles with my friends that are also going through it. I like hearing the different

treatments and responses. So... I'm iffy on this one. I don't agree with him but I don't disagree.

6. OMG... I can't believe I didn't list this one sooner. He has a "wife psycho level" rating system. Yes, he does. With his discussions about the tests and treatment options, he includes which "psycho level" the wife will be at. I was irate when I got to that part of the book.

If you want your partner to let you take on infertility while he is a supportive bystander, then maybe this is a good book for you/your partner. If you're looking for a book that will help you and your partner with understanding the process, this is NOT the book. B had never treated this as my problem. He has never (at least to my knowledge... and if I'm wrong, he may see a "psycho level" kazillion) talked to his buddies about my "psycho level." He wants children as much as I do. I don't know about you, but sex is sex. I find it good... all the time (except the mornings... mornings are hit or miss for me). Sorry buddy but your procreation sex may need a sex therapist not a Reproductive Endocrinologist. My opinion, the book is not worth $12.95. It's not even worth getting from the library.

THURSDAY, MARCH 31, 2011

UPDATED: Getting Closer

I'm sure you're all checking this for updates on my retrieval. I REALLY should post updates every day. I've just been feeling so crappy. Also, our computer is upstairs in my craft room. By the time I get home from work and finish up with dinner, the last thing I want to do is walk upstairs. I know... sounds like we either live in a Mansion or I'm really lazy. Let's pretend I live in a Mansion.

My ultrasound yesterday went well. I had ten follicles measuring over 12:

Three - 12mm
One - 13mm
Four - 14mm
One - 15mm
One - 16mm

I had a couple hovering 11mm and about 15 less than 12mm. My estrogen was a "healthy" 1,200.

I was so uncomfortable at my ultrasound this morning that I didn't write down the exact numbers. I had about 11 or so measuring over 12. The ranges were 12mm-18.5mm. So, if my estrogen is high, I'll trigger tonight. If my estrogen is low enough, we'll stim one more night and trigger tomorrow. Although I'm insanely uncomfortable, I'd prefer to stim one more night and trigger tomorrow. I'd like to get those smaller ones a little extra time to cook in there.

I'm sure I sound like a baby when I whine about being uncomfortable. REALLY, I'm huge. This picture was taken last night right after I took my Gonal-f. See... I'm not exaggerating. I am HUGE. I'll update this once I get the call from the nurse (after 2:00 pm EST).

UPDATE:

My estrogen was 1,700... again, "healthy." I will be taking another dose (112.5 units) of Gonal-F and returning in the morning for ANOTHER ultrasound and Blood work. I'm fairly certain that I will not go any longer with stims. The lead follicle was 18.5 and we can't let that one get too much bigger.

SATURDAY, APRIL 2, 2011

ER Tomorrow

The past 24 hours have not been fun. This cycle is my lowest follicle producing cycle. I'm getting really nervous for the retrieval tomorrow. I know Quality is much more important than Quantity. When you go through this process you tend to create "ifs." If I get pregnant this cycle, I'll be due on my anniversary. If this cycle works, I'll be a bikini pregnant lady." This cycle... my "if" is... "If I get less than 15 eggs, we're not going to get any normal embryos." I know that makes zero sense. Even though I think it's ridiculous, I can't help it. The lowest number of eggs we've gotten is 15. So far, we've retrieved 67 eggs total. 67 eggs and still no baby. I keep thinking that if we don't get at least 15 eggs, the chances of a normal embryo are slim to none. I'm always encouraging others with "it only takes one." Yet here I am, unable to convince myself of that.

I cried at my ultrasound yesterday when the nurse said I had nine mature follicles. What I heard was "cycle over." I knew going into this cycle that I wouldn't produce as much as usual because we started off on really low doses. We had to because of the OHSS that I got last cycle. Dr. P said "Your perspective is skewed because you've always had a million eggs but these numbers are still great (and still better than 90% of our patients)." I know, I know... why can't I just be relaxed about it?

Not only have I been stressing about that, I also feel like complete crap. AND, I'm nervous as heck for the Progesterone injections. I wish I could explain how a needle phobe feels. I have injected myself with THOUSANDS of needles. You would think it gets easier. For me, it hasn't. I still have anxiety... every single time. That's with a tiny needle that goes into your fat. The PIO needle is huge and long and going into my muscle. I may need a tranquilizer just to take it. Aye Aye.

My retrieval is scheduled for tomorrow morning at 9:00. I'll update this as soon as I'm back (and not puking). I'm going to warn you now, I'll probably be Debbie Downer.

SUNDAY, APRIL 3, 2011

ER

I'm going to be quick because I am still not feeling great. My throat is on fire. I think it's a combination of having oxygen while under anesthesia and puking my brains out after.

We got 14 eggs. It's our lowest number yet. I'm trying to be positive since 14 is still a GREAT number. It's not only a great number, we also got them in a healthy way. No insanely high estrogen, no OHSS... just a fat pregnant looking belly. I'd rather be healthy.

Now we just hope and pray that those 14 eggs were mature and all fertilize.

I'm super nervous about the PGD... I'll talk about that tomorrow, when hopefully, I won't be so sick.

MONDAY, APRIL 4, 2011

UPDATED: ER Details

Here's how the day went...

We got to the clinic, checked in and then headed to the 5th floor (surgical floor). The way it works, is you check in on the 4th floor, head up to the 5th, sit in a waiting room until a nurse comes out and calls you. While we were waiting, I was giving B a hard time for making a coffee while I couldn't eat or drink anything. He was torturing me. Needless to say, the hormonal wife won and he didn't make a coffee until I was called in. As soon as the nurse said my name, she stretched out her arms to give me a hug. You know you've been around a while when the nurses hug you, tell you that you're on their prayer list, give you updates on their children, grandchildren and vacations. I'm more like a family member than a patient. Anyway... I changed into the hospital gown and surgical slippers. After vitals were read, medical history was discussed, and I was weighed (vomit), it was time for the anesthesiologist. As he was spraying my hand with the numbing agent, I kept trying to scheme how I could steal it to be used with the PIO injection. Hahahaha... my scheming got as far as me thinking "that would be great to numb my butt before we do the PIO injection. I should steal it." Obviously, I'm not a good thief.

OH! I almost forgot the coolest part of the morning. I take part in all sorts of support groups. We have the AGC girls, AGC digital (email chain) and I do an online support group. There is a girl on the forums that's screen name refers to the Red Sox. I sent her a private message to see if she was from the same area as me. Turns out, she also sees Dr. P (in another location). The night before the retrieval we realized that she was having her retrieval at 8:00 and mine was at 9:00. All the procedures are done at the clinic I go to, so we would be there at the same time. While she was being walked into the surgical room and I was having my vitals done, we got to meet. Pretty cool... small world.

I think I mentioned in a post during my last cycle that in the old building, they would knock you out before wheeling you into the surgical room. In the new building, you walk yourself in and you help put your legs in the medieval stirrups. As I was being put in the Jesus pose, I started to feel light headed. I asked Dr. M if he gave me something. I vaguely remembering him answering me... then I was out. The next thing I know, I was in recovery. As I was waking up, I heard a voice that sounded oh so familiar. Dr. Hottie. Dr. Hottie was not there when I walked into the surgical room.

I woke up to Dr. Hottie standing next to me, holding my hand saying "you didn't wait for me." Oh Dr. Hottie. I'm waiting! He had a case at the hospital so he didn't make it in time for my ER. After trying to choke down some crackers and water, it was time for me to change. I couldn't get the knot untied off one of the johnnies. I walked out to the nursing station looking for help. Who was there to help me? You guessed it, Dr. Hottie. As he was untying my gown I said "This was my plan to get him to undress me." The nurse kept saying "Anesthesia, the truth serum."

When I was relaying this story to B on our drive home, his response was "what are you two in Love?" Oh B... while you get to go into the secret room full of porn, I get to look at Dr. Hottie. I call that fair, not love. Bwahahahaha

I had a fairly rough night with my throat. At one point (in the middle of the night, early morning) I thought I may have strep throat. It's feeling a little better now. I've had a dry mouth after surgery but never like this. My throat was/is not only burning, it feels roughed up. I'm sure the puking didn't help.

Today was the day I had to start the PIO injections. I can NOT express how freaking scary it was. Imagine being afraid of snakes and then having to sit in a room full of them for a few minutes every single day. Or imagine being afraid of flying and the only way for you to get to work every day is to fly there. That's what needles are like for me. A HUGE fear that I have to deal with everyday... some days, multiple times a day. My mother has Multiple Sclerosis (I think I've mentioned this before). For 13 years, she has done daily shots. She told me that if you ice the area first, it actually makes it more painful. She suggested that I take a hot shower before I do the shot because the hot water will soften the skin. I woke up, fed the fur babies, then took the hottest damn shower possible. I'm surprised my skin didn't burn. As soon as I was out, I brought the filled syringe to B. All night and morning I was psyching myself up. I kept saying to myself, you'll just do it. No waiting, no thinking... just do it. Nike style. I gave him the needle, grabbed a pillow, put the pillow on our dresser, leaned my fat ass over, shoved my face in the pillow, and said "just do it." B wanted to talk me through it but I told him not to. Just do it. Do it. Do it. The needle going in didn't hurt. The PIO going in burned. Taking the needle out had a little sting. It was actually easier for me because I couldn't see the needle. My stomach ones hurt more than this one did. I think those hurt more because I'm holding the needle. I'm controlling the injection. Which means, I'm seeing the needle the entire time. My butt is already a little sore. So as easy as it was today, I can see how in a week or two they're going to get more painful. At least it's done and over with!

I will talk to the lab after 2:00 today. Once I get the fertilization report, I'll update this post. Come on eggs and sperm!

UPDATE

12 out of the 14 fertilized. Grow Embies Grow!

TUESDAY, APRIL 5, 2011

UPDATED: Wait Wait Wait... All day long

This waiting! Ahhhh! Today's call will inform us on how the 12 embryos are developing. Usually, at this point, they're looking decent. Day 3 (tomorrow) is when some start to slow down or arrest in development. All the embryos with more than 4 cells tomorrow will get biopsied. Dr. PGD told us that even the ones that arrest in development will get biopsied so we can see what was wrong with them. This waiting is torture!

I must say, we are fortunate to have frozen embryos. Even if they haven't been biopsied and may result in another miscarriage. At least I have the comfort of knowing that no matter what happens with the 12 embryos, we will definitely have a transfer on Friday (with the frozens).

So... I was all talk yesterday when I said the PIO injection didn't hurt that bad. HOLY MOLY... by lunch time it felt as if someone beat my butt cheek with a sledge hammer. It is BEYOND sore. This morning's shot did actually hurt. The pain is hard to explain. Having your eyebrows threaded is more painful than the shot. It's more of a burning discomfort. I jumped a little when B broke my poor skin with the needle. I think the jumpiness was more from my anxiety than the actual shot. My boobs are killing me. KILLING me. At least I know the PIO injections are working!

I've gained a few pounds this cycle. Four to be exact. Boooo. I can't completely blame the cycle and the meds. My youngest niece and brother are in town. They live on the West Coast (I'm on the East) so I only get to see them a few times a year. How can I have my youngest niece here and not make milkshakes to drink while watching the Wizard of Oz? I definitely gained a couple of pounds from the cycle though... I swear.

Again, I'll update this once I hear from the embryologist.

UPDATE

I just got off the phone with the embryologist. All 12 embryos are dividing normally. They're all between 2-4 cells. I didn't ask for a break down for each embryo. If they continue to divide normally, all 12 will be biopsied tomorrow.

WEDNESDAY, APRIL 6, 2011

Biopsy Day

Today is not my favorite day. My day started out with my PIO injection hurting so badly that I yelled "ow ow ow" while B was giving me the injection and then I cried when he took it out. Effing needles. I hate them.

All 12 embryos were biopsied. Although I'm happy that we'll get some answers, I'm totally bummed about their development. I don't know why I thought this time would be different from all the others. Every cycle, our embryos follow the same path of development.

Retrieval: We get a lot of eggs

Day 1: We have 90-100% fertilization rate

Day 2: All the fertilized embryos develop normally and reach 2-4 cells

Day 3: The embryos shit the bed

This has happened with 67 of our eggs. I don't know why I thought eggs 68-81 would bring us different news. The embryologist basically said that they all got biopsied but they all slowed down in development. We had one 7 cell, a couple of 6 cell and the rest were "slow." Normal division of cells doubles every 24 hours. Which means, if our embryos were developing normally, all the four celled ones we had yesterday would be eight cells today. Mother effer.

I really, truly, 100% believed that with 81 eggs and a bajillion sperm, there would be a combination of the two that made a normal, viable embryo.

I hate life today. I hate infertility. I hate how my ass is effing killing me. I hate needles. I hate our stupid embryos. I hate science. I hate medicine.

The embryologist told me to call tomorrow, between 2:00 and 4:00 to get my transfer time. Also, Dr. PGD will call me as soon as she gets the biopsy results (which should be late afternoon/early evening).

THURSDAY, APRIL 7, 2011

UPDATED: PETA... WHAT?!?!

A friend of mine brought a PETA campaign to my awareness. Win a Vasectomy from PETA!

Every year in the U.S., an estimated 6 to 8 million lost, abandoned, or unwanted dogs and cats enter animal shelters. The best way to combat the companion-animal overpopulation crisis is to have your cat or dog neutered. And with a global population of almost 7 billion humans, more of our species could use a (voluntary) snip too.

Now, one lucky man can be reproduction-free, free of charge, just like his pooch or feline friend. In honor of National Infertility Awareness Week (April 24 to 30), PETA will give one free vasectomy to a man who has recently had his companion cat or dog neutered.

WHAT!?!?! In HONOR of National Infertility Awareness Week, you're giving away a Vasectomy? Are you kidding me? This is disgusting, distasteful, tactless, and any other adjective that means repulsive. I'm not against vasectomies. If you are done having children, go ahead, have a vasectomy, or get your tubes tied. Consume as many birth control pills as you can. I'm not disagreeing that some people should curb their reproduction. I've come across many men and women that should stop reproducing. Just walk in a local mall. You'll see plenty of people who should stop reproducing. It's not the reproduction preventative measures that I'm disgusted by. It's PETA's use of Infertility Awareness Week as a means to promote this campaign.

B and I have fought tooth and nail. We have gone through hell and back. We have spent thousands of dollars. I have faced fears (not just fears, phobias) on a daily basis. We have done all these things in attempts to conceive a child of our own. Having our struggle; our fight; our propose being compared to the spaying and neutering of animals is repulsive. Over the past couple of years, the infertile have stepped forward. We have shared our pain. We have made ourselves vulnerable. We have fought hard. We have educated others on the topic. We have broken barriers and taboos. We have been advocates for those afraid to speak about their struggle and loss. This campaign is NOT bringing awareness or honoring the infertile. It's making the topic trivial and insignificant.

Why not Honor Diabetes Awareness week by giving a lucky winner a year's worth of cupcakes and candy? Because that's honor and not offensive, right??

I am going to honor my fellow infertile friends by sharing my thoughts with president of PETA. I suggest you do the same: Ingrid Newkirk, at ingridn@peta.org.

Now, updates on our cycle...

The definition of Indifference (from thefreedictionary.com) is:

indifference n

1. The fact or state of being indifferent; lack of care or concern
2. Lack of quality; mediocrity
3. Lack of importance; insignificance

That is how I feel about this cycle. I have given 3.5 years of strength, hope, care, and optimism. All I have received in return is disappointment. I've been up since 4:00am because my brain is on overdrive. While I'm sitting here pondering our next steps (and the rest of the country is sleeping) I'm getting closer and closer to indifference. I just don't care right now. I don't have it in me. Maybe it's my rage from reading about the PETA Vasectomy? Does this mean I don't think I'll be a mother? No. I am a mother. Plain and simple. I just don't have it in me to care right this moment. I'm confident that our PGD results will be disappointing. I'm even more confident that IF we have normal embryos, they will arrest in development before we make it to transfer. For now, I get to watch Ellen DeGeneres with my fur babies until the sun comes up.

I'll update this once I hear from Dr. PGD. All I will know are the results of the biopsies and the time of our transfer. I won't know how the embryos are doing. Once the biopsy is complete, the lab doesn't like to disturb the embryos until the transfer. So even if they have arrested in development, I won't know until we show up tomorrow.

UPDATE

So... we had four normal embryos. I'm insanely relieved. The eight that were abnormal, all had one of three abnormalities:

Extra Chromosome 14: Will fertilize, divide, implant, and eventually miscarry

Trisomy 22 (cat eye syndrome): Will fertilize, divide, implant and most often miscarry although, some trisomy 22 babies are born. Cat eye syndrome is very rare due to the fact that the babies often don't carry to term.

Chaotic: Basically there are multiple chromosomal abnormalities. Chaotic embryos rarely make it to transfer.

I did ask about the abnormal embryos and gender. Seven of the eight abnormal embryos were one gender. I don't know which gender... we chose not to know because then it would imply which gender our normal ones are.

I have to arrive at the clinic at 9:45 tomorrow for a transfer at 10:45. They will look at the embryos in the morning and decide which two to transfer. Please, please, please keep growing!

SATURDAY, APRIL 9, 2011

1dt5dt

Am I the worst blogger? Yesterday, my blog had the most hits it has ever had in a day. I'm really sorry for not posting the details of the transfer. We got home from the transfer at about 12:30. We had my parent's 35th anniversary party last night. So after a nap, I had to put on my party planner hat. Sorry for the delay.

Of our four "normal" embryos, two of them developed into blasts, one was 4-cells and one was 5-cells. Dr. PGD said it's very common for embryos to stop developing after the biopsy because it's so stressful on them. First they have to burn a whole in the outer layer of the embryo. Then they biopsy (remove an entire cell) the embryo. Even the healthiest of embryos can get stressed and not recover. That's basically what happened to two of them.

The result? We transferred all four. The two small ones will never implant. They most likely won't even develop anymore. Although it's not scientific (Dr. PGD's exact words), embryos have shown to do better in groups. They help each other out. I'm good with non-science. If they have seen better results with large groups, then so be it. I'm all for being PUPO with Quads.

We asked if we had not done PGD and we did a 3-day transfer, would they have picked any of the four normal ones to be transferred. They said no. On day 3, the top three "looking" embryos ended up being abnormal. Dr. PGD believes (we agree with her) that this cycle is validation that we have been transferring abnormal embryos all along. You definitely can't judge a book by its cover. We're proof of that.

Now we wait. I'm not all that anxious to POAS. Normally, I would have started by now. This cycle has given us a lot of answers. Having answers has settled the urgency (at least for now). I may test on Monday or Tuesday to see if hCG is out of my system. Maybe I'll start POASing full time starting Monday. Who knows. I kind of like not being anxious about it.

I've mentioned a few times that we use the PICSI dish to find the best sperm. I believe ALL clinics should be using this dish. A friend told me today that the manufacturer of the PISCI dish has a video on their website of how it works. I just watched it. It's pretty cool. You can view it at:

http://art.biocoat.com/products.htm

I'll tell you one thing. I'm so over the Progesterone injections. Those bad boys HURT! I tried the icing method. Never again. It hurt so much more than taking a hot shower beforehand. It just made it burn and sting more. If you're going be doing PIO, heat the area first, don't ice it.

SUNDAY, APRIL 10, 2011

2dp5dt

Between Progesterone injections, being under anesthesia twice in a week and enlarged ovaries, I have been incredibly constipated (TMI... sorry). Yesterday I made veggie juice (broccoli, carrots, celery, cucumber, collard greens, wheat grass, apple, and pear), I took three Colaces, and we had Mexican (TONS of beans) for dinner. I even went for a couple mile walk. Nothing. NOTHING! Today, I remade the juice (I make it every morning), took another Colace, ate food I would never eat with hopes it would upset my stomach and went on a 3.5 mile walk (MS Walk). Nothing. Nothing until about ten minutes ago. You have no idea how painful that was but how good I feel now. Ahhhh, the joys of IVF.

Nothing to report today. I'm slightly crampy today. It could be GI related. Who knows. I'm going to start testing tomorrow morning. It's very early but you know how much I love those darn sticks.

MONDAY, APRIL 11, 2011

3dp5dt

My sick love affair with peeing on a stick has started today. My entire pay check will go to plastic covered hCG test strips. I love it!

Since getting all the faint positives last cycle, I decided to test every morning with two different brands (same urine). That way I can't question if I see evaporation lines or true lines.

Today's result? Two faint positives. I'm only 3dp5dt (to the non-infertile world, that's the same as eight days past ovulation). So it's early. Very early. Most likely the tests are picking up the trigger. I triggered 11 days ago. Tomorrow will gives us a better reading. If it is the trigger, it will be lighter or negative tomorrow. Joyous.

No matter what the result of this cycle ends up being, I feel much more relieved with the answers we got. I know that if it doesn't happen this time, it will happen soon. It's only a matter of time.

My 7 year old niece has been in town for the past week. She has been going back and forth between my house and my parents. The other night, B and I were teaching her how to play Scrabble. The next morning, she wakes up and says "You'll never believe the dream I had. It was so crazy..." This is how it went...

She was going to the gas station with her Dad. Her Dad asked her if she wanted anything inside. She did, so she followed him into the gas station. Once she entered the gas station, it turned into a police station. I was the police officer standing behind the counter. As she entered, I said "I'm here to give you a ticket." Then I gave her a scrabble ticket.

Hahahaha... Maybe my dreams aren't caused my Lupron. Maybe it's in my genes to have messed up dreams!

TUESDAY, APRIL 12, 2011

4dp5dt

Yesterday's positive tests were definitely the trigger. The two I took this morning couldn't be any more negative. The embryos would have implanted by now. From what I've read online (I know! I can't help Google things!) 5dp5dt is the most common time people see positives. We'll see...

My niece and brother left this morning. It was nice having them around. The house is going to be eerily quiet without my niece. I'm glad we're going on vacation tomorrow... we won't have a chance to let the quietness of our lives settle in.

Other than a nasty cold, I have some dull cramping on my sides. I'm 99.9% sure that it's my ovaries going back to their normal size. Other than a cold and cramps, I have nothing to report. The waiting is boring for all of us. Actually, I take that back. I have a weird rash. It's more like clusters of acne all over my chest. It goes from shoulder to shoulder. It actually follows my bra line (including above the cleavage area. Dr. P thinks it's a reaction to the PIO. If it's a rash caused by the progesterone, I have to discontinue it. If it's acne caused by the progesterone, I just deal. It makes me nervous to switch medications at the end of the cycle. So I'm hoping (as gross and ugly as it is) that it's just acne.

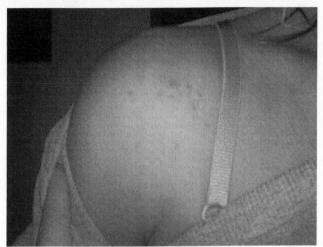

WEDNESDAY, APRIL 13, 2011

5dp5dt

I am going to be quick because I went to the Sox game last night and didn't get around to packing. I have about 45 minutes to shower, get a shot in the rear and pack. I can't wait to be in sunny CA. Ahhhh...

This morning's POAS results:

I took three tests 1) Doctor office tests (a doctor I used to work with gave me a bunch of them) 2) Answer 3) First Response

The in-office test is stark white negative. The Answer test has a faint line... so faint, it may be a shadow. I'm not sure if that's a line. The First Response has a faint, faint, faint line. It's faint but clearly pink and not a shadow. I'm not sure what to think. Last cycle, when Dr. P called me to tell me my beta was 15, I went home and took a test (Answer). I saved that test and the line is MUCH darker than what I'm seeing today. I know Answer can pick up a beta of at least 15 so I'm not sure what to think of today's results. The only thing I can do is Pee again tomorrow! Wahoo! You should see the amount of tests I have to pack. I have enough for three a day until beta. Yep, I'm packing 15 tests. That includes three digitals. I'm saving those bad boys for the end of the cycle.

Speaking of tests, I've learned that the BEST place to buy them is Wal-Mart. They are a few dollars cheaper than all the other pharmacies. I know a lot of people like the dollar store ones. I had my share of false positives with blue dye tests to not care about the price. I'd rather pay a little extra (and if you're a good POAS shopper, you can always get them cheaper with sales and coupons) for the pink line tests.

I'll write more tomorrow. For now, I have to pack.

CA BOUND!

THURSDAY, APRIL 14, 2011

6dp5dt

We only have our Mac with us on vacation. When I'm on the Mac, I can't respond to comments. I will as soon as I get home!

So... our lines are getting lighter. I'm afraid to say it out loud but for the sake of blog transparency, I will... I think we're experiencing a chemical pregnancy. Basically, an embryo implanted but stopped developing. My HPTs so far have looked like this:

3dp5dt (Monday): FAINT line

4dp5dt (Tuesday): Stark white negative

4.5dp5dt (Tuesday late afternoon): Faint line

5dp5dt (Yesterday): Faint line but much darker than Tuesday's

6dp5dt (today): Faint line... faint like it was two days ago

Best case scenario (but still a stretch) is that more than one implanted and one died out and the other is still growing. It's a total stretch... I'm thinking we're out for this cycle. I knew something was up last night. My back was killing me and I was insanely crampy. I felt how I always feel a day before I miscarry.

I always get lots of "I'm sorry" and "It's not over until the beta." I appreciate them but don't feel bad. I feel like we got so much information this cycle. It's the first cycle that I feel like a negative was worth it. I truly feel like this was our first real shot at a live birth. All the other cycles, we were transferring abnormal embryos. Finding a chromosomally normal embryo is just step one in the process. It took us many years and many let downs for us to get there. If this cycle doesn't work, it was worth it.

Every cycle, I pray that it works out. After the miscarriages, I even started praying for an abnormal child. I would say "I know the miscarriage is my body's way of self-aborting an unhealthy child but I can handle it. I would do great with a disabled child." After learning about the abnormalities of our embryos, I am at peace with "why" we have gone through what we have gone through. It's so easy to wonder "why us?" I've realized, we're going through this because it's God's (or whatever you believe in) way of protecting us from a difficult life. He's not just protecting us, he's protecting our future children. I now understand and appreciate why we're going through this. So, to me (I can't speak for B), this feels like our first failure. We're 0 for 1. Sure, we've been going through this for years. Sure we've invested a lot of time and money. Sure my body had seen enough needles to last a lifetime. Sure we have dealt with so much heartache. BUT all of those things got us answers. I can't complain about that.

I will say, knowing (or having an inclination) that this cycle didn't work, made the progesterone injection this morning totally suck. My beta is Monday. Only four more days of those damn things.

I've already thought about our next cycle. Now that we have answers and now that I've officially missed the deadline to get the good maternity leave with work, I'm not in a rush. We were using Clomid to force ovulation (doing so many medicated cycles screwed up my natural ovulation). This cycle, I'm going to let my body do its thing. Even if it takes a month or two to ovulate, I don't mind. I will however, not skip a cycle. I'll get a period right after stopping the progesterone. Then I will start Lupron once I ovulate. That could be in two weeks... it could be in two months. Either way, I'll be spending the time getting my butt back in shape.

I will say this... If you are going to deal with the grieving process of another failed cycle, doing it on vacation is awesome! Seriously, I'm not joking. It hasn't put a damper on our vacation. I actually think I'll have more fun. I won't be too nervous to do anything. We have a wedding on Saturday... you better believe I'll be dancing my booty off!

FRIDAY, APRIL 15, 2011

7dp5dt

Well, my digital "pregnant" has turned into "not pregnant." I didn't bother taking a test this morning. I figured I would save my tests for cycle #6.

I woke up in the middle of the night will KILLER cramps. I asked Dr. P if I could stop the Progesterone... of course she said no. Boohoo. My right butt cheek is absolutely killing me. I can't lay on that side and I can barely sit. It's awesome.

Yesterday, I felt a little more "okay" with this cycle. Today, I'm freaking bullshit. Honestly, it's crap. We're good people with good jobs that would make good parents. There are plenty of blessings in this cycle but they don't make this easier. I thought they would. Then again, I wrote my post yesterday when I was still getting positive tests. Even though I knew it wasn't looking good, I guess I had a glimmer of hope. I was still getting "positive" on the digital test so why wouldn't I have some hope? However, my boobs did start to deflate. That's a sure sign that things are going in the wrong direction. I know... someday we will have kids. Until you have walked in the shoes of a person struggling with infertility and repeated loss, you can't imagine how painful it is to think you may never have a biological child.

Our embryos have always arrested in development. We've always known our issue is with that. I was really hoping that finding the chromosomally normal ones would prevent that from happening. Clearly, it didn't. We had two normal ones that arrested in development before transfer day. Finding the chromosomally normal embryos is just step one. 3.5 years, three failed IUIs, two failed IVFs, one failed FET, two successful IVFs ending in miscarriage, one IVF ending in chemical pregnancy and we're only at step one. I guess you always hope that the current cycle is going to be the one exception to all the others. Apparently, it doesn't happen that way. This blows.

SATURDAY, APRIL 16, 2011

8dp5dt

I'm miserable. I have cramps like you wouldn't believe but I won't bleed until we stop the progesterone... which is in another two days. We went out to dinner last night with a couple of friends and I had to leave before we even ordered. My cramps were so bad, I was sweating at the table. That's not normal, right? What the hell?

I'm not sure what we're going to do. We agreed that we would keep trying until we financially couldn't anymore... which is four more cycles. I don't think I have it in me. I think I'm done. We've created 81 embryos. 81. AND we don't have one child to show for it. This whole process puts my body and my body alone through torturous tests and exams. My body has been through hell and back and all I have to show for it is 15 pounds.

We've missed weddings and parties. We've missed vacations. I've been sick through birthdays and holidays. I haven't had a freaking glass of wine in what feels like years. I don't get to enjoy the things I love, like working out. All these things would mean nothing if it meant we would have a child. But for nothing... I'm all set.

For now, I'm going to take my bruised ass to the pool. Maybe a little vitamin D will lift my spirits. We are on vacation... can infertility just let us enjoy this??

Beta Day

As we all knew, the beta was negative. I am SO glad I don't have to do those damn injections anymore.

I'm not sure what our next step is. As for right now, I'm pretty down. I guess all the years of being positive have caught up to me. At some point, I had to break. I'm not used to being so depressed and crying all the time. It's not just another let down. We're that much closer to realizing that having a biological child may not be in our cards. I can clearly get pregnant (when we have healthy enough embryos)... but even our healthiest embryos stop developing after a few days/weeks. We have created 81 embryos and haven't had one make it longer than seven weeks. How can we expect any to make it nine months?

My WTF appointment is on April 29th with Dr. P. We'll see what she has to say. As of right now, I'm done. Maybe I'll change my mind in a couple of weeks. We shall see.

MONDAY, APRIL 18, 2011

Now What?

Dr. P and I briefly talked yesterday. Basically, these are our options:

1. Stop trying all together.

2. Do another cycle with PGD.
3. Do another cycle without PGD but implant four or five (knowing that more than half won't make it).
4. Do a trial cycle with my eggs and donor sperm.

They all sound like crappy options to me. I always said I would keep trying until our finances forced us to stop. However, my body is burnt out. I'm physically exhausted. How many times we can force menopause, get pregnant, and miscarry? When is enough, enough?

Doing another cycle with PGD is probably the most appealing. Although, do we really want to keep spending thousands of dollars and not have a guaranteed live birth?

If we do another cycle without PGD and transfer four or five embryos, there's a good chance some will implant and die out. What happens if our one survivor is in that mix? What happens if/when I miscarry the ones that stop developing... does the healthy one suffer through it or will it be a forced miscarriage as well?

I have wanted to do a trial cycle for a long time. However, what happens if/when the donor sperm embryos are viable and healthy? What happens to them? I can't and will not willingly destroy healthy embryos.

So... all the options sort of suck. Dr. P said, "You have every right to be discouraged but I think the fighter in you will win." If she's right... which option is a winner? None of them seem appealing right now.

We're still in the adoption process (we're still a year-a year and a half away from the matching process). We know we will be parents. I'm not worried about that. Not being able to share a biological child with my husband is heartbreaking. When you date, you look for traits and characteristics in a person that not only blend with who you are but also are traits you want your children to have. When you get married, you look forward to starting a life together. Having little B's run around has always been something I dream about. Breastfeeding, delivery, pregnancy... they're all events that I have wanted to experience my entire life. Grieving the loss of those needs and wants is a very difficult task.

What about our relationships? They've already changed so much. When friends start having babies, you're automatically pushed to the outside. We're not invited to hang out on weekends because weekends are full of play dates and mommy hang out time. Life goes on for those around us and slowly, we get pushed aside. A lot has changed and will continue to change. So this grieving process isn't just about the loss of a biological child. It's also about accepting that our life is different and will be different than we planned.

THURSDAY, APRIL 21, 2011

I'm baaaack

I'm back. Sorry for the sabbatical. I needed a few days to be angry, sad, depressed. Sometimes all it takes is a 6 mile run and a package of Oreos to bounce back into normalcy. I'm much better now. Well, I'm still sad but at least I'm functional.

I went for a run yesterday. I was traveling for work, so I was running on a treadmill in a hotel gym. Around mile 2, I was dying. I was dripping with sweat. My heart rate was through the roof... at one point it was at 187. All I wanted to do was finish a 5k. I kept focusing on the mileage and timing. That's the worst. If you're running on a treadmill, don't stare at the stats. Looking at them only makes the run seem like it's taking forever. I took my shirt off and put it over the information so I could no longer see it. NO, I wasn't topless. I had a long sleeve shirt over my t-shirt. Anyway, I kept playing mental games with myself. I kept saying "If you can have three miscarriages and still push forward, you can run another mile." or "How can you expect to kick infertility's ass if you can't fight through a cramp?" I just kept playing mental game after mental game. Then, my hand swung and hit the emergency cord. The treadmill stopped. Once you stop... or at least... once I stop, I'm done. I'm no longer sweating, I'm DRIPPING. My heart is no longer beating fast, it's about to explode. COME ON! All I want to do is run a few miles. I take the shirt off the top of the treadmill and saw that I not only ran 3 miles... I ran 6.5 miles. That's a big "Effff You Infertility."

B and I have been discussing our options. I'll definitely update you all over the next couple of days. We're still working it out and I don't want to post about it until we talk about it more.

I'm back. That's the most important thing. Seriously, I was a mess!

FRIDAY, APRIL 22, 2011

Happy Birthday Dr. P!

Dr. P...
Our future baby's conception creator...

You cry with us when we miscarry. You are as heartbroken as we are when our beta is negative. You put up with my crazy emails. You answer my too much information messages as if I'm asking the most important question in the world. Sadly, nothing I have to say is important and I send messages that say, "Can I have sex today?" or "I can't poop." You love Dexter and P90x. You look like you belong on the set of Private Practice. You always are wearing fabulous shoes. You make statements that give me hope (and you have no idea that you're doing it). You run into the sterile operating room because you don't want me to go into surgery without a hug and a "good luck" from you. You call me because you want to make sure the information I received from the nurse is fully understood. You present our case to the department to make sure there isn't anything you're missing. As you once stated, you have made getting us pregnant your life's work. You brought Dr. Hottie into our lives. You're the best and we love you.

Happy Birthday Dr. P!

MONDAY, APRIL 25, 2011

iPod Man

I hope everyone (who celebrates Easter) had a wonderful Easter. We spent the day with B's family. We just had my parents 35th anniversary party a couple of weeks ago (day of transfer) so we saw my side recently enough to not split the holiday between the two families. It can be tough driving back and forth.

Funny story...

Friday, after work, I went for a run. My 6.5 mile run was done a treadmill. Running on the streets takes a lot more out of me so I wasn't sure how far I'd make it. My goal was to run a 5k loop that is around my house. I was running against the elements... hills, wind and allergens. I don't even think I made it a mile before I started feeling tired, winded, and sore. I knew I was just being a wimp so I kept going. Around 2.5 miles in, I mentally started to shut down. I kept thinking "You ran far enough. You can stop here." But then, something inside of me said "don't stop." I kept fighting through the urge to stop. Then, the iPod voice said "RUNNING ON LOW BATTERY." Hahahaha... NO KIDDING! I couldn't help but laugh at myself. Of course, just when I want to give up, the damn iPod reminds me that I'm running on low battery. About a half a mile or so after that, I started to feel like I needed to stop. I wasn't in pain. Other than my lungs burning (from the pollen), I was fine. It's just so easy to give up on yourself. It's so easy to think "I can't do this." Again, I started telling myself that I could do it and I was just being a wimp. As I'm talking to myself (don't worry, these conversations all happen in my head) I run over "PUSSY" that some punk spray painted on the bike bath. First the iPod man tells me I was running on low battery. Then I'm reminded that I'm a "Pussy" by spray paint. I was laughing so hard at the timing of both of those. I ended up running the entire 3.2 miles.

This is just a simple reminder that even when I think I can't do it, I can, and I will. With that being said, I'm pretty sure we'll go for another cycle. I just need medical and scientific reasoning to do it. I need Dr. P and Dr. PGD to give us information that makes us think that next time will be different.

I have a list that is two pages long of questions and tests I want run. After our appointment on Wednesday I'll post about them. I'm sure I'll add a bunch more between today and Wednesday.

WEDNESDAY, APRIL 27, 2011

WTF Appointment

I'm going to do my best to cover every detail of our appointment.

B and I were presented again at the patient care clinic or session... I forget what it's called. Basically, it's like grand rounds. If you watch Grey's Anatomy, it's when the entire department is sitting in a lecture hall, one physician presents a case, and they all discuss treatment options. Anyway, we have been presented often... and we are very grateful for that. I love that we are getting 30 or so opinions and treatment ideas.

I gave Dr. P my two page list of tests that I wanted done (to me). She graciously took the list. I'm sure it's really tough competing with Dr. Google. Anyway, she took the list and said "we've already done these." I wanted a RPL (recurrent pregnancy loss) panel done. We already did it. I wanted thyroid tests done. We already did it. I wanted immune testing done. We already did MOST of it. There were two tests we hadn't done. We decided to only do one. There is only one treatment that has proven benefits. So instead of spending the money on the test, we're just going to act as if I have an autoimmune issue. So, the next cycle, I will be on steroids. That actually gives me a sense of relief. I know I'm testing negative across the board. Women know their bodies incredibly well. I know that something physiological happens to my body right before I miscarry. I don't know if it's normal or not, but my gut is telling me it's not. As advanced as reproductive medicine is, they don't have all the answers. I know I'm testing negative for all the "known" miscarriage causes however, I'm not convinced I don't have something else... something our tests aren't sophisticated enough to find. So, with that being said, we're going to suppress my immune system to see if that will help maintain a pregnancy.

I know we're just doing this for my piece of mind. Both Dr. P and Dr. PGD said there is no harm, so why not? Instead of me writing the full list of tests that I wanted done (and had no idea I already had done), I'm going to refer you to my friend Whitney's blog. She has a great post about them.

http://www.whitneyanderick.com/?p=2539

When we were discussing the autoimmune disorders, I mentioned to Dr. P that even if my levels were slightly abnormal, I would just get a surrogate. She said that she would never suggest a surrogate for us. If it came down to donor anything, she would suggest donor embryo over donor uterus. Her reasoning for this makes sense. Our first miscarriage, my levels started to show signs of miscarriage before I had any physical symptoms of a miscarriage. I was sent home to wait to start bleeding. I didn't have any cramps or pain. All we knew is that my levels weren't rising as fast as they should be. Also, our embryos are dying before they are even placed in my body. If it was truly an issue with my body, the embryos would be looking great before transfer. We have always known that our embryo quality is poor. We knew this from cycle one. It's hard for me (B too) to accept that we just have crap luck. It's hard to accept that there really isn't anything we can do to fix it. So we're constantly trying to self-diagnose and find solutions to what we think is the problem. I'm forever grateful that Dr. P has allowed us to do this. I'm sure she gets annoyed as I know it's not easy to compete with Dr. Google. However, she has always followed up our concerns with tests and treatments (even if they are crazy).

As far as the PGD goes, we've decided not to do it again. We got a lot of information out of the last cycle. We also know that our embryo quality is very poor. The stress of being in a dish for five days and the stress of the biopsy is not good for them. Instead of doing PGD, we are going to transfer more than usual. We don't know the number, it will all be based on the formula they came up with. The thought is, we will transfer more knowing that 2/3 of them won't survive.

Something I haven't talked about on the blog because, this is my blog. It's about me and my thoughts. Although this is an issue that WE as a couple are going through, it's not fair for me to put B's side on here. If he wanted the world to know his feelings and issues, he'd have his own blog. However, I did ask if he was okay with me talking about the sperm. He is. So for the first time we're going to talk about the sperm.

The only issue that we seem to be dealing with is low morphology. When a semen analysis is done they look at several parameters: Count, Motility, Volume, and Morphology. B's counts and volumes are those of a teenager. They're actually insanely high. The motility is the speed and direction of the sperm. The WHO (world health organization) defines normal motility as 60%. B has never even come close to being lower than 60%. He has some speed racers in there. The only thing that came up low but not low enough to cause the issues we're having, is the morphology. Morphology is the size and shape of the sperm. Just like all the other parameters, every male (including those considered super fertile) have some degree of abnormal morphology. You will never find any male that has 100% normal morphology... or motility. Putting all the pieces together, with his high counts/volume, having a lower count of normal morphology shouldn't be an issue. Even with 1% morphology that gives us WELL OVER a million sperm that are considered to be morphology normal. Even with slightly lower morphology, that still doesn't or shouldn't put us in the position we're in.

This brings me to DNA fragmentation. DNA fragmentation is a new concept. Until recently (2006 or so), the reproductive world has thought of the semen analysis parameters to be the end all and be all for sperm testing. Until DNA fragmentation entered the reproductive world, if a couple endured miscarriages or several unsuccessful IVF attempts and the semen analysis were normal, the egg would then be faulted. Now, science shows that DNA fragmentation is a completely separate variable... independent of the semen analysis.

Malereproduction.com states:

Men with otherwise normal semen analyses can have a high degree of DNA damage and men with what was called very poor sperm quality can have very little DNA damage. More importantly what has also been demonstrated is that the degree of DNA fragmentation correlates very highly with the inability of the sperm to initiate a birth regardless of the technology used to fertilize the egg such as insemination, IVF or ICSI. Sperm with high DNA fragmentation may fertilize an egg and embryo development stops before implantation or may even initiate a pregnancy but there is a significantly higher likelihood that it will result in miscarriage. By testing for sperm DNA fragmentation, many cases of formally "unexplained" infertility can now be explained. Many of those couples who have been previously unable to conceive with what would be considered extreme measures have been diagnosed with high sperm DNA fragmentation and treated. It is now very clear to see that having this information about the quality of the sperm can be tremendously helpful to couples and their physicians.

There are tests that can be done to determine the amount of DNA fragmentation. However, the results wouldn't matter. The test is only done on a sample of the sperm. With a formula, they (the lab) come up with a percentage of sperm that have DNA fragmentation. However, that percentage is only representative of the sample, not the entire count. Really, it's not all that accurate. Also, studies have shown that men, who have tested with high DNA fragmentation, have gone on to create successful pregnancies and men who have shown to have low DNA fragmentation have not been able to create a successful pregnancy. Although medical advances have allowed us to test for DNA fragmentation, it's still a work in progress. We still don't know enough. We decided that we're not going to spend the money on the DNA fragmentation testing. Instead, we're going to do what we're doing with me and the autoimmune disorders... we're going to act and treat us as if it is an issue.

Now... that brings me to treatment of DNA fragmentation. Well, there isn't any. There is the thought that somehow from the testicles to ejaculation, the sperm gets damaged. The theory is based on the structure (I'm not going to get into the details of the structure of the male reproductive system) the sperm have to travel through and also natural elements it is exposed to. Believe it or not, the semen (which is the fluid that helps the sperm travel) has chemicals that can be harmful to the sperm, i.e. fructose. That's also the theory behind an IUI (insemination). They remove all seminal fluid and only inject pure sperm. There are two thoughts with IUIs. 1) Removing the seminal fluid gives the sperm a chance to survive without the harmful components of the seminal fluid. 2) During an IUI, they are injecting the sperm and bypassing the cervix. Basically give the sperm a head start in their swim.

What does this mean? Well, there is a thought... again, just a thought, that if you remove the sperm directly from the testicles, then you can avoid some of the damage that can occur. For our next cycle, B will have a TESA or a TESE done... Basically, a sperm extraction from the testicle. From what I read online, it's like having a biopsy done. I don't know... it doesn't sound pleasant. It is painful and zero fun. We're still working with theories so I think it's incredible that B didn't even hesitate when it was brought up. We will meet with the urologist next month. We still don't know the details. I'm not sure if the TESA is done the day of the retrieval or if it is done before and they freeze the sperm. Once I have those details, I'll let you know.

We're dealing with multi-factorial infertility. We don't have one particular issue to work with. Dr. PGD said "With you, it's a matter of fine tuning all these little things." Here we are, fine tuning away. Dr. P and Dr. PGD think we can still conceive naturally. Uhm... yeah. If that ever happens, I will name our child The Fat Lady Sang or Pigs Flew.

Now we just wait for me to ovulate and then we can start good old Lupron.

TUESDAY, MAY 3, 2011

Urology Appointment

Today, we had our appointment with Dr. S, the male infertility specialist/urologist. It was a very strange feeling being on the "other side." Normally, I am the one being examined and poked. B's exam was no more than two minutes. When they came back I said, "That was quick." Dr. S replied with, "These exams are nothing compared to yours." No kidding! I want balls!

We discussed two tests and their possible outcomes and treatments.

The first test is called a Sperm FISH (Fluorescent In Situ Hybridization). Say that three times! Honestly, I don't even know what that means. Basically, the FISH tests the chromosomes in the sperm. Each of us have 46 chromosomes. The sperm has 23 chromosomes and the egg has 23 chromosomes. FISH test will determine if the sperm carries the correct number of chromosomes or an abnormal number (too many or too little). In the medical world, they call this aneuploidy. If there is an abnormality, you will get genetically abnormal embryos. We obviously fit this category. HOWEVER, I pray that the results come back with a decent number of chromosomally normal sperm. If the results show 99% of the sperm is abnormal, then it's game over for us. If the results show a decent percentage of normal sperm, then we can keep trying. B and I were discussing the possible outcomes. We both agree that there is no way that we won't fall into the grey area. That's just how this process is going for us. We figure whatever the cut off is for being able to produce a normal embryo and successful pregnancy, we'll fall on the cut off line. We'll be in the grey and have to make some sort of difficult decision. Dr. P believes that we'll have a good percentage of normal sperm. Her thought behind this is since our PGD embryos resulted in some normal ones, that he must have normal sperm. I really hope she is right. I can't do game over right now.

The second test we discussed is the sperm DNA Fragmentation test. This is the test we discussed at our WTF appointment. Originally we decided not to do it. Dr. S suggested that we do it because the outcome will determine how he extracts the sperm from the testicle (TESA). A friend of mine sent me video of a TESE procedure. HOLY MOLY! I had to watch it in segments. B wanted me to send it to him and I refused. As we were waiting for Dr. S to come into the consultation room, B says, "I am not going to have it done unless I see it." Ya right. Nice try buddy. I guess the procedure I watched is mainly for men who have very poor counts. Dr. S said since B's counts are always great, he most likely can extract the sperm via a needle in the office (as opposed to cutting the testicles open in an OR). Yowzers.

We want answers from the DNA Fragmentation test. We do not want answers from the FISH test. I guess I should say, we do not want negative results from the FISH. If the answer is a good portion of chromosomally normal sperm, then I'll take that. Nothing else.

Having some sort of answer as opposed to "unexplained" would be really nice. I just hope the answer is a treatable one. Right now, B is scheduled for the DNA Fragmentation test on Tuesday. We're still waiting on the office to call us back about scheduling the FISH test.

The kicker to these tests is that they take a few weeks. A few weeks to the fertile may seem like nothing. A few weeks in treatment land, is an eternity. This means we'll most likely not be doing another cycle for a bit. Booo hooo.

WEDNESDAY, MAY 4, 2011

The skinny on skinny

I had a lady (total stranger) tell me that I was too skinny today. Really? Too skinny? I'm 5'8" and weigh 130 lbs... I'm not too skinny. In fact, I have lots of loose, jiggly stuff that I'd really like to get rid of.

First, it's completely inappropriate to comment on how a stranger looks. I even find it inappropriate to comment on how friends look. Unless, of course, the comment is a compliment.

Throughout our cycles, I've heard it all. I've been told I look fat. It has been brought to my attention that I have gained weight (no, really?!?!). I've been told that I look too skinny. I'm too big, too little... I can't keep up.

Here's the thing with fertility treatments...

We all know that women going through fertility treatments get their bodies pumped up with hormones. One day we're ovulating. The next day we're going through menopause. The following day we're producing eggs. The day after that we're ovulating again. Then we're pregnant. Talk about hormone overload. During menopause a female's estradiol levels start to decrease. Lupron stops your body from producing estradiol. Hence using Lupron for the induction of menopause phase of treatment. What you may not realize is that estradiol also impacts the body's fat distribution. When estrogen levels decrease the body starts to distribute fat unevenly. Mainly it starts to get distributed to abdomen area. ALSO, when estrogen levels drop, the percentage of subcutaneous fat drops and the percentage of visceral fat increases. When it comes to fat, you want the subcutaneous version. Subcutaneous fat is just under the surface of the skin. It's what causes the ripply/cottage cheese look as we age. It is also easier to lose. Visceral fat is deep in your body. It's bad fat. Bad bad bad. It's linked to hypertension, diabetes, strokes and more. With that being said... our bodies are going through more than just simple hormonal weight gain. Our bodies are distributing fat to places that we can't even see. We're gaining weight in areas that are so hard to get rid of.

What's my point? My point is, if you think I look fat, I probably am fat. If you notice my weight has shifted to my mid-section... it's because it has shifted to my mid-section. I don't need you to point it out. I don't need anyone to point it out. I get in the shower every day and see it for myself. What I wanted to say to the lady today was "I don't look too skinny. I look damn good!"

My body has gone through "menopause" five times, I have been pregnant three times and I have been on hormone therapy for years. I realize that I may never look as I once did. BUT I think I look fantastic! So no old lady, I don't look too skinny!

SUNDAY, MAY 8, 2011

Mother's Day

Happy Mother's Day to all the mothers out there.

To all the others, I'm thinking of you all.

I go to birthday parties, baby showers, and hospitals when babies are born. I discuss baby rearing obstacles and struggles. I rejoice in baby milestones. Day in and day out, I face, head-on, the most difficult struggle in my life. In a time of social networking and all the other technology advances, Mother's Day is even harder than it once was. Friends send friends "Mother Awards." Facebook statuses are full of baby delivery information. Although today is a day I will be celebrating the mothers in my life, it's also a day full of sadness. I am reminded of the years of struggle B and I have been through. I am reminded of all the Baby Ls and their loss. I am reminded of needles and pain. I am reminded of the control over my body that I once had. I am reminded that at some point in this journey, I lost control of my plans, hopes, and dreams.

Last night at dinner, B and I were talking about friends' of ours and their kids. They are honestly two of the cutest kids on earth. Their daughter (the older one) is by far the funniest child I have ever met. She has the best personality on earth... she's only 3. We were talking about them last night and B said "When we get kids..." As soon as he said it my stomach turned over. Although the idea of a biological child is pretty much a fantasy in our world, I've never heard him even hint at the idea of it not working. He's always the optimistic one. He has always believed that this will work. When he used the word "get" over "have," I made a joke about it. Joking is better than falling apart, right? Why are we the couple that has to get children? Why can't we have them? Those weren't pity questions. I realize that sounds like "why us" or "whoa is me." I meant it seriously. Why? Some test at some point has to tell us something... right??

Women dealing with infertility are the most incredibly strong women I know. They fight day in and day out for what they deserve. My love and thoughts are with all of you today.

WEDNESDAY, MAY 11, 2011

Blessed

Hello Friends!

I know it's been a few days since I last post. Not much has happened since Mother's Day. Well, I consumed enough calories to feed an army. Not to worry, B and I went for a run when we got back from dinner. The run wasn't pretty. I thought I was going to puke up Boston Cream Pie. At least I worked off a portion of my emotional eating.

B went in for the DNA Fragmentation test today. The lab that does the test is in the same State that we live in. They should get the sample tomorrow and we should have results in a week or so. The Sperm FISH test will be done either next week or the week after. I must say, it's extremely frustrating working with the Male Infertility/Urology office. They are not as efficient as Dr. P's office. Dr. P orders a test and you have it done immediately.

Since we won't cycle again for a while, I'm enjoying working out again. I went back to boxing last week. HOLY CRAP! My arms were shaking so badly after! I went this morning before work and I thought I was going to puke. Not once, but twice. I could feel the liquidy burn in my throat. Thankfully, I didn't embarrass myself and survived without puking. At one point during the training, we were paired up with another member. As I was round housing my partner, she mentioned not seeing me for a while. Normally, I wouldn't share my struggles with a complete stranger. I'm not sure what it was that made me share the details of my life for the past year, but I did. She then shared a story about her niece...

Her niece, who was only 15 when she got pregnant, had a healthy pregnancy from the start. At nine and a half months, her baby died. The doctors had her vaginally deliver the baby that she just carried for 38 weeks. 15 years old, dealing with an unplanned (I assume) pregnancy; dealing with the emotions of deciding to keep her baby; dealing with the struggle of being in high school and pregnant; dealing with the loss of the baby she carried two weeks shy of full term.

I also met a girl this weekend (at a 3 year old birthday party) whose husband passed away in Iraq. At the time of his death, their daughter was around 2 years old. She ended up meeting and getting engaged to a nice guy. She got pregnant and delivered a healthy baby. Then the baby died at 3 months old of SIDS. By the age of 30, she lost a husband and a baby.

Hearing stories like that and I can't help but think we are nothing but blessed. We have had our share of crap luck. What's crap luck when you have the happiness that we give each other? I'd take a childless life with B over a life full of children without B. We are blessed to have found each other. We are blessed to have the life we have. We are blessed. Remind me of that the next time a cycle fails!

FRIDAY, MAY 13, 2011

Small Boobies

Okay. When did I forget that I had small boobs?? I guess with all the medication, hormones and being pregnant, I was lucky to live as a full breasted woman. Since going back to my old workout routine and not being on any medication, I have learned or should I say remembered, that I have little boobs. BoooHooo. For the past couple of years I have been busting out of bras. Now I barely fill them. At least they're easy to run with.

Last night I had a patient program. The speaker was a neurologist from NH. At the end of the night we were talking and of course infertility came up. She then shared her story...

She tried for years to get pregnant. They tried naturally and they did several fertility treatments (I didn't ask for specifics). After several failed cycles and miscarriages, she was told she could not have children. She and her husband decided to pursue adoption. She said "at the time, I needed a baby so badly. Emotionally, I needed one. I was about to break." She eventually was matched with a newborn baby boy. After he was brought home, she noticed that she was gaining weight. She decided to pick up running. After a few months of running like a "crazy lady," she went to the doctor. She went to the doctor with only one complaint "I'm getting fat and I don't know why." The doctor ran some tests, one of them being an ultrasound. The ultrasound tech said "HOLY SH*%! There's a WHOLE baby in there." She was not only pregnant, she was 4.5 months pregnant. After years of fertility treatments and eventually being told they could never have a child, she was pregnant. So now her first two children (yes, she had a third) are only 11 months apart. I love that!

Today is cycle day 21. Sure enough, what do I get with my ovulation test? A smiley face. Yep, when I don't need to ovulate on time, I do. Of course, right? My cycles typically run 34 days. Normally, I ovulate between days 17-20. I'm not 100% back on track but I'm pretty darn close. Go figure.

B is scheduled to do the FISH test on Tuesday. The test is done at Baylor in Texas. We won't see those results for a couple of weeks. The urology office told us that if we don't get the results of the DNA fragmentation by mid-week (next week) they will call the lab to see what's going on.

For 10+ years, my Dad has participated in the MS 150. It's a 150 mile bike ride run by the MS Society. I rode with him/his team a couple of times. I wasn't able to ride for the past two years because of cycles. I finally get to ride again this year. The ride also happens to be on my birthday :) I started training for it last week. Before work yesterday, I went on a 15 mile ride. Don't forget, I got my butt kicked in boxing on Wednesday. Yep, boxing then riding. I can barely walk today. Seriously, getting off the toilet is a workout!

THURSDAY, MAY 19, 2011

Fragmentation Results

Finally! We have results. Great news but still leaves us "unexplained."

The DNA Fragmentation test consists of three parts (I explain what they all mean below).
1. DNA Fragmentation: 25
2. Oxidative Stress: Normal
3. "something else to do with DNA" (Those were B's words, not mine): Normal

DNA Fragmentation:
0-20 is normal
20-30 is borderline
>30 is abnormal

B's number was 25... borderline. Not perfect, not bad. Grey... just as we suspected it would be. I did a lot of research on what this means. Basically, if you fall into the abnormal range, the chances of you producing a natural conception are slim to none. Also, IUIs wouldn't work. IVF is the only possible chance of conception for the abnormal group. The borderline group may take a little longer to conceive (greater than four months). IUI and IVF would work in this group. The normal group would naturally conceive within four months. According to these results, we should be fine. Go figure. If you're interested in this topic (it is quite fascinating) this site explains it all very well. If you can't click on the link, cut and paste this:

http://www.reprosource.com/pdf/SDFA_info_sheet_rs-CF7BL7.pdf

Oxidative Stress:

It is easier for me to use Dr. Google to explain it. B's results were normal.

Oxidative stress to sperm from free radicals can cause both loss of motility and DNA damage in sperm. This oxidative damage can even sometimes occur in the laboratory during assisted reproduction procedures. It occurs more readily in infertile men as they often have only about half of the levels of naturally occurring antioxidants in their semen, as compared to fertile men.

Obviously I can't discuss the "something else to do with DNA" test since I don't know what it was.

We're still waiting on the FISH (chromosome) test. We should get that back in the next week or so.

Since I'm not cycling while we wait for tests, my posts have been sporadic. To keep the blog going daily, I'm going to go back to what I used to do when I first started the blog... discussing the myths of infertility. People loved when I wrote those and I loved writing about them so starting tomorrow, we'll welcome them back

SATURDAY, MAY 21, 2011

Myth: Infertile means Sterile

I can see why this myth exists. If you were to look up infertile in the dictionary, it uses sterile in the definition. The dictionary editors should correct that. Being sterile means you can NEVER conceive and/or carry a child. Being infertile means that you have a reduced ability to conceive and/or carry a child.

What would make a woman sterile?? I guess not having pieces/portions of the reproductive system... Like not having a uterus or eggs. Men without sperm would be sterile. As I'm typing these words, I'm recognizing why the dictionary would define them as synonyms. When dictionaries were created, they were the same. Medicine wasn't advanced enough to see that a woman does have eggs but they need to be removed and fertilized in a dish. Semen analysis didn't exist in the early 1900s (or at least I couldn't find documentation of it). So yes, before the advances in reproductive endocrinology, infertility and sterility were virtually the same. Thankfully, research and technology has given us the ability to separate the two. People who were told years and years ago that they couldn't conceive... that they were sterile... would have options for treatment these days.

So, don't call me sterile. Don't call B sterile. We're not sterile.

SUNDAY, MAY 22, 2011

Decisions Decisions

I know I said I would start back up with daily myths. I had and still have full intentions of doing so. I just had a really crappy week full of decision making that I really didn't want to deal with.

First off, we decided to not go through with the adoption financing. You're probably thinking "what adoption financing??" I just realized I never made it public knowledge that we moved forward with private adoption. We did and it's costing us about $45k. No joke. Anyway, the adoption agency offers financing. At first it sounded great, then we got the details. The agency finds you a loan through the bank. We got approved and the interest rate was low so we were happy with that. Then we got a ton of paperwork. First thing that was bothersome was that we had to sign the entire loan over to the agency. Then the agency sets up a trust and cuts checks as we need it. I know its agency policy and they have been doing it for years. I searched high and low for complaints about the agency on adoption websites and with the Better Business Bureau. I did find a couple of complaints about couples not getting matched and they felt wronged. I get that. However, I couldn't find any legit complaints regarding how they function as a company and/or any complaints about finances. Even with that, it made us uncomfortable to have financial responsibility (we would still pay the bank) yet have zero control of the loan. With all that being said, we decided not to go with the financing. Instead, we're going to save the money. We think we should have it by the end of the summer... we hope. Since we already started our home study, we're just going to finish it and then wait for our bank account to grow.

Then I decided to email Dr. P about doing a FET while we waited for the tests to come back. We have some frozen embryos, so why not? Even if the probability is low, it's better than doing nothing. At least it's better in my mind. During the email exchange, the MS 150 came up. I mentioned to Dr. P that it makes me uneasy to do a cycle while B is wearing tight spandex all the time and keeping his balls nice and warm. Dr. P said she didn't think it would be an issue but she would look into it. Then she sent me this abstract:

Physical activity and semen quality among men attending an infertility clinic.

Wise LA, Cramer DW, Hornstein MD, Ashby RK, Missmer SA.
Source
Slone Epidemiology Center, Boston University, Boston, Massachusetts 02215, USA. lwise@bu.edu

Abstract
OBJECTIVE:
To examine the association between regular physical activity and semen quality.
DESIGN:
Prospective cohort study.
SETTING:
Couples attending one of three IVF clinics in the greater Boston area during 1993-2003. At study entry, male participants completed a questionnaire about their general health, medical history, and physical activity. Odds ratios (ORs) and 95% confidence intervals (CIs) were derived using generalized estimating equations models, accounting for potential confounders and multiple samples per man.
PATIENT(S):
A total of 2,261 men contributing 4,565 fresh semen samples were enrolled before undergoing their first IVF cycles.
INTERVENTION(S):
None.
MAIN OUTCOME MEASURE(S):
Semen volume, sperm concentration, sperm motility, sperm morphology, and total motile sperm (TMS).
RESULT(S):
Overall, none of the semen parameters were materially associated with regular exercise. Compared with no regular exercise, bicycling $\geq$ 5 h/wk was associated with low sperm concentration (OR 1.92, 95% CI 1.03-3.56) and low TMS (OR 2.05, 95% CI 1.19-3.56). These associations did not vary appreciably by age, body mass index, or history of male factor infertility.
CONCLUSION(S):
Although the present study suggests no overall association between regular physical activity and semen quality, bicycling $\geq$ 5 h/wk was associated with lower sperm concentration and TMS.

Yep, bike riding is bad for the sperm. BUZZ Kill. So then we had to decide if B should continue training. Also, sperm that is ejaculated is about 70 days old. Which means, when we're ready to cycle again, the sperm we will be using will be the effed up biking sperm. We discussed (along with Dr. P) if we should wait even longer to do a cycle. Her suggestion was to freeze sperm now so if the fresh sperm looks bad we will have back up. Aye aye aye.

THEN, Dr. P mentioned that there is a nationwide shortage of Lupron. They don't know when it will be resolved. If it isn't resolved before the start of my next cycle (FET and Fresh would need Lupron) then we would have to switch protocols.

On top of all that, we got 3 pregnancy announcements in less than 24 hours. I nearly had a freaking meltdown. Actually, I did have a meltdown. I was explaining to B that it's not just a baby. It's not just pregnancy. We have to make decisions and have conversations on a daily basis (most of the time, it's many times a day) that most people never have to have. Most people can't even fathom the decisions we have to make. We have a daily stress. I get medical bills a few times a week. Not only do we have to make these decisions and deal with this stress, we can't make a baby (naturally or in a lab), we can't adopt a child in foster care (we're still at least a year and a half away from finishing that) and we can't buy a baby... AND then, we get it thrown in our face (not intentionally) all the time.

So. I'm sorry that I haven't followed through with my word of daily posts. I was just an emotional wreck and wasn't ready to write about infertility until I calmed down. I'm calm again. Lots of swearing came from this girl.

Right now, my book club is reading a fantastic book. Sing You Home by Jodi Picoult. Picoult is one of my favorite authors. The Pact and 19 Minutes were my favorites. I don't know much about the book I'm reading now (I don't read the back of books... I like to be surprised). All I know is what I have read thus far as well as what a friend told me (although she kept it vague). So far there are two themes, Infertility and Gay rights. Some parts of the book are really hard for me to read. Other than the hard parts, it is fantastic. I can't put it down. I'll let you all know if it's worth picking up.

SATURDAY, MAY 28, 2011

FISH Results

Finally, the FISH results are in. I got a call from the Urology office at 9:05 yesterday morning. The conversation went like this:

"A, it's Sharon from Dr. S's office. I just wanted to let you know that the FISH results were on my fax when I got in this morning."

"Great."

"Dr. S is in the OR all morning so I don't have the results since I can't interpret them. I just wanted to let you know they're here."

"When should we expect to hear the results?"

"I put the results on Dr. S's desk. He will get back to you later today. I will have him try B's cell phone first then yours second."

I waited ALL day with every phone possible by my side. As I was getting ready for a fundraiser last night, I had the phone with me in the bathroom. I ran upstairs to grab my dress from the closet (this was about 5:30PM). I was literally gone about two minutes. When I came back into the bathroom, I saw that I had a message. I said "Crap, I missed the call." B said "Ya, the phone was ringing." BAHH! We have been waiting for weeks for these damn tests and of course, the two minutes I step away from the phone, they call. So, now we wait until Tuesday.

Does anyone else see a theme here? All we do is wait!

MONDAY, MAY 30, 2011

Memorial Day

Thank you to all the courageous men and women who are currently fighting and have fought for our freedom. Today isn't just about cookouts and burgers, it's also about remembering those who sacrificed their lives for us. <3 KRV<3

Every Memorial Day weekend, we have an annual (obviously, if it's every year) cookout at our friend's house. B and his college friends have done a remarkable job of keeping in touch. We see most of them a handful of times a year (some more) and the rest, we see every year at the cookout. This was the first year I debated not going. The cookout started out with just a bunch of people in their mid-twenties without children. As we progressed in life, babies started appearing. Now the cookout isn't just a few babies, it's full of babies and toddlers. When I say full, I mean full. I wasn't sure if I could handle it yesterday. Needless to say, we did what we always do, we sucked it up and went. The entire drive I had knots in my stomach. I knew I wasn't going to be as social as I'd like to be. This cookout is the only time we see most of the people there. So of course, I wanted to see and talk to everyone. I wanted to but I couldn't. I avoided the areas that were baby central. I stationed myself in areas that I felt comfortable and whomever passed by me, would get a conversation. I was very aware of how snotty it may look to some people. I didn't want to seem snotty but I guess looking snotty is better than not going at all. The entire day was overwhelming and uncomfortable. It's hard to imagine that the rest of our life may be full of overwhelming and uncomfortable events. I don't even want to think about that right now. That totally blows.

Speaking of thinking of that, on our drive home from the cookout, I asked B if he thought we would ever have a biological child. The question got us talking about if we are fooling ourselves. We wonder if we're in some kind of denial. The kind of denial where everyone else sees the outcome that we do not. We still have hope. I wonder if having hope is a bad idea. Of course we want to believe it will all work itself out but is the hope doing more damage than good? I wish I could see the end. I never read the backs of books. I like to be surprised about the plot of a story. I like to be surprised about the characters' lives. I like the mystery of the story until the very last word. However, if my life was a book, I'd jump right to the last page and get every detail of how it ends. This story needs a serious twist. The storyline we're in is getting old!

Guess who called at 5:30 yesterday? Yep, the Urologist called right when I was trying to hold it together at a cookout. I wasn't expecting him to call on the Sunday of Memorial Day weekend so my phone was in my purse. I missed the call again. I have had my phone glued to me all day. He hasn't called again.

TUESDAY, MAY 31, 2011

Myth: Miscarriage Is Like a Period

We got the results of the FISH test. I will share them with you when we are ready. B and I need to have a lot of discussions and decisions have to be made before I share the information on a blog. While we work through it, you're going to get a myth...

No, miscarriages are NOTHING like a period.

If your period is full of clots and heavy enough to bleed through pads and tampons, then I would suggest you seeking medical advice. If your period has pieces of tissue (no, not Kleenex) coming out in strings, then I would suggest you call your doctor. The blood from a period is caused by your body shedding the uterine lining that thickened after ovulation in preparation for an embryo. The blood from a miscarriage is a combination of fetal tissue along with the shedding of the uterine lining. It's a totally different consistency than just uterine lining.

If your period involves cramps so painful that they cause your body to tremble, then I would suggest seeking medical treatment. The medical term for miscarriage is "spontaneous abortion." Just as the name suggests, your body spontaneously aborts the pregnancy. I always got (which is very common) severe back pain. It was always the first sign of a miscarriage happening. When I say severe, I mean severe. They were brutal. During a miscarriage, your uterus is contracting. If you have felt a contraction before, I'm sure you'll agree with me that contractions are NOTHING like menstrual cramps.

Please, the next time you know someone experiencing or has experienced a miscarriage, do not compare it to a period.

THURSDAY, JUNE 2, 2011

Myth: You're thinking about it too much...

I don't care if you have been trying for one month, one year, or ten years to have a baby. No one wants to hear "You're thinking about it too much. If you stop trying, you'll get pregnant." Let's try to think about this rationally. I just have to block it from my mind and all of a sudden I'll be pregnant? When there is a medical reason for not conceiving, how do you suggest I go about taking my medicine mindlessly? Has research proven that thinking about getting pregnant prevents pregnancy? I'll answer that, no, it hasn't. In fact, a study came out not too long ago (I read about it in the New York Times over the winter... although, it was in a doctor's office so it could have been an old issue) that proved that emotional distress before an IVF cycle did not change the outcome of the cycle. The study was a multi-centered (in ten or so countries), meta-analysis consisting of over 3,000 women. This wasn't a small study done in some random clinic in the middle of nowhere. This was a large study done in many clinics all over the world. So no my friends, you cannot think about it too much. I do believe that you should be mentally healthy while you're trying. You don't need to be but should be. There is a big difference between should and need.

I will say this, if you are stressed to the point of messing up your ovulation, then yes, you can have trouble getting pregnant. Ovulation is very much needed in order to conceive. With that being said, you have to be insanely stressed out to stop ovulating.

This myth was on one of my first few blog posts "What Defines Me." I haven't read it in a long time... probably since I wrote it. I really should read it more often. It's a great reminder of how strong I knew I was and would be... even at the early stages of this journey.

I am going away with girlfriends this weekend. I'm not sure how often I'll be able to get online to post. I'm still not going to go over the details of the FISH results just yet. I know making you wait is implying terrible news. It's not terrible news. It's not great news either. B and I have a lot to talk about. We have a lot of hard decisions that need to be made. I think it's unfair to share the basis of those difficult conversations on a public forum before having time to work it out as a couple. I will go over every piece of the information, when the time is right. Soon, I promise.

TUESDAY, JUNE 14, 2011

Changes

There will be some changes with my blog. For the past week or two, I've been thinking about what I want and should do about this blog. My intentions with this blog was/is to write about our struggle from my perspective. Over time, our treatment started to shift... leaning more towards tests and less towards treatment changes. The shift has made it very difficult for me to write what I want to write while maintaining privacy for B. Here are my thoughts...

1. I stop writing all together and close out the blog.
2. I continue blogging with less openness about our cycles, treatments, and appointments.
3. I continue blogging on a different topic.

I have received all of your texts and emails. I apologize for not responding. I'm trying to figure out what I should do and what is best for everyone... you and us.

FRIDAY, JUNE 17, 2011

You're stuck with me

I've decided to stick around. My posts may be more vague than usual but vagueness is better than nothing.

You're probably wondering where we stand?? We are meeting with a geneticist tomorrow. We've already come up with a plan with Dr. P. The geneticist will just talk to us with some medical mumbo jumbo but we're not expecting any surprises. We basically know what she (I believe she is a she) is going to say. You can never get too much information when it comes to your personal health and medicine.

I'm also waiting to ovulate. I'm on day 24. Remember last cycle when I ovulate in a timely manner and I said it was because I didn't "need" to. Yep, here I am, needing or wanting to and I'm still waiting. I'm not in a rush, so I don't mind.

Yesterday was a fun day for me. I'm going in for a colonoscopy today. My father's day was spent with our families (both sides) at our house for a cookout. It was fun hanging out with everyone and pure misery to be surrounded by such great food and not be able to eat any of it. I drank lots of chicken broth and Gatorade yesterday. I'm starving! The colonoscopy is being done as an "emergency" so they had to fit me into the schedule last minute. Which means, all the scheduled scopes go first, then me, at 2:00. I have no problem with the time. I just cannot wait to eat!

A couple of years ago, B and I traveled Asia. We went to China, Japan, and the Philippines. During that time, I got really sick. I couldn't walk down the streets of Hong Kong without getting diarrhea (sorry, TMI). When we came back to the states, my GI system was all out of whack. I could eat a piece of toast and get sick but then eat a burger and fries and be totally fine. There was no rhyme or reason to what was making me sick. I was also very sluggish and exhausted all the time. My primary care did a large panel of blood tests that showed my platelets were really low (cancer low). He sent me to a hematologist that followed me for about a couple of months. After ruling out some of the more minor causes (spleen, bacterial infection) he decided that I needed a bone marrow biopsy. Two days before the biopsy, the doctor did another blood test to see how I was doing. The day before the biopsy, he called me to tell me my levels jumped back up and I didn't need the biopsy. He again followed my levels and after a month or so, they brushed it off as most likely an infection/bacteria that I caught in China that took my body several months to fight off.

I was fine for a few months. After my first miscarriage, all the symptoms started coming back. I figured my body was out of whack because of the miscarriage. The symptoms were sporadic (every few months). I went to a GI who ordered a bunch of tests including a colonoscopy. I cancelled the colonoscopy because I was in the middle of a cycle. That was a year and a half ago. My symptoms or what I call "episodes" have become more frequent and more severe. After a really rough Wednesday evening (last week), I called a new GI (I wasn't a fan of the old one) asking to be scheduled as an emergency patient. They took me the next day. The new GI is part of an all-women's GI group. They are extremely knowledgeable not only about the GI tract/system but also about the female body. During my appointment, the doctor and I discussed everything including fertility treatments. She knew side effects of all the drugs. She knew timing during a Lupron cycle. She knew the timing of an antagonist cycle. I'm so glad I switched. To make a long story longer, she said I fit into two profiles.

1. I caught an infection/bacteria in China that went untreated. My body showed signs of resolving it but really it was just laying dormant. Then my miscarriage triggered it to be active again. Since a miscarriage is your body trying to rid itself of what it sees as an "infection," other infections will arise in the process. An untreated infection, especially as long as it has been for me, will trigger a disorder (which I totally forget the name of) that mimics IBS. I asked if we just treat the infection with antibiotics and then it will all go away. Unfortunately, when it goes on this long, it becomes chronic. She said "We'll treat you with antibiotics and probiotics then I would suggest you invest in Imodium." Awesome.

2. I fit the profile of some random, rare disease. It presents in a rash (remember when I had to show Dr. Hottie my chest because of a rash??), night sweats (which we aren't sure if it's the Lupron or my body) and diarrhea.

Both diagnoses (I think that's the plural of diagnosis. Someone correct me if I'm wrong) have the same result... invest in Imodium. Joyous!

So today, I'll be getting a scope up my rear. I don't mind the test at all. Everyone said I was going to hate the prep. The prep was a piece of cake compared to my episodes. Yes, I went to the bathroom every 20 minutes for about five hours but it wasn't painful. I'm also 5 pounds lighter. I haven't been this weight in years! There's always a bright side to everything!

MONDAY, JUNE 20, 2011

Time for a change

So, the colonoscopy was a piece of cake. Everyone makes them out to be torturous. Although they tried to sedate me, I never fully fell asleep. So I got to watch the colonoscopy being done on a screen. It was really cool. As gross as it sounds, the colon and intestinal system are pretty fascinating. I didn't have any masses or polyps. They also didn't find any signs of Crohn's or colitis. She took just about ten biopsies to see if there is a microscopic infection going on. My Celiac's test came back inconclusive. Of course right?? Even with the shits, my results end up in the grey area. I went back yesterday for more tests to confirm or rule out Celiac's. Although it would stink, Celiac's would actually be a fantastic diagnosis. It's not only linked to GI issues, it's also linked to infertility and miscarriages. While we wait for the biopsy and blood tests, I have appointments with an allergist (to rule out food allergies) and a hematologist (my blood tests showed low platelets, white blood cells and IGa deficiency). Needless to say, I'm staying away from IVF until I figure out what's going on in my belly.

We met with the Geneticist on Tuesday. I'll write about that disaster tomorrow. Holy Moly nightmare!

You know how sometimes you feel like you're stuck in a rut... You feel blah and need a change?? I've been feeling like that for a few weeks now. I've been working out a lot (the 150 mile bike ride is this weekend!) and taking care of myself. Generally, that helps the blah feeling. This time, it didn't help. So, I decided to change my hair. I change my hair all the time anyway. I go from light brown to blond to dark brown to platinum. I go from short to extensions to short. I get so bored with my hair. Anyway, I dyed my hair chocolate brown. I tried to find two pictures that were similar so you can see. I found two in the same dress... Old hair, new hair (the new picture is fuzzy but you get the point).

FRIDAY, JULY 1, 2011

Test results

I just got a call from the GI office. All of the biopsies from the colonoscopy are normal. No Crohn's or Colitis. No infection, no parasites. Nothing was in my stool either. Basically, I've been sick as a dog for unknown reasons. Awesome!

I still have to tell you about our appointment with the Geneticist. I can't tell you how angry we were leaving that office. We were called into the office by the Geneticist herself. After introducing us to the student that she was with, she said "Okay, why are we here? I have no information on you... just an email stating that you were being referred to us." I responded with "we're here to go over the results of the FISH test." "I don't have those results." No shit you don't, you just said you know nothing about us. I then told her to call the Urologist and have them faxed. At this point, we had only been there a few minutes and my blood pressure was already through the roof. How dare she schedule an appointment and not look into our history.

She then had the student drawing a "circle and square" map of our families. How many siblings do you have? Did your brother have trouble conceiving? Did your mother have trouble? Seriously? Are you seriously insulting my fertility knowledge right now? At some point during the drawing session, the doctor asks me "Have they tested your hormones?" You've got to be flipping kidding me! I forget my exact answer but it was something along the lines of "of course they have." She then asks me what tests we have had done. I rattle back, "I have had an HSG, two sonohystograms, two hysteroscopies, an endometrial biopsy, immune testing, anticoagulant tests." Honestly, I can't put into words how annoyed I was. I was literally sweating and about to jump out of my seat.

During the questioning (she also asked about each cycle) the FISH tests came. She barely looked at them. Seriously, BARELY looked. Then she proceeded to talk about how sperm are produced every month (I didn't correct her but I should have... it's produced every 70 days or so). Anyway, she was talking about how sperm is produced every month and how eggs are just the eggs we were born with. Our eggs are suspended in time... blah blah blah. Basically, she decided that the issue was with my egg quality. Then she also decided that I needed to be on Doxycycline for a cycle to kill infections that are in my body and killing babies.

I was losing my shit. I was so incredibly pissed off that she was diagnosing a patient without any medical information. Zero. She completely wasted our time.

When we got to the car, I said to B "How unethical of her to make a medical diagnosis and provide medical treatment for a patient that she has not done one test on and has not seen any labs, tests... anything on." B said "How dare she insult our intelligence by thinking she could just wing an appointment. She thought we weren't smart enough to know that she was wasting our time."

So, we went to the appointment and we got nothing out of it. Nothing.

SUNDAY, JULY 3, 2011

More Baby Showers

Every day, week, month that passes without us being in a cycle, is another day, week, month that we are that much further away from having a child. We're kind of in a standstill right now... which you all know, I can't stand. I'd rather stick myself with needles and gain a million pounds than sit around and do nothing. I get so frustrated that we can't just have sex like everyone else. Well, we can have sex but not for the purposes of reproduction. People so quickly say "just give it time. It will happen." Time? Who has time? I'm certainly not getting any younger. Money doesn't grow on trees and unfortunately for us, it costs money to attempt to have children.

I know we're going to be parents. I have said that time and time again. Being a parent doesn't replace the experience of conceiving, being pregnant and delivering a child. There are two reasons why I don't talk about adoption on this blog.

1. If/When we adopt, I don't want people thinking they can openly discuss the adoption with us/our child. We will have a story to tell our child and our child will have a story to tell. It will be up to us to keep that private until the child is ready to share it.

2. People assume adoption is a fix to infertility. It's not. Even with a child in our arms and in our home, there will be a void. B will never get to share stories with his buddies about the delivery room. I will never get to experience pregnancy or delivery. I will never get to ask B to run to the store for pickles and ice cream (which by the way, is actually really good). Being a parent and experiencing pregnancy are two totally different things. One doesn't replace the other.

I'm not sure where this is coming from. That's not true, I do know. I started getting baby shower invites again. I had a nice break for a couple of months. I didn't check the mail for a few days so when I got it today, I had a ton of mail... including a couple of shower invites. For 3.5 years I have willingly exposed myself to one of the most painful situations. I celebrate pregnancies, buy presents, look at swollen bellies, and sit through oohs and ahhs of motherhood. I willingly expose myself because I am genuinely happy for the parents to be. Being happy for them doesn't mean it's not a punch in the gut with every conversation and every baby event. We go to cookouts and parties full of babies and children. We are constantly surrounded by the one thing we want most in this world and can't have. We don't know if we can or will ever have biological children. With that hanging over our head, life can get hard to stomach.

THURSDAY, JULY 14, 2011

4th of July

It has taken me a while to post since 4th of July. We all knew the weekend was going to be difficult. What I wasn't expecting, was it to be one of the most difficult weekends we've had. Last year was tough because there were pregnant people and babies everywhere. I guess I forgot that those pregnant people would have babies and those babies would become toddlers. Everywhere you went, you were surrounded by them. Don't get me wrong... I love babies. There is a huge difference between hanging out with a friend or two and their children than going to a cookout with babies and children everywhere. It was an infertile's nightmare. Of course, I was still the same silly Auntie A and B was the same fun Uncle B. I still held babies, "oohed and ahhed" over their developments. I was still the person having dance parties and crawling around in the grass with the kids. I did what I always do; I put on a happy face while feeling like I was going to puke at any second. A couple of times, I noticed B wistfully watching me holding a baby. I could see right through his masked smile. Behind that smile, was a desire and yearning that I'm not sure will be resolved. We were overwhelmingly reminded, yet again, of what we want and what we have lost.

Last weekend, we had another cookout for a friend of B's. All day, I kept saying that I wasn't sure if I was up to a day full of parents. Even knowing that I didn't think I could do it, I went anyway. That's what I do. I keep telling myself that I will never be able to shield myself unless I turn into a hermit. Being a hermit is out of the question. So, of course, we went. Well, what B forgot to mention was that the cookout was a joint birthday party for his friend's two children. As soon as we were walking up the driveway, I felt nauseous. The loud shrills and screams of the children were making me cringe. We turned the corner into the backyard and there were two inflatable slides/jumpies and about 30-40 kids running around and screaming. We walked into a PTA filled cookout as the childless couple. After a tour of the house, I walked myself to the furthest point in the yard and sat on a swing until we left. I couldn't get out of there fast enough.

I have had some tests done to figure out what is going on with my GI issues. All tests have pointed towards Celiac's disease. They're not definitive for a positive result nor a negative result. What else would you expect from a test result? I always fall into the gray. I should be called Auntie Gray A instead of Auntie Silly A. I'm not exactly sure of the test names or parameters. I do remember one needing to come back at 6 to be positive for Celiac's or a 2 to be negative. I came back at a 4.5. Really?!?! The next step is to do an endoscopy. However, I have been doing a Gluten free diet for a while. Mainly because I didn't want the shits while doing a 150-mile bike ride. In order to get accurate results, I need to be on a Gluten filled diet for six weeks. So we scheduled an endoscopy for August 15th.

I went to the allergist for a food test. I found out that I'm allergic to beef, wheat, and buckwheat. I'm not surprised at all. When I first started getting sick, it was often happening at cookouts. I kept telling B that I thought I was allergic to red meat. I only ate red meat (in the form of a burger) at a cookout. Then I did some research and found that it's insanely rare to be allergic to beef. When I read that, I thought maybe I was allergic to white bread since I only ate white bread (in the form of a hamburger bun) at cookouts. It's nice to know I knew what it was all along. As good as it is to know I'm allergic to those things, they can't be the reason behind my GI issues. They were definitely a trigger but there's something else going on as well.

We also did a bacterial overgrowth test. We all have bacteria in our GI system. Good levels of bacteria are vital for normal digestive processes. Normal levels are less than 10. An hour before my appointment, I had to drink a syrup that activates the bacteria. Then I had to breathe into a machine every 15 minutes for an hour and a half. What the test is looking for are not only high levels of bacteria but high levels that spike, drop, and spike again. My levels looked like this: 9, 12, 18, 40, 24, 39. Yep, less than 10 is normal. The test is supposed to be conducted for two hours. Since I tested positive early, with insane numbers, they ended the test and told me to go fill my antibiotic immediately. The entire time I was there, I was miserable. The syrup activated the bacteria that had been making me sick. So, while I was there, I would go from breathing into the machine, to running to the bathroom. I went from being comfortable to being drenched in sweat. It was zero fun. At least they found what was going on.

A nurse conducts the test, so I was unable to discuss with the doctor why I would have this. From what I have read online, it seems that it's common in people with certain disorders. One of them being Celiac's. We shall see what the endoscopy shows.

Am I a hot mess or what?

MONDAY, JULY 18, 2011

So Small

It's days like today that I ask myself, how can life be so cruel?

I have found solace in an amazing group of women. You have all heard me refer to them as the AGC. Those girls have a strength that is remarkable. We're constantly sharing news with each other. Negative, positive, exciting, scary... it's all news that we welcome. We share encouraging words. We vent about our latest woes. We tell funny stories. We exchange birthday and holiday presents. We support one another through baby showers, births, pregnancy announcements, cookout, and parties. Most of us... nearly all of us... have never met. They're a support that understands how you are feeling. They wait for test results with anticipation as if the results were their own. Every appointment, every consultation, retrieval, transfer, fertilization report, stick pee'd on, we anxiously wait for the results. We send emails, texts, and phone messages with encouraging words and requests for updates. We're as impatient with waiting even though they're not our tests. So when something negative happens to one of my ladies, my heart breaks as if it happened to me. Today, one of our girls got terrible, horrible, no good, very bad news. News that this couple shouldn't have to get. News that this couple doesn't deserve. News that this couple has endured time and time again. All I can say is Fuck. Fuck infertility. Fuck life's cruelty. Fuck all the injustices in this world. Fuck.

We all have our crosses to bear. We all have struggles. Some people think their life is bigger or better than others. Some people think they have it all. No one does. We all have a struggle. What differs from person to person is how the struggle is handled. I can say wholeheartedly, that the women that I have learned to love and depend on are the strongest women I know. They handle themselves with grace and integrity. They stand up for what is right and they fight for what they deserve. If there is any justice in this world, they will prevail.

The next time you are in the grocery store and you're pissed off because the line is long, think about the person fighting a terminal illness. The next time you fight with your spouse about the laundry not being folded, think about the mother who lost her son to a killer. The next time you get all heated at a driver for speeding past you on the highway, think about the person who just lost yet another baby.

I love many things, one of them being Carrie Underwood (and Michael Jackson... of course, I had to add that in here). The lyrics to her song So Small are incredibly inspirational. If you haven't heard it yet, you should look it up on YouTube.

What you got if you ain't got love?
The kind that you just wanna give away
It's okay to open up
Go ahead and let the light shine through

I know it's hard on a rainy day
You wanna shut the world out
And just be left alone
But don't run out on your faith

'Cause sometimes that mountain you've been climbing
Is just a grain of sand.
And what you've been out there searching for forever
Is in your hands

And when you figure out
Love is all that matters after all
It sure makes everything else
Seem so small

It's so easy to get lost inside
A problem that seems so big at the time
It's like a river that's so wide
It swallows you whole

While you're sitting around thinking 'bout what you can't change
And worrying about all the wrong things
Time's flying by, moving so fast
You better make it count 'cause you can't get it back

Sometimes that mountain you've been climbing
Is just a grain of sand.
And what you've been out there searching for forever
Is in your hands

Oh, and when you figure out
Love is all that matters after all
It sure makes everything else
Seem so small!

Sometimes that mountain you've been climbing
Is just a grain of sand.
And what you've been out there searching for forever
Is in your hands

And then you figure out
Love is all that matters after all
It sure makes everything else
Oh, it sure makes everything else
Seem so small

WEDNESDAY, JULY 20, 2011

Rain, Rain Go Away

When it rains, it pours... right?!?!? We had another AGC heartbreak today. Really, this is getting old. I'm sick of it. The worst part about it is that we get used to it. The heartbreak never goes away but we become so hardened on the outside... it sucks. We (our email chain) were just saying the other day that we wish we could just be like everyone else. Why can't we just have sex and get pregnant? Why can't we just get pregnant and be excited about it? Why can't we just have a baby shower without thinking that it's the kiss of death to fertility (a friend once said that to me and she's so right)? As screwed up as it is, we are more like everyone else than we realize. There is a 10-25% chance of miscarriage. Research shows the number would actually be a lot higher if women knew they were pregnant. A lot of women experience a miscarriage before they even knew they were pregnant. There are around 90 million couples (globally) that suffer from infertility. 11 million of those couples are from the US. Male infertility accounts for 40%, Female infertility accounts for 40% and both male and female infertility accounts for 20%. We want to be like "everyone else." we already are, we just don't see it that way. We want to be like the fertile everyone else. We were dealt some shitty cards.

I'm looking forward to our vacation. We're heading out tomorrow evening. We're spending a couple of days in Spain (Madrid) then flying over to Portugal (Lisbon). We'll spend a day or do there. Then we plan on taking a drive (B had to get his international driver's permit) up the coast for a few days. Then we head back to Spain for a day. Ten days of pure awesomeness.

TUESDAY, AUGUST 2, 2011

HIIIII!

Hello Friends!

I feel like we were in Europe forever! Even Forever didn't seem like enough time there! It was amazing! There are so many things I want to share! I'll give details of the trip later. Right now, I want to urge all of you to contact your local Senators to take part in a briefing about infertility and the S 965 Act, Family Act (tax credit for out of pocket costs for treatment).

My call to one senator was under 45 seconds long. The other call will a little over a minute (I talked a lot) long. Both calls were directly sent to voicemail so if you're nervous about actually talking to a person. Don't be... all you'll do is leave a message.

If you want guidance on what to say, I took this script off the RESOLVE site. As you all know, fertility treatments aren't a luxury, they're a burden. Infertility is as much of a disease as all the other diseases out there.

Here's what you can do: (Note: you will repeat these instructions twice, once for each Senator in your state.)

1. Call the main U.S. Senate switchboard at 202-224-3121.

2. Ask to be transferred to your Senator's office.

3. Here is a sample script for your call:

"Good morning/afternoon. I live in... and I'm calling to speak with the Healthcare Aide."

Once you're connected:

"Hi. My name is and I live in... On Wednesday, August 3rd, there is a briefing, done in conjunction with Senator Gillibrand's office from 2:00 - 3:00 p.m. in Room 562 of the Dirksen Senate Office building. The briefing is very important to me as it is about infertility and S 965, the Family Act. I hope you can attend.

THURSDAY, AUGUST 4, 2011

Charm

Tuesday night, the local AGC girls and I had dinner. I got to restaurant 30 minutes early so I decided to head to the charm store to exchange a charm. For each of my miscarriages, I have an Angel of hope charm on my bracelet. For my birthday, both B and my friend K bought me an angel (for the miscarriage in April). I put the one B gave me on my bracelet and planned on exchanging the other one. This was my encounter at charm store...

Me: I'd like to exchange this charm (I then handed the employee an unopened package).

Sales Man: What's the name it was purchased under?

Me: I spelled K's name

SM: It's not in the computer. Maybe it's under your name.

Me: I gave my name

SM: I don't see a recent purchase for the Angel of Hope. It says in here that you already have two.

Me: Yes, I purchased those for friends. I actually have three.

SM: Why would you want three of the same charm?

I ignore him

SM: Our store policy is we can only do exchanges and returns for 30 days after purchase. Without a history of a purchase, I can't exchange it. Why don't you ask her where she bought it?

Me: I can't do that. It's a very personal gift. I do not want her thinking I don't want it.

SM: I don't understand why you can't ask her.

Me: Like I said, I can't. So, I can't exchange an unopened, brand new item from your brand at this brand store?

SM: No.

Me: That seems ridiculous. It's clearly your brand.

SM: Yes, it is our brand. Our store policy states ...blah, blah, blah. What I think is ridiculous that your friend would buy you a fourth Angel of Hope when you already have three.

Me: Blank stare

SM: Why would you want so many of those? Why can't you just ask her where she bought it?

Me: It's none of your business (I believe I swore a few times as well) why I have three Angel of Hopes. Although it's none of your business (I think some curse words were here too), the reason I can't ask her is because each angel represents a miscarriage that I have had. She bought me a very personal gift that I do not want her thinking I do not want. So, can I exchange it or not?

SM: I just don't understand why she would buy it for you.

I start to tear up

Me: May I please just have my charm back? Then I lose it. I'm not just tearing up, I'm bawling.

SM: I'm sorry that you're so upset about our store policy. Our store policy states (yes, the idiot goes into his store policy again)

Me: May I please have my charm back?

SM: Store policy... blah, blah, blah.

I was so annoyed, frustrated, and upset, that I was like "screw it" and I just walked out of the store. A younger employee (female) came running after me with tissues and a small bottle of water.

Nice Girl: I'm really sorry that just happened. I'll exchange it for you.

Me: Okay.

We walk back to the store.

NG: What would you like instead?

Me: I honestly couldn't think straight. I don't know. She gave it to me for my birthday.

SM was about 5-10 feet away from us talking to another employee. When he heard me say it was a birthday gift he said in a very snide tone.

SM to other employee: She just said it was a birthday gift. She probably made up the miscarriage thing.

At this point, I'm a mess. I have mascara all over my face. I'm doing the hiccup thing from crying. The NG had a cupcake charm in my face. I agreed to that one. I paid the difference and I left.

Really Sales Man? Really? You think I give a shit about your stupid policy that much? You think your stupid policy is worth crying over? Idiot.

Needless to say, the AGC dinner couldn't have been more needed!

AUGUST 16, 2011

Fatima, Portugal

After we spent a couple of days in Madrid, we flew to Lisbon, Portugal. We spent a day in Lisbon and then drove up the coast of Portugal. Leading up to the trip, my mother kept telling us that we should visit the Lady of Fatima Shrine. After talking to our hotel concierge, we found that we would be driving through (well, it was a 30 minute detour) Fatima during our drive up the coast. So, we decided to stop. I'm so glad we did. It was amazing. I didn't know the story of Lady of Fatima. All I knew is what my mother kept telling me, which was "miracles have been known to happen to those who visit." This is the story behind Fatima (I got this off the Internet...the English translation isn't that great but it's fine enough for you to understand).

On 13 May 1917, three children were pasturing their little flock in the Cova da Iria, Parish of Fatima, town of Vila Nova de Ourém, today the diocese of Leiria-Fatima. They were called: Lucia de Jesus, aged 10, and her cousins Francisco and Jacinta Marto, aged 9 and 7.

About midday, after praying the Rosary, as was their custom, they were amusing themselves building a little house of stones scattered around the place where the Basilica now stands. Suddenly they saw a brilliant light, and thinking it to be lightning, they decided to go home. But as they went down the slope, another flash lit up the place, and they saw, on the top of a holmoak (where the Chapel of Apparitions now stands), "a Lady more brilliant than the sun", from whose hands hung a white rosary.

The Lady told the three little shepherds that it was necessary to pray much, and she invited them to return to the Cova da Iria during five consecutive months, on the 13th day at that hour. The children did so and the 13th day of June, July, September, and October, the Lady appeared to them again and spoke to them in the Cova da 0a. On the 19th of August, the apparition took place at Valinhos, about 500 meters from Aljustrel, because on the 13th of August the children had been carried off by the local Administrator to Vila Nova de Ourém.

At the last apparition, on October 13, with about 70,000 people present, the Lady said to them that she was the "Lady of the Rosary" and that a chapel was to be built there in her honor. After the apparition all present witnessed, the miracle promised to the three children in July and September :the sun, resembling a silver disc, could be gazed at without difficulty and, whirling on itself like a wheel of fire, it seemed about to fall upon the earth.

Afterwards, when Lucia was a Religious Sister of Saint Dorothy, Our Lady appeared to her again in Spain (10 December 1925 and 15 February 1926, in the Convent of Pontevedra, and on the night of 13/14 June 1929, in the Convent of Tuy), requesting the devotion of the five first Saturdays (to pray the Rosary, meditate on the mysteries of the Rosary, confess, and receive Holy Communion, in reparation for the sins committed against the Immaculate Heart of Mary), and the Consecration of Russia to the same Immaculate Heart. This request had been announced by the Apparition on 13 July 1917, in what is called the "Secret of Fatima".

Years later, Sr. Lucia related that, between April and October of 1916, an Angel had appeared to the three seers on three occasions, twice in the Cabeço and once at the well in the garden behind Lucia´s house, who exhorted them to prayer and penance.

Since 1917, pilgrims have not ceased to come to the Cova da Iria in thousands upon thousands from all parts of the world, at first on the 13th of each month. later during the summer and winter holidays, and now more and more at weekends and any day all the year round.

When we first got there, there was a service going on. I'm not sure what the technical term for it is... there was an outdoor mini church (that's what I'd call it). It didn't have walls. It was wide open, held up by pillars on the four corners. The first thing I noticed were people crawling around the building on their knees. Some people were crawling with their spouse and children holding their hands. Some people were crawling by themselves. Some people were crawling with people following them. I didn't understand the significance of the crawling until much later. Actually, I didn't understand until right before we left. We stopped in the gift shop and we saw that they sold knee pads. I asked the cashier what the significance of the crawling was. He said that when people's prayers have been answered, they paid their debts for the miracles by crawling on their knees. I couldn't believe how many people had answered prayers. It was extremely moving to witness.

There was a section on the grounds that you could light prayer candles. There were several different sizes of candles. I have LOTS of miracles that I wanted to pray for. Not just for me, but friends and family as well. So, we purchased a good amount of candles. I bought the monster of all candles for the AGC girls. It was 3" in diameter and 3-4 feet tall. It was huge. I wanted that bad boy to burn for days. B and I both lit our candles and said our prayers... which of course was touching and emotional. The whole place felt Spiritual. Even the bathroom felt Spiritual.

The main Chapel was amazing. After the shrine was built, the bodies of the three Shepard children were exhumed and moved into the main Chapel. The details of the Chapel were exquisite. You almost felt like you were doing something wrong as you are walking around it. There were nuns and tourists praying. There were people crying. It almost felt like we were breaking into a sacred place without permission. Again... very emotional.

Outside of the main doors to the Chapel, there was a desk with a prayer book on it. Although there was a line, I wasn't going to miss out on adding my prayers to that book. We stood in line for 15 or so minutes before it was my turn to write in the book. I tried reading what other people read (not to be nosey but so I could pray for them as well) but there wasn't one prayer that was in English. I sat there and I wrote. I wrote, I wrote, and I wrote. B said that people were getting a little antsy and annoyed with how long I was there. I'm sorry - I'm in a place of miracles. I'm going to take my sweet time and write a prayer for every single person in my life that needs prayers answered. I didn't care how long it took. It took as long as needed.

All in all, the Fatima stop was one of my favorite parts of the trip. It was spiritual, emotional, beautiful... it was amazing.

My pictures are in random order because they're a pain to move around on Blogger.

Image of Shepard Children (off the internet)

Statues of the Children that is in the center of the town

Statue on the Fatima Grounds

The tree that one of the apparitions were seen at.

Inside the main Chapel

Lighting the prayer Candles

B lighting his prayer candle

Main Chapel

Main Chapel

Outdoor Service building (I couldn't take pictures up close because the priests were there and you aren't allowed to take pictures of the priests and nuns)

Monestary

MONDAY, AUGUST 29, 2011

How many times?

Last week I had a bizarre cycle week. This cycle, I ovulated on day 22 (which is close to my norm). That would make my period due on day 36. As day 36 approached, I started to get cramps. The cramps got worse and worse. Then day 36 came and went. I was talking to a friend and she reminded me of the three things that can bring on a period, a bathing suit, white pants, or take a pregnancy test. So I took a pregnancy test. Of course it was negative, I actually didn't even wait more than 30 seconds before throwing it away. I just took it for the sake of bringing on a period. A couple of days pass and still nothing. On day 40, my cramps started to resemble ovulation cramps. So I took an ovulation test. Sure enough, I got a smiley face. That means, I ovulated on day 22 and day 40. Bizarre, right?? The following day, I had lunch with friends. After a couple of hours of sitting with them, I started to get really nauseous. Not only was I nauseous, I was sweating and really crampy. I started to think my GI issues decided to all of a sudden show up again. I went to the bathroom thinking I was going to be sick. Nothing. I got back to the table and randomly (and awkwardly) said "You ready to go?" Right in the middle of good conversation, I felt like I had to get out of there. Of course, right?!!? Anyway, we paid our bill, walked outside, talked for a bit more, and left. I was about 20 minutes from home. That drive home turned into a torture fest. The pain got so bad that I wasn't sure if I was going to make it home (don't forget I was thinking I was about to poop my pants). Once I got home I had severe diarrhea (TMI, sorry) and was vomiting. Once I was done, I put on pajamas and laid on the couch. I was rolled up in a ball trying to watch TV. The cramping was excruciating. I was texting with a friend asking her for her opinion (B wasn't home but his phone was at home so I couldn't reach him) on what to do. She said that she is too impatient and would drive to the ER. I am too impatient as well, so I went to the ER.

When I got to the ER the triage nurse took me right away. Of course, the first round of questions were...

Are you expecting?

No.

Have you ever been pregnant?

Yes.

How many times?

Three

How many children?

Zero.

Once triage was done, I sat in the waiting room that was conveniently full of pregnant people. It is a labor and delivery hospital so I can't expect anything else. None the less, it sucks to be sitting there. After about ten minutes, I was called into a room. The nurse then asks me...

Are you pregnant?

No.

Have you ever been pregnant?

Yes.
How many times?
Three
How many children?
Zero.
Did you terminate all of those pregnancies?
Terminate? No, None.
What happened to the pregnancies then?
Miscarriages.
So you didn't terminate them?
No.

She then tells me to get naked from the waist down and hands me half a sheet to throw over my vajayjay. Then THREE hours pass and not one person comes into the room. THREE. Let me remind you that I was half naked with barely a sheet over me. I was freezing. At one point, I got up and went through the cabinets to find something to throw over my legs and feet. I found a couple of hospital gowns that I threw over my feet. As the third hour approached, I got up, got dressed, and walked out of the hospital. I know there was an emergency. My room was across the nurses' station so I could hear all the details of the emergency. However, there was always a few of them standing there the entire time. One of them could have come in and asked me if I needed anything or told me that there was an emergency and it would be a while. At least I could have asked for a darn blanket. I was in so much pain that I just wanted to go home and take Tylenol. So I did. I got in the car, drove my freezing, cramping self home. I took a pain reliever and laid down. The pain reliever helped enough so I wasn't buckled over in pain. It didn't take it away, it just made it manageable.

The following day, I woke up feeling like I had the hardest ab workout of my life. I was no longer in pain but I was extremely sore and tender. My belly was tender all the way up to my rib cage. I called my OBGYN to see if I should come in. The nurse said the double ovulation and the lack of menses is strange in itself and the pain adds to the oddness of it. They had me come in (four days later) for an ultrasound and then appointment with the doctor. At the ultrasound, the nurse says...

When was your last menstrual cycle?
Day 1 was July 12.
Are you pregnant?
No.
Have you ever been pregnant?
Yes.
How many times?

Three.

How old are your children?

Zero. I had miscarriages.

Now to the diagnosis. The ultrasound showed a lot of fluid in/around the uterine area. The fluid was result of an ovarian cyst rupture. The doctor said by the amount of fluid floating around, it looks as if it were of decent size. She also is running a couple of blood tests to see what on earth is going on. This could be a fluke thing but with our reproducing history, I'm sure it's not. Or, I will fall into the gray area of test results. We shall see.

THURSDAY, SEPTEMBER 1, 2011

Lady of Fatima

I'm sure by now you have all read my post about Lady of Fatima. Remember when I talked about burning massive prayer candles for the AGC girls and how I spent so much time writing in the prayer book? Well, this is an update on the AGC girls...

One girl had a surprise natural pregnancy. Her betas have been high and strong. At five weeks, her beta was over 10,000. Another girl (after five IUIs, two IVFs, two FETs all resulting in failed cycles, and two chemical pregnancies) did a cycle and her first beta was 700 (unheard of) and her second beta was 1320 (also insanely high). A third girl (after two IUIs, two IVFs, two FETs, all resulting in failed cycles, two miscarriages and an ectopic pregnancy) did a cycle and her first beta was 318 and her second beta was 1210.

People have been known to experience miracles after visiting the Sanctuary of our Lady of Fatima. Are these pregnancies with astronomical betas a coincidence? Maybe but I think not. I think my prayers are working. Now if they could just work on me...

Tonight I am starting a boot camp with some girlfriends. YIKES! I'm in great cardiovascular shape. I run five days a week (usually). I haven't lifted a weight in ages. I'm going to crumble with 3 lbs. I'm excited but nervous at the same time. The boot camp is going to be at my house... I asked my former trainer to do a boot camp just for my friends. He said if I can collect money from five people, he would. We have eight coming! I was really hoping since we'll be outside that the weather would cool off. No such luck. Let's hope I/we survive!

THURSDAY, SEPTEMBER 8, 2011

It never ends...

I have yet posted about all the findings of the tests they were running. I had another strange medical mystery last week... which meant more testing. Finally, I have results from everything.

First off, I do not have Celiac's Disease. We found that I do have a wheat allergy. My endoscopy looked normal and the biopsies all came back normal. The doctor diagnosed me as Celiac's Intolerant. Basically, I have the allergy but not the autoimmune portion of Celiac's. I should stay on a Gluten Free diet but if I cheat, I may get GI upset but nothing more. I have been doing 75% Gluten free. I'm Gluten Free at home but not being overly careful when I go out.

So where does that leave me with my GI diagnosis? Since the antibiotic they put me on for the bacterial overgrowth, my GI symptoms are pretty much gone. I think most of the issues I was having was from the bacterial infection. She gave me the final diagnosis of Post Infectious IBS. Basically, you can get an infection that is so bad and goes so long untreated. Your body is able to fight off the infection but your intestines cannot. The only part of that diagnosis that I hear is BS. Hopefully she's wrong because I do not want chronic, unexplained shits. Hopefully by clearing up the bacterial overgrowth, we got rid of the symptoms for good.

The final diagnosis of my blood issues is ITP. Idiopathic Thrombocytopenic Purpura. ITP is defined as chronic low platelets. Fortunately, my platelets have been able to maintain themselves around 104, which is a decent number. The hematologist warned me of getting upper respiratory infections (bronchitis, pneumonia, etc), bruising, rash called Petechiae. I need to get my platelets checked four times a year. If I notice any of those things, I'll need to go in for a Platelet check as they are symptoms of low platelets. If my levels get below 100, I'll need to go on steroids and/or IVIG treatment. IVIG contains immunoglobin G (IgG) immunoglobins from the plasma of a thousand or more blood donors. IVIG is given as an infusion. The treatment is temporary and short term... only lasting a few weeks. It's just enough to get my platelets high enough to fight the infection. My platelets have dropped below 80 but have pretty much maintained themselves at 104 so I think I'll be fine without treatments.

This brings me to now. I posted about having a ruptured cyst. After that cyst, things got a little weird. I felt pretty good for about a week. Then I started getting really crampy. I figured it was finally my period coming. Eventually, I started to bleed (on Wednesday). I guess bleed isn't a good word for it... I had some sort of funky ass brown gook coming out. It looked like what your (or at least mine) period looks like at the very end. Anyway, I had that for a day. Then the second day I had regular bleeding. At 10:15 at night, I went to the bathroom and I noticed that my period seemed really clotty. Then I looked down and I had a freaking foreign thing (that I keep referring to as an alien) hanging out of me. I started screaming for B. By the time he came in, I had pulled out the alien and was just sitting on the toilet. We just kept repeating, "what the fuck is that?" Then, came another piece. I have a picture but I'm not going to post it. I took the picture to send to Dr. P. The best way to describe what they looked like is this... it looked like if you were to butterfly a shrimp. It was solid but squishy (like a gummy worm) and had the rippled texture of a butterflied shrimp. One piece was 4" long by 2" wide the other was 3" by 2". They were huge, thick, and scary. I was freaked out. I sent the picture to Dr. P and she replied with "I don't know what to say." She had me save it and the following morning I brought it in for testing. The Pathology report came back with nothing. They basically called it inflamed menstrual tissue. What the hell?!?! Dr. P is putting me on Doxycycline just to be sure I didn't or don't get an infection from it. So I delivered an alien. Awesome.

The alien delivery sparked some blood tests. I went in on Saturday for regular day 3 labs (FSH, E2, AMH) and a couple of other tests. Yesterday, I met with Dr. P to discuss future cycles and the test results. For the first time ever, I had a test come back abnormal. My Prolactin came back at 27.8 (or something like that). The general cut-off for normal is 26. Dr. P said that if my level was that high but my periods and ovulation were still regular, she wouldn't be concerned. The fact that all of a sudden my cycles became irregular and with my increase of Prolactin. They have checked it several times. The last time they checked it was in April/May and it was 9 - is concerning. That's a huge jump in six months. I asked her what we do about it and she said I need to start medication (Bromocriptine) right away and need to have an MRI. Apparently the main cause of increases/high levels of Prolactin is a Prolactinoma... A tumor in the Pituitary Gland. I've been consulting with Dr. Google all night. Prolactinomas are generally benign tumors. They are sporadic and the causes are unknown. They are more common in women than men. The medication, Bromocriptine, is used to reduce the levels of Prolactin which ultimately shrinks the tumor. If that doesn't help, then the tumor can be removed surgically. Of course, I'm freaking out. The earliest MRI I could get is Monday at 5:30. So I have Today, Tomorrow, Saturday, Sunday and all of Monday to be worried. I guess I'll have more time since we have to wait for the MRI to be read and results to be sent to Dr. P.

I went from very healthy, with no health issues to having chronic shits and a brain tumor. What the eff?

THURSDAY, SEPTEMBER 15, 2011

Just another Manic Monday

Monday proved to be our lucky day.
1. First thing in the morning, I got an email from Dr. P stating "Totally normal MRI!" Yay! I'm totally normal. Well, what is normal?
2. We became active on the adoption agency's website.

A couple of things about #2...

We are very open about our fertility struggle and our desire to have a baby. I have always said that we will be parents someway, somehow. I have only mentioned adoption as an "if and when" and never a definite. There are a few reasons for this.

It's a scary process. It's scary and emotional. Realizing that the way you will have a child and start a family is by being advertised on a website with pictures of yourself and letters to potential birthmothers is a very hard concept to accept. It's hard to accept with the judgments of yourself always going through your head. Having outside opinions and judgments would make the process even more brutal than it already is.

This isn't just about us anymore. This is about us and our child. This is his or her story to tell when he or she is ready.

We have been quietly (only a small handful of people knew) going through the adoption process for months and months. We interviewed many agencies and selected our agency about six months ago. Then we quietly went through the Home Study Process; finishing that step in June. Then, we went through the process of sending checks (huge ones), gathering photos, writing birth mother letters, and filling out questionnaires. After a few struggles and road blocks (which I'll share another time), we were FINALLY activated on Monday evening at 9:30 pm.

I've been battling a chest cold... seriously; health is not on my side this month. During the Patriots game on Monday, I kept falling asleep on the couch. At one point, I woke up to B saying

"Apeyyyy." I was groggy and had no idea what was going on. I saw that he had his computer streaming through the television. We do this often to watch shows on Netflix. At first I thought he was singing my name to watch a show. After a few seconds of being awake and yawning off my haze, I realized our home and our faces were on the TV. Finally... active!

It's a strange feeling... being active. It's what we have been working towards and excited about. We knew we would be active sometime Monday. We received notification via email early Monday letting us know that we "should" be active by the end of the day. I was anxious and excited all day. Once it happened, I was initially excited then instantly sad. I just kept thinking "this is how we have a baby?" We have to advertise ourselves and wait to be judged then selected?!?! I was sad and frustrated but B's excitement deterred me from staying feeling sorry from myself. I had been excited all day and there was no reason for me to stop feeling that way.

Tuesday afternoon, I received an email from B that said something along the lines of, "Selected by a birthmother. Less than 24 hours of being live." When I saw the email, I got a knot in my stomach, my hands were shaking, and I thought, "Not funny." I called him a few seconds later and asked if it was a joke. Of course it wasn't a joke. Why would he joke about that? Then everything else happened so quickly, an emailed picture of the birthmother, a conference call with the adoption advisor, calls to Dr. P and a decision was made. We accepted the match early Tuesday evening. Our birthmother is due November 18th... in two short months. It's a surreal feeling. We honestly thought it would take months, years, to be matched. We are that rare story (which we are beyond grateful for) that got matched immediately. Less than one day. Holy shit.

With all that being said, there are a few things that I want to emphasize. This is our baby. We are expecting our first child in two months. We cannot wait to have this baby. Having a baby isn't just about having it come out your vagina or belly. We cannot wait to have our baby in our arms, our home, and our hearts.

We ask that you respect our privacy and our child's privacy when it comes to the details. We ask that you not refer our child as adopted. We will be open with our child about having a birthmother from the beginning. We will share his/her story with our child the way we feel is best. If and when our child is ready, he/she will share that story with you. Until then, we are expecting a baby in November... plain and simple.

We are having a baby. A real human baby... one without fur. A baby. Yay!

FRIDAY, SEPTEMBER 16, 2011

Friday

A real HUMAN baby without fur. HOLY SHIT.

That's all I have for today. We're beyond excited. Too excited for anything other than HOLY SHIT.

WEDNESDAY, SEPTEMBER 21, 2011

Updates

You're all due for updates. AND by the number of hits my blog is getting daily, I know you're all waiting for them. Work has been crazy this week for me. Things will slow down tomorrow evening. I will update you all either tomorrow or Friday.

Just so you know... I'm still thinking HOLY SHIT!

SATURDAY, SEPTEMBER 24, 2011

Baby Crazy

Since we got the clearance call/accepted the match, we have been crazy. Work has been nuts for both B and me. Monday evening, we had a conference call with us (B and myself), the social worker, and the birthmother. Everyone was slightly nervous at first but once the call got going, we were all comfortable and talked non-stop. The call lasted about an hour and twenty minutes. According to the social worker, that's not the norm. She said most of her calls are only 30 minutes long. She generally has to ask a lot of questions to keep conversation going and she usually cracks jokes to lighten up the mood. She very impressed with how she felt like a bystander on our call. She loved that she really wasn't needed. During the call we discussed various things like, why the birthmother chose us, how B and I were raised, how B and I met, and some other things. We also found out that our birthmother is expecting to have the baby by Halloween. She said, "I will be extremely shocked if it's not out by Halloween." UHM... that's in a MONTH!

The social worker said generally, they advise adoptive parents to have their bags packed a month before the due date.

However, in our case, she suggested we pack and get all our ducks in a row within the next two weeks. So, on top of our crazy work schedules we have been doing the following...

Cleaning out the nursery (it was our storage/laundry room).

Purchasing a bajillion baby items.

Washing all the items people loaned us (car seat, high chair, swing, etc.).

Putting the nursery together.

Washing all the baby items we need to pack (onesies, receiving blankets, swaddling blankets, socks, mitts, hats, etc.).

Making a list of the contacts we need (attorney, social worker, hospital, car rental, airlines).

Making a list of all the flights and departure times for every airline.

Interviewing pediatricians and making appointments.

Meeting with lactation consultant (I attempted to pump for two days. I ended up having terrible side effects from the medication so I can't breast feed).

Figuring out Parental leave with work.

Those are just the major things...

Originally, our plan was to fly out a couple of weeks before her due date. That way, when she goes into labor, we will be close by. Since they don't think she'll make it that far, we're not sure what we'll do. As it stands right now, we'll get a call when she's in labor. Once we get the call, we will head to the airport. We need to have everything packed and ready to go. There will be no time for thinking.

My sister-in-law's wedding is October 9th. Let's hope we make it through that!

SATURDAY, OCTOBER 1, 2011

Anti-Baby Shower Luncheon

Today I had my anti-baby shower luncheon. Of course, I despise baby showers. They are a reminder of our struggle and our losses. They induce anxiety and bitterness in me. I do not like them one bit. I have stopped going to them and I most definitely do not one for myself. Plus, I'm Italian. Italian culture is not a fan of showers either. It's considered bad luck to have a shower before the baby is born. Things happen and unfortunately for MANY people, the things that happen aren't good. So, as a compromise to my friends wanting to throw a shower and me being completely against it, we had an anti-baby shower luncheon today. It was very small, just a few of my closest friends and sister (and sister-in-law). There was a champagne toast and plenty of food. I did get some wonderful and thoughtful gifts. I cried a few times but mostly we just enjoyed conversation without focusing on a baby. It was perfect. Plus, I got my period today. The mother-to-be at her anti-shower, drinking champagne while having her period. How ironically perfect. Periods and alcohol... the perfect opposites of pregnancy. LOVE IT.

We got some really great items, convertible car seat, play gym, clothes, newborn photo shoot (in the state and city where the baby will be born), books, sheets... it was fantastic.

Speaking of my period. Today is Cycle day 31. Did you hear me? THIRTY-ONE! Finally, I'm starting to be back to normal. That magic little pill being used to lower my prolactin is working.

We put together our high chair this morning. I LOVE IT. I'm actually obsessed with it. I did so much research on the crib and high chair. I was a psycho researcher. Seriously, psycho. I wanted something that was first and foremost safe... obviously. I also wanted something practical. I wanted to be able to use it for long term as opposed to short term. The high chair I got is the Stokke Tripp Trapp. I love the look of it, I love the practicality of it. What I love the most about it, is the baby, toddler, child will always be table height with us.

B is out grabbing some last minute things for his sister's wedding (which is next weekend!). When he gets home we'll put the crib together. A crib. This home is going to have a crib. I can't believe it. We have fought so hard and so long for a family. It is mind boggling that it is actually happening. Wahoo!

SUNDAY, OCTOBER 9, 2011

It's a BOY!

That's right! Our little gift has made an early arrival. What did I say in one of my earlier posts??? I think it was something along the lines of, our birthmother will go into labor either the night before my sister-in-law's wedding or mid-ceremony. We got the call during the rehearsal dinner that he was born. We are so insanely excited but sad that we will miss the wedding. B was playing Over The Rainbow while his sister and father walked down the aisle. He has been practicing like crazy. We'll have to Skype into the wedding! I'll upload pictures as soon as I can!

WEDNESDAY, OCTOBER 12, 2011

Finally, Motherhood

Sorry for the birth announcement and then disappearing. It has been a crazy four days. As soon as we got the call, we left the rehearsal dinner and started making travel plans. Fortunately, I have had all the baby stuff packed and ready to go. All we had to do was pack for ourselves (which we're learning, we did a very poor job). We got on the earliest flight Sunday morning. We had a short layover (30 minutes). We boarded our second plane and sat on the runway for a while. After 20 minutes or so they told us there was a problem with the plane and we needed to deboard. I went up to customer service and told them that our baby was born and we are just trying to get to him. They were able to get us on a flight that was leaving in five minutes. It wasn't to the city we needed to be in but close enough that we could rent a car and drive. So we ran through the airport (I feel like we always end up running through airports) and got there just as they were closing the door. Fortunately, they let us on the plane. Our drive to the hospital was just under two hours but it seemed like it took us days. We thought we would get there and they would let us right in. Not so much. We waited forever. First in a waiting room then they put us in a freezing cold old, no longer used, Triage room. The charge nurse informed us that before we get to see the baby, we have to meet the birthmother. Originally she didn't want to meet us so I had them double check that she was okay with it. After they did, we went in to her room. I'm not sure what I was expecting but I was surprised at how tiny she was or is. We sat down and starting talking. We pretty much let her steer the conversation. She told us about M's delivery... it was fast, 45 minutes from the start of contractions. He came seven minutes after the ambulance got her to the hospital. It was a bumpy ride, "M" has a scraped chin to prove it. The charge nurse came in and abruptly ended our conversation. It was actually quite uncomfortable. B and I got up, hugged the birthmother, and walked out the room. As soon as I turned my back to her, I started bawling my eyes out. I just felt so badly for her. I can't imagine being in her shoes. Then, we met M. Ah. It wasn't weird. It wasn't uncomfortable. I didn't think for one second "who is this baby?" As soon as I saw him, I thought "You finally have arrived." He was and still is, perfect. He smelled how I imagined. He looked how I imagined. He felt how I imagined. Finally, we were looking at our baby.

Once we got M. We had M. The hospital was not only a dump but it was also filled with crappy staff (mainly crappy... we did get a good nurse on day 2). A few hours after we had him, I had to call the nurse and say "Can you bring us some food. We have had the baby for a few hours and I'm assuming he needs to eat." They sucked. Oh and due to budget cuts, they don't perform circumcisions. We couldn't get out of there fast enough.

The day after we were discharged, we had an appointment scheduled with the pediatrician. We quickly learned that we are still not legally M's parents. M's birthmother told me that they called her to confirm the appointment. It was bullshit. She knows our first names... that's it. She doesn't know where we live or our last names. Yet they had us both listed as his parents. Billing errors happen all the time. They could very easily send our info to her address. I asked them to remove us or her from the file... not as easy as it seems. We were able to remove her and "inactivate" our account but that's all we could do.

After fighting with the pediatrician, we spent the day driving to lawyer's offices and filling out paperwork. Halfway through the paperwork, my blood pressure was through the roof. For privacy purposes, I'm not going to get into the details of why I was angry. Just know, I was angry.

Now, here we are. In a hotel room. With a perfect little nugget.

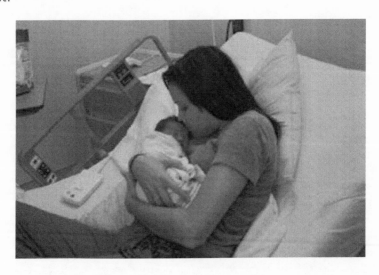

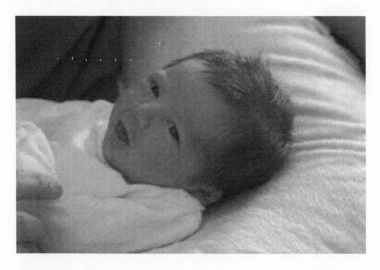

FRIDAY, NOVEMBER 4, 2011

M at one Month

First off, the fact that the title of this post is "M at one Month" is not cool. I've only posted twice since he was born. That's pure laziness. It really is. Our computer is on the second floor so I've been finding every excuse under the sun to not climb the stairs. In my defense, I only have a handful of minutes a day to do it. If I'm not feeding M, burping him, changing his diaper, changing his clothes, reading him books, telling him stories, doing tummy time... I'm cleaning, washing bottles, doing laundry, cooking dinner, or attempting to shower. Oh, and trying to fit in a meal for me. I'm not complaining one bit. I'm just trying to justify my lack of posting.

There is so much to write about. Where shall I begin? Let's begin with my cycles...

Two months in a row, I ovulated on time. This month, since we were back from picking up M, Dr. P had me come in for a Progesterone check and a Prolactin check. My progesterone was nice and high (confirming ovulation) and my Prolactin was nice and low (confirming the Bromocriptine is working). When I found out my Prolactin is low again, I asked if I can discontinue the Bromocriptine. Nope. The Bromocriptine is the only reason my Prolactin is staying low and I'm ovulating normally again. So, until we're done having children, Bromocriptine is part of my nightly routine.

The last I wrote, we were having some legal difficulties. Eventually, it was all worked out. While we were out West picking up M, we had him circumcised. The hospital he was born at didn't do it after birth due to budget cuts. Seriously... that's absurd. We were very fortunate to be matched with a birthmother who lives a couple hours from where B and I lived for a few years. So we had many friends that were able to visit us and were able to visit with. It also provided us with pediatrician referrals. I have a good friend that has three children under 3. The youngest two are twin boys. When we were dealing with the circumcision debacle, she was able to refer us to her pediatrician and the person who performed her boys' circumcision. M left the hospital weighing 5lbs 11oz (peanut!). The day of his circumcision (he was 8 days old) he was 5lbs 13oz. He was finally putting some weight back on!

The circumcision was interesting. Both B and I watched. Originally, I wasn't going to go into the room, only B was. But when it came time for them to leave, I couldn't bear the thought of not holding his little fingers. To be honest, it wasn't as bad as you would expect it to be. It's bad but not that bad. They gave M some Tylenol and they injected Lidocaine directly into his penis. The only thing he didn't like was being strapped down. He screamed and arched his back. Other than that, he just stayed wide eyed and kept sucking B's finger. He was a trooper.

Waiting for the clearance to come home seemed like an eternity. We were very fortunate to stay with generous friends. Who not only gave up their bedroom for us (we did protest... a lot), they cooked us dinner every night and loved M endlessly. Even with their generosity, we were anxious to get home. We wanted to have M meet his fur siblings and our families. We wanted him to get used to his surroundings at home. We wanted him to get used to his bassinet and his crib. We got the call late October 20th. We were on the first flight home on the 21st. We were there for two weeks and we have been home for two weeks. Four weeks of pure bliss.

This has been a long, painful road for us. I'm not sure if parenting comes naturally to us or if the length of wanting this makes us appreciate everything... including screaming, sleepless nights. I'm sure it's a combination of both. Either way, we are loving every second of M... even the last 48 hours of 100% fussiness. I was really sick last week and unfortunately, M caught what I had. On Wednesday night, he got a fever that required a late night call to the on-call pediatrician. After a 15 minute conversation, the pediatrician said, "You are the most poised and calm mother I have ever conversed with." It was not only nice to hear but it was also nice confirmation that what we have been fighting for is what were and are supposed to be doing all along.

Being parents is what we are meant to be. It's who we are and who we have always been.

Now, that leads me to "What about Infertility." where does that stand. It stands. It stands right where it was before. I have not forgotten what we have been through and what we have lost. I have not lost anger towards the unfairness of it all. I have not lost the want and need of having a baby or carrying a baby. I still can't look at big bellies and glowing pregnant ladies. Pregnancy announcements still knock me off my feet. So yes, we are still fighting for that. Which means, yes, we continue with IVF.

My ten minutes of quiet have ended. My poor little sick skadoosh needs his mama. I'll upload some pictures tomorrow (B will be home and I'll have some more time).

TUESDAY, NOVEMBER 8, 2011

Let's set a few things straight

Today M is one month old! Can you believe just seven weeks ago, we were activated on the agency website and matched a day later??? Now we have this perfect little nugget. I'll share some photos after I set a few things straight.

1. I will not get pregnant now that we have M. So don't feel that you have to tell me that I will every time we talk. If I get pregnant, it's not because of M and "not thinking about it." It will be due to the fact that we have tried for several years and we have exhausted all medical technologies. It will be because I have injected myself with a million needles and ounces of drugs. It will happen because we surgically removed my eggs and injected them with B's sperm. It will be a result of seven IVFs, not because I have relaxed and stopped thinking about it since we have M.

2. Just because we have M, doesn't mean our history is erased or forgotten. I am still hurt and scarred by what we have dealt with and what we have lost. I still mourn the loss of all our babies. Yes, I remembered that two due dates of Baby L's just passed. Yes, I cried and yes, I mourned. M brings us joy but doesn't erase history.

3. I still cannot look at pregnant bellies. M didn't grow in my belly. I didn't feel him grow inside me. I didn't feel him kick or flip. I don't know what pregnancy butterflies are like. I don't know what it's like to be exhausted from carrying a child in my womb. I still have trouble with

pregnant people. I don't think that will ever change... even if I end up pregnant sometime before I'm 70.

4. Pregnancy announcements still knock me off my feet. Being sensitive to my situation is still needed. I may never get a chance to announce that I'm pregnant (well, longer than several weeks). I will never have the SURPRISE we're expecting announcement. Never.

5. Yes, M is adopted. However, his story, his history, his birthmother is just that... his. I know you're all curious and want to hear about it but it's no one's business but his. If and when he's ready to share that story, he will. Please respect that and not ask me about it.

M had his one month checkup yesterday. He is 7lbs 13oz. He's gaining an average of 2 ounces a day (they want to see a half an ounce a day). He's tiny but doing great. Don't forget, his due date isn't for another 10 days. He was very early.

M and Bear at 2 weeks

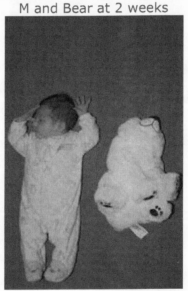

Hmmmmmmm

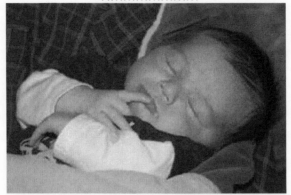

Reading with Daddy

Snuggles with Mommy

THURSDAY, NOVEMBER 10, 2011

Sick Sick Sick

I was puking last night. M was puking last night and today. B had a bunch of meetings scheduled so he had to go into work. So it was just sick M, the fur babies and me today. Well, it's like that every day but I am sick so that makes a big difference. Anyway, M kept puking all over me. I felt like I was hit by a bus and I smelled shit. No, I didn't smell like shit (well, who knows), I smelled shit. I was carrying a puking baby around the house trying to find the smell. Then I found it, on the dog. He rolled in shit. I couldn't put M down all day. I don't blame him. If he feels the slightest bit as I do, he's miserable. I had to drag the dog upstairs (our down stairs shower is being renovated) and wash him while I was holding a pukey M. Three minutes into the bath, the hose to the shower head exploded. I was holding a puking baby, shampooing a shitty dog while getting soaked by the broken shower hose. OH, I can't forget that M didn't pee all day so I had to drag my shitty smelling self (yes, I then smelled like wet, shitty dog) to the pediatrician to make sure M wasn't dehydrated. We sat him naked for a long time and finally he peed. Thank goodness! Going to the hospital so he could get fluids was not on my top ten things to do today. Yes, it was that kind of day. And no, I'm not complaining. In fact, it's awesome. Everything went wrong that could have gone wrong... on a day that I don't have the energy to deal with it... yet, it was perfect. I wouldn't want it any other way. This is what we fought for. Even on the worst of days, I am on cloud nine.

Now, if I could just get rid of this virus...

AND

If I could just get knocked up.

WEDNESDAY, JANUARY 4, 2012

It's been a while

I realize I have been a terrible blogger. To be honest, my life is consumed by M. This blog is about infertility for those looking to understand it better and those looking to relate. Although I'm still one big infertile, I don't feel this is the place to talk about my daily baby routine. But then, I had a couple of things happen...

B and I took a CPR course through the hospital. What I didn't realize (however, I should have) was that everyone that would be taking CPR through a hospital would be expecting. B and I drove to the wrong building. So by the time we got to the correct one, we were late. We walked into a room full of pregnant women and their spouses. And then there was us. Just as I was staring at all the bellies, all the bellied women were staring at me. Or least it seemed. Since M's arrival, I haven't realized how much bellies still affect me. I haven't given myself the chance to think about how I feel when I see a pregnant woman. My life belongs to M now. He comes first. B second. Me third. I know, if I were on Oprah, she'd say I have to make time for myself. Sounds nice but that's not how us ladies work. Everyone before us... that's just how it is. Anyway, my life is about the boys and not about me. However, when we dropped M off at my parents for the night, our life temporarily went back to just us. When we walked into that pregnantly packed room, I had nothing else to think about except, "HOLY FUCK." I was dizzy, nervous, anxious. I felt like I was going to vomit. I've been walking around for a couple of months as Mommy and not as the infertile. I have been living my life as proud and not disgraced. I have been confident as women and mother. For the first time since M has arrived, I felt like a failure.

All during the class the instructor kept saying, "expecting mothers, this may be hard for you to hold this position so why don't you sit down and let the Daddies do this." Ah, the Daddies and Me. When it comes to infertility, it seems like there are two categories: 1) The world 2) Me. When do I get to fit in with the world? Who knows if I ever will. All I know is that my wounds have not healed and I still have holes in my heart. I know that M has changed my life forever. He is our baby. He is meant to be our baby. I know that infertility brought us to him. Our loss and struggle was the beginning of the journey to M. I can't imagine life without him. He may have grown in T's belly but he grew in our hearts long before. He is the most amazing, perfect little man. If perfection can't heal wounds, what will?

This week I keep hearing horrible stories about loss from friends. It's heartbreaking. Then you see those who take it for granted. Those who think pregnancy is just something that happens when you want it to. Or those who get angry for it happening. Or those who abuse and neglect their children. It's devastating that there are so many deserving, wonderful people wanting and waiting to become parents. Sadly, those are the people that fit into the category of "Me." I wish they didn't.

SATURDAY, JANUARY 21, 2012

Blogger, what's that?

Blogging:

Verb: Add new material to or regularly update a blog.

Ha! I guess I can't consider myself a blogger that takes part in blogging. I have been terrible. In my defense, well, I don't have one. I have been blogging but I haven't been posting. I secretly went through IVF cycle #6. Yes. #6. I blogged during the cycle but didn't post because I wanted to be able to go through a cycle in privacy, without questions or pressure. I'll start publishing the posts tomorrow.

I briefly mentioned that a lot has happened but I never mentioned what those things were.

The handful of weeks leading up to Christmas, I noticed a change in M. He seemed very irritable. Not seemed, he was very irritable. He screamed day in and day out. He screamed anytime he wasn't sleeping. I brought him into the pediatrician and was told he was Colicky. Colic and I do not get along. I think it's a BS way of saying "I have no idea what's wrong." After about a week, I went back to the pediatrician stating that "something is wrong with M." The pediatrician not only defaulted to him being Colic but she also added "You're a new mother." She told me that babies can be overwhelming and sometimes they feed off your stress. Colic can make that stress worse. "Don't worry, it usually gets better around four months." That was on December 16th.

On Christmas Eve, M screamed all night. We literally did not sleep one minute. I have some pictures of us on Christmas morning (which I'll post another time, I am at a hotel, on my work computer and all my pictures are on my home computer) and I look like a zombie. On Christmas day, M cried anytime he was awake but wasn't really awake all that often. He slept most of the day. On December 26th, M slept 14 hours straight, without waking to feed. We would try to wake him and he would just turn his head and continue sleeping. We thought it was strange but brushed it off as being exhausted from a couple of days of screaming and not sleeping. On December 27th, B and I were packing for a trip to Florida (we were leaving the next day). I was in the kitchen, bouncing M around, trying to soothe him. He was screaming bloody murder. M was screaming and I was bawling my eyes out. I kept saying, "Babies cry. This isn't a cry. He is in pain. What if he has cancer of his kidney and can't tell us it hurts? Something is wrong with him and no one will listen to me." I told B that I was going to call the pediatrician and get an appointment to "have his ears checked" since we were flying. It was complete bullshit but I didn't want to travel until someone helped me.

We ended up getting an appointment right away. We also ended up getting an appointment with a pediatrician that wasn't our usual one. The doctor checked his ears and said they looked great. He then proceeded to discuss with me what to look for if he gets an ear infection from flying. I started bawling my eyes out as he is telling me this. I then said, "I knew his ears were fine. Something is wrong with him and no one will believe me." The doctor then told me that I should never have to lie. If I think something is wrong, then they will see him and treat him. Of course, I had to tell him that I came in three times over the last few weeks and I got brushed off as "new mom." I'll leave that part of the conversation out... he was pissed that it was my fourth time coming in. Anyway, he weighed M. M only gained a few ounces in over three weeks. He also listened to M's heart and found a new, loud, murmur. Those two things, combined with the 14 hour stretch of sleep concerned the doctor. Finally, I heard what I wanted to hear, "you're right, something is wrong with him."

We ended up at the hospital. We first had to go through the ER. The ER ran a battery of tests... some useful and some a total waste of time. One of the tests was an EKG. The EKG came back abnormal, indicating the M's left ventricle was enlarged. That EKG combined with his "failure to thrive" (poor weight gain), got us admitted.

The next morning, we met with a nutritionist who discussed monitoring M's formula intake, his urine/stool output, and his weight gain. They also switched M's formula because his symptoms were similar to those of a baby with a milk protein allergy but his tests kept coming back negative for that. They switched the formula anyway to see if he would gain more weight.

We also met with a team of cardiologists to discuss their concerns about his heart. OH, I almost forgot, his blood pressure was consistently 125/60. Totally normal for an adult and insanely high for a baby. His should have been around 80/40. The cardiologists ordered a renal scan to see if he had any renal issues that could be causing his high BP. That came back inconclusive because he was moving too much. I was pretty pissed about that because the poor kid just laid there, sucking down a bottle of sugar water. It wasn't a squirmy baby that made it inconclusive, it was the poor work of the ultrasound tech.

The doctors actually said they didn't want to redo it until another tech was working. So at least they agreed with my thoughts.

December 28th was our second night in the hospital and it was also our anniversary. We ordered pizza to celebrate. B was in the lobby waiting for the pizza man while I stayed in the room with M. M was screaming and puking non-stop. Again, I was crying my eyes out. I kept asking the doctors and nurses to do something. AND I kept saying "It's the formula, he is much worse on it." They all said to give it time.

Fast forward a couple of days...

At this point, they are leaning towards an Aortic Coarctation. Basically, a narrowing in the arch of the aorta. They are talking about cutting his chest open (if it turned out to be that) and doing heart surgery. We were a mess. The only way to verify or rule it out was to do an echocardiogram (an ultrasound of the heart). In order to do that, M needed to be sedated. In order to be sedated, he needed to fast for several hours before the procedure. The procedure went well. The heart was totally normal. No narrowing of the aorta or any part of the heart. M slept off the sedation for several hours. When he finally woke up, he was all smiles. Not only was he all smiles, his blood pressure was back to normal. The doctors wanted us to stay another night to monitor the BP. The next morning, his BP was still normal so they discharged us with a diagnosis of "Possible stomach bug and bad reflux."

M continued to throw up a lot and have major bouts of diarrhea while we were home. We went back to our pediatrician and they reran the tests on the stool (blood in the stool is how they test for a milk protein allergy). That time, he had TONS of blood in his stool. TONS. There is a 1% chance that babies can be allergic to the allergy formula. M was one of them. So when I was crying and saying that the formula was upsetting him, I was right. Bastards.

All of the "Colic" and all of those medical issues were because the poor kid was starving. He was literally starving. He had been malabsorbing formula/nutrients for weeks. Most babies are not born with the allergy, it develops over time. I knew exactly when it happened. There was a change in him and I knew something was wrong but the pediatrician wouldn't listen. I hate this story for the details of what M had to go through, how sick he was and how it could have been resolved much sooner if I wasn't brushed off so quickly. Thank GOD, I am not a pushover and I knew to keep fighting for him. I love this story because it goes to show you, that genetics do not matter. You know your child as well as anyone who shares genes with their child.

Maternal instinct and maternal bond has nothing to do with whether or not you carried your child, used your eggs/sperm or donor eggs or sperm. It doesn't matter how your child became your child. Your child is your child. And that's that.

FRIDAY, FEBRUARY 24, 2012

January 11, Day 1

Dr. P decided to switch up my protocol. For no reason other than, why not? Instead of starting Lupron with Ovulation, I'll be starting Gonal-f (stim) with my period. Today is cycle day 3 so I had my baseline ultrasound and blood work. Driving to the clinic, I had some anxiety. I'm not sure why. I haven't cycled since our last miscarriage in April. Nine months. I've never had that much time off in between cycles. Maybe the time off gave me some new anxieties or maybe the anxiety was just hiding out for a bit. Either way, I was nervous. I forgot how gross it is to have a vaginal ultrasound done with your period. Not only is that gross, but you also get dressed behind a curtain. You basically wipe your lubed, bloody vajayjay with wet wipes and get dressed. It's nasty.

I got the call from my favorite nurse (whom I will no longer have because of their new scheduling) around 4:30 to let me know that I was to begin my stim drugs tonight. I'm starting with the same dose of Gonal-f that I always use, 187.5. Taking the injection wasn't bad. I was hesitant but I didn't freak out. I freaked out more on the poor phlebotomist that had to draw my blood. I flipping hate needles. Hate them.

Day 1 is done. It feels weird. What am I doing?!?!?

SUNDAY, FEBRUARY 26, 2012

January 12, Day 2

I'm sick. Sick, sick, sick. I had my boss with me all day both yesterday and today. I thought I was going to die. Not die, that's harsh. I thought I was going to fall apart. My entire body is aching. As my boss was reviewing reports with me, all I could think about was how I felt like I was hit by a truck. You know that feeling when your skin is just crawling? When you brush up against something, you feel like you got shocked? That's how I feel and how I felt all day. I went to the doctor with a fever of 103. Yep, 103. No wonder I felt so terrible. Needless to say, my shot tonight felt like I was being shot with a rifle and not a syringe. Holy brutal. I have a bad feeling about this cycle. Definitely starting off on the wrong foot.

To make matters worse, M is sick too. He's very congested in his chest. He's whiny and I assume he's achey just like his Mommy. No fun for the little man. No Fun at all.

WEDNESDAY, FEBRUARY 22, 2012

January 13, Day 3

I just took my last dose of Gonal-f before going in for a check. I'm not sure how I feel about this protocol. I stim really fast and really well. I'm afraid I'm going to respond too well and will end up with a poor outcome. Normally I freak out and Dr. Google every little thing. This time around, I'm just blah. I don't have high hopes or expectations of this cycle. I guess I'm burnt out. You all know how badly I want this and need this. I haven't lost that. I have just lost a little bit of fight. If I lost all of the fight in me, I wouldn't be cycling again. So I'm not completely lost... just slightly lost. I hope this cycle proves me wrong. I hope this cycle proves to be the one that works. M needs siblings... lots of them. Now this isn't just about B and I. This is about M. It's one thing to fail yourself and your husband. But it's another thing to fail your child. I refuse to do that. That can't happen. It just can't.

TUESDAY, FEBRUARY 28, 2012

January 14, Day 4

Ugh. I have a bad feeling about this one. I had an ultrasound and blood work this morning. First let me say, vaginal ultrasounds are NOT the same without Dr. Hottie. Anyway, I have four follicles on my left ovary measuring between 12mm-18mm and one on my right ovary measuring about 18mm. HOLY MOLY. That's too big too fast! I knew this would happen. I respond insanely well to stim meds. I am afraid that I'll have a few lead follicles that are huge and all the others won't have time to mature. Tonight I start taking Ganirelix. I will also start taking Menopur. Three shots, one belly. Seriously, I'm going to have a panic attack. OH! And M is NOT feeling well. We have had a few long nights at our house. Here's a little info on the two new drugs... well, new to me.

Ganirelix is a gonadotropin-releasing hormone (GnRH) antagonist. It is indicated for inhibiting premature luteinizing hormone (LH) surges in women undergoing controlled ovarian hyperstimulation with FSH and hCG, followed by subsequent assisted insemination or reproductive technology (ART) procedures. The main advantage of GnRH antagonists versus GnRH agonists (e.g., Leuprolide) is that they reduce the required days of fertility drug therapy per cycle from several weeks (three weeks) to several days, thereby increasing patient convenience. Secondarily, the onset of GnRH antagonists occurs rapidly after drug initiation, and the effects reverse rapidly, allowing pituitary function to return to baseline within about two days after discontinuation. Thus, pituitary and hormonal release is essentially normalized at the time of embryo transfer or implantation.

MENOPUR® is a highly purified preparation of naturally derived gonadotropins, called hMG. MENOPUR® contains equal amounts (75 IUs) of two kinds of hormonal activity: follicle-stimulating hormone (FSH), which helps stimulate egg production; and luteinizing hormone (LH), which helps the eggs mature and release (ovulate). MENOPUR® helps stimulate eggs to mature in women whose ovaries are basically healthy but are unable to develop eggs. It is not used for women who suffer from ovarian failure.

MENOPUR® is usually used together with human chorionic gonadotropin (hCG), and is indicated for the development of multiple follicles and pregnancy in women participating in an Assisted Reproductive Technology (ART) program.

WEDNESDAY, FEBRUARY 29, 2012

January 15, Day 5

AHHHHH! Okay, a few things happened last night.

1. I took a million shots.

2. No one warned me that Menopur burns like a mother effer!

3. I called the on call doctor with a question on how much solution to use with the Menopur powder. The fellow gave me the wrong info. I injected 2ccs of saline mixed with 75 units of powder, into my belly. Not only did it burn like heck, I also had a MASSIVE bubble of fluid under my skin. I kept saying to B all night, "there is no way this is correct." I finally emailed Dr. P and she said that I was to only use 1cc of solution. No wonder I had a massive bubble of fluid.

I'm starting to have my usual cycle anxieties. All the "what ifs" are running through my head. What if it doesn't work? What if we don't get any eggs? What if I have another miscarriage? I don't know what to think. I generally get pregnant every other cycle. Our last cycle, which was in April, I got pregnant. Which means, if this cycle follows the pattern, it won't work.

Thus far, I'm not a fan of the antagonist protocol. I will say, I haven't gained 20lbs. That is the only positive I see thus far. I'll keep searching for more.

On top of all this, M is getting worse. We brought him to the pediatrician today and he tested positive for RSV. It's just a virus that we all get often. However, it's serious when a child under 1 gets it... especially a preemie. We did a few nebulizer treatments in the pediatrician's office. We couldn't leave until his oxygen levels came back up. We were trained on some back compressions to help M cough up the mucous. We have to do medicated neb treatments every 3-4 hours with a saline treatment in between. My poor little man.

THURSDAY, MARCH 1, 2012

January 16, Day 6

We had a long rough night. M's cough is brutal. Not only is it brutal, he's having apnea episodes. We didn't want to leave his side because of the apnea so we took shifts staying awake with him. We just camped out in the living room. One of us would sleep and the other would stay awake with M on our chest. Poor little guy.

I'm starting to feel pain in my ovaries. I'm still not feeling this cycle. I just don't think these meds are working for me. I know each cycle is different and you can't compare one to the other. I have done this so many times and I know my body so incredibly well, it's hard for me not to compare. If I had a million dollars, I would bet it all that this is going to be a bust of a cycle. I have an ultrasound tomorrow to see how my little ovaries are doing. I hope the lead follicles are hanging tight. They can't get too big... if they do, we'll have to trigger and all the immature ones will be wasted.

March 1: M and I are heading to Indiana, tomorrow morning, for one of the AGC girl's baby shower. I can't wait! I'm a tad nervous about traveling with him by myself. He's a little curious George and he is hard to keep still. We'll be fine traveling through the airport... being on the plane may be difficult. I booked flights around his nap times so hopefully he sleeps...

hopefully. M was AGC baby #2, then Baby A was born a few weeks later. Now this baby, Baby J, will be AGC baby #4. Finally, AGC is having prayers answered! If I get around to it, I'll publish the posts from the cycle, if not, I'll start publishing them again on Monday. They're all written, it will just be a matter of me getting to it or not.

WEDNESDAY, MARCH 7, 2012

January 17, Day 7

So, lots of things happened last night. Yesterday, I mentioned M having RSV and some episodes of apnea. I was changing his diaper late afternoon/early evening when he started to choke on his phlegm. This has happened a handful of times throughout his bout of RSV. The pediatrician taught me some back compressions to help him pass the phlegm. When he started choking, I first tried to suction out the phlegm with the bulb... but the phlegm was too deep in his throat. Then I flipped him on his belly and started doing the back compressions... and nothing happened. At this point, it has been 12-15 seconds and he's a deep purple color. His arms were going crazy as he struggled to breathe. So, I did what any other person would do, I slapped him on his naked bum. The slap made him take a huge, deep breath, and let out a massive wail. That scream, forced the phlegm back down and opened his airway. As soon as his airway was open, I started a nebulizer treatment and called the pediatrician. She told us to go right to the hospital and to get there via ambulance (so if it happens on the road, we have the means to help him). So, we called 911 and took a ride to the hospital. When the ambulance arrived, M had most of his color back. His upper lip (between lip and nose) was still blue. His oxygen levels were still incredibly low. After a battery of tests, we were admitted to the hospital. Even with nurses and doctors poking him with needles and tools, he is the happiest baby. One nurse blew out his vein trying to put in the IV. Initially, he gave her a nasty look, then laughed at her.

We spent the night with M in a mist tent and giving him frequent nebulizer treatments. It was actually nice to have him hooked up to machines because it gave us enough comfort to be able to sleep. We hadn't slept in days.

I had to leave early morning to get to the clinic for my ultrasound. It was about an hour drive... it wasn't too bad.

My E2 was 1,349 (decent... hopefully low enough so I don't have to trigger yet). I had six measurable follicles on the left ovary (18.5mm, 15.5, 14.5, 13.5, 12.5) and multiple under 12mm. I had two measurable on the right ovary (19, 12) and multiple under 12mm. This totally blows. The 18.5 and the 19 are going to get too big and I'll have to trigger before the rest mature. Hopefully I will make it one more night before having to trigger. Either way, this cycle sucks.

Sick, sick, sick and still smiling

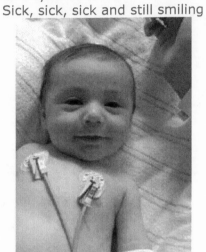

Hanging out with my favorite toy, Octopus Walker Hines, while in my mist tent.

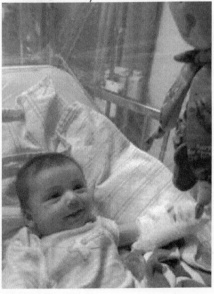

THURSDAY, MARCH 8, 2012

January 18, Day 8

This morning, I had an ultrasound. I have a two day meeting to attend as well. I wouldn't make it to my meeting on time (which I hate having to go to with M in the hospital. B stayed with him but still... I hated it) if I went to the clinic first. Dr. P's office has some satellite locations... fortunately, one is near my meeting location. I went there early in the morning. It was a fiasco. First off, it's in the city so parking is a nightmare. Second, I had to go up a few floors to check in, down a few to have blood drawn, up to check in, back down to register and back up for ultrasound. The appointment usually takes ten minutes at the location I go to. This morning, it took a full hour. I like my comfy location much better!

M is doing much better. His oxygen levels are normal when they turn it off. His lungs are crackly but not wheezy... which is fantastic. I think we'll be here a couple more days. I'm getting more sleep here than I was at home so I don't mind staying! We are getting a little stir crazy though.

And the results are...

E2 - 2,408

Left ovary follicles - 21.5, 21, 18, 16.5, 16, 14

Right ovary follicles - 20.5, 13

Blah. There is no doubt that I will have to trigger tonight. I am not going to get many mature eggs from this crappy batch. I KNEW it from the beginning. I am not meant to do the antagonist protocol. I respond very well to the Lupron protocol. I guess we just have to wait and see how this goes...

FRIDAY, MARCH 9, 2012

January 19, Day before retrieval

Not much to post about today. It's a non-drug, appointment day. I had to pull the trigger last night. Of course, I expected it but it still makes for a blah day. I know those lead follicles are going to ruin it for the others. My retrieval is tomorrow morning at 7:00 am. We shall see what we get.

M is doing much better. MUCH better. I think we're going to get discharged today. We're still waiting to see the doctor. Getting discharged would make the logistics of the retrieval much more simple. Anyway, off to keep my mind occupied before tomorrow.

Is it strange that the thing I'm most nervous about is the IV needle going into my hand? I HATE needles.

SATURDAY, MARCH 10, 2012

January 20, retrieval day

Of course, I slept zero last night. I couldn't get the thought of the IV needle going into my hand, put of my mind. The anesthesiologist on duty this morning was new. At least he was new to me. He didn't use the freezing cold spray that supposedly "numbs" your skin. I always think that spray makes it more painful. Anyway, he didn't use it and the IV needle wasn't as scary as usual. The actual procedure was standard. Nothing exciting. In fact, without out Dr. Hottie around to wake up to, it's even less exciting than usual. Normally, when I first wake up from surgery, I immediately ask how many eggs were retrieved. Today, I could have cared less. It wasn't that I just didn't care... I also didn't want to hear a crappy number. In so used to high teens; 15, 18, 19. After all these years of needles and surgeries, I didn't want to hear a depressing number. At one point the nurse in recovery asked if I got my number yet. I responded with, "I don't care to." she then told me that I would be pleasantly surprised. Finally, Dr. R came over to tell me they retrieved 11. He also then discussed how in Europe, they try to not get more than ten because quality tends to be better. I know he said all this to keep my calm but I know better. Eleven may be a decent number but I know they won't all be mature. For now, all I can do I sleep off this sedation, take some pain meds and wait for the fertilization report.

MONDAY, MARCH 12, 2012

January 21, Fertilization report

Ready for it?????

Only 4 out of the 11 eggs are mature. I knew it. I effing knew it. Of the four, three fertilized. THREE. I have never had a cycle with such small numbers. After the embryologist called me, I messaged Dr. P one sentence... "Antagonist is not my friend." She ended up calling me a few minutes later. She allowed me to bitch and moan about this crappy cycle and how I'll never do this protocol again. Then we discussed our game plan...

You usually wait until day 3 or day 5 for transfer because it gives the embryologist time to watch the embryos develop. That time allows for better selection of the embryo(s) that will be transferred. Since we are going to transfer everything, there is no reason to wait. Dr. P called the lab and told them to schedule me for a day 2 transfer. I go in tomorrow morning for transfer. I will say, as disappointing as the numbers are, the three we have, look really good.

Until tomorrow...

WEDNESDAY, MARCH 14, 2012

I'm not going to torture you

There is no point in dragging this on. The cycle didn't work. Another bust. We did end up with four embryos to transfer. One excellent, and three good. All were four cells (perfect for day 2). I ended up with an early beta just so I could stop the progesterone injections. It totally effing blows.

I'll write about my WTF appointment tomorrow.

Three IUIs
One FET
Six IVFs

Seriously?~?~

WEDNESDAY, MARCH 21, 2012

WTF and WTF!

I'm sorry I haven't posted about my WTF appointment. That last cycle hit me really hard. Really hard. For some reason, I have associated six cycles as the end of the road. I don't know why. Needless to say, I agonized over this BFP much longer than I usually do. For the first time ever, I walked out of a beta crying. No matter how many times you have been faced with loss, you always have this little glimmer of hope. Hope. What is that anyway? Wishful thinking? A positive attitude? Being Naive?

A few things happened at my WTF appointment.

1. Dr. P suggested I go to another clinic. I kept joking with her that she was firing us. She kept reassuring me that

she wasn't. She just felt that maybe unbiased set of eyes might be beneficial. Having someone look at us, without having so much invested in us, would help. She gave me a clinic to look into. I did. They look like duds. I already don't like them.

2. I told Dr. P that I was finally going to pull the trigger and see Dr. Kim Kwak. Dr. Kwak is a reproductive immunologist in Chicago. She's the best of the best... although, there are not many Reproductive Immunologists out there. From what I have read, very FEW couples walk away from her care without carrying to term. She's not very well respected in the Reproductive world because she uses medications off label and in unconventional ways. A lot of her medical treatments are not supported by research. Studies or no studies, it works. In my mind, that's good enough. There are a couple of AGC girls who have seen her. One is now in her third trimester and the other is in the process of doing an FET. Her body has shown major improvements and should be a much better environment for those little snowbabies. I have lurked on many immunology boards over the past couple of months. Many of them have women seeing Dr. Kwak. These women have suffered many, many losses. They have undergone several IVFs without taking home a baby. Many of those women, are now pregnant... and far along. How can I not go see her?

Initially, Dr. P was against it. She was afraid that Dr. Kwak would basically throw everything "but the kitchen sink" at me when it isn't necessary. At the WTF appointment, Dr. P said that she felt it was a good idea. So, I filled out all the paper work and sent in my medical records (I did all of this before my beta. I guess I was more prepared for a BFN than I thought). The first available appointment is May 7. Yep, she's that high in demand. So, we wait...

So I thought...

You may have noticed the title of this post has two WTFs in it. Are you ready for the second WTF??

Last week, I found out I am pregnant. YES, a NATURAL pregnancy! WTF! In 4.5 years of trying every single month (outside of IVF months), I have never been pregnant naturally. I know what you are thinking... only because everyone keeps saying it to us... it's because of M and I stopped thinking about it. You know how much this drives me bonkers and it is NOT true. Does anyone really believe we stopped thinking about it? Seriously, me, the infertility freako, stopped thinking about conceiving? I don't think so. In fact, this past month, I was more stressed out about it than ever because I just had the failed cycle. So NO, this isn't because of M. NO, this isn't because we weren't thinking about. NO, I wasn't relaxed. I still used the fancy fertility monitor. I got the egg on March 27, 28, 29. I STILL put a pillow under my ass to keep my hips elevated after. I STILL laid there for 45 minutes. I STILL refused to pee for hours "just in case." YES, that's a person STILL thinking about it and STILL stressing about it.

How does this happen? I don't know. Both Dr. P and the geneticist said they strongly believe we would be able to get pregnant naturally, it would just take 7-10 years. 7-10 years, who has that time when you're already in your 30s? No matter what higher being you believe in, you have to believe that something greater than us made this happen. I have no doubts that this is a miracle and a blessing.

My first beta was 54.

Second beta (44 hours later) was 134

Third beta (4 days later) 1,088 (doubling every 22 hours).

I have a beta on Monday then a viability ultrasound on Wednesday.

Ahhhhhhhhhhhhhhhhhhhhhhhhhhhh!

WEDNESDAY, MARCH 28, 2012

28dpo

I haven't purposely not been keeping you in the loop. I have been waiting for a good chunk of information that I could pass along. I finally feel like I have enough...

Last Friday morning (at about 1:00 am), I woke up with insane cramps. Excruciating cramps. At first, I thought "here it is, my fourth miscarriage." I knew if that was the case, there is nothing that can be done. So I tried to tough it out. After about a half hour, I decided I should go to the ER. The sharp pain was on my right side, shooting into my back. I was worried that it could be an ectopic and I feared something happening to my tubes. I got in the car and drove myself to the hospital. They took a urine sample and a blood sample. The Urine was "beautiful" and my beta came back at 3,540 (a few days before it was 1,088). They did an ultrasound and saw the yolk and sac... measuring 5wk 6d. Exactly where I thought I was. They told me that the pain was ligament tearing that usually doesn't happen in the second trimester but of course, it happened in the early weeks for me.

I am still POAS every morning. I know the lines don't mean anything at this point; however, it gives me a little comfort knowing there still there. I pee, see the line, and say "phew. Still pregnant." This past Monday, my POAS freaked me out. The test line seemed the same exact color as the control line. The past few tests, the test line is much darker than the control. Of course, I nearly lost my shit. I messaged Dr. P and asked if I could have another beta (I wasn't due for one until today). It came back at 6,991. I probably should have or could have canceled the scheduled beta that I had today. COULD have but didn't. I knew I wouldn't be able to wait from Monday until Friday without any information. Today's beta came in at 12,588.

What's next? Viability ultrasound (the please, please, please have a heartbeat ultrasound) is scheduled for Friday. We lost our first baby after we saw/heard the heartbeat. Friday will for sure be a milestone but it won't ease the worry.

I feel sick with worry every second of the day. When I have cramping, which is often, I'm worried that something bad is happening. When I don't have cramps, I'm worried that something bad already happened. I pee every two minutes and every single time, I check the toilet paper for blood. I am a freaking internal mess. I'm a mess but it's a mess I am beyond thankful for having.

Betas:
14dpo 54
16dpo 134
20dpo 1,088
23dpo 3,540
26dpo 6,991
28dpo 15,288

FRIDAY, MARCH 30, 2012

103...

I nearly had a panic attack on our way to the appointment. I was sweating bullets on the table. B was holding M (who was just pure smiles and giggles the entire time) next to me. Dr. P didn't waste one second. Well, she held M for a few seconds then said, "Ok, let's get going." She knows me all too well... or she has done this a kazillion and a half times. Either way, she knew not to keep me sitting there.

First, she started the ultrasound by saying that they (there was a student... a very pregnant student... with her) were just going to do their thing. Those weren't her exact words but it was something along the lines of that. My heart was practically beating out of my chest. I couldn't hear anything. Right away, Dr. P said "I see a flicker." I couldn't see the screen but B could. I'm pretty sure I asked if she was sure. Then she moved the monitor towards my direction so I could see. The sweet little flicker of a 3.8mm baby. It measured 103 (right where it should for this early on).

There were a couple of things that freaked me out.

1. I have fluid on my right side, above my uterus. Dr. P explained it to most likely be blood. Blood that will either eventually come out or get absorbed into my body. Yes, come out. As in, I may see blood on toilet paper. No! She did say, "It will freak you out. It will freak me out. But it will be fine." It is OUTSIDE of my uterus so when I see the blood, I have to remind myself of that. It's also in the exact spot that I've been having the crazy cramps. I'm going with Dr. P's ultrasound (you could clearly see the blood) over the ER's (who couldn't find my uterus for a good three minutes). I am slightly glad to know that I am not ripping apart my ligaments. I was so nervous and flustered that I didn't ask how it gets there. I will at my next appointment.

2. I was measuring two days behind. The fetal pole measured 6 weeks 1 day. I know I'm 6 weeks 3 days. After doing some research and consulting with friends, it seems that there is a +/- 4 day measurement window. With that information, I will not (or try not) to think about it again.

Technically, I'm not supposed to go back for another two weeks. Ya, that's not going to happen. Dr. P suggested we do weekly ultrasounds to keep my sanity in check. I 100% agree with her. It's a necessity. We will start doing them every Wednesday. Is it Wednesday, April 4 yet?!?!!?

For now, we have a perfectly, healthy, flickering grain of rice.

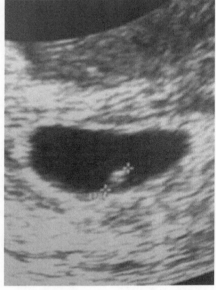

TUESDAY, APRIL 3, 2012

Is it tomorrow yet??

I have a Mac so I can't comment on your comments. I can from my work computer but that thing is so freaking slow. Thank you all so much for reaching out to me. Hearing similar stories, hope and excitement keeps me going. Thank you!

I'm sick as a dog. I'm nauseous 24 hours a day... literally 24 hours. I wake up in the middle of the night thinking I'm going to puke, only to dry heave for a few minutes. I puke about once day. Sometimes I force it because I know I'll feel better... sometimes it just happens. This is NOT a complaint. I feel like shit and love every second of it.

I'm still terrified out of my mind. I keep telling myself that since I'm not seeing blood, then I must be in good shape. Until today. One of our AGC girl's went in for an ultrasound (8 week) and both babies (twins) no longer had heartbeats. She didn't have spotting or bleeding. My heart just breaks for her. My heart breaks and my mind is filled with even more worry.

I am so nervous about tomorrow's ultrasound. If tomorrow's ultrasound looks good, I will officially be carrying for the longest time yet. We miscarried our first baby (the heartbeat baby) at 7.5 weeks. We knew that it wasn't looking good so we were expecting it. If tomorrow goes well, I think we'll pass that milestone. Fingers crossed. Prayers needed.

Oh, if you don't watch Giuliana and Bill, you should. It starts back up tonight! They have done an amazing job on documenting their fertility struggle.

WEDNESDAY, APRIL 4, 2012

7 Weeks and counting

Let me just tell you... ultrasound days are a blessing and a curse. It's so great to have weekly updates. It's fantastic. However, leading up to the ultrasound, I'm a mess. I'm basically one big panic attack. I can barely function. On top of my insane nausea, I have nervous nausea and knots in my stomach. On top of my pregnancy puking, I have nervous puking.

The ultrasound went well. The baby grew 5mm in five days (great!). It's heartbeat was 121 bpm (perfect). The heartbeat is amazing to see. The baby is only 9mm in length and it has a one chamber, blood pumping heart. Crazy.

The free fluid has not absorbed into my body. It actually traveled down and is now sitting below my uterus... which means, above my cervix... which means, its canal to exit my body. Dr. P told me that I will freak when I see the blood. It can be spotting, it can be clotty, it can be quick, or it can last weeks. GREAT! More anxiety for weeks! Hopefully it comes out quick! She did say that if/when I start bleeding, she will do whatever I need to be comfortable. Really?!?! Okay! I won't be comfortable unless we're doing daily ultrasounds! Daily ultrasounds sound wonderful but that's a lot of upkeep on my vajayjay. I only shave her up for Dr. P now (poor B). I can't keep up with daily shaves.

Dr. P also offered to write me a prescription for the nausea. I'm terrified to do anything, never mind take meds. As much as I want to feel better, I can't do it. I'd rather feel like death.

It's crazy, even after good news and a good ultrasound, I'm a wreck. I'm just as nervous as before, if not more nervous. I can't shake the feeling like the ball is going to drop at any moment. Dr. P and I talked about this for a while today. She said that once I hit 20 weeks and I can feel the baby, the anxiety will settle a little. I hope she's right. I hope she's not just right about the anxiety settling but also right about hitting 20 weeks! That sounds like an eternity away.

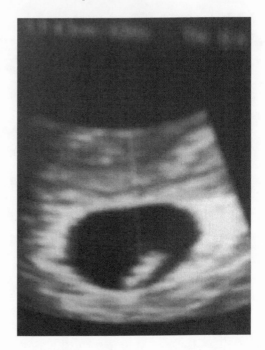

WEDNESDAY, APRIL 11, 2012

Car accident? Sure, why not?

Easter Sunday we were hit (from behind) by a young kid. He reeked like beer and was a nervous nelly. M screamed his head off when it happened. I think we (my mother, B and I) scared him. We all screamed when it happened. We're all fine. We had some sore backs and stiff necks but other than that, we are fine. However, I had some major cramping all night. Dr. P had me come in for an ultrasound first thing Monday Morning. Everything looked great. The baby's heart rate was 145. It was measuring on track and grew lots. I have a picture but it kind of stinks so I'm not going to bother scanning it. Dr. P was in the satellite office so I had a dude doctor do the ultrasound and apparently good pictures aren't a dude's priority.

I am so sick. The other day I puked up a smoothie. A smoothie. Can't a sister hold in liquid?!?! You will never, ever hear me complain about being sick. Being sick is part of pregnancy. I want pregnancy so I don't care about being sick. I look like hell, I feel like hell, but it's all worth it. Speaking of looking like hell, who knew you could get acne on your boobs? Or how about your earlobes?!?! Did you know that? Well, you can and I do.

B asked me the other day what kind of sick this feels like. The only thing I could think of is... this feels like your worst hangover, all day, every day. Nothing fixes it. Throwing up only temporarily settles your stomach. I can't look at protein. Meat makes me want to rip out my stomach and hurl it at a wall. The only things I can consume right now are carbs. Even sips of water send me face down in the toilet. I've been buying Gatorade and really watering it down. I'm so afraid of getting gestational diabetes from my horrible eating. I'm used to eating fruits, veggies, and lean meats. Not bagels, pasta, and sugary drinks. This baby is thriving off my diet so for now it's fine. Hopefully, I make it to the second trimester and feel better. Although, B's aunt threw up every day for nine months. Holy Shit.

I have an ultrasound on Monday then another one on Tuesday the 24th. After that, I have to leave Dr. P. Noooooo! I can't believe it. A regular, pap smearing OB?! What about weekly ultrasounds? What about messages with my fabulous doctor? What about the place that became my second home for over four years? Ahhhhhhhhhhhhhhhh

WEDNESDAY, APRIL 18, 2012

Phenergan

I finally caved and filled the prescription from Dr. P. I had a hard time with it... filling it. My hesitations were this...

I have wanted to experience pregnancy for years and years. I've been jealous and angry at every puking, pimple infested pregnant woman I have crossed paths with. Filling a prescriptions to help with nausea felt like I was skimping out on the experience. I want pregnancy. I want the good, the bad (excluding loss), pretty, and the ugly. I want it all. The reason I finally agreed to fill it... well, technically I didn't fill it, she called it in... Anyway, the reason I finally allowed her to call it in, was that I was getting extremely dehydrated from the vomiting. My lips were so chapped they were bleeding. My head was constantly pounding. My pee was the brightest shade of yellow/orange. My body was not doing well. At one point Dr. P responded to my comment about feeling like I'm skimping out on the experience with "Except when you're so dehydrated that it's bad for you and the baby." OKAY, OKAY, I'll take the pill!

She called in Phenergan for me. I can only take it at night because it knocks me out instantly. So, during the day, I am still beyond nauseous. However, I'm not puking anymore. I THINK it's because the Phenergan is helping me sleep. The more sleep

I'm getting, the less pukey I am during the day. I can't cook food. Forget about it. I can barely prepare M's food without gagging/puking. All food grosses me out. Not grosses me out in a simple food aversion way... grosses me out to the point of dizziness and vomiting. Oh but I LOVE every second of it. I will come out of the bathroom, with tears running down my face, boogers dripping, puke on my breath but feel completely satisfied that I look and smell that way because of a perfect little bean growing inside of me. I will never understand the pregnant person that complains... never.

I had my ultrasound on Monday (I know, I'm late to posting. I have my boss for a couple of days so I've been a little stressed). The baby's heart rate was 175... WHOOP WHOOP! We saw a head, eyes, arms, legs, heart, body, spine, chord (We've never made it to umbilical cord stage before).

Next Tuesday is my last appointment at the clinic. I can't believe I have to leave there. What will I do??? I have my first OB appointment scheduled for May 3. Holy Moly. An OB that is not going to squeeze my boobs and scrape my cervix. I can't believe it...

Nine weeks down, 31 to go (hopefully)

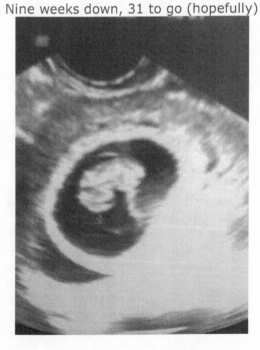

MONDAY, APRIL 23, 2012

9wks 4days

Saturday was a weird day for me. Every day (other than Saturday) I have been sick as a dog. I have been puking with severe nausea 24 hours a day. Saturday, we had a friend's wedding at 2:00. Leading up to Saturday, I was insanely worried about how I would handle functioning as a social human being. Strangely, I woke up Saturday morning feeling perfect. No nausea what so ever. I took the opportunity to eat eggs and get some protein in me. After the eggs... still nothing. Then it was time to leave for the wedding. I felt great. The reception was at 5:30 so we had some time to have appetizers and drinks (water for me) with some friends. At the restaurant, I had some pizza. At some point, I was expecting my nausea-free minutes to end. They never did. Dinner came and went. Dessert came and went. Then I danced my tail feather off all night. Nothing. Not one thing.

Now, how do you think I slept? I didn't. I stayed up all night pushing my boobs to see if they were still tender and peeing every ten seconds to see if there was blood. I was convinced the baby died. Finally Sunday morning, I told B that I had to go to the hospital. A few things were running through my mind...

1. If the baby died, I don't want Dr. P to be the one to see it on Tuesday.
2. If the baby died, I'll need a D&C.
3. We're leaving for Aruba on Wednesday. If I need a D&C and they don't see that the baby has died until Tuesday, then we won't be able to go to Aruba. Infertility has already taken so much from us. I'm not missing another vacation because of it.
4. If the baby died, the hospital will see it, and then I can schedule a D&C for Monday and maybe still go to Aruba.

So, I went to the hospital.

First let me say, I was a mess. I was bawling my eyes out. On top of expecting horrible news, I was getting looks from the staff as if I was a crazy person. "What do you mean you don't have any symptoms? Why are you here then?" That's my point bitchface! I DO NOT have any symptoms. I have been sick as a dog for weeks and weeks. I have barely been able to put a bra on without my boobs feeling like they're being cut open with razor blades. I haven't been able to consume food or even look at it for weeks. AND Today, ALL of that is gone. In my world, that means the baby is gone too.

The doctor finally came into my room. There I was, crying, half naked and being judged by a person who is supposed to understand me. Before she did an ultrasound she said "You know, normally when a person hits nine weeks, they are generally happy and relieved because they're in the safe zone." NORMALLY? One of the most frustrating parts of Infertility is the assumption of normalcy. Normal to one person is not normal to another. Maybe in her perfect, fertile world, nine weeks is safe. In my normal world, nine weeks is far from safe. My world is surrounded by losses at 6, 8, 9, 10, 11, 12, 16, 18, 21 weeks. Nine is not 40 and even 40 weeks doesn't guarantee a healthy living baby. In my normal world, a loss of symptoms generally means a loss of pregnancy. In my world, a loss doesn't necessarily come with cramping and blood. In my NORMAL world, worry is healthy.

Athletes squirt Gatorade down their throats when they are thirsty and in need of a boost. In my world, I need you to squirt some KY Jelly on the Ultrasound wand and show me a heartbeat. That's what I need. I shouldn't be judged on it.

The doctor (very quickly) did an ultrasound. It was the first time I had an over the belly ultrasound. She had the screen turned away from me. My throat was in my stomach and my heart was on the floor. I was shaking and just waiting for the words of "I'm sorry." Although, I wouldn't be surprised if the biznatch didn't say I'm sorry. With the monitor turned away from me and the sound off she said "Yep, there's a heartbeat. All is good." She then proceeded to shut it all down. HELL NO. I did not drive all the way here to be treated like crap and turned away with a "All is good." You best turn that machine back on, turn the monitor towards me, measure the heartbeat, turn the volume on and let me see/hear it beating with my own eyes and ears. After I yelled at her, she repeated the ultrasound while letting me see it for myself. So yes, all was well.

I know what you're thinking, my sickness is on its way out. NOPE. By Sunday afternoon, it was back with a vengeance. We had a 3rd birthday party for a friend's daughter. I threw up a TON there. Today, I can barely look at food. I just had one good day. I was able to enjoy the wedding. I enjoyed the food and dancing. I enjoyed talking with friends. I had one good day. That's it.

My last ultrasound with Dr. P is tomorrow at 11:45. Then I'm off to my OB on May 3. Yowzers.

WEDNESDAY, MAY 9, 2012

Discharged from Dr. P

I'm sorry I haven't posted in a while. My last appointment with Dr. P was the day before we went to Aruba. I had all the intentions in the world to update you all before we left but that didn't happen. So, I have two appointments to update you on.

The first is my last appointment with Dr. P. Dr. P was actually working in the satellite office that day. We had a plan for me to take the last appointment in the morning (Tuesdays the doctors have a meeting at the location I go to). I would see Dr. PGD then Dr. P would make it in time to see us and say goodbye. When we were on our way, she messaged me to let me know that she was just leaving and didn't think she'd make it. I was sitting on the table, half naked, when I heard sex kitten heals clunking down the hall. I said to B, "Those are Dr. P's feet." He made a joke that it would be funny if I was right. Sure enough, two minutes later, Dr. P walks in. She didn't do my ultrasound, she had Dr. PGD and the student do it. The baby looked great. He/She was doing a party dance for Dr. P. It wouldn't stop moving and jumping around.

Leaving the clinic was bittersweet for sure. Of course, leaving means we're in a good (hopefully) place with the pregnancy. At the same time, leaving means I lose all my sense of security. That office has been one of my rocks for the past 4+ years. If I have a mental breakdown, no one judges me when I call (or at least they don't act judgmental). They know that waiting is one of the most brutal parts of this process, so they call you as soon as they get any information. Dr. P would check the computer a million times a day for my results. I would get them as soon as she would. It's more than just getting answers sooner. They're empathetic, sympathetic, and understanding. Although they may have not gone through what their patients are going through, they get it. Leaving the office means entering the world of the fertiles. A place that sadly outcasts the infertiles and rarely acts or tries to understand. Ahhhhhh...

Baby L at 10 weeks (Just shy of 10)

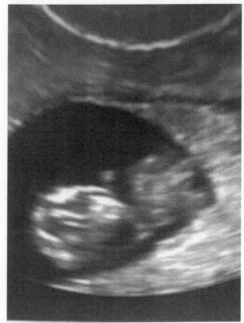

My First OB Appointment:

Needless to say, I was terrified for my appointment. I didn't know what to expect. I was convinced that as soon as I walked into the office the baby would spontaneously terminate. After getting some paperwork that I needed to update, I looked around the waiting room. Pregnant bellies and newborn babies everywhere. EVERYWHERE. It doesn't matter that we have M or that we are currently pregnant, our history, struggle and loss stays with us all the time. I had the same sick, gut wrenching feeling in my stomach that I always got when I go there. I'm not walking in there happy go lucky. I'm not walking through a field of daisies as I enter the office. I'm walking in there a nervous wreck. I'm walking on pins and needles. It only took me two seconds to recognize a face that I all too well and understand. There was a girl, probably in her late 20s/early 30s, that had her face turned to the wall. Anytime a pregnant person walked in, she quickly turned her head to the wall or floor. Her legs were shaking and her hands were jittery. As soon as I saw her, I started crying. I knew that she was surrounded by her biggest desire and her greatest struggle. I have been there several times... just there for a routine PAP and you have no choice but to be slapped in the face over and over again until the nurse calls you into a room. My heart broke for her.

I'm still not comfortable showing my belly. I try to hide it as much as I can. We had a birthday party this past weekend that I knew a friend (who recently lost her baby late in the second trimester) would be there. I must have tried on a 100 outfits before walking out of the house. The last thing I wanted to do was to walk into that party looking pregnant. I didn't want her to have to see that. I have been there. I that's all I have been... the person who just lost a baby and has to see someone else's fat, swollen belly. As much as I want to enjoy this and experience it, I don't want to flaunt it. You'll never see a sonogram photo on Facebook from me. You'll never see a pregnancy announcement from me. I'll enjoy this and love it, in the privacy of my own home or in the privacy of a conversation... not publicly.

So, after the waiting room cry fest, I was called into a room. The medical assistant that triaged me had no idea what she was saying or doing. After answering a bunch of questions about my period (you do know I'm 11 weeks pregnant, right!?!) she proceeded to ask me the following...

Have you ever been pregnant?

Yes.

How many times?

This is the fourth.

How many live births?

Zero.

Were they all abortions?

Were they all what?

Abortions?

No. I lost them all... as in not voluntary. As in, miscarriages (Biotch)

At this point, I'm messaging Dr. P, telling her that I hate being at an OB and I want her to take me back. After my brief conversation with the OB, I ask her if she can do the Doppler. I laid on the table and she started searching for a heartbeat. Nothing. One minute passes. Nothing. Two. Nothing. Three then four. Still nothing. At this point, I'm sweating, and thinking to myself "I knew it. I knew I should have stayed at the clinic." After four excruciating minutes, she says, "I'm going to see if we can get an ultrasound." She comes back a few minutes later and tells me I have to wait ten minutes but the ultrasound tech will take me after she's done with the current patient. I go back to the brutal waiting room and I wait. And wait. And wait. 25 long minutes later, they call me in.

The ultrasound tech knows my history (she has seen me for cysts in the past). She asks about M, updates me on how her sister's two adopted kids are doing and then says, "Look at the screen." There on the TV, was Baby L, jumping around like a madman/woman. It wouldn't sit still. Jumping, jumping, jumping.

THANK GOD! Apparently, with a uterus tilted backwards, the Doppler doesn't really work. WOULD HAVE BEEN NICE TO TELL ME THAT BEFORE!

At one point, the baby was measuring a week behind. I kept telling the tech that I couldn't leave until it measures exactly right. After a few minutes of not being able to get it, I started crying and saying, "Something's not right. Something is wrong." As soon as I said that, the baby literally looked in our direction, gave us a two arm wave, and flipped its body to the side. She got the correct measurement, it waved again and then went back to how it was sitting before. Call it coincidence but I swear the baby knew what I needed so it helped me out. Smart little lemon sized fetus. Smart.

I initially turned down the Downs testing. The results don't matter to us. If this baby carries to term, whatever its health may be is what we deal with. No amount of information beforehand would change how we feel or what we do. All it would do is worry me. So I turned it down. Then my OB told me I wouldn't see her again for a month. A MONTH. NO effing way. Once she said that, I quickly requested the Downs testing. I can't wait a month without seeing/hearing it. My NT scan is today.

I'm not feeling much better. So much for the "12 weeks and you'll feel great" mark. Puking and feeling like shit is all just a reminder of how blessed we are. So bring it on!

Baby L at 11 weeks... this is the "wave, flip" picture

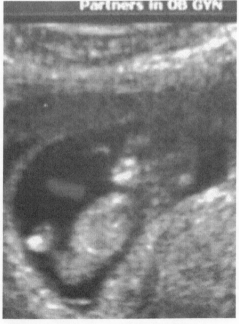

MONDAY, MAY 21, 2012

UPDATED: Approaching week 14

A week and a half ago I had my NT scan. For the scan, they like you to fill your bladder an hour and half before the ultrasound. So, I drank the 32 ounces... well, actually, I knew 32 ounces was an absurd amount, so I drank 20 ounces. Then we waited... and waited... and waited. They took me an hour late. Which means, I was holding a full bladder for 2.5 hours. I could barely walk. I was so pissed. Emergencies happen. I get that. However, let me empty and refill. Why torture me.

The scan went well. The baby looked great. It has a bladder, kidneys, arms, legs, brain, heart... all those good things. The fluid scan measured Normal. 1-3 is considered normal, we measured 1.34... perfect. I will try to scan a picture today. The OB ultrasound pictures suck. They are not nearly as clear as Dr. P's. They must have older, crappier machines.

Today, I'm convinced the baby has died. I'm sort of... not sort of... I am freaking out. I called the OB to see if I could come in for a scan. That was two hours ago. I haven't heard back yet. Ahhhhhh!

I talked to one of the AGC girls, M (an original) and she was saying it's because this is the longest I've gone without seeing/hearing the baby. She's right, it is. I just need to know it's okay. Right now, I'm Googling what you do with a 14 week loss... deliver, D&C...

Will they just call me back? I hate OBs!

UPDATE:

The nurse called me back around 11:00 am. She was incredibly nice and understanding. She told me to come in as soon as I can and she would scan me with the Doppler. I went in at a little after noon. The nurse took me immediately... I didn't wait more than ten seconds. It took about 1.5-2 (excruciating) minutes for her to find the heartbeat... but she found it. It was there and healthy at 156 bpm.

We had a nice chat about my history (she was aware of it but didn't realize I was the person she was always speaking to on the phone throughout the years). She told me, anytime I have a freak-out, to give her a call and she would take me right away. She also said, it's totally normal to freak out and that given my history, I have the right. She's right. All I know is that babies die. I don't know anything else. I witness others having healthy pregnancies and live births. But at the same time, I witness just as many others, including myself, deal with heartbreak after heartbreak. I can worry. It's what I know and it's how I protect myself. So worry I will away... with a Doppler check here and there.

I tried to scan a photo of the baby from the NT scan. It is such poor quality you can't tell what it is. I'm going to ask about that next time. Hey, by the way, why do your u/s images suck?

FRIDAY, JUNE 1, 2012

15+ Weeks (WARNING BUMP PICTURES)

I have included three bump pictures. They are on the bottom and there is a spacer in between. If it makes you nervous or uncomfortable, don't go beyond the scan images.

Yikes, 15 weeks?!?! What does that even mean?!?!

Wednesday, I had my first cervical length scan which means, I also got a little peek at Baby L. First off, my cervix was 4.1 (nice and long). I had a LEEP back in 2001ish. My OB does bi-weekly cervical length measures with anyone who had a LEEP. It's nice to be able to get in there more frequently. As Dr. P said, "Who knew a LEEP would come in handy?"

The baby is looking great. It has all the right parts and is measuring all the right measurements. It's weighing 4oz and is a little gymnast. Most of the images we got were of the baby upside down and tumbling around.

We're not going to find out the gender. We have not had enough surprises throughout this whole conception ordeal. Not finding out gives us 10 months (really 9 after realizing you're pregnant) of excitement full of wonder. I think girl...

A friend that I met through one of the fertility forums sent me her Doppler. It's actually really nice to have. I listened to it as soon as I opened the package. Then my mom wanted to hear it, so I used it again. Then a friend who was thinking about buying one wanted to hear it, so I used it again. I'm not being crazy like I thought I would be. I actually haven't had a moment of worry in a couple of weeks (knock on wood). You know who loves listening to it? M. He LOVES it. He screeches with joy every time he hears it. I used the Doppler this morning just I could see his excitement.

I'm feeling pretty good. I'm not yet comfortable with all the congratulations and questions. I still squirm and awkwardly say "Thank You." I'm not comfortable talking about how I'm feeling. "Good" seems much easier than "Well, the other day I thought it was dead so I called the nurse. While I was waiting for her to call back, I was freaking out. I also now have a Doppler to ease my mind. I'm only puking a few times a week as opposed to a few times a day. I am not sure if the baby will make it, I hope it does." Good. That's what you'll get if you ask me how I'm doing.

It's a weird thing. I have always wanted to be pregnant. Now that I am, I'm not sure what I'm comfortable doing. I have only known loss and struggle. I am a pro at loss emotions. I am an expert with struggle emotions. But pregnancy? I don't know. I'm excited yet guarded. I'm not sure when that will go away. I'm also clearly pregnant. My belly is now a bump. So there is no pretending anymore. I am pregnant. Plain and simple. Now I just need to get used to acting pregnant. What do pregnant people do anyway? I have the eating down. What else? Should I walk different? Should I talk different? Other than looking large, what do I do?

Here are the most recent scan pictures. As I said before, I am not impressed with the images. They're so cloudy.

Upside down little gymnast

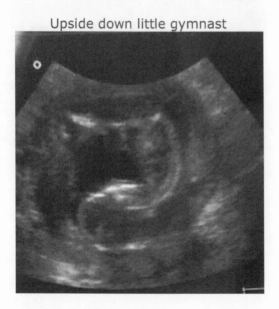

Profile

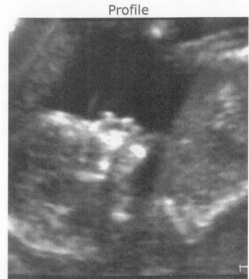

M holding the Doppler... so excited listening to the heartbeat

****
BUMP PICTURES
****

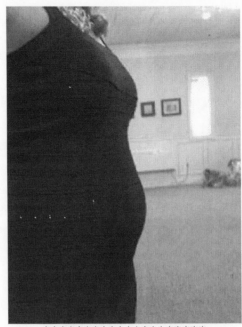

****

These were taken at 14 weeks (last week). I had a function to go to. After trying on a million and a half dresses, I went with the tight, non-maternity dress. The last one is an aerial view that someone had asked me to text them. Sorry about my unpedicured beach feet!

FRIDAY, JUNE 8, 2012

And M becomes a legal L

Today M turned 8 months old. Today is also the day that we finally went (via power of attorney) to court to finalize his adoption. M is no longer Baby Boy... he's MJL.

I never really thought of him not being ours. When he was in the hospital, we had to contact the state he was born in (and legally belonged to) so of course, during those times, I thought about it. More than anything, I would get frustrated. Then I woke up today, thinking about the call with the Judge and Attorney. I couldn't wrap my head around what was happening. How could there be a proceeding for something that already exists? He's our baby... has been since the moment we got the call. How do we go to court to legally obtain something that is already ours?

Eight Months. Eight glorious, beautiful months with the most amazing little man on earth and many more years of bliss to come.

MJL

THURSDAY, JUNE 14, 2012

And the ball has dropped...

I've been waiting for the ball to drop, today, it did.

As you all know, I had a LEEP back in 2000... maybe 1999... regardless, a long time ago. As result, my OB wanted to monitor my cervical length bi-weekly throughout the duration of my second trimester. I went in today for my scan. First, the baby was amazingly cute. It was sitting breached position, legs stretched out and crossed at the ankles, arms folded in front of its chest and its head resting on its forearms. It was sleeping like most people sleep on a plane. She had me eat some starbursts and do a little dance to wake it up. When it woke up, it flared its arms around like it was annoyed and went back to sleep. Seriously, the cutest.

After the belly scan, she had me empty my bladder for the transvaginal cervical scan. Two weeks ago, my cervix measured 4.3. Today, it measured 2.7. Uhm, ya. 2.4/2.5 is when they start to freak and worry about labor. The ultrasound tech kept trying to remeasure and remeasure. Once she got the longest length that she could, she said, "I'm going to get the doctor."

The Doctor came in and said, "okay, I'm not freaking yet so I want you to stay calm." Right, not happening. Dr. D discussed injections of Delalutin. She explained that it works well in most patients but isn't a guarantee. Fingers crossed and prayers that I fit into "most." Although, I am far from average or "most" when it comes to reproduction/pregnancy. In fact, I'm the polar opposite.

Dr. D then went into the possibility of a clercage (stitching of the cervix). She said, the first sign of pre-term labor is the cervical length shortening. After the shortening, the cervix opens. The opening is what the clercage prevents. If we can stop the shortening, a clercage wouldn't do anything except be a risk. But if we can't control the shortening, the clercage is a benefit that outweighs the risk.

We left the ultrasound room to set up everything... injections, appointment for next week... blah blah blah. As I'm scheduling the appointment, the receptionist tells me that they will call me, "most likely Monday," with the details of the injection. UHM, MONDAY?? I don't think so. Of course, this is when I start to freak out. As I'm freaking out, the ultrasound tech starts frantically yelling, "this is her fourth pregnancy, no live births. She's not going anywhere without an injection." I'm a mess, she's a mess. We're all a mess. THEN, the insurance/prior authorization person comes over. She starts explaining the process of getting a medication approved. First of all, I work for a pharmaceutical company as a pharmaceutical rep... I KNOW the process. Second of all, who gives a shit? You get the medicine and you try to stop this baby from coming out. Third of all, I don't give a shit about co-pay. I'll pay endless amounts, out of pocket, right now to get my hands on that medication.

After a lot of yelling and crying on my part, Dr. D comes out (at this point she saw another patient and was finished with that patient. A lot of time had passed). She starts telling the insurance chick that I need this now and no later than tomorrow. After about 30 minutes, I get the medication. Turns out, they gave me another patient's medication and my shipment that arrives tomorrow, will replenish the meds I used.

Now on to the Delalutin. Delalutin is an IM injection, in the ass. Yes, back to PIO like injections. Only this time, my husband isn't doing it. Some strange nurse that I have never met is doing it. She tells me to lay on the table and roll onto one side. Oh sweetheart, have you never had an infertility patient before? There is a method. A method that prevents me from screaming and punching you in the face as you inject my swollen, pregnant ass. I tell her that I would like to stand, on one foot with my weight on the leg opposite of the injection site. She looked at me like I was crazy but, I know what I'm doing. The injection was painful. It's thicker than PIO so it took about a minute longer to push it all in. After she removed the needle, it stung like I had a bee hive on my butt cheek. But in the end, I survived and hopefully the baby will too.

For now, no work... seriously, I'm out on leave at 17 weeks... and weekly injections/scans. I am cursed.

A friend of a friend gave me the most thoughtful, amazing gift yesterday... a prayer shawl. She knew of our history through our mutual friend. When she heard I was pregnant, she asked her mother to add us to the prayer shawl list. The women in the shawl group, pray (specific prayers) for you as they are knitting the shawl. She had it made when we first found out we were pregnant. She wanted to give it to me when we saw each other about a month ago but wasn't sure if I was still pregnant. I went to visit my friend yesterday and she gave it to me. It amazes me how people that you barely have contact with, can be so kind and generous. I love this shawl. I'm going to live in it for the next 23 weeks.

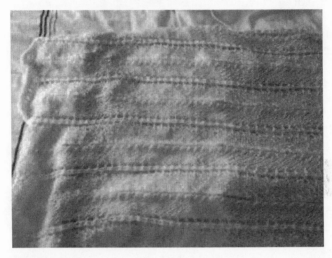

MONDAY, JUNE 25, 2012

Hello Crinone

I was waiting to update you all. When I get my weekly checks and injections, I do not see the doctor. Today I had my 19 week appointment and I wanted to wait until I talked with my OB before giving you an update.

Wednesday, my cervix measured 2.89 (with human error that's considered the exact same measurement as it was the week before). I received another injection and that was that. I was feeling pretty good about things until I heard a story about a girl who went into labor at 20 weeks and lost the baby. Of course, that had me freaking out. Fortunately, I had my appointment today and I could ask a million and a half questions. It's amazing how badly I wanted this and how badly I wanted to enjoy it... yet it seems at every chance I get to enjoy it, another curve ball is thrown my way. I can tell you this, I am NOT enjoying it, however, I am appreciating every second.

Last Thursday, my OB attended a grand rounds topic of "Progesterone, Clercage, and a Pessary to Prevent Preterm Birth in Women with a Short Cervix." The lecture was given by a world renowned maternal fetal medicine physician who specializes and had done extensive research on this topic. As a side note, I am so blessed to live in an area with such respected and well trained specialists. During his lecture, he presented a few studies that showed vaginal progesterone (such as Crinone) has a much higher success rate at reducing preterm labor than IM progesterone (Delalutin). Because of this research, my OB is taking me off the weekly injection and having me start daily Crinone (1xday at night). She also said that the MFM criteria for shortened cervix are generally 1.7-2.0... which means, I don't even fit the criteria for shortened cervix. My OB's personal criteria is 2.4/2.5 because she would rather be considered too cautious than take the risk her patients go into preterm labor. With that being said, although my cervix is shortening, it's not technically short. With the progesterone and being out of work, she's confident that we can stretch me out to at least 36 weeks (fingers crossed).

On a side note, today is my birthday! It's my Larry Bird birthday... 33. Last night B, M and I had dinner (M has the appetite of a teenager) and then my family came over for cake and dessert. Today, my sister and the two boys she nannies for are taking me out to lunch. Other than that, I will be listening to MJ (RIP MJ) while trying to organize my closet (seems to be low impact on my body but high impact on my life... it's a disaster).

We have our anatomy scan and cervical length recheck on Wednesday. I will be sure to update you all once I get home. BUT you will not find out the gender because we are not finding out either :) We have waited so long for this and the first half of the pregnancy was spent worrying about every kink and cramp. I was constantly on guard for losing it. Now I am worried about my damn cervix. Having the mystery and not knowing what the baby is (I'm thinking girl) keeps me excited. So no Pink or Blue announcements from us.

WEDNESDAY, JUNE 27, 2012

Anatomy Scan Day UPDATED

I'm a few minutes away from heading out to my appointment. I just got this and I wanted to share it. It makes me feel so much BETTER!

Hi!

I have been following your journey forever and wanted to say congrats most of all! Second, I saw your update on your blog and wanted to share my experience with the wonderful nightmare of a short cervix!

At 19 weeks, my cervix went down to a 1.8... I freaked... took forever to get there and now this (exactly what you thought too, right?!) Well my MFM put me on Crinone and monitored me weekly (he was going to do bi-weekly but he knew I was scared!)

I did the Crinone at night as directed because it absorbs better, and it worked!! Had a full term successful pregnancy.

So just wanted to share and wish you the best!

UPDATE:

The anatomy scan went well. NO, we did not cave and find out the gender. I will admit, when the ultrasound said, "oh, turn your head we're getting a clear shot in between the legs," I was dying to know. But that soon passed and now I'm glad we don't know.

The baby is measuring on track. Everything looks great (I can't believe how many different little body parts they measure). The baby's legs are measuring a week behind which means, it will have the L side legs... short and stumpy. I was hoping it would get my long legs! Hopefully it's a girl because those short legs for a boy would be a bummer!

My cervix measured a 2.9 and a 3.2 (they measure the longest and shortest length to get a range). I have been giving you all my longest measurement which means, it has grown a bit. The progesterone is working :) Fantastic news!

FRIDAY, JULY 6, 2012

20

I'm 20 weeks... halfway there. It feels strange. It feels great but strange. The first trimester went by brutally slow. Now I'm just a few weeks away from entering my third trimester. Bizarre (wonderfully bizarre).

I had my weekly cervical check yesterday. Every time H (my ultrasound tech) starts measuring, the only thing I focus on is the measurement on the right of the screen. She puts the cursor on the left side (top side of my cervix; closest to baby) and then drags it to the right side (bottom side). I never know how much longer she has to drag the cursor because I'm just watching the numbers and anxiously waiting for it to pass 2.5. Yesterday, I saw 1.0, then 2.0, then 3.0, then 4.0 and THEN 5.0. I'm pretty sure I said, "Shit" or "holy Crap" or something along the lines of that. H always takes the shortest measurement and the longest. Your cervix is squishy like a sponge so you can actually stretch it and elongate it by pulling up and pushing down near your belly button. My shortest measurement yesterday was 4.88 and my longest was 5.32. HOLY CRAP! THANK GOD for living in an area near academic centers. If my OB hadn't gone to those grand rounds, I would still have a shorter cervix and be getting injections in my butt. I'll take the Crinone vaginal leakage, migraines, acne, bloated face, and GI issues ALONG with a 4.88 cervix any day!

I'm not sure if I mentioned on here that Dr. Hottie was doing a documentary on Infertility in Africa. At one point (he said it was when he heard we were pregnant) he made the decision to bring in a few couples from the States as well. B and I were one of them. We had a film crew in our home and Dr. Hottie interviewed us (most of the questions were based on blog posts). It was a good day. Lots of tears, lots of laughs but mainly, it was a good reminder of how far we have come.

Dr. Hottie brought the footage to his editor and she made some comments that irked me. One, she said that it is hard to relate to a couple with a nice home, clothes, make up, etc. She also said since we are pregnant we are no longer fertile.

As Dr. Hottie was telling me these things, I was pissed at the comments but thought there must be some artistic view she has that I don't understand. This isn't my documentary so if we don't fit the mold, we don't fit it. BUT then the day went on, and I couldn't get those damn, ignorant comments out of my head. I felt like I had to say something to her but I have no idea who she is. I opted with an email to Dr. Hottie so he could pass the message along. I am going to post the email on here as well... maybe she reads my blog and she'll realize how she is sadly one of those people who have NO IDEA what infertility is and means. If she is going to edit a documentary on infertility, then she needs to get a clue.

Okay...

So after lots of thinking about this (over and over again), I decided I should email you some things that your editor should know. I can't let the comment "they're no longer infertile" slide without clarification. The whole purpose of my blog is to break the assumptions and misconceptions about infertility, if I let that go, then I would be self-defeating my own goals.

Once you're infertile, you're infertile. We are very fortunate to have modern medicine that allows us to continue to try to have children. Infertile does not mean sterile. If we were sterile and got pregnant, then one could say "they're no longer sterile." However, we're not sterile, we're infertile. Big difference. Infertility is a medical condition. Just like every other medical condition out there, there are treatments and medical procedures that MAY help that condition. It may be a temporary fix, it may mask the condition, but it won't cure the condition. There isn't a vaccine to prevent infertility. There isn't a pill that takes it away.

There are just methods that help you fight it. If a cancer patient goes through 4.5 years of treatment then finds themselves cancer free... that unfortunately does not take them out of the category of cancer patient. It puts them in remission. It doesn't take away their diagnosis, it just gives them some time (hopefully a long time) without the disease.

Although our story doesn't line up with the direction of the documentary (I totally get that), I do need to clarify another point the editor brought up. Yes your documentary is about Africa, infertility and the social ramifications of infertility. Yes, many African countries and regions do not have money or means that we have here in the States. However, just because one person has a nice house, great spouse or some make-up, doesn't mean the pain, the loss of friendships, being socially out-casted, the fear, hurt... any of it, less of a struggle than a person who doesn't have money. The emotional and social (religious included) impact are the same. We feel just as rejected by society, by our bodies and by many religions or God, as a person living without the monetary and material means that we have.

Infertility unfortunately doesn't have boundaries. It doesn't care who you are, where you live, and what you have. It doesn't care if you're emotionally stable to handle it, it doesn't care if it could destroy your marriage or your life. Infertility doesn't care if you're black, white, purple, or orange. It doesn't know that you're a fighter. It doesn't know that it will destroy you. It doesn't know what hemisphere you live in. It is without boundaries and limitations. I don't want people to forget that. I don't want people to think because we have means here in the States that we're less of a victim. We're not.

WEDNESDAY, JULY 25, 2012

17 to go

First off, I apologize for my lack of blogging. I have a friend who is very ill and being on the computer is the furthest thing from my mind. Watching a friend in the last days (unless he experiences a miracle) of his life is emotionally heartbreaking. When that friend is one of your best friend's husbands, it's even more heartbreaking. When you are taking their two and four year old on play dates so the house is calm and quiet, it's even more heartbreaking. I'm exhausted but the exhaustion I feel, is nothing compared to what they are dealing with. The past handful of days have looked pretty bad, with a rapid decline in the disease (Stage 4 colon cancer that spread to liver, lungs, bones, spine), so many of us spent the past few days at the hospital. We ate cafeteria food, slept in waiting rooms and laughed at who farted in their sleep. We slept maybe a few hours a night. A couple nights, even less. Needless to say, I have thought about Baby L and updating you often, I just haven't had the time to do so. I don't know how many times I have reminded myself that "I have no problems." All of this puts your own life into perspective.

My 21 week scan looked great. My cervix was measuring 4.4-5.2. My scan last week measured about the same; 4.8-5.04. My cervix is a trooper and responding well to Crinone and not working. Everyone keeps telling me that they're worried about me... not sleeping, not eating enough, stress. I'm okay. Fortunately and unfortunately, I'm a comfort eater. I have consumed more calories in the last couple of weeks (particularly the last four or five days) than I have in the past year. I'm getting plenty of food. In fact, at my last appointment, I was weighed. 12lbs have been added to my frame. My boobs have gone from a 34B to a 36DD! They're gigantic. I basically live in sports bras. I am tired. Pregnancy feels like mono anyway, I just feel like I have a bad case of it. But I'm okay. I'm getting sleep and when my body feels like it's had enough, I make sure I go home and rest. I'm doing right by the baby so no worries. I do miss M. He has been shuffled between babysitters and/or seeing mostly B. It breaks my heart. I just keep reminding myself that M doesn't need me, he wants me. My friends, need me, we all need each other. He won't remember that I wasn't around often for two weeks of his life.

M had is 9 Month check up a few weeks ago. He weighed in at 19lbs 4oz (43%) and is 28" long. He's happy, funny, and full of life. He's the best.

Baby L has been kicking and punching like crazy. He/She (I think she) has a strong punch. Baby L is weighing in at a little over a pound. Has a button nose like B. He/she loves snuggling and gets annoyed every time we wake him/her for an ultrasound.

Between the massive boobs, fat ass, huge belly, and acne, I finally have accepted that I am pregnant. I am pregnant and only have 17 weeks to go. How did this happen???

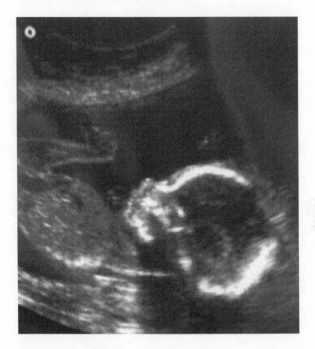

FRIDAY, AUGUST 10, 2012

Viability

The last time I posted was July 25th. I came home for less than 20 minutes. During that time, I wrote my blog post, played with M, then I got a call that Mark had taken a turn for the worse. I immediately left. Just a couple of hours later, Mark passed away. My emotions are all over the place. I'm confused as to why such a great person was taken from his wife and children. I'm saddened for his family. I'm relieved that he's no longer suffering. I'm angry that the suffered at all. Most of all, I realize that tomorrow is not promised to anyone. It's not promised to an unborn child or a parent of a child. I don't understand it. I just don't.

Missy, Mark's wife, is one of my best friends. His children may not come from my blood line but I love them as I do my own nieces. They're strength is admirable. Yet, I wish I didn't have to witness it. I wish they got to enjoy all the things that life should promise... family vacations, father daughter dances, football games, high school drama, college applications, walking down the aisle. Missy and the children have been robbed. Instead of worrying about Mark leaving his wet towel on the floor or what to make for dinner, Missy has to worry about finances and what's next. Totally and completely unfair.

Baby L is doing well. My cervix was 4.8 at my last scan. The baby is measuring in the 43rd percentile. Perfect. 24 weeks is the week of viability. It's crazy to me that a baby can be born that early and have a good chance at living. I actually didn't know it was considered the week of viability. It wasn't until the ultrasound tech and Dr. P (Yes, I still talk to her regularly) mentioned it to me. I will be 26 weeks on Tuesday. I will officially be in my third trimester. How on earth did I get here?

The baby is moving like crazy and I'm loving it. I'm fat, HUGE and I don't mind. My ass is gigantic, my arms have cellulite, my face doesn't even look the same... oh, and my boobs are disgusting (I went from a 34B to a 36DD) and I don't care. I care. I do care but I don't. Make sense?

Nice shot of my massive boobs

SATURDAY, AUGUST 25, 2012

28

WARNING: BUMP PICS AT BOTTOM OF POST

I'm approaching week 28. At most, I have 12 weeks to go. My OB is taking me off progesterone at week 34. My guess is, once we stop that, the baby will come soon after. I'm just hoping to make it through M's 1st birthday party.

WHAT did I just say?!?! M will soon be ONE. Holy Crap! I feel like it was just yesterday that I was crying over our adoption profile... feeling sorry for myself and for B. I hated that marketing was how we were going to have kids. Now, I am so incredibly grateful for that stupid website with our dumb pictures of us gardening and riding bikes. I can't imagine life without M in it. A year... holy Moly.

My last scan was good. My cervix was measuring 4.4-5.04... slightly shorter than usual. However, this is when the cervix should start shortening. As the baby gets larger and starts to put more pressure on the cervix, the cervix will shorten. Baby L has decided the best place to chill out is deep down low. He/She has its head right on my cervix. When I do my cervical length check, I have to try and lift the baby's head out of the way. Needless to say, my cervix should start to shorten now. I just hope it goes nice and slow.

I have my gestational diabetes test this week. Hopefully I pass. To be honest, I haven't been very good about controlling the sweets. It's the summer and ice cream is fantastic in the summer.

I'm starting to get really uncomfortable. Everything is hurting now. This is NOT a complaint. It's totally worth it. It's just not as "pretty and wonderful" as I imagined it being. I'm just so happy and blessed that I get to experience it... all of it... including the hard parts.

I'm finding that I'm getting increasingly nervous about something happening to the baby. I know part of it is because this is all so surreal. Having a baby has been a dream/wish/prayer for years and years. Losing babies and having failure after failure has been my reality. So now that I have this swollen (massively swollen) belly, I don't feel like me. I feel like this is another person's body. I just can't believe it. Any of it. It's crazy. It's surreal. It's HOLY SHIT.

BUMP PICTURES:
****

The first couple are from about three weeks ago. The last one, of me in a pink tank top, was yesterday at a concert (which I may add, going to a music festival sober is quite funny. It's amazing for people watching). I cropped out my friends so the picture is pretty small.

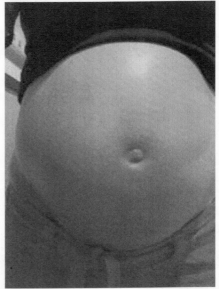

SATURDAY, SEPTEMBER 1, 2012

28.5

I had my 28 week scan and appointment this week. So far so good. I have gained 18lbs, which is average. However, the baby is growing but slowed down in its weight gain. I've been instructed to eat more protein or a daily milkshake or bowl of ice cream. How about those doctor's orders?? The baby is in the 38th percentile... which is fine... but it dropped from 48 so my OB just wants me to increase my diet a little. I will say, I totally get why my weight gain has slowed down. My summer diet seems to be mostly cucumbers and tomatoes from the garden. They're just so good!

I had my glucose screen as well. My sugar levels came back at 91. I guess the diabetic level is above 130. Bring on the sweets!

B and I are going through a sad time. As you all know, I love my fur babies as much as I love any human baby. Our dog Cappy started getting skittish towards M once he started crawling. On Thursday, Cappy jumped off the couch and pinned M on his back. He didn't bite and he didn't attempt to bite. BUT he was trying to show dominance over M... not good. I was losing my shit. I was screaming and crying. M was laughing (after he stopped crying) as if Cappy was playing with him. Cappy was cowering in the corner. I was paging B at the YMCA where he was swimming. I didn't know what to do. I put Cappy out on the deck for a bit while I cried hysterically. Even though M was fine, I knew that we wouldn't be able to keep Cappy. We called the trainer we used and he told us that some dogs are very intimidated by crawling babies. They look like other animals to them. He said there is nothing you can do except keep them separate until M is no longer crawling. That's not fair to M, Cappy or us. We'd always have to be on guard. We'd always have to keep them apart. Cappy wouldn't be comfortable in his own home. So, we found him a new home. I have been a mess. I have cried non-stop for three days now. My heart is broken...

I know it may seem silly to be so upset over a dog but people who have gone through IF or any struggle, will understand how a fur baby helps you through that.

When B had to go to China for six months, Cappy was my husband. We ate dinner together. We watched TV together. He warned me when animals or people were approaching our house.

When I had to give myself shots and I was freaking out, he would stand by my side. He would lick my legs and let me know that it was okay.

When I lost the babies, he never left my side. He would practically sit on me until I was out of my depression.

When a cycle didn't work, he would lay with me while I cried. He wouldn't even let me go to the bathroom without him following me to make sure I'd be okay.

When M was first born, he would sit by M and make sure he was breathing. As soon as M cried, he would get up to let me know that the baby needed me.

Cappy got me through the worst 4.5 years of my life. He has been by my side every step of the way. Now, I feel like we just betrayed him. He didn't give up on us yet, we gave up on him.

I know M comes first, which is why we did what we had to do. Even though I know we did right by M, I feel like we failed Cappy.

My heart is shattered.

TUESDAY, SEPTEMBER 4, 2012

Boy? Girl?

I love not knowing what we're having. Sometimes I think it's a girl. Other times, I'm convinced it's a boy. I have no idea. Some people "just know." I'm not one of those people. Maybe it has something to do with my disconnect from this pregnancy for the first 24 weeks. Although I was pregnant, I was trying not to get attached. However, how do you honestly know?? Attached or not?

If you go by old wives tales, I fit every category. One tale suggests I'm having a girl, another tale suggests a boy. The baby's heartbeat is all over the place. One day it's at 124, another at 160... most days it's steady at 145. Who knows, all I know is that I can't wait to find out.

At my 28 week appointment, I had a gender reveal scare. The medical assistant (the same one who asked me how many of my losses were result of abortion) asked me to sign a waiver allowing me to deliver at the hospital. She had it on a clipboard, signature page face up. I have never heard of needing a waiver to deliver at a hospital. That, on top of never signing anything without reading it, I flipped it over to read the details of the waiver. At the top of the page it said, "BABY BOY LANE." I instantly started crying. First off, I was by myself. B wasn't with me. Second off, we waited over seven months and I was finding out from some freaking waiver. She quickly took it away and said, "sorry, wrong form." Then she handed me the right form. When I mentioned that we weren't finding out the gender, she just brushed me off and replied, "sorry, imagine if I just told you what you were having." Then she walked out of the room. For 15 minutes, I sat there, texting my girlfriends and B and hysterically crying.

Once the doctor came in, she explained that EVERY SINGLE pregnant person in their office, has to sign the consent for a circumcision (if they choose to have one). They do not want you signing any consents medicated. They like to have everything all set before you go into labor. She also explained to me that the only person that knows what we're having is the ultrasound tech. It's not in my file anywhere. Not one person (besides the tech), including my OB, knows what we're having. When I STILL doubted her, she explained what she meant by EVERY SINGLE pregnant person is EVERY SINGLE pregnant person... including the ones who know they are having a girl. The only expectant person excluded from that waiver is the person who had an amnio since that is the only fool proof way to know what you're having.

Phew.

I nearly lost my shit there.

Oh, and the reason for the original waiver... it wasn't to deliver at the hospital. It basically said they can rip out my insides, paralyze me or kill me and I have no rights to sue them. I didn't want to sign it but it was the only way my OB could deliver. So let this be my legal waiver of me saying, if they do any of those things to me, the crap waiver I signed in the office is null and void. I will sue if you rip my insides out and B will sue if you kill me. Thanks.

TUESDAY, SEPTEMBER 18, 2012

9 to go

I can't believe I am down to single digits. Only 9 weeks to go.

My last appointment went well. My cervix measured 4.2 or 4.5 (I forget). It's still measuring above normal and super long (especially for being this far along). The result of a long cervix, no more scans. AHHHHHHH! My OB said we could continue them if I would like but I felt like I had been spoiled long enough. I'll go back to normal scans like everyone else. My next scan won't be until I'm 34 weeks (just three more weeks). After that scan, we will discontinue the progesterone. Then it's just a waiting game. Ahhhh... so weird.

My "shower" is coming up this weekend. I have really struggled with people understanding my needs for a shower. I didn't want a shower. I don't want a shower. However, I do want to celebrate this miracle. I just don't think it needs to be done in the traditional way. I don't think gifts and oohing and ahhing over the pregnancy is the way to do it. In fact, that way makes me really uncomfortable. People are more than welcome to bring gifts if they really want, however, I will not be opening them. It's not that I'm not appreciative of the gifts. It's not that I won't enjoy opening them eventually. It's that I'm not comfortable with it.

When the topic was approached, I told the people planning it that I would love to have a celebration but I did not want to accept gifts. I suggested that we choose a charity or two that people could donate to or bring items to be donated instead. In lieu. It's a term often used yet somehow has caused an uproar amongst those that know me. I am astonished at the complaints and criticism I have received or heard about because of this no gift thing. I don't get it. Aren't you supposed to be coming to celebrate me and this pregnancy? So shouldn't this be about me and my pregnancy? Why does it have to be about everyone else? It's mind boggling to me. Seriously.

First off, I don't believe in "showering" a life before the life is given. Tomorrow isn't promised to anyone... especially my babies. If I were to sit and open presents, every piece of tape that I rip off, would feel like a jinx. It would feel like I'm slowly killing my baby. It's not post-traumatic stress, it's not anxiety.

It's history. I do not have a history of delivering babies. I have had four pregnancies with zero live births.

Secondly, when did celebrations become about what the guests want? When did they turn into "well, I will feel bad if you don't open my gift?" Huh? You? What?!??!

M's first birthday is coming up (no kidding... holy crap!). I put on the invitation a suggestion for donations in lieu of gifts. I'm getting the same complaints about the birthday as I am the shower. M doesn't need a million toys. He has plenty. B and I don't want him growing up thinking that birthdays are about getting gifts. We want him to grow up knowing that birthdays are about celebrating his life. We will get him gifts. Our immediate family will get him gifts. He won't be deprived. I don't get how that is such a horrible thing. Or why it's worthy of judgment. I guess, I don't understand judgment at all... but that's a whole different blog post.

I'm in love with this pregnancy. I'm not in love with it the same way many women are. I don't have dreams about the baby. I don't feel this immense connection with every kick and roll. I love it... I love that I'm experiencing it. I love that I have been blessed with it. I love that my ass is the size of Texas because of it. However, I will not be in love with it, until the baby is here, in my arms. I know those who don't understand infertility are going to judge this and try to say that I won't connect or bond with my baby properly because of it. That's just bullshit. Many people do not carry their child and have no issues with bonding. Look at M. I didn't carry him. I didn't even see him for the first 12 hours of his life. We couldn't be more bonded or connected. Bonding and your love for your child has nothing to do with how you handling the gestational portion of the life. Nothing. So please, don't start an uproar over me saying I'm not having dreams of a little girl or boy dancing through fields of daisies. In fact, I'm not having dreams at all because I'm not sleeping.

Wow, that was a rant. I guess I'm sick of people complaining.

WEDNESDAY, SEPTEMBER 19, 2012

Ungrateful

I have just a quick response to all the responses I'm getting about my previous post. The most frustrating one... "Ungrateful."

I am extremely grateful. I am beyond grateful. However, I want to celebrate this pregnancy being surrounded by those who know and understand me. If and when the baby comes to life, then people can spoil the crap out of it. I will not mind at all. But for now, I want to do this my way... how I'm comfortable.

I know I will get gifts at the shower. I will open them... at home. In my home, where I can cry in privacy. In my home, where I can freak out and stop opening them whenever I want... without a bajillion eyes on me.

If I was truly selfish; if I was truly ungrateful; then I would be asking for gifts and not opening them in front of the guests. I'm not asking for gifts and then saying I'm not comfortable opening them. I'm saying I'm not comfortable opening them so please consider such and such charity (I don't know the charity because I didn't plan the shower). By requesting a charity donation in lieu of gifts is far from selfish and ungrateful. I'm simply requesting that my wishes to celebrate this pregnancy be respected. There is no difference between myself and someone with a registry. They're asking for hundreds of items that they want. I'm only asking for one.

For Christmas, my siblings and sibling-in-laws, adopt a family and buy the gifts they need. We do it because we have what we need and in the spirit of celebrating the holiday, we want to give a family less fortunate what they want/need. Are we selfish for doing that?

I'm going to wrap this up then stop talking about it because it's really annoying (in fact, I'm not sure if anyone else deals with this when they have requests for their shower). I want to celebrate overcoming 4.5 years of suffering, seven IVFs, eight IVFs if you include the FET, three losses, four million vaginal ultrasounds, 10 trillion needles in my stomach, veins and ass, bruises, weight gain, hot flashes, acne, night sweats, induced menopause and endless days of crying. I want to celebrate a victory over a disease that brought us nothing but heartbreak and pain. There is NOTHING wrong with that. More so, there is NOTHING ungrateful about that.

I don't expect everyone to understand this. No two people are the same. No two situations are the same. Until you have walked in my shoes, you can't judge.

MONDAY, SEPTEMBER 24, 2012

Victories worth celebrating...

32. I have made it to 32 weeks. Yowzers!

I am posting Celebration pics below... which means... bump pictures are included

Yesterday was Baby L's celebration. It was beautifully done. My wishes and anxieties were so well respected. I couldn't have asked for a better day.

4.5 years, eight IVFs (including the one FET), three losses, a bajillion needles and oceans of tears. This victory over IF is beyond worth celebrating.

The girls (a friend, my sister, and B's sister) had adorable mason jars for drinks (I'm in love with mason jars for some strange reason) with damask lids (damask is another obsession of mine). They had two signature drinks, one pink and one blue. The recipes for the drinks were on the jar. There was just enough "baby" to know what we were celebrating and to not make me feel overwhelmed. It was perfect. It really was.

In lieu of gifts, everyone brought diapers that would be donated to local hospitals for families in need. Many people brought us gifts for baby L. We did enjoy opening them at home. We opened them at our own pace. We opened them without eyes on us and without feeling like we were jinxing the next eight weeks. We got lots of checks in cards that are for a charity of our choice. I love that everyone who attended came to support us, to celebrate our victory... all while respecting who we are and what we have been through.

****

BUMP PICTURES BELOW

****

M making his grand entrance.

Baby in a bassinet Fruit Salad made by my sister in law

Life Saver and Tic Tac Pacifiers

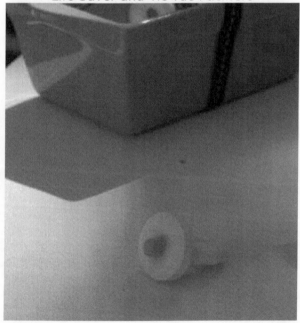

Floral Sock centerpieces

Cake made by my amazing friend... who by the way just makes cakes for "fun"

We actually did NOT plan on matching. The color coordination is totally random

SUNDAY, SEPTEMBER 30, 2012

Approaching Larry Bird

I'm approaching my Larry Bird week... 33. It's surreal. I by no means feel comfortable. I don't think I will until the baby is in my arms... then all sorts of other worrying kicks in.

Last night... well, this morning, at about 3:00 am, the baby went crazy. He/She was kicking, punching, rolling, and doing a booty shake for about 20 seconds. It was fast and hard. Then all of a sudden, nothing. Not a kick. Not a punch. Not even the slightest flutter. I started to panic that something happened. I worried that what I felt was the baby fighting for its life. I thought maybe it got tangled in the cord. Thank GOD I still have the Doppler. I waited a few minutes to see if it would move again. When it didn't, I pulled out the Doppler. I found the heartbeat immediately. Goes to show you, the fear Infertility instills in you never goes away. Never.

Moments like that make you realize that life is too short for non-sense. All the drama about the Baby Lane shower made me realize who my true friends are/were. It made me realize that true friends are NOT just around for trauma. They're not just there for you when you're down. True friends are there for you to celebrate the good times too. They are around to know that you just had a panic attack in the middle of the night thinking your baby died at 33 weeks. They are around for everything. They never have to ask "what is going on in your life" because they already know. This pregnancy and all the events surrounding it didn't make me realize all of this. But it did make me realize that I'm constantly making attempts to make things work that I shouldn't. I really need to let that toxicity go. It's not good for me to be worrying about why so and so is upset. Or what could I do to help them or fix it. Life is too short and too good for anything but love and laughter. All the other BS can go. I have enough to worry about than petty drama... like if my baby will make it to term. AND, celebrating M's 1st birthday! I still can't believe he will be one next week.

One year ago, I didn't have one baby. I had a lot of tears. A ton of wounds and many scars. Now, in just seven short weeks (at most), I will have two babies, tons of scars, but endless wounds healed. I'm making huge strides in my struggles. I can't surround myself with any unnecessary negative energy. Life is good. It's unfair and painful... but the strong get through it.

"Strength does not come from physical capacity. It comes from an indomitable will" ~ Gandhi

MONDAY, OCTOBER 1, 2012

October 2012

M is taking a nap so I have to capitalize on this time and take a shower... so this post is just a quickie.

OCTOBER! I can't believe it.

In exactly one week, I will be a mother of a one year old.

Next Month, I will be a mother of two.
Exactly one year ago... being a mother seemed impossible.
Nothing is impossible.

SUNDAY, OCTOBER 7, 2012

First Step!

Today is the big birthday party! Woot! Not only are we celebrating M's first birthday... we are also celebrating his first step that was taken shortly after his breakfast. Soon enough he'll be walking. Whoooot!

A friend passed this article by Catherine Pearson (Catherine.Pearson@huffingtonpost.com) on to me and I thought it was worthy of sharing with you. Interesting...

http://www.huffingtonpost.com/2012/10/02/infertility_n_19 33500.html?ncid=edlinkusaolp00000003

Michelle was still nursing her daughter, born through in vitro fertilization, when she found out she was pregnant again. It was entirely unexpected - she wasn't using any fertility drugs.

Several years earlier, the Indiana mother found herself so determined to have her first child, she resorted to using donor eggs. She and her husband made the decision following a string of devastating failures: Michelle suffered two miscarriages and gave birth to a stillborn baby at 20 weeks. She tried three failed rounds of intrauterine insemination -- a procedure in which her husband's sperm were placed directly in her uterus using a catheter. Then she moved onto IVF, which involves joining an egg and sperm together in a laboratory dish, and placing the fertilized egg into a woman's uterus. Michelle tried one round using her own eggs.

That failed, too.

In early 2003, at the of age 42, Michelle, who asked that only her first name be used for this article, made the difficult decision to place another woman's fertilized egg in her body. She gave birth to a daughter, whom she lovingly describes as bright, daring and, at 8 years old, "all girl --pink and purple and sparkly." Initially, she worried about using donor eggs and giving up a genetic link to her daughter. But now she cannot believe she ever, even fleetingly, doubted her ability to love a child who wasn't genetically hers. That feeling was re-confirmed when she give birth to her second child, her biological son, now 7. Both feel entirely hers, she said, and both feel miraculous.

"Sometimes my husband and I hear them playing in the other room and we look at each other and say, 'Can you believe how lucky we are?'" Michelle said.

Lucky, perhaps, but not alone.

Though few studies track how often a spontaneous pregnancy after use of assisted reproductive technology occurs, those that do suggest it is not uncommon. Most recently, a French paper published this summer in the journal Fertility and Sterility found that 17 percent of women who gave birth after IVF became pregnant again within six years — this time on their own. Among couples whose IVF failed, the rate of spontaneous pregnancy was even higher: 24 percent of the women became pregnant in the years after treatment. A 2008 German study found that 20 percent of couples who conceived a child by intracytoplasmic sperm injection — a form of IVF in which a single sperm is injected directly into an egg — and who subsequently tried to get pregnant naturally, succeeded. Estimates suggest that normal, healthy women have around a 20 to 25 percent chance of getting pregnant per menstrual cycle.

Many fertility doctors say the findings bear out, at least anecdotally. "I tell my [IVF] patients, 'You know, after you have your baby, your OB is going to come to discharge you and tell you to use birth control if you don't want to get pregnant," said Alice Domar, an assistant professor of obstetrics, gynecology and reproductive biology at Harvard Medical School and executive director of the Domar Center for Mind/Body Health. "And my patients look at me and say, 'You've gotta be kidding me. I've had 18 cycles of IVF.' And then they get pregnant."

Though no expert has ever offered her a definitive explanation, Michelle believes her first pregnancy somehow healed her body.

"With my boy, it's like I had one golden egg in there. I don't know how to explain it," she said. "But I don't think it would have happened without my daughter. It's like she taught my body what to do."

Scientific theories do support Michelle's hunch, particularly for women with certain conditions. For example, about 50 percent of women with endometriosis, which causes the tissue that normally lines the uterus to grow elsewhere, have problems getting pregnant. Whether induced or natural, pregnancy "suppresses" the condition, Domar explained.

"For somebody who has a history of endometriosis, if she manages to get pregnant, those nine months of pregnancy are very healing to her pelvis," she said. "It would make more sense that she would be able to get pregnant after."

An underweight woman faces a similar prospect, as long as her weight is a reason for ovulation problems. If she manages to get pregnant, even a window of several months to lose the baby weight may be long enough for her to become pregnant naturally with a second child.

AN INEXACT SCIENCE

An even simpler explanation is that some women are rushing into assisted reproductive technology and that given more time, they might have gotten pregnant on their own. Much about infertility and its roots is still a mystery, and to have a baby, the complex processes of ovulation and fertilization need to go just so. Around one-third of infertility cases are traced to female problems, such as ovulation disorders and structural complications; one-third stem from male problems like deficiencies in sperm count and ability to swim; and one-third are due to both partners, or are unexplained.

Knowing how much time to give biology to work is an inexact science that changes from couple to couple and from situation to situation. The most commonly agreed-upon definition of primary infertility is when a woman has tried to get pregnant, and failed, for at least 12 months, and of the 15 states in the U.S. that provide some form of coverage for IVF, most stipulate that a woman must have been trying to get pregnant for at least that long before enlisting help. But groups like the American Society of Reproductive Medicine stress that earlier evaluation and treatment is warranted for women over 35. Indeed, for someone like Michelle who was 40 when she began trying to have a child, a viable pregnancy is that much less likely.

"It's all statistical. So long as a couple doesn't have any of the absolutes — completely blocked tubes, no sperm — as long as you have some chance each month, then statistically you will find that some couples will get pregnant on their own," said Dr. Robert Oates, president of the Society for Male Reproduction and Urology. "We have to hold back our enthusiasm for getting to interventions like IVF too quickly and need to give biology some time to work when there's a sense that it might."

Nearly 12 percent of American women between the ages of 15 and 44 have sought some form of fertility assistance and, though only a small percent pursue the most aggressive options, more than 146,000 cycles of assisted reproductive technology — namely IVF — were performed in the U.S. in 2010. The Centers for Disease Control and Prevention estimates that 1 percent of babies born each year are now conceived using some form of assisted reproductive technology.

"Because IVF is so successful now, I think some people are probably getting it who don't really need it," said Courtney Lynch, an assistant professor of obstetrics and gynecology, epidemiology and pediatrics at the Ohio State University Wexner Medical Center, whose research centers on risk factors for fertility problems. Lynch said there is something of a don't ask, don't tell policy with reproductive endocrinologists and their patients. Rather than pressing for details on how often they have been having intercourse and how carefully they have been timing it, doctors take their patients at their word that they are good candidates for fertility treatment.

But IVF is a grueling, logistically challenging process, not a quick fix. Women are given drugs to boost their egg production, often hormones that must be injected daily. During that time, patients must undergo pelvic ultrasounds and blood tests to check their ovaries and hormone levels. Next their eggs are retrieved, an outpatient procedure that usually involves some form of sedation. That is followed by insemination, or the mixing of the sperm and egg in a lab. When a fertilized egg divides, it becomes an embryo which is monitored and, given that everything looks okay, transferred into a woman's womb several days later.

The process is expensive — in the U.S., the average cost per cycle is at least $12,400 — and not without risks. There is a small chance of ovarian hyperstimulation and pelvic infection, as well as the possibility of multiple pregnancies if more than one embryo is transferred to a woman's uterus. According to the American Society of Reproductive Medicine, babies conceived by IVF have a slightly higher risk of birth defects — between 2.6 and 3.9 percent, compared to just to 2 to 3 percent in babies born naturally.

And then there is the enormous emotional toll of treatment.

"Those years were the low point in my life," said Cortney Carroll, a bubbly 34-year-old with a wide, pretty smile who recently moved from Ohio to Virginia." They were the saddest. I was crying constantly — every day, it was this up and down. You'd get excited, you'd think, 'These numbers are good! Yay!' And then you'd just crash."

Cortney grew up wanting to be two things: a dancer and a mom. After a stress fracture in college ended her Broadway dreams, Cortney eventually ended up working in pharmaceutical sales. In 2001, she married her husband in front of 200 guests and the pair started trying for a baby in September 2004, when Cortney was 26.

"I thought it would be easy," she said. "That was a dumb assumption."

After about six months of trying, Cortney went to an OBGYN who preached patience — women under 35 are generally not considered infertile until they have attempted to get pregnant for one year. A few months later, she saw a different OBGYN who found a blocked fallopian tube, not necessarily enough of a hindrance to make pregnancy impossible, but enough for Cortney to be put on Clomid, a pill that induces ovulation. She tried two rounds of the medication; neither worked.

By then Cortney was moving along a treatment trajectory familiar to many of the 7.4 million women in the U.S. who have used some form of infertility services in their lives. She was referred to a reproductive endocrinologist and tried three rounds of IUI, all failures. In November 2005, Cortney began preparing for her first round of IVF. Cortney found out she was pregnant on December 21, but seven days later her hormone levels had dropped.

"At that point, in doctors-speak, it's called a 'chemical pregnancy,'" she said flatly. "But it's a miscarriage."

Cortney's next two rounds of IVF were also unsuccessful. One was canceled because there weren't enough ovarian follicles to retrieve, the next because none of her eggs had fertilized. Her fertility doctor said there was nothing more he could do and suggested she try a more pioneering out-of-state clinic. At that point, she had spent more than $12,000 out of pocket on co-pays, medications and anything her insurance didn't cover.

In September 2006, Cortney took a medical leave from her job and flew to Las Vegas where she spent three weeks shuttling between various hotels and the Sher Clinic, part of one of the largest networks of infertility clinics in the U.S. She left Las Vegas hopped up on her highest dose of medication yet and the maximum number of embryos Sher's doctors were able to transfer. She was certain she was pregnant. She was not.

A month after returning from the failed trip, Matt and Cortney started pre-adoption parenting classes at their local hospital. They planned to return to Las Vegas in January for another IVF cycle, the final one that would be covered by insurance (her company's plan covered a portion of her treatments), but they were beginning to wonder if conception was even an option for them.

The adoption classes were almost over when, on a November day in 2006, Cortney took a home pregnancy test. She watched the line start to grow, tossed the test on her bathroom counter and got in the shower.

"At that point I was so used to negatives, it was like 'Whatever,'" Cortney said.

A few minutes later she stepped out, looked at the test, and called her husband in tears. A blood test hastily scheduled for that afternoon confirmed what the home kit had told her: Cortney was finally pregnant, all on her own. And two and a half years later, she gave birth to a second child who was also conceived naturally, this time a girl.

"It was just up and down, up and down," Cortney said, "and all the time trying to just have hope that it could happen." Though the ordeal strengthened her marriage — Cortney and her husband began going to church together and praying together every night — she confessed there were times when she felt desperate and completely alone.

'JUST ADOPT, IT'LL HAPPEN.'

Those feelings of fear and anxiety are the basis for another popular explanation for these unexpected pregnancies, which hinges on the role that stress plays in women's efforts to become pregnant. Research on the relationship between stress and fertility is far from conclusive, in part because of the chicken and egg challenges of mapping a woman's stress. Does stress lead to her infertility, or is infertility the source of her stress?

These complexities help explain why recent scientific evidence tends to contradicts itself. A 2011 study in the journal Fertility and Sterility (on which Lynch was an author) used saliva tests to measure certain stress biomarkers in 274 women who were trying to get pregnant. Stress appeared to significantly reduce the probability of conception, and at least one small study has found emotional stress can hurt sperm quality. But a review published in the venerable British Medical Journal in 2011 found that a woman's stress levels do not appear to affect her chances of getting pregnant after a single cycle of assisted reproductive technology.

"At this time, there has not been a clear link between stress, depression, anxiety, and successful outcomes in infertility treatment," said Dr. Marlene Freeman, an associate professor of psychiatry at Harvard Medical School and director of the perinatal and reproductive psychiatry program at Massachusetts General Hospital in Cambridge.

Nonetheless, the connection flourishes in the public imagination. Ask a handful of women who have dealt with infertility and they'll roll their eyes over the number of times they heard some version of: "Just relax. If you stop stressing out, it'll happen."

"People say all those things that they think are helpful," said Tracy Birkinbine, 40. "I heard them all the time: 'Just adopt, it'll happen.'"

Tracy started trying to have a baby in 1996 at 24 and taking Clomid soon thereafter. Earlier in her 20s she was diagnosed with polycystic ovary syndrome, a hormonal disorder that can make it harder to have children, but everything else looked good. Her doctors checked her tubes for blockage and analyzed her husband's sperm.

By 26, Tracy was referred to a reproductive endocrinologist, who suggested she move on to IVF. She dove into three cycles, carrying around a fishing tackle box with needles to give herself injections of the fertility drugs needed to stimulate egg development. The medicines made her "not very nice" to her husband, she said.

Tracy, like many women in this situation, was so driven to birth a baby that she felt inadequate when she could not. "I would say really stupid things, like, 'You need to just divorce me and find somebody else who can give you a baby,'" Tracy said. "Or I would get really angry and say mean things that were not true and were hurtful. I knew it when I was saying it, but I couldn't stop. I almost felt like a different person."

But the most fraught period was the stretch known in infertility-speak as "the two-week wait," the time between the end of treatment and before the pregnancy test.

"It's excruciating," Tracy said. "Every move I made, I was afraid I was going to push [the embryos] out. I was crazy. We lived in an old house, and I went to open the windows and used my abdominal muscles. I was like, 'Oh my gosh! I strained when I did that!'"

Harder still was trying to keep herself from seeing everything as a sign of pregnancy. "You start having the, 'Oh, am I going to the bathroom a little more? Are my breasts starting to ache?'"

During Tracy's second IVF cycle, the answers to those leading questions became "yes." She was pregnant. Then three days later, her hormone levels dropped and it became clear it was only a chemical pregnancy. Altogether, Tracy underwent three cycles of IVF before she and her husband decided to adopt a child through foster care, and soon took in a 3½-year-old girl. Four months after the adoption was finalized, Tracy discovered she was pregnant with a girl. Just over a year later, she was pregnant again, this time with a boy.

"I wasn't adopting, thinking, 'If I adopt, I'll get pregnant,'" Tracy said, acknowledging that she followed the exact pattern people told her she would.

None of her doctors ever gave her an explanation for her infertility, nor did they give her a reason why she was able to have children after failing with IVF and adopting.

The lack of clear answers can make it extremely difficult for women to know what to make of their bodies throughout the infertility process, particularly when, after years of pipe dreams and treatments, they suddenly have a baby on their own.

Should they feel betrayed? Elated? Can they muster any sense of trust in their own reproductive systems?

Kari Harris, 29, took ovulation drugs for three years and had multiple IUIs — having her husband's sperm injected into her uterus — as well as two miscarriages before she gave birth to her son. Now 2, he was conceived during her second cycle of IVF. As she and her husband were preparing to start another cycle to try for a second child, Kari found out she was pregnant, naturally. She is due in December.

Her reaction to the news surprised her. "My first feeling was that I was angry. I was angry that this was happening after everything we had been through," Kari said. "My feeling was, 'We're going to end up having a miscarriage.' I was like, 'This isn't fair. How is this happening?'"

When she got pregnant with her son, Kari was already on several medications to help prevent miscarriage; this time she was not. Though she and her husband are "over the moon" and "beyond excited" about the prospect of having another baby, that joy is tempered by the fear that her body will fail her, as well as the guilt she feels about being able to have a second baby naturally when so many women cannot.

As an alum of the IVF world, her feelings about pregnancy — natural or otherwise — are defined by the turmoil of the process. "I just wanted to have a pregnancy I could enjoy, a normal pregnancy where I wasn't scared all the time," Kari said. "This was supposed to be that pregnancy for me, but it hasn't been. I'm still in complete shock and disbelief that this is really happening."

This story originally appeared in Huffington, in the iTunes App store.

MONDAY, OCTOBER 15, 2012

October 15- Pregnancy and Infant Loss Remembrance Day

Thinking of all those babies who never made it to life. Thinking of all those Mommies and Daddies who never got to meet their baby. Thinking of all the broken broken hearts, shattered dreams and oceans of tears. Today is the day for all of us to remember not just what we have lost but how far we have come. Our babies are forever with us and never forgotten. Although today is a day dedicated for those who have suffered loss to come together with friends and family to remember their losses... I know we all remember our losses daily. We don't need a specific day however, it is nice to have the recognition by those who have never dealt with loss.

We are all still standing for a reason... we are all strong.

I don't feel right posting about my pregnancy on a day that is meant for loss remembrance. I will update tomorrow.

FRIDAY, OCTOBER 19, 2012

35+

Lots going on here...

First thing is first... the baby.

The baby is doing great. Last time I had an ultrasound (two weeks ago) the baby was measuring 4lbs 7oz... which was somewhere around 50th percentile. Average baby... my vagina likes that.

Recently, I started to feel really worn out. EXHAUSTED. Barely functioning exhausted. I only have 4.5 weeks to go so that's to be expected. At my appointment on Thursday, I mentioned to my doctor that I'm having a little issue with fluid leakage. I said, "I'm either peeing my pants all day long or I'm leaking some sort of fluid." I knew it wasn't the Crinone because that comes out clumpy. This stuff is like water... or pee. I change my underwear four million times a day. When she did my exam she said, "oh yes, I see all that fluid you're talking about." Seriously? It just pools up in there? Who knew?!?! She said it's definitely not pee (phew) nor is it Amniotic fluid (phew phew). My cervix is closed, however, it's really thin. She told me that when the cervix starts to thin, you start to have all sorts of extra fluid. Mine just like to leak out like an incompetent bladder. Whatever, if it means I'm progressing properly, I'll take it. She could also feel the baby's head... which explains the feeling like I've been kicked with a steel toed boot.

I'm going to stop my Crinone on Sunday. Although, I'm contemplating using it a little longer. My OB said I could stop any time after Sunday. I'm thinking I may hold off until my appointment with her on Wednesday.

M has to have his adenoids removed. His surgery is Tuesday. I do not want anything happening that will prevent me from being by his bedside until he is 100% better. Recovery is quick (two to three days) so hopefully he doesn't have any infections or complications and he's back to his normal self quickly. I'm actually relieved at the removal. He is CONSTANTLY sick. His colds are never normal baby colds. They start boogery like normal kids then within a day or two he has a full blown chest infection. Asthma runs in his genes so it wasn't farfetched to assume he had asthma. We have been treating him, off and on, with Nebulizer treatments, antibiotics, and steroids. Finally, the pedi said we needed to see an ENT. Sure enough, his adenoids are large. The surgery won't make him 100% better. The ENT said he can guarantee at least a 50% improvement. Plus, they're getting so large, that his breathing is affected. He started snoring and only breathing through his mouth. When he eats, he chews with his mouth open. When he drinks, he has to take breaks because he can't breathe. He needs this surgery... even though I'll be an emotional wreck... he needs it. I'm sad that his Demi Moore voice will go away but psyched to have an improvement on his health.

His birthday party was a blast! He had so much fun with all his friends. My craftiness looked fantastic. I'll post some pics

One more thing about this pregnancy. I'm starting to get really sad that it is almost over. I am beyond uncomfortable and beyond excited to meet this little boy or girl. However, I can't believe that this is what we fought so hard for. We dealt with heartache after heartache to get here. We spent years crying. Years fighting. Years watching the world move forward and our life be at a standstill. We put my body through hell and back. We lost hope. We gained hope. We lost hope. We put on a happy face for others when we were at our lowest low. Then came M. He brought us peace, joy and an insane amount of love. He made us realize that genetics don't matter. The love for your child... no matter how they are brought to you... is unconditional and endless. Then our battle became about pregnancy. Not about a baby. Not about being a parent. We were fighting for the experience of pregnancy. Here we are, nearly five years later, and we're approaching the end of what we wanted so badly. I just can't believe it. What does that make us? Are we survivors? Are we victorious? Lucky? What? I don't know. It's almost like my identity is becoming a mystery. I guess it is. I am infertile. That doesn't change. But who am I in a few weeks? Who am I when we want to try to have another baby or when we try to use our frozen embryos?

****

1st BIRTHDAY PICS

****

Smash cake and cupcakes

Thing 1 Thing 2 Cotton Candy Cupcakes

12 Months of M

Sugar High!

Apparently I'm the most excited about music time!

THURSDAY, OCTOBER 25, 2012

Update tomorrow

I have been trying to find time to update you all. M didn't have his surgery... he needed prednisone which meant they had to postpone the surgery (to a week before my due date). I feel like we will be in a vicious cycle of trying to get the surgery done and keeping him healthy enough to do so.

My 36 week appointment went well. I will update tomorrow. Right now, I'm exhausted (I have been up since 3:00 am) so I am going to crash.

FRIDAY, OCTOBER 26, 2012

36+

Less than four weeks to go. F-O-U-R. Crazy.

Update on the baby...
Weighing 5lbs 15oz... estimate birth weight just under 8lbs
Head is nice and low... really low
Cervix is 80% effaced and half a centimeter dilated (or as my OB stated... I can get my fingertip in there)
So I'm progressing as I should. I still can't believe it. I just can't.

I have a KILLER UTI right now. Holy brutal. I'm on day 4 of antibiotics and it still feels like my vagina is being shredded by razor blades every time I pee.

I'm starting to get really anxious to find out what this little bean is. I go back and forth all the time. As one of my friends said recently "it has to be one or the other." True. Very True.

Last weekend, I went away with some girlfriends. Before our friend passed away in July, he bid on a beach rental house at a benefit. M (his wife) decided that we should use the house as a girl's get away. The house was AMAZING! Multimillion dollar home, on the water. Each and every bedroom had a full bath. I was trying to figure out if that meant it had five master suites. Anyway, the weekend was bittersweet. It was incredibly relaxing. We spent hours upon hours laughing our faces off. We cried. We laughed. We ate. We laughed. We ate. It was just what we all needed. Two of my closest girlfriends are widows (both under the age of 32) and now single mothers. At one point, someone mentioned that they couldn't believe that I was not only pregnant but that I would have a baby soon. That lead us into the conversation of how weird it feels for me. It still doesn't seem real. I'm still waiting for something to go wrong. I don't feel like I have been pregnant. I can't imagine actually having to deliver a baby because it doesn't seem real to me. I also mentioned that I feel like part of my identity is leaving me. Where do I fit in? What am I called? One of the girls said to me, "Even if I get married in 30 years, I will still be a widow." Right. That makes sense. I'm still infertile. I will always be infertile. That will never leave me.

I'm an infertile pregnant woman... sounds like an oxymoron.

MONDAY, NOVEMBER 5, 2012

37+ (BUMP PIC INCLUDED)

Here I am... just shy of 38 weeks and I still can't imagine this working out. It's been a wild ride and soon it will end.

At my appointment last week, I was no longer dilated (huh?). Dilation measurement is purely subjective based on the size of the doctor's hands... well, fingers. My OB was on vacation last week so I saw a different OB. The one I saw was also 9.5 months pregnant... she was also super swollen. She said I was closed up. In my head I was thinking, "no kidding, those sausage fingers aren't fitting into anything of mine." My contractions are getting stronger. My damn UTI is back. I just finished my second week of a second antibiotic and of course, today, I can't pee again. I just left a voicemail on the nurses line at my OB. My lower right back is killing me again. I'm hoping it's just my sciatica making another appearance and not my kidney.

Other than pressure, hip pain and pure exhaustion, I feel pretty good. I am doing more than I think I am supposed to... or maybe more than the average person?? I don't know. Often, when I am out and about, someone offers help or comments on how I should be home resting. I lift things, I go on long walks, I go to the park with M, I drive around, I clean... B has to work so how else does this stuff get done? M weighs 22lbs... I lift him all day so I'm pretty sure I will be okay lifting groceries or a basket of laundry.

I wasn't going to pack a bag. For some reason, I didn't find it necessary. Then everyone and their mother kept telling me I'd want a bag packed. So I caved and packed one. It's just sitting at our bedroom door waiting to be used. It feels weird to have it and it feels weird to be waiting to use it. All of this is weird. All of it.

In July of 2010, I had a post that mentioned funny onesies I would have made if/when I were to ever have a baby. I thought it would be great to bring that back. I DID have one of these made. I have a "worth the wait" one from when M was born... so it's not that one.

Pigs Flew
Made in a dish
One night in a lab
I cost thousands
I was worth the wait
I kicked infertility's ass
FINALLY

One tough Mommy
Three years in the making
Made by an Embryologist
Retrieved, Fertilized and Transferred
Here is a pic of me last week (37 weeks).

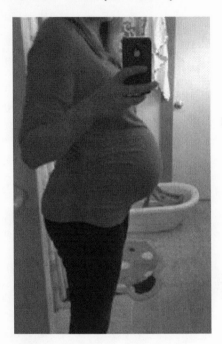

TUESDAY, NOVEMBER 13, 2012

Next week

I'm due next week. Next week. Holy shit! How did we get here?

I had my 39 week appointment this morning. The baby is super low... low enough where I can now see my feet. I haven't been able to see my feet in months. I'm 3cm dilated. My OB stripped my membranes. Now we just wait. I have been waiting nearly five years for this. FIVE. I can't believe how far we have come.
Three IUIs
Seven IVFs
One FET
Three Miscarriages
Endless needles

Endless exams
Endless tests
Endless amounts of money

And here we are. Infertility didn't define us. It didn't stop us. It discouraged us then it drove us. It motivated us. It made us fight even harder. Struggle gives us purpose. It gives us drive. It gives us something to overcome. I never imagined we would struggle so much for the one thing we both wanted most. I never imagined the pain and suffering we would not only endure but we would overcome. And now, here we are, at the end of our struggle. We're victorious. We kicked infertility's ass. Time and time again, we were losing. Our loss gave us strength. That strength gave us hope. That hope turned into reality.

I have so many friends still struggling. I have so many friends who are just starting their struggle. I have so many friends who have had to stop fighting. I just hope and pray that their struggle too turns into victory. There is no greater feeling in the world than saying F*@! You struggle. You can pressure me, you can hurt me, you can bring me down... but you can't beat me.

M will be a big brother soon. I cannot wait for that. He is so sweet and gentle. He feeds his baby a bottle. When he is having a snack, he shares it with his baby. He gives his baby hugs and kisses. He burps the baby. He is going to be such a great brother. I'm beyond grateful and extremely blessed to be able to give him that opportunity.

Speaking of M...

His surgery went ok. Not well, just ok. We have had a rough few days here at the L house. First, he had a bad reaction to the anesthesia. The anesthesiologist called it "asthma like reaction." Basically he had bronchial spasms that eventually stopped his breathing. They gave him emergency meds (prednisone and albuterol) which got him stabilized fairly quickly. Once they took the tube out, he couldn't swallow and was choking on his saliva. So then, they had to give him morphine. The poor kid. The entire time this was happening, we were in a waiting room freaking out. The surgeon told us it would be 30 minutes at most. Thirty minutes passed, then 45, then an hour. At the hour point, B was looking for someone to talk to and I was losing my shit. Finally, after nearly an hour and a half, they came out to tell us what was going on. We weren't allowed to see him until he was stabilized and well. He was the saddest looking little boy I have ever seen. They gave him a bottle of sugar water. He had the bottle hanging out of his mouth, being held by a weak little hand. He wasn't drinking it. It was just hanging there. His eyes were half open and rolling around. It broke my heart.

His recovery has been equally as bad. He can't eat. He wakes up screaming every couple of hours. He just wants to be held... which is no problem for me! I'm loving the extra snuggles. He's on alternating Tylenol and Motrin, every four hours. He has about an hour and a half of feeling good after he gets meds. He will play, eat, and be wild. Then he starts getting fussy again.

HOWEVER, amongst all his surgical woes, he has started to walk! It's so amazing to see. He is so proud of himself. We are so proud of him. He has been taking steps since the day before his first birthday. Yesterday, he just ran across the room to me. Now he's walking when he feels like it but still crawling. Apparently crawling is more time efficient.

I will keep you posted on the progression of the baby. Yikes. The baby.

TUESDAY, DECEMBER 4, 2012

Big Brother M

I promised I would keep you all updated and I didn't. The arrival of the baby was a whirlwind of events that kept us on our toes and away from the computer. It all started Thursday November 15.

Thursday November 15...

I was in Target when I felt a huge gush of something. I said to my mother, "I either just peed my pants or my water broke." I came home, checked my underwear, and found the fluid to be unscented and clear. I called my OB office and she told me to monitor the fluid. At this point, my contractions were about every seven minutes apart. I leaked enough fluid to have to change my underwear three times. Finally, late afternoon, we decided it would be safe to head to the hospital. Once we made it through triage, they hooked me up to the monitors. Within 45 seconds of being monitored, they were pressuring me to induce. No lie... less than a minute. It was crazy. I just kept asking, "Is something wrong?" I was there no more than a minute and all of a sudden there were a million people in the room and a lot of demands being thrown around. "Roll to your left, roll to your right, get an IV, she needs oxygen." My contractions were irregular. They were every 5 to 7 minutes or so. The ER mid-wife did an exam to see how far along my dilation was along with a test on the fluid. The fluid was not amniotic and I was only 1cm dilated (which I was confused on how I could be 3cm at an exam a few weeks prior and only one in the ER). However, they kept me on the monitor because the baby's heart rate was showing some decelerations following contractions. I had no answers, just a whole lot of worry. At this point, I'm angry at the forcefulness of induction and the lack of explanation. After an hour or so, a nurse said, "I'm sorry, when we see decels, we legally have to act." Okay... so everything is fine?? In the end, they kept me overnight for monitoring. By the morning, my contractions had been consistently two minutes apart with no cervical change. The baby never had any more decels (they only saw it when I was first hooked up to the monitor). They gave me the option to be induced or labor at home. I chose laboring at home. I didn't see the point of introducing all those drugs when the baby was fine and I was fine.

So we went home...

Then on Saturday, I was soaking through underwear again. I called the on-call OB and they told me to head to the ER for an exam (to check cervical change) and fluid levels. My cervix hadn't changed again and my fluid looked great. I basically was gushing out non amniotic gook. They sent me home with instructions to follow up with a non-stress test, fluid check and exam on Monday.

Monday comes...

At this point, my contractions have me moaning and stopping me in my tracks. To me, they felt like they were never ending. I kept thinking, "my cervix has to be dilated to at least six." There was no way that I wasn't in active labor. I was in so much pain. We get to the clinic for the NST and Fluid check Monday at 1:30. My fluid measured 11 (fantastic). My NST showed some late decels with my contractions. Late decels are far worse than regular decels. Regular decels they just call variables. It happens with contractions. Late decels is when the baby's heart rate drops after the contraction and takes some time to bounce back. It means either there is compression on the cord or the baby has had enough. Either way, it's not good. The clinic called my OB and asked if they want me to show up to my 3:00 exam or go straight to the hospital. We were sent straight to the hospital. At this point, I'm thinking the baby will arrive any second. I was on day 5 of active labor... well, active with contractions less than five minutes apart but not active with my cervix. We get to triage and we were immediately sent to a room for monitoring. Who walks in?? The resident who was forcing us to induce. She walks in and says, "so now are you ready to induce?" Well, no, I'm not. I need information. I had a million and a half questions about what the medications would do to the baby. If it's already under stress, couldn't we make it worse by making the contractions stronger (which, may I add, could NOT possibly get stronger)? At one point, I asked why someone from my practice wasn't with us discussing the options. She replied with, "You mean a real doctor and not a resident?" No. That's not what I mean at all. I mean a doctor from my practice... one who knows my history. One who will have a decent conversation with me without being a total bitch. The conversation went on with me asking a lot of questions and her not being honest. She lied to me about the side effects of Pitocin. What do I do? I whip out my iPhone and pull up the package insert. Right there on the side effects of the PI, I catch her in a lie. Maybe she wasn't lying... maybe she didn't know the answer. Either way, I didn't trust her. When I called her out on it, she left the room. She came back a few minutes later and said, "You have too many questions and I'm not comfortable treating you. We are going to admit you and let a physician from your practice meet with you in the morning." I got fired as a patient. Hahahah. I should have been pissed. I think we were pissed at one point... but we found it more humorous than anything.

Tuesday morning comes...

All night Monday, I was up in agony. My contractions at this point were either a minute apart or they were continuous. Yet, my cervix still had no change. The doctor from my practice came in around 8:00 am. She suggested we do a Foley Balloon and Cervidil. The Foley balloon is basically a catheter with a balloon that inflates to 3cm with saline. They put it in your cervix, inflate it, and wait for it to fall out. Once it falls out, it means your cervix is beyond 3cm. The Cervidil is a tampon like swab that is soaked in a medication that helps soften the cervix. We had both of those things put in around 9:00 am. Right before she put them in, she did an exam. She felt the scar tissue from my LEEP procedures. She mentioned that if my cervix doesn't dilate within a few hours, she may have to manually break up the scar tissue. The procedure itself was far less painful than any of the other infertility procedures I have had done. Hysteroscopies are way more painful. Sonohystograms are far more uncomfortable. Endometrial biopsies are far more painful. Ovarian stimulation is far more uncomfortable. Both the doctor and the nurse mentioned how calm and well I handled it... apparently they have never dealt with an infertility patient before. We are far more stoic and strong than the fertile (no offense fertiles).

The Foley Balloon did nothing but make my contractions hurt more. I was in so much pain. SOOO MUCH Pain. I was swaying, rocking, squatting. At one point, I was squatting on the floor, moaning through a contraction when a nurse comes in, picks up my monitor strip, and says "wow, you're having strong continuous contractions. Can you feel any of these?" EFFING idiot, do you see me on the floor?!??! At this point, we have requested to see a doctor a million and a half times. We have gone through a million shift changes. With each shift change, no one takes me seriously. They think since my cervix hasn't changed that I'm not in active labor. I'm on day 6. DAY SIX. My politeness has worn off. Our patience is at zero. The poor nurse who walks in next is getting it. And sadly, she did. I dropped "Fucking," "Idiot," "this is a fucking Joke," "Fucking," "Fuck," "fuck," "FUCK." I felt bad but seriously, this is a top 25 OBGYN hospital in the country?? We kept asking about having the scar tissue broken up and each and every nurse kept saying that it wasn't in my protocol. I don't give a fuck what's on the protocol, get me a doctor. I hadn't seen a doctor since the Foley balloon was placed. I had a nurse pull the Foley balloon out after 8.5 hours because I couldn't handle it anymore. I hadn't slept in weeks. I needed a competent doctor.

After all my swearing, the nurse comes back and says that since I'm not asking for pain medication, she wasn't going to send a doctor up to do an exam. Are you fucking kidding me? I am trying to do this NATURAL... which means NO Pain meds... that doesn't mean I'm not in Pain. We lost it again, and demanded we be sent to labor and delivery. The only way this could happen was if I were to agree to Pitocin. Whatever, I don't need my contractions to progress, I need my cervix to. But whatever I need to say to get off that damn floor, I will say it. Finally around mid-night, we are brought to labor and delivery. Once we got there, we experienced the top 25 hospital care.

Right off the bat the nurse recognized that my contractions were active labor (THANK YOU JESUS). She called in the doctor and he did an exam. First thing he said was, "you have scar tissue that is really tough and preventing your cervix from dilating. Do you mind if I manually break it up?" AHHHHH! PLEASE! Do it and do it NOW! I agreed to an epidural because I was beyond exhausted after nearly a week of labor. I wasn't sure how I would handle the Pitocin contractions. They also told me it could be another 12-24 hours of labor. So I caved and got an epidural. I wish I didn't. It was nice to have pain relief but I had made it six days without pain meds. Had I known the baby would come in just a few hours, I would never have agreed to it. Anyway, I got the epidural and the doctor came back in to break up the scar tissue. Once he did, my cervix dilated from 2cm to 10cm within an hour. AN HOUR! All I needed was someone competent and we would have delivered a baby a week earlier. He broke the scar tissue, my water broke within 30 minutes, and I was pushing within 30 minutes of that.

6:30am: Wednesday, November 21...

Time to push. I wasn't sure how I would be at pushing. I never took labor classes. I never asked anyone about it. I just figured I would do what my body needed me to. The nurse told me it could take 30 minutes to 3 hours of pushing. Once we got close to delivery, she would call the doctor. After one push, the nurse said, "I think I should get the doctor." I pushed for 25 minutes with a total of five pushes. I found one of my reproductive skills. DELIVERY. Not to toot my own horn but I am a rockstar in delivery. Seriously. I may not reproduce like many of you but I can get a baby out like no other.

At one point, the baby's head was out, the baby was screaming and the doctor turns to B and says, "Ok Dad, one last chance, do you think it's a boy or a girl?" B says, "That's a girl face. Girl." The plan was for B to announce the gender. However, my legs are being held by the nurse and B. I'm giving one last massive push so my head was right up in between my knees. When the baby comes out, all I have in my face is BALLS. BALLS! I yell, "OH MY GOD THERE ARE BALLS!" We didn't know what we were having and we weren't leaning one way or the other. Yet the balls shocked me. I couldn't believe that it was a boy. MJL (named after our friend who passed away in July) was born at 7:00 am (on the dot), weighing a teeny tiny 6lbs 3oz and 19 3/4" in length.

I can't explain the feeling. It was all surreal. We knew I was pregnant. We knew a baby would come eventually. But we really didn't know. It was all steps in a process that never had the ending we wanted. Yet, the ending was here and it didn't seem like ours. It didn't seem like we were the people looking at a screaming baby. It didn't seem like we just had a baby. I needed an episiotomy. The doctor was stitching that up and I turned to him and asked if the placenta had come out yet. It had. I was in such a state of disbelief and amazement that I didn't realize all these things happened. We just had a baby. Never mind the seven days of labor leading up to it. Never mind the massive, gigantic body I was lugging around. A baby. A real baby came out of my reproductively challenged body. Out of me. What on earth.

I will post more on my emotions later this week. Big M is sick (we all are) and he has a pediatrician appointment shortly. I need to get going but I really wanted and needed to get this post written. Here are some pics of the two MJLs.

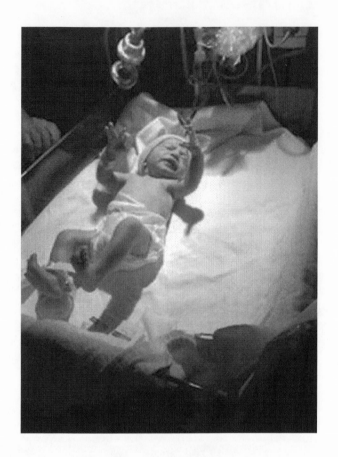

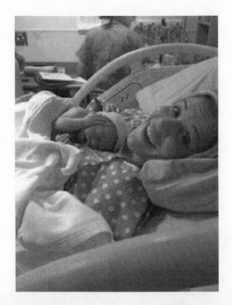

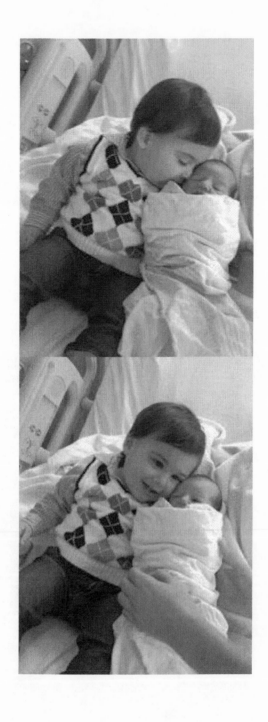

NOVEMBER 17, 2013

Epilogue

Nearly 5 years, three IUIs, eight IVFs (including the frozen cycle), three losses... so now what?

I've often think about who I am and the life we are living. We went from our lowest low to parents of two amazing boys. We always hoped and dreamed we would get here but with each passing day and each failed cycle, we felt that our dreams would remain dreams and not become a reality.

I have a really unique perspective on having a family after infertility. I did not carry Miles and I did carry Mark. Miles is not genetically ours but he's ours. Mark is genetically ours but he's ours. I love them the same. I love how I got to them the same. I love their stories the same. Miles returned some hope into our lives. Mark instilled faith in miracles.

My pregnancy with Mark did teach me a few things...

I kept saying that I was fighting to be a mother. After Miles' birth, I thought that I was wrong all those years, I wasn't fighting to be a mother, I was fighting for pregnancy. I always said that I knew we would be parents, it was just a matter of how we would get there. Then came perfect little Miles. I was a mother. It was and is amazing. Even with motherhood, I had this fight in me. I felt like our fight was over. I thought I was fighting for motherhood, but I realized that I was fighting for pregnancy.

I wanted to experience having a child the traditional way. I wanted to experience morning sickness, back aches, an expanding belly and labor. Once I was pregnant with Mark, I realized that even though I achieved it, infertility took it away. I was fighting for something that was already gone. I was bitter, scarred, angry, and most of all, terrified. I thought if I enjoyed the pregnancy, something would go wrong. When I felt okay, I found myself in an ER thinking that the baby passed. When people commented on my pregnancy, I would have anxiety that they were jinxing it. I wanted so badly to have this experience. There I was, in it, and I couldn't enjoy it. I realize now that Infertility makes you feel damaged and needy. You feel like it's all unfair (and it is). You end up fighting for all these things that other people take for granted. Then, if you're lucky, you get to experience them and you find yourself terrified to ruin it.

I absolutely feel that our family is incomplete. We're not done having a family. I am done with putting my body and my psyche through what it went through. I only recently read my blog/this book for the first time. Reading the changes in my perspective on life was heartbreaking. What I felt in the early chapters is certainly not how I felt in the end chapters and certainly not how I feel now. When I read how sick I was, ALL the time, I can't believe I functioned that way. Would I change a thing? Absolutely not. Back then, if you told me in order to get pregnant, I would need to cut my eyeballs out, I would have done it. Even now, if I knew that cutting my eyeballs out would lead me to Miles and Mark, I would do it... in a heartbeat. I wouldn't even think twice about it. However, I do know now, that sometimes life changes you. It can change you for the better and it can change you for the worse. Infertility changed me. It changed how I see pregnancy. It's a miracle and a privilege. It's scary and painful. It's heartbreaking and dark. It's a life event that most people take for granted.

I pray that we are blessed with more children one day. Maybe we will adopt. Maybe one of our two frozen embryos will result in a live birth. Maybe we will have another miracle natural birth. I don't know. I do know that I have holes in my heart. Maybe I have three of them, one for each lost baby. Maybe I have eight of them, one for each failed cycle. Maybe I have 11 of them, one for each failed medicated cycle. Maybe I have 96 of them, one for each month of trying. Maybe some will heal. Maybe some will forever be part of me. However it ends up, my life is the way it is because of infertility. It may have left me damaged, but it also left me with two amazing children. I realize that I am one of the lucky ones. I thank God every day for that.

I have a new fight in me. My fight is not only for my family, it's for yours too. I promise to commit myself to all those couples out there dealing with Infertility. I will do everything in my power to help you fight your fight. I will continue to go to DC and lobby for our rights. I will continue to run support groups to help support you through your cycles and losses. I will work my tail feather off to make sure that AGC Scholarships are able to financially assist as many couples as possible. Every one's family deserves a chance at existence.

"But there is suffering in life, and there are defeats. No one can avoid them. But it's better to lose some of the battles in the struggles for your dreams than to be defeated without ever knowing what you're fighting for." Paulo Coelho

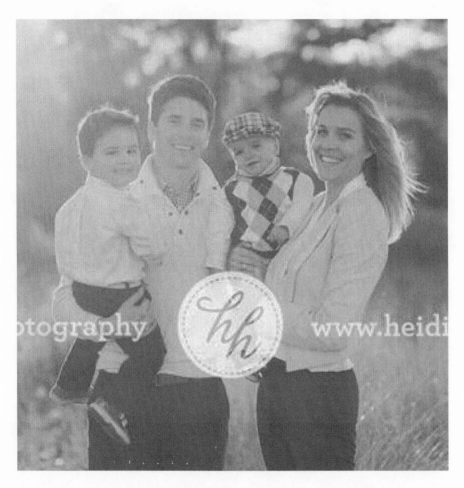

From left to right: Miles, Brian. Mark, and Aprill Lane

To order a copy of this book from the publisher visit:
www.fountainbluepublishing.com

If you would like to be notified by email when new books are released from Fountain Blue Publishing send an email to info@fountainbluepublishing.com with SUBSCRIBE in the subject line.

27398125R00234

Made in the USA
Charleston, SC
07 March 2014